Europe's Leadership Famine

Portraits of Defiance and Decay (1950-2022)

Tom Gallagher

First published in the United Kingdom in 2023
by Scotview Publications.

ISBN: 9780993465444

DEDICATION

The British state and most of the political world swiftly moved on from the Manchester Arena bombing of 22 May 2017, which left 23 dead and over one thousand injured.

The book is dedicated to these innocent victims of terror.

ABOUT THE AUTHOR

Tom Gallagher is a Scot who pursued an academic career as a historian in England for over three decades and is currently Emeritus Professor of Politics at the University of Bradford. He lives in the Lake District and travels widely in Europe and further afield.

Among his books are:

Glasgow The Uneasy Peace: Religious Tension in Modern Scotland
Manchester University Press, 1987.

The Balkans Since The Cold War: From Tyranny to Tragedy
Routledge, 2003.

Romania and the European Union: How the Weak Conquered the Strong
Manchester University Press, 2010.

Scotland Now: A Warning to the World
Scotview Press, 2015.

Salazar: The Dictator Who Refused to Die
Hurst Publications, 2020.

Europe's Leadership Famine

Portraits of Defiance and Decay (1950-2022)

CONTENTS

PART 4

PART 5

ABBREVIATIONS

AfD	Alternative für Deutschland
CDU	Christian Democratic Union
CSU	Christian Social Union
CSCE	Conference on Security and Cooperation in Europe
DC	Christian Democrat
DDR	Deutsche Demokratische Republik
DSP	Democratic Socialist Party (Montenegro)
ECJ	European Court of Justice
ECSC	Coal and Steel Community
EDC	European Defence Community
EEC	European Economic Community
EFTA	European Free Trade Association
ENI	Ente Nazionale Idrocarburi
ERM	Exchange Rate Mechanism
ECB:	European Central Bank
EMA	European Medicines Agency
EOKA	National Organisation of Cypriot Fighters
EPP	European People's Party
FCMA	Friendship, Cooperation and Mutual Assistance Treaty
FdI	Fratelli d'Italia
FDR	Federal German Republic
FDF	Front Democratique des Francophones
FRY	Federal Republic of Yugoslavia
GDR	German Democratic Republic

GRR	Gender Recognition Reform
IKL	Patriotic People's Movement
JNA	Yugoslav Federal Army
LGBT	Lesbian, gay, bisexual, and transgender
NATO	North Atlantic Treaty Organisation
ND	New Democracy
OECD	Organization for Economic Cooperation and Development
OEEC	Organization for European Economic Cooperation
Pasok	Panhellenic Socialist Movement
PCI	Italian Communist Party
POB	Belgian Workers Party
PP	Popular Party (Spain)
PS	Socialist Party of Portugal
PSI	Italian Socialist Party
RPR	Rassemblement pour la République
SKDL	Finnish People's Democratic League
SNP	Scottish National Party
SPD	Social Democratic Party
UDF	Union pour la Démocratie Française

PREFACE

The main underlying theme of this book is that democratic politics is in increasing disarray across much of Europe. The seeds of the malaise have been long in the germination process. But they have sprouted vigorously due to a series of recent crises. The often-inadequate governmental response means that competitive politics is coming to be viewed as a source of difficulty rather than a handy route to reduce them or escape from them altogether. Hard-pressed citizens often look in vain for effective figures at the top of politics who can provide an anchor of stability in a time of intensifying hardship. An uplifting hallmark of democracy is that it often has strong corrective tendencies but, of late, examples of democratic renewal have been increasingly hard to spot. Calls to restrict, or even remove, democracy now come not just from the extremist fringes of politics, but from groups in society who enjoy imposing weight in the economic and media worlds. They would be far less persuasive, especially to the young, if political decision-makers were good at what they were supposed to do and ready to mount a vigorous defence of open and free politics. But increasingly, whether it is routine tasks, complex challenges, or sudden emergencies, politicians often seem dazed or listless in the face of them.

There is no single explanation for the decline of the effectiveness of representative systems of democracy. But several factors stand out. Recruitment has not kept pace with the increasingly complex demands that the profession of politics faces. Over the last eight decades surveyed in the book, the calibre of leaders holding high office has slumped. In a growing number of societies there is declining commitment for democracy, which is true especially among younger age groups. Parties struggle to keep in touch with voters and display credibility in dealing with their problems and those of the broader polity. Politicians who scheme or campaign to get to the top often turn out to have no programme or prefer instead to act as tools for other forces which have not sought electoral validation. There is too much evidence of late that politicians are far more interested in advancing their careers than in offering public service by demonstrating governing skills. They increasingly resemble not Machiavelli's proud energetic lions but the cunning foxes adept at deception, whom he juxtaposed with this monarch of the animal kingdom in his study of human political behaviour.

As a result of this slump in quality, those in the political class standing for election face rejection from the voters with increasing regularity. Elections come to be seen as obstacles to circumvent, rather than as opportunities for aspirant officeholders to draw closer to voters and understand their concerns. The European Union is arguably rather more of a hindrance than a help in preserving the relevance of democracy in uncertain and even dangerous times. In the past thirty years, it has acquired a central role in law-making and policy-enactment, extending far beyond its original one as a trade facilitator, but has never felt the need to be legitimised by popular ballots. It places emphasis on processes, five-year plans, binding treaties and protocols rather than personalities, parties and consultative processes. Yet the age-old struggle of individuals to acquire power, impose ideological agendas, and influence the direction of an entire continent, continues unabated. Thierry Breton, the EU trade commissioner, displayed an imperious outlook in October 2022, when the news broke that Elon Musk had acquired Twitter, the influential social media platform. The tech entrepreneur displayed an image of an uncaged bird, declaring that 'the bird is freed'. But the former high-flying French bureaucrat quickly retorted: 'In Europe the bird will fly by our...rules'.[1]

This might seem an incongruous remark, since Article 11 of the EU's Charter of Fundamental Rights reads that: 'Everyone has the right to freedom of expression. This right shall include freedom to hold opinions and to receive and impart information and ideas without interference by public authority and regardless of frontiers'.[2]

In the past, much of the EU's appeal had rested on its identification with the search for peace and the promotion of a political freedom, in a continent most of which was under authoritarian rule when the integration process began at the start of the 1950s. But its structures have grown increasingly opaque and cumbersome, and few gifted planners, innovators, visionaries, and conciliators subsequently emerged from its ranks. Instead, the entity became an arena for ambitious administrators, often happy to break free of electoral politics, and instead rub shoulders with powerful financial and other business interests which soon learned how to benefit from the EU's enhanced role as a regulator of the economy and the market.

The tendency of household names in business such as Volkswagen, Siemens, and Renault to acquire an outsized role in politics had already spread to the national arena. Inevitably, the types of politicians who often flourished in an era of growing corporate influence and shrinking popular participation were technocratic and managerial ones. Their agenda for government often bore little relation to the core identity of their parties or the interests of its electorate. When difficulties arose, it often proved hard to prevent parties becoming factional and strife torn. Politics grew more volatile, and even normally cautious commentators expressed gloom about the parlous state of democratic politics in some of its European heartlands.

This book examines how, initially high hopes in different quarters, that in Europe, polarised politics that had led to disaster between 1933 and 1945, could be replaced by a more effective model enjoying long-term legitimacy, were gradually eroded. It does this in perhaps an unusual way - by profiling twenty political figures who were at the front rank of politics in their respective countries from the late 1940s almost to the present day. The selection made is designed to illuminate, by means of a personal profile, particular traits that indicate the direction Europe has gone in since the 1950s. The gallery of profiles aims to show what the circumstances were that brought an individual to prominence, what motivated his or her entry into politics and how did this vary over time, what talents or skills enabled the politician to stand out, and what was his or her overall impact on the national stage and sometimes in European or even global affairs. It seeks to explore how a cross-section of politicians used their power and influence in a range of crises, frozen conflicts, power struggles, controversies, and political experiments. A premise of the book is that as time passed, politicians, especially in the old democracies, were increasingly disinclined to show tenacity, display courage, or take risks in order to secure an important outcome. The book is less a set of profiles in courage, and closer to being one that could be called profiles in procrastination.

These interpretative essays defy convention somewhat by endorsing the view that the role of personality continues to matter. The human dimension plays out sometimes to a crucial degree in shaping epochal events like the Cold War, the creation and rise of common European institutions, the retreat of communism, the crisis of the Eurozone, and growing friction arising from territorial cleavages or clashes of psychological identity spilling over into politics. But few individuals managed to have any strong bearing on the *underlying* long-term evolution of politics. A lot of the features which hollowed out democratic politics and made it an exercise with a shrinking number of active and committed adherents, were beyond the power of one individual to shape, although policies which they pursued could accentuate a particular direction that national politics took. The changing role, quality or importance of education, religion, demography, manufacturing industry, leisure activities, other voluntary roles, forms of media, and the way politics was practised and laid before citizens, also undoubtedly had a transformative influence on the evolving shape of politics.

An observant reader may find that while I am sceptical about the merits of perhaps most of the figures profiled, my scepticism grows the closer to the present the narratives reach. This is perhaps because even in a communist one-party state like Josip Tito's, there was pressure to fulfil popular expectations and acquire legitimacy by doing so, a consideration that faded in importance with the passage of time.

There are five thematic sections in the book, into which the profiles are placed, that cover Cold War struggles, Franco-German efforts to refashion Europe, the political economy of Mediterranean Europe, the rise of identity politics in states affected by territorial cleavages, and finally, the return of strong or self-absorbed individuals to a fractured political landscape who seek domination by making direct popular appeals via charisma or demagogy. The emphasis is not on providing intricate or detailed personal biographies, but instead on placing the career, formative experiences, outlook and intentions of the subjects, in the context of how their nations, and Europe as a whole, evolved politically in the seventy-five years covered by the book.

A sizeable introductory essay in each of the sections (chapters 1, 6, 11, 16, 19) offers an analysis of the themes that are covered. Competitive democracy, or concessions to popular sentiment, while predominating in the first half of the book, increasingly give way to rising impatience with the constraints of electoral democracy on the part of many in the political class. The book aims to show how the agenda of often strategically-placed groups shaped around economic, ideological, ethnic, or transnational factors, increasingly acquired greater priority over what could be seen as the preferences of national electorates on various issues, including ones that went right to the heart of representative democracy.

At least from above, the demand for politicians who were good Machiavellians, adept at juggling interests, concealing intentions, and neutralising pressures from below, grew greater. But arguably, the impact of shapeshifters or chameleon-type figures on the health of the body politic across Europe has not been a beneficial one. With the decline into stagnation or worse of formerly achievement-orientated democracies, has come endorsement for unruly figures who (in elite circles) are felt to question democracy or even show contempt for it. When such figures pose an electoral threat to established political forces, any epitaph of disapproval flung in their direction often seems merited. But when unambiguous anti-democrats happen to be in control of a large nation, the language of influential elite figures is often tempered and can shade into outright approval or at least admiration.

Thus, in December 2021, Hubert Védrine, longstanding head of the François Mitterrand Institute and France's foreign minister from 1997 to 2002, described Russian president Vladimir Putin in the following terms:

> 'I found him very strong. Very wired. Very dialectical. Very intelligent… He's a very meditative guy, who reads a lot. You can't say that about a European leader today. There is a solidness in Putin that no longer exists in politicians.[3]

Any respect Védrine may have merited for ditching the festive club atmosphere at the top of European politics in favour of stinging frankness about the philistinism embedded in the elite, was surely forfeited by this outsized tribute to a dictator who already had an impressive record of murder and chicanery to his credit. Putin was just weeks away from launching what would soon be the biggest war seen in Europe since 1945. It was one which quickly revealed that his image as a masterful planner left much to be desired.

After the war in Ukraine commenced, there was candour in other quarters about the leadership famine which had crept up on Europe. It meant that there was more readiness to point to some of the least edifying features of the political profession and the various ills spawned. Scepticism towards elected politicians has grown. The profession has found it increasingly difficult to recruit from a broad range of talent and experience. Party memberships have slumped along with electoral turnouts. Disenchanted voters feel that the only choice they have is to choose between the lesser of two evils. Political volatility has affected a growing number of countries, sometimes spilling over into social unrest or more serious political fractures. Those on the government benches were often neglectful of their duties and even behaved like opposition politicians. By contrast, those facing them on the opposition side showed no desire to rule because of the scale of the problems that they were likely to encounter.

As the finishing touches were being put to this book, a deep-seated crisis in the British Conservative Party, arguably the most successful vote-winning force in the last two hundred years, seemed to bear out various concerns discussed in the book. In office for twelve continuous years, five leaders had come and gone in the last six of them. They struggled to deal with complex and unexpected challenges such as a growing epidemic of violent crime as well as serious urban disruption caused by climate protesters. Ministers often seemed out of their depth as they were confronted with the surge of migrants from across the English Channel, which arguably, predecessor administrations would have nipped in the bud. Their performance produced deepening scorn and anger, with one poll in October 2022, showing that only seven percent of people under the age of fifty were still prepared to back the Conservatives. Policy blunders and personal shortcomings meant that loyalty to the party was no longer capable of keeping factionalism in check. Increasingly, it was harder to see what the Conservative party believed in, other than the right to rule. However, staying in charge was difficult because of diminishing authority at the top. In the summer, mutinous MPs had managed to topple Prime Minister, Boris Johnson, and, in the autumn, failed to rally behind an inexperienced successor who soon got into serious difficulties over the economy. A frantic struggle then ensued between the deposed Prime Minister and Rishi Sunak, the man who had tried but failed to succeed him. The race for the succession revealed a chasm between activists and elected politicians. Disorientated voters looked on, appalled that the world of British politics seemed so mixed up and populated by people unqualified to offer effective direction. The opposition Labour Party soared in popularity, but it was more due to being the only viable alternative across most of the country: it too was beset by ideological splits and regularly-occurring scandals and, lacking answers for pressing problems, was felt to be in no hurry to return to government while crisis conditions persisted. Instead, with the assistance of allies in the media, it contented itself with heavily personalised attacks on ministers grappling with the heaviest problems, even though, when pressed, it struggled to show how it would handle issues like the Channel migrant crisis any better or differently.

The British imbroglio badly dented the country's image of being a sentinel of stability in Europe. But the cocktail of troubles was equally great in other sizeable European countries. They were burdened by sclerotic political classes that seemed paralysed in the face of economic decline and mounting societal woes. Europe's political winter had a varied set of causes and had slowly crept up on what had previously seemed the most resilient of continents. Given the political shortcomings which it explores, this book suggests that it might be harder, this time, for Europe to recover from its difficulties than perhaps at any other point in recent history.

---

[1] Thierry Breton, Twitter, 29 October 2022.
[2] https://eur-lex.europa.eu/legal-content/EN/TXT/?uri=CELEX:12012P/TXT
[3] Brigitte Bouzonnie, ‘Védrine: “J'ai rencontré Poutine”’, *Lettre politique de Brigitte Pascall,* 19 December 2021, https://brigittebouzonnie.substack.com/p/vedrine-jai-rencontre-poutine-je, accessed 29 October 2022.

INTRODUCTION

Europe's lengthy post-war epoch, stretching from the fall of Nazi Germany to the commencement of the Russo-Ukrainian war, was one when low-key politicians, increasingly technocratic in outlook, flourished. Typical practitioners of politics usually shunned flamboyance. Perhaps times in which authority was often fragmented and different interests competed for ascendancy, suited such low-key operators. At their best, the late 20th century politicians were smooth pragmatists effective in committees, able to manufacture consensus, and clever at selling schemes which possessed short-term merits. They were adept at bureaucratic manoeuvre and party management. They often rose due to being good at alliance building, thwarting adversaries, and disempowering the party grassroots which had nominated and supported them. They relied initially on bureaucrats and planners overseeing national reconstruction. Soon their horizons had expanded, and it was the transnational officials, planners and lobbyists of the entity known as the European Union from 1993, which they collaborated with. This was especially the case after the EU started to amass powers which previously had been the domain of the nation-state.

Finally, many became willing participants in an emerging cosmopolitan elite that was increasingly explicit about detaching itself from the nation-state and replacing identities shaped around loyalty to a fixed territorial community with commitment to building a new and self-styled progressive global order. Increasing government control over the lives of citizens was also matched by growing concentrations of wealth, as corporate giants in the new tech industries surged ahead while economic small and medium-sized companies struggled to compete or survive.

George Orwell, writing in 1946, had predicted the rise of such a managerial state, one with outsized ambitions that was ready to sweep away obstacles preventing it directing the planet in the purposeful way that a successful corporation was run:

> 'What is now arising is a new kind of planned, centralized society which will be neither capitalist nor, in any accepted sense of the word, democratic. The rulers of this new society will be the people who effectively control the means of production: that is, business executives, technicians, bureaucrats, and soldiers, lumped together...under the name of "managers". These people will eliminate the old capitalist class, crush the working class, and so organize society that all power and economic privilege remain in their own hands'.[1]

However, the author of *1984* and *Animal Farm*, books which delivered chilling warnings about the onset of a totalitarian society, may not have foreseen the staying power of competitive democracy. It would survive in non-communist countries and even expand to ones which had thrown off the yoke of Soviet communism. Arguably, it has displayed more vitality and staying power than competing authoritarian systems, principally centred around first, the Soviet Communist system, and then the kleptocratic nationalist order established by Vladimir Putin after 1999.

Orwell grew increasingly pessimistic as, in the final years of his life, Stalin imposed his rule on half of Europe. It is quite possible that he would have been shocked by the ability of an initially, seemingly infirm Ukraine to unleash an internal revolution in defence of freedom. But he would possibly have been far less surprised by the struggle for ascendancy being waged in a number of pluralist states, between elected tribunes committed to national government within a framework of popular sovereignty, and figures whose authority stems from global or regional bureaucracies expanding in size and power. This new cohort of decision-makers prefer a tutelary version of democracy, in which the verdict of voters can be overridden by non-elected guardians.

The contrasting choices were thrown into sharp relief when Ursula von der Leyen, the unelected head of the European Commission, a body now with more power than nearly all European states, declared on 23 September

2022, that the EU had the 'tools' to deal with wayward member states.[2] This was in response to a question put to her about the possibility that the Italian general election, due in two days' time, would produce a result which ran counter to the EU's centralising vision for Europe. If it was a warning shot across the bows of the Italian electorate, it failed dismally. Instead, the Brothers of Italy (Fratelli d'Italia: FdI) centre-right coalition won a strong electoral endorsement.

It is unlikely that such a name for a contender for power would readily be adopted in many other parts of Europe. Its clearly masculine overtones may well have sounded jarring for those committed to gender equality in politics. The choice of name for the electoral alliance was perhaps palatable owing to the fact that the FdI's leader was a woman, 45-year-old Giorgia Meloni. Her canny and pugnacious discourse and bearing conveyed echoes of Machiavelli and his celebrated discourse on political power, *The Prince*, published in 1513. It is often assumed to have been inspired by the Renaissance thinker's belief that Italy needed a ruler capable of uniting the peninsula and shaking off foreign overlordship. In a work that has enjoyed enduring influence, he explored the qualities needed for a ruler to succeed. He emphasised effectiveness as a warrior possessing courage and endeavour. But he also underlined the importance of 'fraud' by which he meant cunning and the ability to deceive.

Especially in the English-speaking world this has harmed his reputation: When James Burnham published his book The Machiavellians in 1943, he wrote that 'his name has become a term of reproach and dishonor'.[3] According to the US political scientist N.O. Keohane, '*The Prince* provides the paradigmatic statement in the Western political tradition of the view that effective leadership is personal, powerful, and, to a large degree, unconstrained'.[4] But the Latin world, spread over several continents, has by no means been as disapproving of Machiavelli. It is possible to argue that Machiavellianism continues to be seen there in a rather more positive light, denoting political artistry, and sophisticated double-dealing. From the age of the Italian enlightenment to the unification of the peninsula, far from being seen as immoral and cynical, Machiavelli and his thoughts were seen as educational and responsible, revealing to many the circumstances and requirements for the successful exercise of power.[5]

The book seeks to explore the political craftmanship of decision-makers in a range of crises, power struggles, controversies, and political experiments from the start of the Cold War to the eruption of the war between Russia and Ukraine. Attention is paid to the human dimension in the various stages of growth of the European Union and its predecessors, and in efforts to alter the structure of governance in various states, incorporating new ideas involving the re-arrangement of state power. The age-old struggle involving ambitious opportunists subverting structures meant to hold unscrupulous behaviour in check, inevitably looms large: such power grabs did not cease even in the most hopeful phases of the seventy-year period under discussion.

A book of this nature, paying close attention to the personal in politics, is obviously swimming against the tide. Strong tendencies have existed in scholarship to take the individual out of recent historical accounts of Europe after 1945. Beforehand, Europe had witnessed heroic and demonic examples of leadership. Afterwards, there seemed to be far less justification for interpretations which emphasised the human dimension. Events seemed to justify placing much of the emphasis on impersonal structures and forces.

Ones that readily spring to mind include: material reconstruction after World War II; the waging of the Cold War; the creation of cooperative economic institutions; and finally, the rise of the environmental movement in world affairs, in which bureaucrats and activists were to the fore in crafting the 1992 Rio deal and the subsequent 1997 Kyoto protocol.

The era of personal politics seemed to recede as, more than ever, universal concepts were used to explain the latest chequered experiences of the human species. The appeal of structural explanations for events, based on concepts and theories in which human agency had little or no role, grew in popularity. As the historian Donald Cameron Watt noted, the use of abstract theories made it easier for some historians to make claims that their work was based on some form of pseudo-scientific certainty.

Watt argued that the policies of states and the course of their interactions could not be divorced from the flesh and blood people, the political, military, and economic elites, who formulated state policies and acted upon them. In assessing his work and its particular focus, Joseph A. Maiolo has pointed out what was distinctive about it:

> 'He urged practitioners of international history to borrow from the analytical vocabulary and concepts of sociology, economics, and above all international relations theory. However, there was a definable limit to how far the historian could and should draw upon the social sciences. That limit was the point at which the real flesh and blood "people" of the past became mere cardboard characters acting in compliance with grand theoretical constructs'.[6]

Countries emerged with particular political systems, due to distinctive historical experiences. Troubling historical features and fissures arising from social, ethnic, and religious cleavages, could cast a long shadow. The responses of elites to new members and the nature of the challenge from below for improvements and representation varied widely. National divisions over the sharing of power or the division of frontiers also contributed substantially to the tumult in pre-1914 Europe, accelerating rather than hindering the countdown to conflict. By the mid-1930s, democracy, as commonly recognised, had disappeared from most of Europe, except the British Isles, Scandinavia, France, and the Benelux countries. The human factor continued to be central in political affairs, and sometimes catalytic, as shown in Britain in 1940 and also in the decisions taken by Britain's adversaries at that time.

A long post-war era overshadowed by the menacing Cold War, and the need to reconstruct shattered economies and disrupted societies, now lay ahead. It offered the opportunity for cunning and calculating figures to hold sway. They were described as realists and pragmatists by their admirers but were viewed as under-hand and untrustworthy by their detractors. Their ascendancy has been an extended one. At their best they displayed flair at short-term problem-solving. But they often struggled to display vision and perspicacity in the face of new and unexpected developments. These ranged from the emergence of neo-capitalist, but still very much communist China, to the challenge of satisfying the desire of well-placed elites for Green solutions for energy needs, when much of the technology remained on the drawing-board. Individual acumen and endeavour were increasingly overshadowed and supplanted by different forms of group think, that could be the fruit of assiduous lobbying to promote an all-embracing idea rather than the outcome of rigorous research or debate.

The tendency was, if anything, reinforced by the rise of full-time politicians who had few organic ties with society. Increasingly, in the major democratic states, there was an emphasis on transferring major decisions to remote global bodies like the IMF and the World Health Organization. They were often staffed by individuals whose ambitions extended far beyond stabilising currencies or improving human health, and whose networks were more powerful than those that the leaders of nation-states could muster. Trans-national deliberations began to eclipse national decision-making, even though the plans and strategies agreed often fell victim to the march of events. National elections lost their legitimacy as medium-sized nation-states increasingly struggled to adapt to decisions being made by global corporations, financial institutions and multi-level bureaucracies.

Invariably, a club atmosphere developed at the senior decision-making levels of an inter-connected world. There was an emphasis on communicating with fellow leaders and with high-profile economic figures who had risen to prominence as a result of the growing inter-connectedness arising from accelerating population movements, trade, and cultural inter-action. What became known as globalisation elevated the status of international institutions, particularly in the economic realm. Electorates were often shut out of the conversation.

Arguably, many politicians have lost the ability to communicate easily because their contact with the wider society has shrivelled. Instead, they have relied increasingly on media communication experts or 'spin doctors' to craft their speeches and sound bites. These influencers often end up as more influential figures in a leader's team than ministers in charge of major spending departments.

INTRODUCTION

The politicians confronted with a malevolent Vladimir Putin, a seemingly deadly global pandemic, and intensifying cycles of economic instability often appeared disorientated and irresolute. The creation of a single currency in 1999 for lots of countries, with disparate economic bases and cycles, had taken major economic decisions out of the hands of most of the governments belonging to this currency zone. Debate was frowned upon, even at elite levels, as the Euro faced severe jolts a decade into its existence. It had emerged in what proved to be a short-lived era of optimism following the anti-climactic end to the Cold War. The historian, Robert Tombs, well-described the late twentieth-century mood: 'No global wars, no revolutions, no uncontrollable economic disasters, no epidemics that could not be treated, but rising wealth and life expectancy. Softer values and looser morals suited this age of safety, as sterner virtues seemed outdated'.[7]

Almost an air of frivolity marked the transition from an era of deadly Great Power competition to one summed up by Francis Fukuyama's influential book *The End of History,* which postulated that the world was entering an era of benignity when ideological struggle and the clash of great power interests were receding into the past.[8] Accordingly, it was a time when not only countless members of the military were being retired in NATO countries, but one where there seemed little need for vigilant and incisive politicians alert to danger. Following the 9/11 attacks in the USA in September 2001, the bubble of quiet euphoria was punctured. Costly, destructive and humiliating intervention by Western powers in Iraq and Afghanistan resulted. But messianic politicians like Tony Blair proved to be of transitory importance. In the United States, President Barack Obama rekindled the sense of optimism that deep-seated differences over national interests, ideologies or economic needs were the product of a bygone age. Simultaneously, the European Union, awarded the Nobel Peace Prize in 2013, a few years after Obama was a recipient, invested heavily in the notion that soft power, based on diplomacy and good example, would render unnecessary the investment in arms and plans for military deterrence. These awards seemed to legitimise the idea of 'leading from behind', one that involved substituting an alert and vigorous approach to international relations with a more consultative or reflective one.

A downplaying of leadership roles in the West during the era, which saw both Russia and China's stature and leverage rapidly expand, gathered pace. Largely gone were the forceful personalities, energetic reformers, raffish diplomats and outspoken tribunes able to hold a crowd. The vacuum was filled by figures who differed in background, personality, and style but who were adept at using their office or high profile to realise objectives that were most dear to them, which often were somewhat removed from their stated aspirations and goals. All of the figures examined here were chameleons or shape-shifters to one degree or another. They fitted well Machiavelli's image of the sinuous and deceptive fox who seeks to outwit the powerful and stolid lion by subterfuge or deception.

Twenty figures are assessed here who had different priorities. They:

- Sought to preserve, modify or dismantle communism through the exercise of personal authority (Josip Tito, Milo Djukanović, and Viktor Orbán).
- Ensured their countries became beneficiaries, and not victims, in interactions with the Soviet Union and later Russia (Urho Kekkonen, Angela Merkel).
- Sought to give the movement for transnational European cooperation key momentum, and benefit directly from it (Paul-Henri Spaak and Valéry Giscard d'Estaing).
- Used their Machiavellian skills to impede reform in Mediterranean Europe and entrench their personal power (Silvio Berlusconi, Andreas Papandreou, Pedro Sanchez).
- Diluted ideology and downgraded the importance of political ethics in order to extract outsized benefit from the exercise of patronage and the acquisition of wealth (François Mitterrand and Gerhard Schröder).
- Manipulated ethnic emotions and identity in order to try and alter the map of Europe (Jordi Pujol, Nicola Sturgeon).
- Thrust themselves forward as emblems for schemes of national renewal or consolidation based on demagogic appeals or contrasting globalist agendas (Mark Rutte, Boris Johnson, Emmanuel Macron).

Such individuals might not have loomed so large or indeed acted in the ways that they did, if the post-1945 story of Europe had evolved differently. It has often been argued that a more resolute approach to Stalin by his Western Allies, could have scaled back his conquests in Eastern Europe. A peaceful and less polarised Europe could have weakened the hold of dictators and demagogues. Moving further ahead, after the Cold War, a more strategic and less haphazard approach to building a stable and economically cohesive European order, could have encouraged brighter talent to enter the political arena. Instead of displaying realism and a sense of urgency, hubristic leaders pursued ill-prepared niche projects. All too often, they were based on the search for a historical legacy rather than any cost-benefit analysis of how they might strengthen a continent emerging from generations of warfare, dictatorship and division, one that was far less strong and resilient than it seemed.

The temporising that prevailed after the eruption in 2022, of the biggest land war Europe had seen since 1945, showed that in the one-third of a century after the breaching of the Berlin Wall, the statesmanship needed to provide a viable design for a peaceful European order was sorely lacking. A leadership famine seemed to stalk much of Europe.

It was becoming ever harder to appeal to the common good and a shared unity of purpose. Internal divisions, based as much on cultural disagreements about the character and purpose of nations and societies as on economic ones concerning the distribution of wealth and priorities for investment, had frayed societies. The inability of politicians to craft appealing narratives accompanying forward-looking policies, meant the political stage emptied of talent. Arguably, this was painfully clear in the build-up to, and early crucial stages, of the Russo-Ukrainian war which the last chapter focuses upon. Politicians who seemed increasingly ill-equipped to motivate and calm their own societies floundered in the face of this return to total warfare in Europe.

The figures profiled in the opening Cold War section of the book, Josip Broz Tito, Uhro Kaleva Kekkonen, Paul H. Spaak, and Giulio Andreotti differed in style, but they displayed the ability to organize a consensus behind policies designed to preserve stability in unpredictable and hazardous circumstances. Coercion was also an arrow in Tito's quiver to enable him to preserve a common polity in an ethnically diverse and volatile Yugoslavia. Kekkonen used guile and Soviet help to preserve his neutral vision of Finland and seek to extend it elsewhere in Scandinavia during the Cold War. Spaak used his energy and resilience to place Belgium at the heart of the emerging Euro-Atlantic political and security communities. Meanwhile, Andreotti's legendary patience and cunning were harnessed to preserve a dysfunctional Italian Second Republic, until it was overwhelmed by corruption scandals in the 1990s.

They were resourceful and energetic politicians who were not cut off from their societies as successors would prove to be. What each had in common was a desire to shrink the political stage upon which they performed, to dimensions that enabled their influence to be perpetuated. None displayed much serious thought about what might come after them.

The next section of the book is devoted to France and Germany. Their political and economic weight respectively was undisguised after the 1950s. They were the directing players in the European entity, as the powers it acquired from nation-states, boosted its strength. The argument made in this section is that these pivotal European nations, by their conduct, highlighted the decline in the effectiveness of European liberal democracy. Poorly-conceived power-plays at home and abroad and an incoherent approach to building the architecture of the EU governance, left them poor stewards of an embryo post-national Europe.

The growing visibility of career-fixated opportunists with a short-term outlook started to be noticeable in these countries. However, there had been an interlude of stability, contrasting in length, after both countries saw their political systems recast in 1949 and 1958. The standing of the federal German model and the central French one, proceeded to fray, as elite cohesion and the mindfulness of office holders to maintain good standards of conduct, diminished. Corruption scandals involving French presidents and the high-handed behaviour of successive German chancellors, had corrosive effects. Growing absorption with European affairs led to deepening interaction with other world-focussed leaders, global technocrats and corporate businesspeople. Fringe forces were able to exploit the feeling that citizens were being left behind, and thus started to emerge from the political shadows. Perhaps the most crucial misstep, which put the political class on a collision with a large swathe of the population, was the decision, chiefly driven by France and Germany, to provide enormous state support for an ailing financial sector after 2008, while doubling down on austerity for much of the rest of the population. This was not the only decision by the leadership of these states that revealed they were drifting away from their own societies. But it was arguably the most momentous one. It meant a loss of integrity for the political class in the eyes of voters that was reflected in electoral abstentions, backing for populists and outbursts of social unrest. President Macron's decision in March 2023, to raise the pension age without a parliamentary vote, is likely to swell the sense of alienation from the political order in France.

Profiles of Valéry Giscard d'Estaing, François Mitterrand, Gerhard Schröder and Angela Merkel, reveal autocratic and sometimes impulsive leaders who benefited from the decline of checks and balances that previously offered restraints on conduct. Their desire to wield power often failed to be matched by a desire to use it for constructive purposes, even though there were a growing number of problems requiring a prudent and long-term approach. At times, they were gripped by hubris, refusing to show awareness of the difficulties and dangers some of their decisions could give rise to. Each shared a distinct lack of enthusiasm for having them debated or subject to any kind of serious scrutiny.

Leadership failings in two such pivotal countries, greatly added to the troubles that bore down on much of Europe, especially after the year 2000.

Historically, it is the countries on the northern shores of the Mediterranean Sea which have been among the first to buckle and collapse into strife when Europe has faced generalised crisis, particularly over economic matters. The decline of economic competence and fiscal prudence that has marked the EU in recent decades, exposed them to the post-2008 financial crisis in raw form. Beforehand, despite Mediterranean states being hailed as successful examples of democratisation, they had been unable to establish political systems where the competing forces displayed restraint in order to best handle precarious economic conditions. Instead, partisanship and a fierce contest for state resources has more often than not disfigured and weakened south European politics. This section profiles four leaders who have sought to monopolise power and, at times, display a reckless approach to constitutional rules. It hardly matters that three of the four led the predominant left-wing force in their countries. In practice, they ruled on behalf of an informal and shifting set of interests that defies easy ideological classification. The defence of the interests of lower-income voters were often far from their consideration. Much of the time the focus was on political warfare and using the state to benefit themselves and their clienteles. They were in politics not so much as saviours or problem-solvers, but as acquisitive political entrepreneurs.

Stronger 'partner' states in the EU have continued to adopt a moralistic tone towards the countries on the southern rim of the EU. But in truth, the politics of the core EU states have increasingly displayed some of the corrosive traits that have undermined representative democracy in Mediterranean Europe. Where adapted, it is naive to assume that aligning with cut-throat financial cartels, or pursuing policies that damage national cohesion in the longer-term, won't undermine democracy, as has occurred in these politically volatile countries.

British politicians are largely absent from these pages, even though many of the holders of the Premiership from 1945 to now, strongly encouraged the post-national tendencies in policy-making which opened up divisions in society. They strongly believed that the world was moving in a more inter-dependent direction and that Britain should be in the vanguard of this process. The majority of the political class was enthusiastic about sharing sovereignty with other European countries, allowing China to be integrated fully into the world economy despite remaining a communist country, and embracing a global strategy designed to control the environment. The two contrasting British politicians profiled here, Boris Johnson and Nicola Sturgeon, shared many of these priorities.

There was perhaps no other large democratic country where projecting soft power was seen as a normative principle to the extent that it was in Britain. At the turn of the century, it pressed ahead with the creation of autonomous political institutions. These were based on historic identities or on the need for a city as important as London to have its own elected mayor. In Spain, a parallel transfer of powers from the central state to autonomous territorial formations had occurred earlier, leaving no part of the country untouched.

The decentralisation process was meant to strengthen identification with newly established democratic institutions after a long period of centralized authoritarian rule. Arguably, more prudence was shown by central rulers there than in Britain, in order to ensure that it did not spiral out of control and raise the spectre of secession.

It was assumed there was sufficient cohesion at the centre to handle disruption from newly-empowered territories. This turned out to be a misjudgement and perhaps it was hardly surprising that Britain was the first sizeable European democratic state where the miscalculation became obvious. The granting of devolution to Scotland and Wales coincided with a tendency for the state to depict Britain as having a mosaic identity shaped by the collective personalities of different ethno-religious, regional and later gender-focused groups. Patriotism was frowned upon as a unifying concept, just as the central state was downgrading national sovereignty.

But if the assumption was that the historic regions of Spain and the Celtic national communities of Britain would go down a similar consensual path, it turned out to be a mistaken one. Highly-motivated purveyors of identity, quite prepared to foster an 'us and them' mentality with the larger state they wished to be distant from, gained increasing ground. In Catalonia, outright separatists have been in charge for most of the period since 1980, and in Scotland for the last fifteen years. Leaders like Jordi Pujol and Nicola Sturgeon, who are profiled here, see themselves as being on a moral mission. They believe in 'a conquest of state and society by nationalism'. They have sought to 'coordinate' and control all political, social, cultural, and educational institutions in the name of national unity. Pujol pursued his strategy craftily and noiselessly. Sturgeon arguably has been more overt and confrontational. Boundaries are emphasised and there is no official backing for overlapping identities, despite the fluid nature of identity in both Catalonia and Scotland. These ethnic identity politicians have boldly pursued social engineering measures designed to alter the character of their societies, in order to make them more susceptible to their bold agendas.

However, viable plans for state-building and continuing with existing levels of state protection for citizens after secession is accomplished, are hard to spot. Yet they remain strongly in contention. One essential explanation may well be that no other political movement has been as effective in manipulating the assertion of feelings and emotions which have spring up as important markers of identity in Western culture, especially among younger generations. Hence, there may well be a strong case for including a section on ethnic entrepreneurs in politics.

Those profiled in the final section, dwelling on contemporary Europe, shed some light on the opacity and incoherence of political affairs. Viktor Orbán, Emmanuel Macron, Boris Johnson and Mark Rutte rejected or transcended the prior allegiances which they had started out with in public affairs. Instead, they went before the nation as tribunes whose personal qualities meant that they could make a positive difference to people's lives. The cultivation of a *saviour* role (or that of *benefactor* in the case of Mark Rutte) was an age-old device for acquiring political ascendancy. It is the principal political technique employed by those who aim to supplant the left-right divide in Europe (or indeed secede from existing states).

Dwelling on the personalisation of politics can all too easily distract attention from deeper shifts occurring below the surface. Since the end of the Cold War, this binary distinction of 'left' and 'right' has grown even less helpful as a tool for tracking the behaviour of both parties and voters. The left has succeeded in moving increasingly closer to business, its leadership having been middle-class in origin for a sizable period already. The alliance hardened, certainly in Anglo-Saxon countries, as bolder titans of the dot-com economy were able to make unprecedented profits from promoting radical progressive themes and merchandise in the companies that they controlled.

Similarly on the right, old commitments have frayed. The popularity of free market economics has waned as it became clear that economic nationalism, containing a bigger role for the state than before, was a formula capable of moving lower-income voters rightwards. Perhaps Orbán is the only one in Europe to have succeeded in making conservative paternalism a formula for enduring success. He had the discipline to create a formidable political machine, Fidesz, whose influence extended deep into the state. Like Machiavelli's *Prince,* he was prepared to take risks to buttress his position, not all of his gambles paying off.

By contrast, Johnson (like Berlusconi before him) seemed a dabbler who lacked the stamina and lucidity to create anything beyond the transitory in politics. Yet such 'men of no quality' have been a recurring presence in European politics in times of flux and upheaval. Perhaps it is not just their own personal shortcomings that account for their failures. They may have benefited from a rejection of mainstream positions that was increasingly seen in some of the older democracies, but their ill-discipline helped to fuel disengagement and depoliticisation. Citizens, especially the young, increasingly absented themselves from democratic politics. Growing numbers were absorbed in millennial causes that ultimately required the validation of progressive elites, not the ballot box.

While a nation like Ukraine astonished much of the world due to the elán it showed in its struggle for democratic freedom, this attribute seemed of steadily diminishing importance to key groups in the West who no longer identified with the norms and values underpinning liberal democracy. Perhaps France is the European country where alienation from the status quo seems most acute. It has been far from a new or recent occurrence. Emmanuel Macron is a tireless and self-confident product of the technocratic French left who has been buffeted by these tensions. One advantage that he has over Johnson, and which makes him comparable with Orbán and Rutte, is that he has displayed an intimate knowledge of how to use political power to his advantage. In his bid to consolidate a liberal capitalist order in Europe imbued with culturally radical features, he has made mistakes. But he has the ability to subdue and mould institutions to his purpose, one which has eluded many conservatives in our own day.

One danger for Europe is that pressures from both left and right will result in the ballot box being gradually abandoned in favour of more consultative forms of rule. The fact that France has had no less than eight constitutions since 1814, shows how unsatisfactory democracy has periodically seemed in a country which, if natural wealth is to be taken into account, should be one of the most stable and satisfied countries in Europe. Influential Frenchmen dispensed with democracy and won enough backing to impose an alternative. If democracy ceases to be useful and becomes an inconvenience for influential citizens, there is no reason why such rejection cannot become a feature of the politics of other countries in the future, ones with which France can be compared.

A final chapter on Europe in the shadow of the 2022 Russo-Ukrainian war, asks what impact the geo-political and military surprises resulting from this clash of arms could have on the exercise of leadership in democratic Europe. It focuses on two individuals, Volodymyr Zelensky and Olaf Scholz, and explores what have been the motivations of key European actors in this conflict. To what extent have decision-makers belatedly realised their mistakes in previously facilitating an imperial-minded leader ready to sweep away internationally agreed conventions? Is the sense of entitlement shown by particular nations, that European affairs should dance to their tune, now in retreat? Will the ferment perhaps even diminish the scale of Europe's leadership famine? In the face of momentous events, this is an apt time to use the medium of biography to highlight and explore a number of deepening problems in European politics.

---

[1] Michael Lind, 'The importance of James Burnham', *Tablet Magazine*, 2 September 2021, https://www.tabletmag.com/sections/news/articles/burnham-michael-lind, accessed 25 October 2022.
[2] 'EU's von der Leyen delivers veiled warning to Italy's right wing', *Reuters*, 23 September 2022, https://www.reuters.com/world/europe/eus-von-der-leyen-delivers-veiled-warning-italys-right-wing-2022-09-23/, accessed 29 September 2022.
[3] James Burnham, The Machiavellians, Defenders of Freedom, London, Lume Books, 2020 edition (from original 1943 one), p. 47.
[4] N.O. Keohane, 'Western Political Thought', in *The Oxford Handbook of Political Leadership*, R.A.W. Rhodes and Paul 'T Hart (eds.), Oxford: Oxford University Press, 2013, p. 30.
[5] See Giovanni Giorgini, 'Five Hundred Years of Italian Scholarship on Machiavelli's Prince', *Review of Politics*, Fall 2013, Vol. 75, No. 4, p.p. 625 – 640.
[6] Joseph A. Maiolo, 'Personalities, Policies, and International History: The Life and Work of Donald Cameron Watt', *Diplomacy and Statecraft*, Vol. 26, No. 2, 2015, p. 207.
[7] Robert Tombs, 'The divided West is enfeebled by declinism and despair', *Daily Telegraph*, 25 June 2022.
[8] Francis Fukuyama, *The End of History and the Last Man*, New York, Free Press, 1992.

PART 1
CHAPTER 1: COLD WAR PARADOX

Conservatives retreat before The Left

Chosen as case studies for the height of the Cold War period are four determined, cunning and resilient leaders who shaped the direction of European countries in the decades after 1945. Both Tito and Kekkonen were durable rulers of states that lay on the front line of the East-West ideological struggle. Tito seems to have known that the chances were high that his brand of one-man rule was a holding operation in a country with plenty of fissures. But he contented himself with tinkering with the details rather than attempting an overhaul which could give Yugoslavia a better chance of long outliving him. Kekkonen also chose to retain a formula for keeping the Soviet Union at arm's length from Finland, which relied on the charisma of a durable leader. But the stakes were less high, even though Finland came near to ceasing to exist several times during his lifetime.

The influence of Spaak and Andreotti stemmed not so much from direct exercise of executive power but through the sway that they exercised across the body politic of Belgium and Italy for many decades. The pair preserved internal equilibrium in the face of a range of threats, projecting themselves as wily guardians of constitutional order, but who were not always beneath acquiescing with dubious forces. Andreotti's clerical air hid a masterful bureaucratic fixer, Spaak was a *bon viveur* whose stubborn imperturbability suited him for the deal-making trans-national aspects of post-war politics. Tito has been described as a communist pharaoh whose charisma and cunning kept a dysfunctional political order afloat, while Kekkonen was as resourceful and competitive in politics as he had been in sport, networking and intelligence work.

These were Marxist, liberal-conservative, secular social democratic, and Christian democratic figures respectfully who hung on to power and influence as Europe recoiled from the political polarisation and massive bloodletting of the 1933-45 period. Few states had emerged untouched. Many citizens, due to the extension of Soviet power deep into Central Europe, saw their freedoms extinguished for nearly two generations. Leadership in the electoral democracies that continued, or were restored, evolved along different lines than before. Candidates for high office sought backing by emphasising their qualifications for rebuilding damaged or shattered economies. Alliance builders who promoted the politics of pragmatism to ward off fresh extremist dangers found it easier to acquire relevance and prestige than in the polarised 1930s. Fewer leaders were visible who sought endorsement through recourse to charisma or demagogic messages. In some countries, the politics of compromise were impeded by internal cleavages or the existence of powerful anti-system parties. Italy acquired fitful stability by 1950, but France would take another decade before its politics settled into a predictable pattern.

Confronting the powerful communist parties in France and Italy were parties that drew their leaders, activists and followers from conventional sections of society. Successive crises and upheavals from 1914 to 1945 had disturbed long-established patterns of life. But civil-war, dictatorship, invasion and physical destruction would arguably have less of an impact on the traditional European way of life than the later growth of prosperity and leisure time, the advance of secularism, and profound changes in the status of women, the role of education, and the impact of the mass media. Politics was still class-orientated and those with higher social status or seniority in the labour movement were usually able to advance quicker and faster than others who lacked corporate sponsorship or access to private wealth.

The career-minded politicians who dominated much of the political spectrum by the 1990s jostled with others whose involvement derived from ideological conviction or a desire to promote reforms or ensure injustices were overcome. Prior to the age of the electronic media and privatised ways of life, civil society was multi-layered and quite extensive. Charitable, educational, religious, sporting and other recreational pursuits proved absorbing for large numbers of people from different social stations. It meant that the main political pillars based on labour, industry, agriculture, local and imperial interests, were reinforced by a wider cross-section of participants. Undoubtedly, the legitimacy of democratic politics benefited from this range and depth of involvement. It became less easy for opponents of conventional democracy to subvert elective systems. The only long-established European democracy to founder after 1945 was the 1919-38 Czechoslovak one in March 1948, albeit with crucial foreign help.

Initially, politics offered far fewer material rewards for elected representatives than it would later when it came to be widely viewed as a lucrative career for ambitious people. But it was also perhaps less arduous in psychological terms than it would later become. Before the onset of electronic media, it was far easier to dissimulate and conceal, than it would later become. An intrusive and politically engaged media has been one of the tools which has enabled a left-leaning intelligentsia to throw opponents onto the defensive after the year 2000. Before the age of high-powered political reporting and permanent campaigning online, conservatives found it easier to preach a message of incremental change or defence of the status quo. In West Germany, the left would be denied office until the end of the 1960s and in France and Italy, it would take much longer before the left emerged from an electoral trough.

But the democratically-minded political centre-right was not master of all it surveyed. It was on the defensive from the outset after 1945. Nazism was associated with the political right, despite *National Socialism* being the doctrine of the Nazi movement. The desire for a redistribution of wealth was most vigorously promoted by trade unions and left-wing parties; decolonisation may not have been a priority for them, but retaining overseas possessions was an uphill task for national conservatives. The French, and especially the Dutch, were tenacious. But it was to no avail.

At home, it was hardly easier to mount a defence of a social order which had clearly benefited those with wealth, status and informal power. The fall-out from fierce internal struggles, some of which even preceded the First World War, meant that the inclination to retreat from class conflict was strong. Gradually, there was a slow acceptance of alternative 'progressive' norms that were extending their hold over wider society. Such pragmatism at elite level made it easier to hold the line against the expansionary communist parties of France and Italy. In 1946, French Communists had over one million members and in Italy, the Communists could already boast 1.7 million members in 1945.[1]

The commencement of the Cold War proved an advantage for the democratic right. The anti-communist climate produced electoral gains and encouraged conservatives to regroup. Christian Democrats (CDs) were their most recognisable and electorally successful brand. Absorption with economic recovery and deterring communist influence marked the tenures in office of Alcide de Gasperri in Italy and Konrad Adenauer in Germany. The pre-existing strength of the Catholic Church in much of Italy and large parts of West Germany may have precluded the CDs from trying to consolidate their influence in society. Meanwhile, in France, the conservative world was compromised by the legacy of the wartime collaborationist regime at Vichy. A series of disastrous colonial conflicts then disrupted French politics until the start of the 1960s.

De Gaulle and Adenauer were symbols of patrician rectitude. But they were unable to promote any fundamental conservative recovery. Before forming the 5th Republic in 1958, perhaps de Gaulle's most significant peace time role had been to nationalise large swathes of the French economy in 1945. Winston Churchill, a long-term conservative totem, had even less time or interest in upholding a conservative programme. He was a former liberal who had never sat easily in Tory ranks. In the 1950s, the British Conservatives were drawing heavily on the pragmatic and adaptable strands of their long-term philosophy, one evolved in the furtherance of shaping Britain's destiny.

The Labour Party leader Clement Attlee remarked privately in 1951 that: 'By far the most radical man I've known in politics wasn't on the Labour side at all'. It was Harold Macmillan, who would lead the Conservatives and the country from 1957 to 1963.

A willingness to allow the diffusion of power across state and society was not matched on the right by any keen attempt to ensure that conservative ideas retained visibility and influence. There was a disinclination to treat communism as a criminal system on par with Nazism. This was combined with a readiness to allow the Soviet regime 'to impose on the world its own ideological understanding of how political systems should be classified. Lenin reduced them essentially to two polar opposites, socialism and capitalism…'.[2] Conservative thinkers lacked a strong base in the worlds of education, the media and even their own institutional churches, to confront the new left that was coming to the fore.

They presided over an expansion of the state very much on left-wing terms. At contrasting rates, a large, intrusive and regulatory state took shape that encouraged a dependent population managed by an army of low-skilled bureaucrats. Little energy on the centre-right was devoted to creating a strong capacity-driven state that, as well as doing things for people, equipped them with the means to do things for themselves.

In the turbulent 1960s, there was a feeling of helplessness as 'authority' became a term of disapproval. As it became clear that the Paris revolt of May 1968 was having a profound effect on politics and society, not just in France, authority became a term of outright condemnation. By now, thanks to the dissemination of works by influential social theorists on the left, commitment to previously mainstream values (regarding morality and religion) was viewed with increasing suspicion and could be seen as concealing a reactionary or even fascist personality.[3]

By the 1970s, right-of-centre leaders, such as Giscard and Andreotti, did not hide their preparedness to incorporate left-wing campaigning demands in order to redefine the family in law. An Italian divorce law was approved in 1970 and eight years later, Andreotti, as prime minister, approved the legalisation of abortion. Christian Democrats in Italy increasingly emphasised that they were a broad platform of opinions rather than a confessional option. Augusto del Noce, increasingly recognised as an important conservative philosopher, quit the Italian Senate in the 1980s, finding himself isolated in a philistine atmosphere.[4] Someone who shared his sceptical outlook about the modern European journey was Joseph Ratzinger, who acceded to the papacy in 2005 as Benedict XVI. He warned in those years that: 'We are building a dictatorship of relativism that does not recognize anything as definitive and whose ultimate goal consists solely of one's own ego and desires'.[5]

For Christian Democrats in both Italy and Germany, promoting European political integration was far more important than safeguarding the essential features of a Catholic society.[6] One French Catholic publicist went as far as to say that by 'the first decade of the twenty-first century (and probably sooner), nominally Christian politicians were not Christian anymore, or at least not Christian enough to challenge the rest of the political class, as their forefathers had'.[7]

Certainly, evidence was accumulating that Christianity was no longer normative in morality and foundational in the culture, values and laws of Europe. The journey taken by Johann Vollenbroek, the Dutch environmental activist, who, with the help of sympathetic judges, waged war against farmers in the name of eco-purity, highlights the extent of the revolt against the church. Raised a strict Catholic, he 'fought against both the religion and his parents' expectations of church attendance'. Looking back in 2023, he had no qualms about stating that: 'I think that Christianity is causing this disastrous attitude toward the climate. Because… if you read the Bible, then mankind is on a much higher level than nature.'[8] Shortly afterwards, the once powerful Christian Democrats suffered a mighty electoral reverse as it headed towards near political extinction while a newly-formed Farmers party, using direct action to resist Vollenbroek and his establishment allies, who came first in the Dutch regional elections.

Replacing any semblance of doctrinal rigour with a kind of festive Europeanism became de rigueur in politically-minded Catholic ranks. It meant that politicians, bankers and bureaucrats with a Catholic background (Helmut Kohl, Jacques Delors and Mário Draghi spring to mind) were – unsurprisingly - to the fore in promoting the single currency at the century's close. There were no 'adequate adjustment mechanisms' between the nineteen heterogeneous states participating.[9] Experts, who warned that a common currency between members who remained fiscally sovereign states was bound to enter crisis because of the absence of a common Treasury, were dismissed as alarmists. When the crisis came along with the Euro less than a decade old, the inability to devalue currencies or adjust interest rates meant that social devaluation was pursued instead, leading to grinding hardship across Southern Europe. No major Christian Democrat or Socialist politician defied the clamour orchestrated in the media for the imposition of 'hairshirt economics' that was mainly borne by lower income groups. It meant that the old blocs soon struggled to avoid being capsized by alternative forces, pejoratively branded as 'populist' even though their priorities were often hard to distinguish from the left and Christian Democracy *before* they jumped on the Euro bandwagon.[10]

By now, a politically-marginalised church was prepared to accept that it was a minority voice in an increasingly post-religious Western Europe. The absence of any kind of cultural fight-back meant that leaders on the right were firmly secular in their outlook. Even in Italy, the church found itself gradually excluded 'from a defined role in the life of modern society'. Thus, it was unable to act as a rallying-point for conservatives in the political arena. European conservatives had shown no inclination to promote a narrative based on preserving age-old values of prudence and restraint in the face of the clamour for experimentation and novelty. The emergence of Giorgia Meloni in 2022 as a powerful foe of abortion in Italian politics, was noteworthy as much for the length of time it took for someone with her traditional outlook to break through, as for her electoral strength.

Helmut Kohl and Margaret Thatcher were notable centre-right leaders. But their lengthy span in office was taken up with major internal and geopolitical challenges. The British leader was a purposeful economic liberal who had an unsentimental and downright wary view of the state. She once remarked: 'If politicians or bureaucrats are given power that is unaccountable and unrestrained, they will, in the long run, be as corrupt as they can get away with. That's the best possible argument for limited government'.[11] But her eventful eleven years in office saw no attempt to 'build ethos-driven institutions' or balance the dominance of the left across education with a conservative approach to socialising young people.[12] The prevalent view was that strategic thinking should be hitched to what brought short-term electoral advantage. Thatcher listened to intellectuals, but if there was any concern on her part about Gramsci's 'long march of the left through the institutions' of state and civil society, it was hardly reflected in any purposeful action. In 1990, she was toppled, with surprising ease, by economic liberals as soon as she seemed poised to frontally challenge the post-national European agenda. They continued to flourish in her party despite its populist conservative branding. The EU's technocratic construct was now steadily encroaching on matters that were hitherto the sole prerogatives of the nation-state. It was a more powerful source of loyalty for many in the ruling elite than *Britain*. Plenty of career politicians had a lofty or even dismissive attitude towards the nation-state, and by the early 2020s, it was not unusual to hear the Labour Party described as a party whose dominant strands found it increasingly harder to conceal their dislike for at least half the country.[13]

Conservatives had been the initial midwives of the European integration project. Adenauer had told his cabinet in 1952: 'the people must be given a new ideology. It can only be a European one'.[14]Across Western Europe socialists had largely remained detached, or even hostile, until the 1980s. But as its competences expanded and the EU started to turn into a pro-active organisation poised to manage and direct the whole of society very much from top to bottom, the complexion of those behind the driving wheel altered. An overseer class not just of bureaucrats and European-minded politicians but also managers, financiers, lobbyists, and radical activists, permitted by decision-makers to draw up numerous social engineering projects, became steadily more visible. The EU left behind not only its Christian roots, but also its identification with trade union rights as the influence of the labour cause steadily withered in its upper echelons. Increasingly, a bureaucratic or technocratic left-leaning intelligentsia came to acquire a hold over the EU machinery. These activists and lobbyists, and not labour organisations or overtly socialist bodies, became the left's primary source of empowerment. Their new Brussels-centred project was secular, post-modern, and post-national, a meeting point of the technocratic right and the cultural left. When drawing up the European Constitution in 2002, it was noticeable that no mention was made of

Europe's religious heritage, and God went unmentioned, despite the profound role of Christianity in shaping Europe.

With the ending of the Cold War and the rise of a fresh set of challenges, it was difficult to conceal that, across Europe, there was a noticeable deficit of leadership. The steady expansion of the EU had discouraged the rise of lawmakers who were keen to make a specific impact on policy within a national framework. Its acquisition of new powers, far beyond the economic realm, naturally weakened national decision-making. This in turn separated the popular will from policy-making.[15] The retreat of popular sovereignty encouraged the rise of an army of politicians, increasingly at ease with the horizontal intra-elite transactions that were at the heart of an opaque trans-national project.

This had unmistakeable advantages. Office-holders in the European Commission or the European Parliament were under far less pressure to perform and deliver in the eyes of electorates. Commissioners were unaccountable and Euro-parliamentarians could pass motions but not enact laws. Politics increasingly revolved around inter-elite dialogue and long-term social engineering projects and processes, often in the hands of internationally-focused 'experts'. Resolving immediate problems only became a priority once a mishandled or neglected problem had turned into a major crisis (such as happened with energy policy after Putin's invasion of Ukraine). Despite rhetoric, the disinclination to prepare long term for adversity remained deeply rooted in politicians, whose preference was to often deflect difficulties and focus attention on their careers outside national politics.

A diminishing number of leaders emerged in the expanding EU (currently 27 members) who were recognisable by their achievements or what they stood for. The decision-makers of the EU were often colourless and nebulous figures. Hermann von Rompuy, the Belgian Christian Democrat who served as the first President of the European Council, travelled from Brussels to Paris in a motor cavalcade.

But he was unrecognisable to most Europeans, a former German Chancellor dubbing him 'Mr Nobody'.[16]

A graduate class educated in esoteric or technocratic subjects and with only a fraction of the experiences of life and work of pre-1980 decision-makers, now increasingly determined the direction of policy and the allocation of resources, both at nation-state level and within the emerging trans-national seats of authority. Perhaps most had not been required to take risks in their lives or careers, not had they had to struggle to acquire a decent income. Few, if any, would have served in the military or fought in conflicts, as was the case with Helmut Schmidt, an anti-aircraft gunner on the Eastern front after 1941. Nor would the new political breed likely have closely engaged with social groups outside their ranks, through voluntary activities, or worked in a wide range of roles involving close interaction with the public. It is no surprise that their decisiveness was often felt to be lacking when crises came along such as that afflicting the Eurozone, the Covid pandemic, or Putin's attack on Ukraine, and the ensuing energy panic of 2022.[17]

The new elites claimed to be directing an exciting fresh project which would extricate Europe from acrimonious territorial politics and instead orientate the continent towards problem-solving on a global scale. But they struggled to define goals and objectives which would strike a chord with the population. Instead, there was often an emphasis on imposing ideological prescriptions, bound up especially with the environment. Employment and moral fulfilment were bestowed on a superior 'priestly elect'. They were slotted into positions of authority, but only to behave in increasingly irksome ways in the eyes of general populations.

Growing numbers of European decision-makers seem absorbed with global issues and thus lack the touch of arguably more capable rulers in the past who, at their best, could rally populations in times of adversity and crisis. It may not be unduly unfair to suggest that some trenchantly advance views on how to solve many of society's problems without having acquired the necessary experience or wisdom to be taken very seriously beyond their networks of influence.

Some of these decision-makers with limited life experiences often struggled when governing the institutions of cooperation and coordination which emerged from the Cold War period. Too many had lost their appetite for electoral politics, and their political antennae may have been blunted by the long years of deceptive peace (at least in most of Europe) from 1989 onwards. Political leaders took their cue from the doyen of European philosophers, Jürgen Habermas, who postulated that Europe was now firmly in a 'post-heroic age' bound up with consumerism and leisure activities.[18] Instead of showing alertness to the continuing communist character of China, European conservative statesmen, like the former British Prime Minister, Edward Heath, and the Italian Christian Democrat, Romano Prodi, head of the European Commission from 1999 to 2004, became enthusiastic defenders of the authoritarian state during its ambiguous embrace of features of Western capitalism.

Putin's Russia had an even bigger list of political grandees from Western Europe ready to be of service. In 2022, it emerged that René van der Linden, a Dutch Catholic politician who became head of the Council of Europe after presiding over his country's Senate, was under the surveillance of the Dutch secret service due to his alleged closeness to figures in the Russian state.[19] Later on, as the governing elite in many Western countries embraced social progressivism, many quite authoritarian and very conformist people who might once have readily identified with political conservatism, instead were happy to switch to becoming promoters of assertive liberalism. What may have counted for them was to be near the centre of power, irrespective of the ideology being advanced.

In what could be described as an age of complacency, it is perhaps no surprise that old problems and dangers were not long in manifesting themselves, from rule-breaking challengers of the democratic status quo to predatory leaders ready to destroy the peace of Europe and jeopardise the future of the world. In the face of such threats, what stood out was the reluctance of so many leaders to analyse past mistakes. Such evaluations had occurred during earlier times of crisis in the democratic age. But a sense of history was required and, by the start of the 2020s, much of the political class not only lacked detailed awareness of the past but had no qualms about sometimes repudiating it, despite being able to offer few signposts for the future.

---

[1] David Reynolds, From World War to Cold War: Churchill, Roosevelt, and the International History of the 1940s, Oxford: Oxford University Press, 2010, p. 274.
[2] See Alain Besançon, 'Forgotten Communism', *Commentary,* Vol.105, No. 1, January 1998.
[3] Arthur Herman, *The Idea of Decline in Western History,* New York: the Free Press, 1997, p.p. 316-17.
[4] James McElroy, 'How Marxism created the West', *UnHerd,* 19 January 2022, https://unherd.com/2022/01/how-marxism-created-the-west/, accessed 19 January 2022.
[5] Edward Norman, *The Roman Catholic Church, An Illustrated History,* London: Thames & Hudson, 2007, p. 186. Casey Chalk, 'The "Dictatorship of Relativism" Has Arrived', *Crisis Magazine,* 14 December 2020. https://www.crisismagazine.com/2020/the-dictatorship-of-relativism-has-arrived, accessed 11 February 2022.
[6] See Michel Gurfinkiel, 'Christian Democracy', *First Things,* Aug-Sep 2020, p. 28.
[7] Gurfinkiel, 'Christian Democracy', p. 28.
[8] Karl Mathiesen, 'The chemist v the Dutch farmers', *Financial Times,* 9 March 2023.
[9] Brigitte Granville, *What Ails France?,* Montreal: McGill/Queens University Press, 2021, p. 101.
[10] Dominic Green, 'Europe's "New Right" Looks a Lot Like Its Old Center', *Wall Street Journal*, 12 November 2022.
[11] Twitter, @realmrsthatcher, 23 December 2022.
[12] Phillip Blond, 'Boris's Red Tory Victory', *First Things,* 13 December 2019, https://www.firstthings.com/web-exclusives/2019/12/boriss-red-tory-victory, accessed 11 February 2022.
[13] See Paul Embery, Despised: Why the Modern Left Loathes the Working Class, London: Polity, 2021.
[14] Tony Judt, *Postwar: A History of Europe Since 1945,* London: Pimlico, 2007, p. 275.
[15] Perry Anderson, *Ever Closer Union? Europe in the West,* London: Verso, 2021, p 180.
[16] Walter Laqueur, After the Fall: The End of the European Dream and the Decline of a Continent, New York: St Martin's Press, 2011, p. 47.
[17] See Alexis Carre, 'Europeans have weapons but aren't warriors', *Foreign Policy,* 4 December 2022.
[18] Daniel Johnson, 'Germany's Crisis of Conscience', *The Critic,* June 2022.
[19] 'Former CDA senator was a 'Kremlin pawn' and monitored by the AIVD', *DutchNews.nl,* 13 November 2022, https://www.dutchnews.nl/news/2022/11/former-cda-senator-was-a-kremlin-pawn-and-monitored-by-the-aivd/, accessed 14 November 2022.

CHAPTER 2: JOSIP BROZ TITO

1892-1980

Josip Broz Tito transcended the deep divisions in his country to become a powerful but transitory symbol of unity. Perhaps more than any of the other figures whose careers are assessed in this volume, he was a gifted improviser, able to experiment and advance often from positions of seeming total adversity. An artful cult of personality underpinned a tenuous unity in a country which had seen much fratricidal bloodletting between 1941 and 1945. For a time, at the height of the Cold War, Yugoslavia enjoyed a position of stature and influence in international relations, one that was without parallel in the Balkan peninsula for many centuries. He was inventive in framing Yugoslavia as a progressive beacon, 'the homeland of the proletariat' which could play a messianic role in a turbulent world.[1]

Tito's popularity rested on the widespread belief that he towered above the communal and ethnic tensions of a country, which had only come into being in 1918 with the formation of the Kingdom of the Serbs, Croats and Slovenes. But having achieved much in unpromising circumstances, he failed to build the institutions and foster the social conditions which would have impeded the return of ancient hatreds. In Western Europe, most of his contemporaries also shrank from confronting difficult issues which, if tackled, might have spared their countries from adversity later on. But there was far less at stake in countries like Belgium or Italy, with their own internal cleavages. The existence of democracy, civil society and a free media provided an outlet for grievances, usually preventing frustrations spilling over into uncontrolled conflict. Tito's capacity for experiment, unusual among communist leaders, had never extended towards allowing citizens the means to challenge state authorities. Civil society remained stillborn. Thus, the society was disarmed and helpless when bureaucratic and military establishments, which he had endowed with authority and resources, launched deadly power struggles less than a decade after his passing.

Unlike other European figures who rose to significance in the twentieth century's second half, his firm grip on power and prestige stemmed directly from his Second World War role. He had forged a resistance army in the western Balkans at the apex of Nazi power in the early 1940s; the authority acquired enabled him to be proclaimed Marshal of Yugoslavia 1943-4. For Tito, legitimate power belonged in the hands of those who had liberated the country. The Partisans made their own revolution in imitation of the Soviet model, but independently. Later, he would be the only Marxist state leader to defy Stalin and get away with it.

Upon his death in May 1980, he was the last leader from that bloody and tumultuous period left alive. His funeral was attended by no less than four kings, thirty-one presidents, six princes, twenty-two prime ministers, and forty-seven ministers of foreign affairs. Six years earlier, West Germany's Chancellor, Helmut Schmidt had pronounced him 'the greatest of the winners of the Second World War.[2]

Tito's poise and charm, his gregariousness and good humour, along with his ruthlessness and determination, could not have been easily honed in the era marked by the rise of the European Union, which left perhaps most politicians with little experience of life outside social science university degrees, assignments with think tanks, or apprenticeships to important politicians. From an early age, Tito's formative experiences were on a much vaster scale.

He was born in 1892, a subject of the Austro-Hungarian Empire. His father was Croat and his mother Slovene. He had fourteen brothers and sisters, of whom only seven lived to adulthood. His formal education was rudimentary. But by 1914, Tito had learned many trades and, as a skilled mechanic, had been in many parts of Germany and the Habsburg Empire.[3] Few politicians today possessed even a fraction of his experiences of life, which left him multi-lingual. In addition to his native Serbo-Croatian, Tito was fluent in Russian, knew some German, Slovenian, French, Czech, Hungarian, and even Kirghiz, and later studied to improve his English.

In the First World War, he was captured on the Russian front while serving in the Austro-Hungarian army. He became a Communist in Russia, but, as he himself later admitted publicly, he participated only minimally in the Bolshevik Revolution. Richard West, one of Tito's biographers, mentioned that such occasional bouts of candour, and even humorous self-deprecation, made Tito nearly unique among Communist leaders.[4] He admitted that he considered emigrating to the USA while in strife-torn Russia, later boasting that if he had done so, he would certainly have become a millionaire.[5]

That such an individual, arguable well-prepared for success in a conventional setting, embarked instead on a revolutionary path, may help to highlight how broken the European order was – disrupted by the slaughter of a world war, an upsurge of political radicalism, and the solidification of hatreds as a result of controversial new borders, not to mention the overturning of empires, and the demobilisation of millions of troops, often returning to empty prospects. The resulting retreat of order proved a recipe for chronic unrest. In the midst of this poisonous brew, new states were hurriedly created, thanks to frantic diplomatic machinations which, more often than not, bore little relevance to trading links, communication systems, ethnic allegiances, and religious affiliations.

Instead of choosing America, Tito instead opted to be a disruptor of the shaky and indeed provisional post-1918 order. By the early 1920s, he was a labour agitator in the Croatian capital, Zagreb. A locksmith by training, he spurned any absorption with communist theories and became a revolutionary cadre, graduating to being a Comintern agent in the 1930s. His temperament suited him for intelligence work. Self-confident, astute, and secretive, he was a born survivor but also a natural individualist.

Tito was arrested in 1928 and spent the next six years in jail. Convicted Communists were treated much better than later prisoners jailed under Tito's orders. He then worked for the Comintern whose aim was to place global communist movements under Soviet control. It was hostile to Yugoslavia which was allied to several of its main enemies. Although it demanded dissolution of this 'prison of the peoples', Yugoslav patriotism began to grow within the Yugoslav Communist party.[6]

When all the significant Yugoslav Communists had been liquidated on the orders of Stalin, he was appointed general secretary of the party in 1939. By now, he had adopted 'Tito' as an alias for underground work. His role in purges carried out in Moscow, and also in Spain during its civil-war, has not been fully explained. But there would be abundant opportunity to show that he was not squeamish in sacrificing large numbers of people in order to assist the cause which he had chosen to make his own.

Following Hitler's invasion of Yugoslavia in April 1941, he quickly organized a Partisan movement, which advocated national equality and a federal Yugoslavia. Brotherhood and unity were the watchwords which would eventually define the entire Tito epoch. But he was implacable to any who questioned his authority. Thus, he did not lift a finger to rescue the imprisoned intelligentsia and activists of the Croatian communist party before the local fascist collaborators, the Ustaša got to them in 1941. He may not personally have participated in atrocities. But others had to commit to carrying out acts that he had authorised.[7] There is Tito's order from October 1944 on the "cleansing" of Vršac (in the Banat) of its German population.[8] Multitudes of people, deemed 'collaborators' were executed in the 'great butchery' after the war, which 'Tito never regretted'.[9] After the collapse in ties with the Soviet Union, he also 'made the decision' to isolate the pro-Soviet 'Cominformists' in the island-camp of Goli Otok, which, according to one victim, surpassed Nazi and Soviet camps.[10] As undisputed master of the country in 1949, his role in the murder, by lethal injection, of imprisoned Andrija Hebrang, a long-term rival in communist ranks, is unlikely to have been negligible.[11]

This sanguinary side to Tito would very likely have been known to the British, but Winston Churchill and his aide, the Conservative MP, Sir Fitzroy Maclean, who fought with Tito and the wartime Partisans, were unlikely to have been swayed by it. In a striking episode that occurred just after the end of the Second World War, 4,000 White Russians and 11,000 of their family members were delivered by Allied officers to Yugoslav and

Soviet communist officials, to disappear without trace. Part of what was known as Operation Keelhaul also involved the British commanders in their zone of occupation in southern Austria handing over some 70,000 'quisling' troops (mainly Slovenes and Croats) who had surrendered to the Western allies in Austria.

Those Russians mentioned earlier had never been Soviet citizens, and their handover was not even in accordance with the Yalta Agreement.[12] Later, a former key lieutenant of Tito's, Milovan Djilas, expressed astonishment that the British showed so little curiosity or concern about the type of justice that was likely to be handed out to the repatriates. Ironically, many of those from the Ustaša movement who had issued the orders for the slaughter of Serbs and Muslims, were able to escape, often thanks to assistance from Catholic religious orders.[13]

Tito had justified British support in wartime because of his prowess in leading armed resistance against German forces. The mastery of the techniques of special warfare that his Partisans acquired under him convinced the British that, despite being a communist, he stood a chance of welding Yugoslavia into a united entity. The energetic and self-confident warrior whom Maclean described in reports to Churchill seemed a protean figure who would be unlikely to end up as a tool of Stalin, and who could be a balancing force in a ravaged post-war Europe.[14]

The polarisation in European politics, offered hope that a working relationship could be established with Tito.[15] Churchill had turned to Maclean in 1944 and asked: 'Do you intend to make Yugoslavia your home after the war?' Maclean said he did not. To which Churchill replied, 'Neither do I. And...the less you and I worry about the form of government they set up, the better'.[16]

Under the Yalta Treaty signed between the Allied powers in 1944, non-communists were meant to have important sway in determining the future political shape of Yugoslavia. But the British allowed Tito to relinquish the treaty, given the total control the Partisans enjoyed over most of the state once their forces had liberated Belgrade (along with the Soviets) in October 1944.

British policymakers were arguably right to assume that Tito's immense prestige at home meant that he would be nobody's subaltern. But the evidence for this view was not immediately forthcoming. Tito proceeded to impose full communism, dispensing with the intermediate stage of the national popular front. The blueprint for a doctrinaire People's Democracy was ruthlessly implemented. Class enemies and perceived ethnic foes, such as the Italians inhabiting coastal Dalmatia and Istria, endured terrible suffering in the Yugoslav regime's most ideological phase.[17] Collectivization and a centrally planned economy were the order of the day.[18]

Tito sought to extend his political influence beyond the Balkans, indeed across much of the north Mediterranean littoral and into Central Europe. His implacable support for the communists in the Greek civil war is a matter of record. Less well known is the involvement of his Partisans in an attempt to overthrow Franco in Spain, his backing for communists in France and Italy, and his attempt to detach southern portions of Austria from control by Vienna.[19] Tensions with the anti-communists in charge of Italy from 1948 were severe and, as late as 1954, he was massing troops on the border with Italy as he sought to acquire control of the city of Trieste.[20]

Britain was fully stretched trying to avert a military clash over the Trieste question. But in the end, it was with Stalin that Tito's freelance operations led to a direct collision, opening up room for a partial *rapprochement* with the West. At Yalta, Stalin had allocated Greece to the British sphere of influence. The Soviet leader preferred Trieste to be an international free port, a buffer zone between Yugoslavia and the West, to which Tito would never agree. The break occurred in February 1948, after Tito rejected Moscow's call for a Bulgarian-Yugoslav union. He knew it would hobble him and make it easier for him to be quietly removed. His excommunication from the communist church would have nothing to do with communist doctrine but was bound up with the strategy for advancing communist power in Europe. Tito dreamed of being a powerful regional magnate and detested the idea of being in charge of a dependency within a Moscow-run monolith.

His 1954 state visit to then royalist Greece, a regime which he had spent years trying to topple, was an unmistakable indication that he was placing himself at the head of a highly personal niche regime, still demonstrably communist, but heterodox in theory and practice. As a counter-doctrine challenging Soviet central planning, a self-management scheme was unfurled. It involved elected workers councils that were responsible for running their own plants and making investment decisions. A hybrid socialist system was thus promoted, but party domination and central planning continued to define the Yugoslav system. For those with eyes to see, workers' self-management was a facade. Tito's Yugoslavia saw no experiment in workers power, and Western believers in the system struggled to explain how it operated.

For a time after the break with Moscow, Tito was dangerously isolated. All communist bloc countries promptly severed economic ties with the heretic state. He had the presence of mind to turn down American overtures to affiliate with the newly founded North Atlantic Treaty Organisation (NATO). At no point was he in danger of appearing a tool of the West. This would have weakened his position at home and reduced his room to maneuver on the world stage.

Lucky timing was perhaps crucial in enabling Tito to break free from the suffocating Soviet embrace. Western leaders, President Truman and British Foreign Secretary, Ernest Bevin, were prepared to offer diplomatic and economic support and sell him arms.[21] The Korean War broke out in 1950, preventing Stalin from taking active measures to liquidate the Tito heresy by direct military invasion or assassination.

This is a point in Tito's story when his ability to survive, and indeed thrive, in a Hobbesian environment of murder and intrigue is striking. His self-possession, cool nerves, ability to scoff at adversity, and a facade of bonhomie, impressed leaders like Britain's Foreign Secretary, Anthony Eden, who met him when he was still embattled and in seeming danger. Tito was past sixty when Stalin died in March 1953 and the most obvious threat to his survival therefore receded. He had been drawn into revolutionary politics at quite an advanced age, in his late twenties, and now thirty years later, at pensionable age, he was aiming to be the great disruptor. But this was on the international stage rather than at home.

Tito neglected domestic affairs once his rule had been consolidated. He showed real agility and flair by acquiring a distinctive platform in international relations, through sponsoring the movement of non-aligned nations neutral in the Cold War. For a decade or more after the Bandung conference of 1955, he carved out an unlikely sphere of influence in the emerging Third World, and some of his actions hastened the retreat of European empires. His stance meant a distancing from the United States, whose intervention in Vietnam he repeatedly criticised.[22] US military aid had been discontinued in 1957 and most favoured nation trading status remained in jeopardy through the 1960s. Efforts were made to establish Yugoslavia as a 'strong moral factor in the world' such as the 1967 initiative to offer $600 million dollars in credits to underdeveloped nations.

There is evidence that Tito played a major role in encouraging Egypt to nationalise the Suez Canal in 1956.[23] He saw President Nasser as a kindred spirit, a populist unencumbered by ideology. Tito even more keenly sought to end French rule in Algeria, arming the rebels and offering diplomatic support.[24] In September 1961, he welcomed dozens of leaders from this promising new neutralist bloc to a conference in Belgrade.[25] Next year, however, China invaded India and his soulmate, Jahawaral Nehru, was forced to turn to the West for help. Thereafter, Tito's international influence, along with the relevance and importance of the non-aligned movement itself, waned.

Solid economic achievements might have endowed the uneasy amalgam of peoples in Yugoslavia with the basic underpinning necessary for a viable state community to be forged. But Tito's system increasingly resembled some of the Third World regimes he had befriended: leader fixated, exotic and deep down not very practical. Melodramatic gestures were preferred to attract the world's attention rather than solid economic endeavours. Thus, in 1973, Tito sponsored one of the most expensive feature films ever made: *Battle of Sutjeska* was a Partisan war movie about the most crucial engagement of the Yugoslav Partisan War. He hired the British actor, Richard Burton, to play a character modelled on himself, and cultivated him and his wife, Elizabeth Taylor, while they were filming the biopic.[26]

Being absorbed by vanity projects like this meant that the hard work needed to implant a cohesive state, that could survive his passing, was neglected. Efforts to devise a Yugoslav identity from cradle to grave via the school, the media and the world of work simply were not made. Instead, Tito became the main integrative force in a country which experimented with federalism without abolishing either the single party's monopoly of power, censorship, or the secret police. His personality cult combined seemingly contradictory features. He was an unswerving socialist, albeit an approachable *comrade* who enjoyed a lavish lifestyle, including numerous homes, luxury possessions, cars, and women. A highly effective propaganda effort managed to instill in many citizens a 'compelling picture of his heroism and dedication to Yugoslavia's cause', leaving the impression that the 'good life' he enjoyed was more than deserved.[27] The personality cult shaped around Tito was maintained without any reference to Marx or Lenin. Tito's birthday on 25 May, not the international workers day of 1 May, was the principal ceremonial event of the regime.

For a population weary of upheaval and murderous conflict, Tito was appealing because of his refusal to identify himself with any ethnic or religious group. He was the only member of his generation of communist bloc leaders to exert long-term attraction and interest.[28] It is not hard to see why. There were tangible economic benefits associated with his rule. Life expectancy rose from 46 in 1938, to 68 in 1972.[29] Citizens enjoyed more access to consumer goods than elsewhere in the communist world. Freedom to travel existed. Ordinary citizens were shielded from the adverse effects of a disfunctional economic system, perhaps longer than anywhere else in the communist world. But by the 1970s, his opaque system was beset by chronic inefficiency and high levels of corruption.[30] It was increasingly kept afloat by the foreign loans secured by Tito, who reminded the Americans and others, that Yugoslavia remained strategically placed on a delicate Cold War frontline and that instability could have dire outcomes for the world. Accordingly, the Western powers failed to extend their critical eye towards Yugoslavia and human rights violations. Uniquely in the communist world, the US government-sponsored Radio Free Europe failed to broadcast uncensored news to the country.

By the end of his life, evidence was building up that he had failed to create a common set of values and interests capable of holding his multi-national state together.[31] It may well be the case that he did not have much of a grip on things during the last five years he was alive. From the early 1950s to the mid-1970s, it was foreign affairs that occupied most of his time. He acquired important breathing-space when Nikita Khrushchev issued an official apology in May 1955, for Soviet mishandling of bilateral ties in the last years of Stalin. When the Soviet leader issued a wholesale denunciation of many of Stalin's crimes at the 20th party congress in February 1956, it looked as if Tito's opportunity, to pioneer an early form of Eurocommunism with some pluralist elements, had arrived. However, in the second half of 1956, revolution erupted in Hungary. Both the Yugoslavs and the Soviets were thrown off balance. Tito accepted the necessity of force being used to prevent Hungary leaving the socialist camp, but he criticised the Kremlin's handling of the uprising. Having offered shelter in the Yugoslav embassy to Imre Nagy and the Hungarian leadership, when Soviet troops invaded on 4 November, he was angry when they were lured out of the embassy by subterfuge (with Nagy and other later being hanged).[32] He declined to attend the 40th anniversary celebrations of the Russian Revolution being held in Moscow during 1957. The traumatic events of 1956 showed that a normalisation of ties between Tito and whoever ruled in Moscow was bound to be difficult.

His ambitions to create a community of socialist states where the Soviet Union was first among equals (nothing more) waned in the 1960s once the Brezhnev era got underway. The aims of Russia and Yugoslavia could never be synchronised. Tito spurned the idea favoured in Moscow of Yugoslavia embracing the kind of passive neutrality that Finland enjoyed. In 1968, he was surprised by the Soviet decision to crush the Prague Spring with tanks. He hadn't assumed that the Kremlin would invoke the Warsaw Pact and go so far when Czechoslovakia's reformist leaders still wished to remain within the socialist ambit.[33]

His long exposure to Leninist concepts of party discipline blunted his reformist ardour. In 1954, he purged the speaker of parliament, Milovan Djilas, one of the architects of the self-management scheme and a close wartime comrade. He had caused a stir by expressing the view that the

Leninist type of party and state were obsolete.[34] Tito's move may have been a gesture to reassure the Kremlin as a thaw in relations was gathering pace.[35] He later received further detention for writing a book, *The New Class*, which denounced unchecked corruption in the higher echelons of the party state and characterised it as an inevitable byproduct of the Soviet model, even in its attenuated Titoist form.[36] He was made an example of because he stated so publicly that a new class of oligarchs, who used their positions to enrich themselves, were 'becoming the dominant faction' in Tito's new order.[37]

Tito's historical reputation might have been enhanced and his country's later grim fate avoided if he had listened to his wayward former lieutenant. In the early 1970s, rather than retreating into authoritarian orthodoxy, he could have backed the new young 'democrats', particularly those within the Serbian Communist Party, who wanted further to democratize the workers' self-management system.[38] They were replaced by sycophantic Tito loyalists presiding incompetently over a wasteful and dysfunctional system. These colourless bureaucrats in Serbia would be easily dislodged in the late 1980s by Slobodan Milošević, as he sought to make the revival of nationalism a passport for survival for large portions of the ruling elite, as the Cold War drew to a close.

A burst of what seemed like political innovation occurred in 1974 when a new constitution was unfurled which reduced the communist party at federal level to a shell and instead located political power and economic decision-making at the level of the republics. This opaque document, perhaps the world's longest constitution, underpinned the confederal direction of the state. Armed with important powers, the republics duplicated services and subsidised their own producers. Important hydro-electric projects which would have reduced dependence on costly oil imports, were only some of the projects held up by disagreement on the share-out of benefits.[39] It has been claimed that Yugoslavia's economy did worse in the 1970s than more centrally controlled Communist ones, thanks to burgeoning inflation and debt exacerbated by a series of unprofitably large investment in unworkable projects funded through foreign loans.[40]

It is perhaps not far-fetched to say that at the end of his life, Tito was Yugoslavia's only integrating force in a land aptly described as 'one country with six republics, five nationalities, four religions (including Communism), three languages and two scripts'.[41]

Tito's political impact on his country is very much bound up with his towering personality. Until the final decades of his long life, he was a risk taker. In the 1940s, he relied on his charisma and strategic skills to forge a formidable wartime military force. He struck up relationships with unlikely allies who abhorred his communism but admired his political prowess, a skill that would never quite desert him. After having taken charge of Yugoslavia, his ruthlessness and cool nerves enabled him to fend off a mortal threat from Stalin.

He went on to project himself as a pivotal figure in Cold War politics, whose sagacity earned him the right to be viewed as a global statesman. Yet his repertoire of political skills largely deserted him when it came to the state-building efforts needed to build a cohesive country that had been scarred by savage internecine strife. In Turkey, Kemal Ataturk managed in less than half the time Tito enjoyed in charge of Yugoslavia, to introduce sweeping reforms that altered the character of society. Arguably, the challenges that he needed to overcome in this stronghold of Middle Eastern traditionalism were far more daunting than the ones that would have confronted Tito in Yugoslavia.

The Yugoslav leader became bound up with his own image as the talisman who was indispensable for the survival of Yugoslavia. A series of one-year presidencies, with the office holders drawn from each of the republics on a rotating basis, was the formula for securing his legacy of brotherhood and unity after he was gone. It was a flimsy basis for keeping together a communist state, one which had become massively dependent on his carefully curated propaganda cult.

No European political leader's handiwork came undone as rapidly and as completely as Tito's. The destruction of his heroic-sounding but tragically mismanaged project proved to be the demise, not just of an unusual political experiment, but of an entire country.

---

[1] See Sergej Flere, 'The Broken Covenant of Tito's People: The Problem of Civil Religion in Communist Yugoslavia', East European Politics and Societies, Vol. 21, No. 4, p.p. 681–703.
[2] William Klinger and Dennis Kuljiš, *Tito's Secret Empire, How the Maharaja of the Balkans Fooled the World,* London: Hurst Publishers, 2020, p. 346.
[3] Istvan Deak, 'The Beginning of the End— Tito and the Rise and Fall of Yugoslavia by Richard West, *The New Republic,* 7 August 1995.
[4] Deak, 'The Beginning of the End'.
[5] Klinger and Kuljiš, Tito's Secret Empire, p. 14.
[6] Aleksa Djilas, 'Tito's Last Secret', *Foreign Affairs,* Vol. 74, No. 4, July-August 1995, p. 119.
[7] Jože Pirjeveć, Tito and His Comrades, Madison, Wisconsin, University of Wisconsin Press, 2018, p. 82.
[8] Klinger and Kuljiš, Tito's Secret Empire, p. 205.
[9] Pirjevec, Tito, p.p. 150-2.
[10] Pirjevec, Tito p.p. 198-99.
[11] Pirjevec, Tito p. 188.
[12] Klinger and Kuljiš, Tito's Secret Empire, p.p. 201, 210-12.
[13] Richard West, *Tito and the Rise and fall of Yugoslavi*a, London: Sinclair Stevenson, 1996, p. 202.
[14] Klinger and Kuljiš, *Tito's Secret Empire,* p.169.
[15] Ann Lane, 'Putting Britain Right with Tito: The Displaced Persons Question in Anglo-Yugoslav Relations 1946-7', *European History Quarterly*, Vol. 22, No. 2, 1992, p. 242.
[16] Fitzroy Maclean, *Eastern Approaches,* London: Penguin, 1999 edition, p.p. 402-3.
[17] Klinger and Kuljiš, *Tito's Secret Empire,* p. 204.
[18] Dennis P. Hupchick, *The Balkans, From Constantinople to Communism*, London: Palgrave, 2002, p. 374.
[19] Klinger and Kuljiš, *Tito's Secret Empire,* p. 200.
[20] See Robert Niebuhr, 'Enlarging Yugoslavia: Tito's Quest for Expansion, 1945–1948', *European History Quarterly,* Vol. 47, No. 2, 2017, p.p. 284–310.
[21] See Lorraine Lees, Keeping Tito Afloat: The United States, Yugoslavia and the Cold War, Pennsylvania: Pennsylvania State University Press, 1996, p.p. 18-19.
[22] 'What did Tito think about Vietnam?', *Quor*a, https://www.quora.com/What-did-Tito-think-about-Vietnam, accessed 21 November 2021.
[23] Klinger and Kuljiš, *Tito's Secret Empire,* p. 265.
[24] Klinger and Kuljiš, *Tito's Secret Empire,* p.p. 293-7.
[25] See Jovan Čavoški, 'Between Great Powers and Third World Neutralists: Yugoslavia and the Belgrade Conference of the Non- Aligned Movement, 1961', in T*he Non-Aligned Movement and the Cold War,* edited by Natasa Miskovic, Harald Fischer-Tiné, Nada Boskovska, London: Routledge, 2014.
[26] Edin Hardaus, 'Did You Know That Richard Burton Played Tito In The Partisan War Movie Sutjeska?' *War History Online,* 29 September 2015, https://www.warhistoryonline.com/guest-bloggers/know-richard-burton-played-tito-movie-sutjeska.html.
[27] See Tamara Pavasović Trošt, 'Personality Cult Transformed: The Evolution of Tito's Image in Serbian and Croatian Textbooks, 1974–2010', *Studies in Ethnicity and Nationalism,* Vol. 14, No. 1, 2014.

[28] See Sabrina P. Ramet, Review of 'Jože Pirjevec's Tito and His Comrades', *Southeastern Europe*, Vol. 44, No. 1, 2020, p. 88.
[29] Dusko Doder, *The Yugoslavs*, London: Allen & Unwin, 1979, p. 65.
[30] See Deak, 'The beginning of the end'.
[31] Tom Gallagher, Outcast Europe: The Balkans, 1789-1989, London: Routledge, 2001, p. 219.
[32] Johanna Granville, 'Hungary 1956 – the Yugoslav Connection', *Europe-Asia Studies*, Vol. 50 Issue 3, 1998, p. 673.
[33] Klinger and Kuljiš, *Tito's Secret Empire*, p.p. 293-7.
[34] François Feijtö, *A History of the Peoples Democracies*, London: Penguin, 1974, p. 57.
[35] Doder, The Yugoslavs, p. 191.
[36] See Urban, 'A Conversation'.
[37] Jasmin Mujanović, *Hunger and Fury: The Crisis of Democracy in the Balkans*, London: Hurst Publishers, 2018, p. 61.
[38] Gallagher, *Outcast Europe*, p. 232.
[39] Djilas, 'Tito's Last', p. 121.
[40] Hupchick, *The Balkans*, p. 423.
[41] Frank Roberts, Dealing with Dictators: The Destruction and Revival of Europe, 1930-1970, London: Weidenfeld & Nicholson, 1991, p. 176.

CHAPTER 3: URHO KALEVA KEKKONEN

1900-1986 [1]

Finland had 26 governments between 1956 and 1982, but only one President, Urho Kaleva Kekkonen. This already seasoned politician established an unusually dominant position in national life during that period, which coincided with some of the tensest moments in the Cold War. For its forty-year duration, Finland could be described as one of the frontline states and Kekkonen acquired his ascendancy by convincing many ordinary Finns, as well as much of the political establishment, that he was uniquely qualified to manage relations with the Soviet Union, Finland's formidable neighbour. Russia had ruled the country for over a century until 1918. Its communist rulers had shown an appetite for relentless expansion since the Bolshevik revolution of 1917. Twice, Finland and the Soviet Union had fought in battle, in the Winter War of 1939-40 and from 1941 to 1944 when Finland was a reluctant ally of Germany.

Kekkonen had been active in politics during these turbulent times. In 1940, he had voted against the terms of the harsh peace treaty negotiated with Stalin after the Finns had put up resolute (and for a time effective) resistance against the Red Army. But in 1945, possibly due to pressure from the victorious Allies, he had supported placing on trial the leaders of wartime Finland who had been in a military alliance with Nazi Germany.[2] He had also refrained from enthusiastically embracing Germany's war effort or Finland's expansion beyond its pre-1939 borders.

In 1945, he met for the first time with Andrei Zhdanov, the chairman of the Allied Control Commission in Helsinki.[3] It was the first of numerous meetings with leading Soviet figures in decades to come. Kekkonen seems to have convinced members of the Soviet elite that he could be a reliable interlocutor in Finland, prepared to accommodate himself at least to the preservation of Soviet defensive interests in Northern Europe. Not challenging Soviet interests meant that Finland held aloof from various international initiatives and was prepared to discreetly advance some of Moscow's foreign policy objectives. This process whereby a smaller and weaker state adapted elements of its policy to the interests of a bigger neighbouring country, typically a great power, became known as *Finlandisation* in the language of international relations. Kekkonen insisted that he was never Moscow's lackey and that his balancing act was designed to safeguard Finnish independence and reduce the danger of the country being overwhelmed in yet another conflict, perhaps a terminal one if it involved nuclear weapons.[4] Nevertheless, he acquired an amount of power unusual in any modern democracy. He supervised the media and security services, controlled key appointments, and kept prime ministers in the dark about his diplomacy with the Soviets. His ability to make foreign policy the pivot of national politics, and himself the indispensable arbiter, ensured that he enjoyed a longer period of continuous power than any other leader of a democratic country in the second half of the last century. The extent of his ascendancy enabled him to engineer an extension of four years to the six-year term he had begun in 1968 and his final re-election in 1978 was largely a formality.[5]

Born in 1900, Kekkonen's hinterland was unusual for a politician, even before the arrival of the era when the political class across much of Europe became dominated by narrowly-focused insiders with little exposure to real life. He had been Finland's national high jump champion during his student days and later served as president of the Finnish Sports League (1932-1947). He was dedicated all his life to skiing, hunting, and fishing. He had shown talent as a writer and public speaker and had been prominent in student politics. Kekkonen was self-assured and tough-minded. In the 1920s, he had served as an officer in the Finnish security police, in which role he had visited Moscow for the first time.

The Soviets had always used Helsinki as a hub for gathering intelligence and he would have been known to them quite early in his career in politics. By 1936, he was minister of Justice and from 1937 to 1939 he was minister of the Interior at a time of rising European tensions. The Soviets would likely have been aware that he had tried to outlaw the extreme right-wing Patriotic People's Movement (IKL) which saw Russia under communism as a mortal enemy (a proposal rejected by the courts).[6] During the early 1940s, he showed dexterity as Finland was menaced from many sides. Initially, with the Germans seemingly on course for victory, he pursued a strongly nationalist line, being intent on recovering lost territories. But from 1943, he figured prominently in the cross-party 'Peace opposition', which pressed for Finland to withdraw from the war. Minister of Justice again in 1946, he did not flinch from overseeing a judicial process which led to the imprisonment of some of Finland's wartime leaders. Thus, he had emerged in his forties as a politician who had offered some proof that he was not a threat to Russian hegemony in North-East Europe. To those directing Soviet foreign policy in the final years of Stalin's rule, when his morbid outlook shaped decisions near and far, Kekkonen seemed to be a man to transact with.

Of relevance here is Stalin's purges of the mid-1930s, which had devastated the Finnish Communist Party. The Soviets seem to have decided that their interests were better served in dealing with more supple and detached figures who could wield influence on their behalf.

It is unlikely that Kekkonen's political star would have risen so easily without the backing he enjoyed from Juho Kusti Paasikivi, President of Finland from 1946 to 1956. He belonged to the realist school of thought existing in Finland since Tsarist times, that believed any pursuit of self-government needed to accommodate itself to the reality of Russian strength and power. In the perilous post-war period, he sought to restrict Soviet influence. The respect that he was held in at home strengthened his hand in confronting the Soviets.

His Presidency is probably best remembered for a landmark diplomatic event, the Friendship, Cooperation and Mutual Assistance Treaty (FCMA) that was signed with the Soviets in April 1948. Finland was then widely seen in the West as a Soviet vassal whose freedom of action hardly surpassed that of Czechoslovakia. It had just entered the Soviet orbit after the communist-led coup in Prague in February of that year. For the previous two years, a communist, Mauno Pekkala, had been in charge of Finland's coalition government and the ministry of interior and thus the internal security services were under communist sway. Finland was unable to seek Marshall aid. Heavy reparations were paid to the Soviets. The FCMA treaty also assumed a continuing mortal threat from Germany, then under 4-power occupation. It laid down that Finland must align its defence policy with that of Russia in order to counter it. In addition, Finland was forbidden from recognising the emerging West Germany, while attempts continued to be made by Moscow to induce it to become the first state to recognise the pro-Soviet German Democratic Republic (GDR).[7]

In return for holding aloof from Western military alliances and recognising the primacy of Soviet defensive interests, Finland escaped Sovietisation. Cooperation with the rest of Scandinavia was also initially ruled out by Moscow. A Nordic Council had been set up by Norway, Sweden, Denmark and Iceland in 1952, focussing mainly on practical matters. The official Soviet line that it was an unfriendly move designed to deepen imperialist influence in Northern Europe was softened once relative pragmatists around Nikita Khrushchev won out in the post-1953 Kremlin power struggles.

A thaw occurred in September 1955 when Paasikivi led a delegation to Moscow and the Soviets agreed to vacate the strategic Porkala naval base, within sight of Helsinki, which they had acquired on a fifty-year lease, in 1944. In return, the FCMA treaty was extended for a further twenty years. In a separate meeting with Kekkonen, Khrushchev offered to lift his objection to Finland joining the Nordic Council if Finland was prepared to recognise the DDR. Kekkonen was amenable, but he backtracked due to the fury in Bonn, the capital of West Germany, when news of the proposed deal was leaked.[8]

Nevertheless, a relationship of wary trust had been established between Kekkonen and the man running the Kremlin for the next nine years. He won the admiration of many Finns by hosting Khrushchev in his own sauna, where they soaked and drank beer, as the Soviet leader recalled in his memoirs with a certain wistfulness. Back in Moscow, he was criticised for having 'gone naked into a sauna with a capitalist and non-socialist.'[9]

Khrushchev trusted the Finn sufficiently to use his influence at the start of 1956 to ensure that his chief contact in the higher political echelons of Finland was elected President. He began the race as an outsider. But a Soviet instruction to Finnish communists meant that they threw their backing behind this outwardly pro-capitalist conservative. Kekkonen thus won by one vote.[10]

From then on, Kekkonen was prepared to accept a level of Soviet influence in Finnish domestic affairs that his predecessor Paasikivi might have baulked at. In contrast to most other European leaders beyond direct Soviet control, he remained silent when the Soviets brutally quelled the Hungarian revolution in 1956. In 1958, he did little to prevent a cabinet being driven from office due, in no small part, to Soviet pressure. Moscow was disgruntled at the exclusion of the communist-controlled Finnish People's Democratic League (SKDL) from a new coalition government, despite being the largest party. The new Prime Minister, the Social Democrat Karl-August Fagerholm (the narrow loser to Kekkonen in 1956), was seen as a foe intent on orientating Finland towards the West. Moscow abruptly halted trade talks and called its ambassador home. By the end of 1958 the cabinet had collapsed, with Kekkonen having offered it little support.[11]

In a fractured political landscape, Kekkonen's long-term aim was to shape domestic policy around foreign affairs and specifically relations with the Soviet Union. The 1958 'night frost crisis', as it was called, enabled him to do so, while still being in a position of relative weakness. In a time of international tension, with the Soviets angrily denouncing growing signs that West Germany was becoming an integral part of the West, the Finnish political world was keen not to provoke Moscow's wrath.

As the end of his first term approached, Kekkonen's opponents still seemed strong enough to deny him re-election. But then, on 30 October 1961, a fresh and seemingly more dangerous breach in bilateral ties occurred. Cold War tensions were dangerously high once again owing to international disagreements over Germany, in this case the disputed status of the divided state's former capital Berlin. The Finnish government received a Soviet note requesting military consultations based on the 1948 FCMA treaty. The 'imperialist threat' from West Germany was invoked as justification, and the note demanded that action be taken against anti-Soviet media voices in Finland.[12] Kekkonen was on the Hawaii leg of an official visit to the United States when the note was sent. It coincided with the detonation by the Soviets of a 50-megaton hydrogen bomb, by far the biggest to date. Kekkonen then flew to Siberia for talks with Khrushchev. Given the way tensions quickly eased and Soviet demands were shelved, he was able to plausibly depict himself as a figure indispensable for keeping the menacing Soviet bear at bay. The united front of parties who had assembled behind a common candidate then dissolved, and Kekkonen was re-elected at the start of 1962.

Historians, who argued that Kekkonen's presence of mind in dealing with the unpredictable Soviets with their lethal arsenal, made him the 'saviour of the fatherland', are countered by those who see him as a Faust who sold his soul to the Kremlin.[13] Sceptics wonder why the Soviet note should have suddenly materialised when Kekkonen and his aides were regularly interacting with officials from the Soviet security service, the KGB. The Finnish leader's confidential channel to the Kremlin was Viktor Vladimirov, the head of Soviet espionage in Finland. A prominent ally of Kekkonen's, the politician Ahti Karjalainen, in a letter written to him in the late 1950s, described the KGB chief as 'a sincere friend of ours.'[14]

Kekkonen, a gifted writer, was known to write material under a pseudonym that was meant to influence the direction of the relationship with the Soviets.[15] Historians who claim that he is likely to have manufactured the 'note crisis' for his own political ends, point to how he undertook a highly unconventional constitutional gambit six months before the crisis erupted, only for it then to conveniently disappear very quickly. On 18 April 1961, he worked out an unusual political timetable in consultation with the prime minister and close allies: parliament would be dissolved in November, with the parliamentary elections to take place a week after the presidential contest, but before the electoral college met to select the President.[16] What later emerged was that Kekkonen showed the plan to the Soviet ambassador the very next day.[17] The envoy would therefore have been aware, long in advance, of when would have been the most advantageous moment for the Soviets to intervene in order to ensure Kekkonen's survival in office. He had already shown his readiness to accommodate key Soviet concerns and was averse to upsetting the political status quo of Cold War Europe.

In 1949, the British minister to Helsinki had described Kekkonen as a man whose 'ability has never been questioned, but his sardonic, mordant wit has earned him many enemies and his various flirtation with the communists has not added to his reputation for "reliability" in right-wing circles.'[18]

Eleven years later, Anatoly Golitysyn, a KGB major based in Helsinki, defected and told the CIA that there were nine pro-Soviet agents of influence with seniority in Finnish politics and that the country's President was one of them. The unusually close contacts Kekkonen had with the Soviets were already becoming well-known, but the advice Western intelligence services gave to their political masters was that it was better not to ostracise him, otherwise there was a risk of pushing Finland far more deeply into the Soviet orbit.[19]

The publication of a book in 2022, showing that Kekkonen had unusually close links with two British citizens who had served in the British intelligence service, is likely to puncture the lingering suspicion about where Kekkonen's true loyalties lay.[20] In 1945, while on a hunting trip, he struck up a friendship with Rex Bosley and James H. Magill. They spoke Finnish and had lived in the country before the outbreak of war. Bosley worked for MI6 and may have later ensured that the Finnish leader received numerous intelligence reports relating to the Soviets and Northern Europe. Magill promoted British exports and was meeting Kekkonen about twice a year in the 1960s.[21]

Kekkonen accomplished the feat of convincing deadly Cold War rivals that he was a person who stood for equilibrium in a tense neighbourhood and was therefore not someone to push around. The respect shown to him by Britain especially, but also the US, was not, however, replicated by West Germany. In Bonn, the capital, top officials saw Finland as a potential Trojan Horse, ready to be used by Moscow to strengthen the legitimacy of East Germany in world affairs.[22] Suspicions only faded when Chancellor Willy Brandt's 'Ostpolitik' initiative of the early 1970s led to 'détente' between the two Germanys.

In the rest of Scandinavia, there was also reticence, and at times annoyance, towards Kekkonen's bids to promote Finland's active neutrality. The Finn's effort to extend that to the promotion of Soviet-Nordic cooperation, failed to strike a chord in Oslo, Copenhagen or even neutralist Stockholm. A proposed visit to these capitals by Khrushchev fell through in 1960. The dearest wish of the Soviets in the region was to promote the anti-nuclear cause in the hope that Scandinavia would drift from the NATO orbit and embrace Finland's strictly neutralist stance.[23]

Kekkonen always claimed that preserving regional peace was his overriding personal vocation. His idea of a top-level meeting in 1962 to discuss cooperation in the Arctic Circle with the Soviets was rebuffed by the leaders of Norway and Sweden.[24] Tage Erlander, the Social Democrat Prime Minister of neutral Sweden, suspected that a different agenda might instead be promoted.[25] A 1965 proposal from Kekkonen, to protect the Finnish-Norwegian border region from possible military action in the event of a conflict between the great powers, similarly got nowhere.

The Finnish leader was an infrequent visitor to other Scandinavian capitals. It did not go unnoticed that the Soviets had no intention of making the north-west of the Soviet Union, adjacent to parts of Scandinavia, nuclear-free and that the main concessions were expected to come from the Scandinavian side.[26]

Max Jacobson, an experienced Finnish diplomat, who had worked closely with Kekkonen (who nevertheless refused to support his strong bid to become Secretary-General of the United Nations in 1971), noted that:

> 'Kekkonen's various Scandinavian initiatives have aroused...irritation and resentment in the other Scandinavian countries... He has been accused of...promoting the Soviet cause at the expense of the security of Finland's western neighbours.'[27]

At home, Kekkonen had more success than abroad in acquiring durable influence. His seeming triumph in the 1962 Note crisis made him an unchallenged political figure for almost the next two decades. His refusal to appoint ministers who might be seen as detrimental to Soviet interests, revealed the arrival of a *de facto* presidential system. Many across the political spectrum sought to advance their career prospects by cultivating his favour and also that of the Soviets. An unofficial President's party emerged, which spread out to the right and the left.[28] Finland, at the apogee of his power, was characterised as 'Kekkoslovakia' by critics who disliked the personalisation of power involved. By 1968, he felt confident enough to propose to Leonid Brezhnev a land swap whereby the Soviets were given the eastern part of Finnish Lapland in exchange for the city of Viipuri and its environs, seized by the Soviets in 1940. He did this without having consulted the Prime Minister.[29]

The diminution of democracy was arguably most evident in the restrictions faced by the media. Kekkonen's insistence that the media's reporting of Soviet-related developments correspond to the country's official foreign policy, was heeded. In 1973, Finland and the Soviet Union issued a declaration whereby the media in both countries acquired a special responsibility in sustaining friendship and trust between the two nations. Self-censorship had already proliferated and would spread from publishing and journalism to cultural matters. The fate of noted Soviet dissident Aleksandr Solzhenitsyn's *The Gulag Archipelago*, published in 1973, illustrated the situation well. A Finnish edition could only be published abroad because of the pressure on Finnish publishers. But, in 1970, the Finnish postal authorities had issued a stamp commemorating the centenary of the birth of Lenin, the architect of the Soviet system, and in 1980, Kekkonen (by now mentally frail) was awarded the Soviet Union's Lenin's peace prize.[30]

Kekkonen had been shaken by the Soviet invasion of Czechoslovakia in 1968. But he regained his poise and, in 1969, made an effective case for Helsinki being the location for the Conference on Security and Cooperation in Europe (CSCE), designed to promote multilateral reduction in nuclear arms. The prospects of East-West détente slowly blossomed with the decline in intra-German tensions and, as a result, Kekkonen's policy of active neutrality enjoyed growing appreciation. He was also engaged in the delicate balancing act, strengthening economic links with the European Economic Community, without antagonising the Soviets. By the late 1960s, much of Finnish trade was already orientated towards Western Europe. Finland had joined the European Free Trade Association in 1960 and a free trade agreement with the EEC followed in 1972. In both instances, and without alerting its West European economic partners, Finland had guaranteed Russia the same trading rights and advantages as it enjoyed with its main economic partners.[31] This concession persuaded the Kremlin that Finland could still broadly be trusted. In turn, the United States appears to have been convinced that Finland was not quietly leaking advanced industrial technology secrets eastwards. By the very last years of Kekkonen's rule, Finland was a producer of advanced technological and communications equipment, quite a leap forward for a country with a rudimentary economic profile a generation earlier.[32]

Amidst this time of economic ferment, confidence-building measures with Moscow were initiated, one of which—controversially—was the passage of an emergency law which extended Kekkonen's third term, due to expire in 1974, by another four years.[33] Opposition to his outsized presence in national life had dwindled to such an extent that this measure was passed by five sixths of parliament. Any defiance of what Kekkonen wanted was now seen as harmful to national unity and regular ties with the Soviet Union. His final election in 1978, was viewed as a charade in different quarters due to media restrictions and the absence of any challenger actively seeking to defeat him.[34]

In his 78th year by now, Kekkonen had long been portrayed as an admirable individual who had risen from fairly modest circumstances in a remote part of Finland to become a statesman, through brains, determination and hard work. He was widely regarded as an *everyman* figure, a sportsman in his youth who remained an avid fisherman, a patriot who could be trusted to protect the national interest in his close dealings with the Soviets, and a figure worthy of the highest honours. One that might have been expected to come his way was the Nobel Peace Prize for services to the cause of European disarmament. To the surprise of many, Kekkonen narrowly lost out to the Soviet nuclear physicist and dissident Andrei Sakharov in 1975. The Helsinki Accords, one of the outcomes of the CSCE process in

Helsinki that year, gave narrow but crucial recognition to opponents of one-party control in the Soviet bloc.[35] It would not have been a priority for a hard-headed devotee of *realpolitik* like Kekkonen. But neither had he acquired sufficient standing in Bonn or the other Scandinavian capitals that would have enabled him to live down his image as someone who, at times, appeared to be an over-eager exponent of Soviet interests.

As ruler of Finland, it was by no means an easy undertaking for Kekkonen to carry out complicated transactions with the Soviets over a span of a quarter-of-a-century. They could be capricious and exacting, particularly in the Brezhnev era which began in 1964. With the eruption of the global energy crisis in 1973, which hit Finland particularly hard, an ageing Kekkonen found himself involved in arduous talks with the Soviets over the price of their oil. Around this time, the Kremlin's chief hardliner Mikhail Suslov sought to increase Soviet leverage over Finland by encouraging the radical wing of the communists to embark on serious labour unrest. At one stage, Kekkonen threatened to resign unless Moscow behaved more reasonably.[36]

Assessed overall, the relationship between those in the Finnish power structure and their Soviet interlocutors was both deadly serious but with an occasional undercurrent of levity. Networking and discreet negotiations often took place in either the presidential sauna or that of the Russian embassy. Perhaps the informal surroundings and the availability of alcohol helped to loosen tongues. KGB officials often slandered one another, and it was not unknown for their superiors to be disparaged. When Brezhnev took over, he was described as 'that stupid guy' by one of the KGB Helsinki operatives.[37]

As discipline slackened in the torpor of the Brezhnev years, Kekkonen found himself dragged into status disputes among promotion-hungry KGB figures. When a truculent KGB official, V.S. Stepanov, asked him to counsel the Kremlin to make him ambassador to Helsinki, Kekkonen reluctantly acquiesced, fearing the consequences if he held back and the official got the job anyway.[38] Stepanov would take to styling himself 'the Vice President of Finland' and in 1978, he managed to talk the Soviet defence minister Marshall Dimitry Ustinov into taking a harder line with the Finns. Ustinov tried to pressurise Kekkonen into holding joint military consultations.[39] In a sauna evening with the marshal, the President tried to brush the matter aside but the Soviets were insistent.[40] In the same year, while on an official visit to the Soviet Union, the head of the Finnish military, General Lauri Sutela, was almost kidnapped, and kept in isolation by his hosts in a presumed bid to crack his resistance to having Finland dragged deeper into the Soviet orbit.[41] What emerges from this imbroglio is that it was not only Soviet machinations but Finnish ones that were in play in order to alter the bilateral relationship. A key member of Kekkonen's entourage, noticing the gradual decline in his chief's mental powers, sought to manoeuvre him into offering a concession to the Soviets, in the hope that he might then succeed him.[42]

But when it was impossible to conceal Kekkonen's neurological decline, he agreed to retire on 26 October 1981 (his presidency officially ending in January 1982). He retreated into private life, and his death was announced on 31 August 1986. By now, a very different politician, Mauno Koivisto was president of Finland. He had demonstrated the shrinkage in Kekkonen's authority towards the end of his presidency by rebuffing a call for him to stand down as prime minister.[43]

Fitful Soviet attempts to pressurise the Finns slackened off with the commencement of the Gorbachev era in 1985. The onset of a new era in bilateral relations strengthened the view of those who believed that the ability of the Soviets to exercise pressure and influence stemmed, in no small measure, from the willingness of influential Finns, and much of wider society, to let them.[44] Not all acquiesced. The military chief General Sutela had set up his own military intelligence operation, which remained beyond the reach of Kekkonen and the Soviets.[45] Kekkonen himself ceased to be a totemic symbol of constrained nationhood even before his death. But three decades later, the accommodating stance towards Russia known as 'Finlandisation' has been revived as an explanatory tool for defining relations between Russia and its 'Near Abroad.' Russia had grown steadily more assertive under Vladimir Putin, while the West was growing divided and introspective in how it sought to influence global politics.

'Finlandisation' has been rolled out in some policy circles as a suitable formula for restraining Russian expansionism in Ukraine and Georgia. Weeks before the outbreak of the Russo-Ukrainian war, President

Macron's open discussion of 'Finlandisation' as a 'possible model' for Putin's quarry, earned him the rebuke of leading Scandinavian figures.[46] Five months later, the French National Assembly was ratifying Finland's decision to set aside its neutrality and join NATO.

It is impossible to know how Kekkonen would have interacted with a predatory figure like Putin, exercising power in the Kremlin without being hampered by ideological scruples? On the eve of his becoming President, a Soviet vice foreign minister V.M. Pushkin complained that the Finn had exploited ties with Moscow for his own personal advantage. The political analysts Raymond Aron and Walter Laqueur saw Kekkonen as a schemer without any firm ideological ballast.[47] But others, such as the US policy-maker George Kennan were more charitable.[48] They would tend to argue that while his own grandeur counted, what was in the best national interest of Finland was primordial for him.

Holding such a nation-rooted perspective can seem anachronistic in an age of European integration and trans-national capital, where there is often scant attachment to the national domain. Across the West, the national interest is a concept that has grown out of favour due to sweeping cultural changes and the inability of the major political forces to agree on almost any transcendent national objectives. At least in both Finland and Sweden, such cleavages were insufficiently serious to prevent a rapid and overwhelming consensus emerging for joining NATO within a few weeks of the 2022 invasion of Ukraine.[49] Political figures both possessing Kekkonen's skills set and his immersion in the social life of the nation may still be easier to spot in Scandinavia. Few other parts of Europe displayed such unanimity in the face of Russian aggression, refusing to flinch in the face of Kremlin threats delivered after the historic shift towards NATO membership.

---

[1] I am grateful to Mika Paananen for providing helpful information and correcting some inaccuracies.

[2] Jukka Nevakivi, 'Kekkonen, the Soviet Union and Scandinavia — Aspects of policy in the years 1948–1965', *Scandinavian Journal of History*, Vol. 22, No. 2, 2008, p. 67.
[3] Nevakivi, 'Kekkonen', p. 67.
[4] Seppo Hentilä, 'Maintaining Neutrality Between the Two German States: Finland and Divided Germany Until 1973', *Contemporary European History*, Vol. 15, No. 4, 2006, p. 485.
[5] George Maude, *Historical Dictionary of Finland*, Lanham, Md & London: Scarecrow Press 1995, p. 122.
[6] Maude, Historical Dictionary, p. 119.
[7] Hentilä 'Maintaining Neutrality', p.p. 473-4.
[8] Hentilä 'Maintaining Neutrality', p. 477.
[9] Mark Bosworth, 'Why Finland loves saunas', *Sauna Times*, n.d., https://www.saunatimes.com/sauna-information/sauna-in-the-news/why-finland-loves-saunas-article-from-bbc-news-magazine-in-the-uk/, accessed 4 October 2022.
[10] Rentola, 'President Urho Kekkonen', p. 278.
[11] Jason Lavery, 'All of the President's Historians', *Scandinavian Studies*, Vol. 75. No. 3, 2003, p.p. 381-2.
[12] Hentilä 'Maintaining Neutrality', p.p. 479-80; Lavery, 'All of the President's', p.p. 384-6; Henrik Meinander, *History of Finlan*d, London: Hurst Publications, 2011, p. 220.
[13] Lavery, 'All of the President's', p.387.
[14] David Kirby, *A Concise History of Finland*, Cambridge: Cambridge University Press, p. 251.
[15] Kimmo Rentola, 'President Urho Kekkonen of Finland and the KGB', in Aunesluoma, Juhani and Kettunen, Pauli (eds.), *The Cold War and the Politics of History*, Helsinki: Edita Publishing, 2008, p.285.
[16] Kirby, A Concise History of Finland, p. 257.
[17] Kirby, A Concise History of Finland, p. 257.
[18] Lotta Lounasmeri & Jukka Kortti, 'Campaigning between East and West: Finland and the Cold War in the presidential campaign films of Kekkonen', *Cold War History*, Vol. 20, No. 3, 2020, p. 335.
[19] Kimmo Rentola, 'Great Britain and the Soviet Threat in Finland 1944-1951,' *Scandinavian Journal of History*, Vol. 37, No. 2, 2012, p. 175.
[20] Mikko Virta's book *Operaatio Kekkonen, Lännen Agitit Tamminiemen Sisäpiirissä* was published in Helsinki by Otava in 2022.
[21] Seppo Varjus, 'gentti piilossa sohvan alla – Kekkosen hurjat suhteet brittitiedusteluun', *Ilta-Sanomat* (Helsinki),
12 October 2022.
[22] See Hentilä 'Maintaining Neutrality, passim.
[23] Nevakivi, 'Kekkonen', p. 78.
[24] Nevakivi, 'Kekkonen', p. 79.
[25] Nevakivi, 'Kekkonen', p. 79.
[26] Nevakivi, 'Kekkonen', p. 80.
[27] Nevakivi, 'Kekkonen', p. 80.
[28] Hentilä 'Maintaining Neutrality', p. 480.
[29] Lavery, 'All of the President's', p. 481.
[30] 'Vladimir Lenin, Finland - Postage stamp, 1970. Lenin Symposium. UNESCO' https://www.pinterest.co.uk/pin/529595237425318841/ [undated], accessed 6 Dec 2021.

[31] Kirby, A Concise History of Finland, p. 256.
[32] Niklas Jensen-Eriksen, 'The Northern Front in the Technological Cold War: Finland and East-West Trade in the 1970s and 1980s', *Journal of Cold War Studies*, Vol. 21, No. 4, 2019, p. 156.
[33] Maude, Historical Dictionary, p. 122.
[34] Maude, Historical Dictionary, p. 122.
[35] Meinander, *History of Finland*, p. 247.
[36] Kirby, A Concise History of Finland, p. 277.
[37] Rentola, 'President Urho Kekkonen', p. 284.
[38] Rentola, 'President Urho Kekkonen', p. 286.
[39] Rentola, 'President Urho Kekkonen', p. 286.
[40] Tarkka Jukka, 'Suomi joutui kuilun partaalle' 'Finland was on the brink of an abyss', Kaleva, 8 July 2003, https://www.kaleva.fi/suomi-joutui-kuilun-partaalle/2044597, accessed 25 October 2022.
[41] Eugen Systems Forum 21 May 2016, https://forums.eugensystems.com/viewtopic.php , accessed 29 May 2022.
[42] Ikka Salo, 'Did Paavo Väyrynen order his own "note crisis" in 1978?' *Uusi Suomi*, 19 February 2016, https://puheenvuoro.uusisuomi.fi/ilkkasalo1/212207-tilasiko-paavo-vayrynen-oman-noottikriisinsa-1978/, accessed 25 October 2022.
[43] Forsberg and Pesu, 'The "Finlandisation"', p. 480.
[44] Lavery, 'All of the President's', p. 397.
[45] Eugen Systems Forum 21 May 2016, https://forums.eugensystems.com/viewtopic.php?t=44782&start=540.
[46] Mike Eckel, '"Finlandization" for Ukraine hits a nerve', *Radio Free Europe*, 10 February 2022, https://www.rferl.org/a/ukraine-finlandization-macron-zelenskiy-helsinki/31697728.html, accessed 6 April 2022.
[47] Forsberg and Pesu, 'The "Finlandisation" ', p. 474; Walter Laqueur, 'A postscript on Finlandization', *Commentary*, Vol. 95, No. 1, January 1993.
[48] Forsberg and Pesu, 'The "Finlandisation" ', p. 474.
[49] Sune Engel Rasmussen, 'Finland, Sweden Apply for NATO Membership, Breaking Decades of Neutrality', *Wall Street Journal*, 18 May 2022.

CHAPTER 4: PAUL-HENRI SPAAK

1899-1972

The pugnacious, squarely-built Spaak was a nimble political figure. Indeed, he could be described as a Marco Polo of West European politics in the mid-20th century, someone who would engage in distant voyages to some of the more far-flung and exotic shores of politics.

Paul-Henri Spaak was keen to identify with causes that seemed to enjoy powerful global momentum, from state intervention in the1930s, to Cold War anti-Sovietism, to European integration. He took risks, as when spearheading the opposition to the restoration of King Leopold III to the throne of Belgium, when his own wartime record was pretty murky. He sat on boards, mixed with the great and the good, played front rank roles in NATO, the Common Market and the United Nations, yet remained an unpredictable *enfant terrible.*

He knew dizzy reversals of fortune. In 1938, he became the youngest Prime Minister in Europe. Two years later, he was a fugitive concealed in a lorry fleeing across Franco's Spain, eventually to reach the safety of wartime Britain. He would later be criticised for hesitating about backing the Allied cause, but he showed no trace of indecisiveness when it came to embarking upon the drive for European integration.

His energy, self-belief and obstinacy proved indispensable for putting wind in the sails of the embryo European project. He was a central figure in early dramas denoting the successes and failures of the search for a post-national Europe. He was less assured in his handling of the linguistic, educational and territorial cleavages that assailed his homeland, Belgium. His forthright opposition to the Soviet Union's expansionary drive led to him becoming the second person to run the North Atlantic Treaty Organization (NATO). Controversies involving France's de Gaulle, over whether NATO should have a role beyond Europe and North America, and later the post-colonial strife in the former Belgian Congo, dogged his footsteps. Perhaps no European politician in the last century was plunged into such a continual round of controversies while still being able to rise to the surface like an unsinkable cork.

It is perhaps fitting that it was the cockpit of Europe in the first half of the last century, which would produce a figure as tenacious and strategic in his focus as Spaak. His negotiating skills and visibility ensured that the headquarters of both the nascent EU and NATO (after 1966) were located in the Belgian capital. He was an eloquent exponent of winding down independent nation states in favour of pooled sovereignty and federal arrangements. But he was also a fierce defender of regional rights and of maintaining European influence and economic advantages in former colonial possessions. These were Belgian preoccupations in particular, and his persistence enabled them to become consistently-held preoccupations of the EU.

He showed bravery and a willingness to take risks in his political career. But he never lost an appetite for the good life. His rarely concealed egoism, combined with a sense of entitlement, made him an increasingly questioned figure within the ranks of his own Socialist party. Unsurprisingly, he determined to carve out power-bases that made him less dependent on fickle electors, or party comrades who recoiled from what seemed like personal opportunism, but which he would insist was adherence to principle. It is possible to contend that Spaak's influence today is most clearly discerned in the number of grandees at the apex of EU politics who essentially share his approach to public affairs.

Spaak was born into a family steeped in Belgian politics. His provenance is bound to have strengthened his lifelong confidence in his own abilities and judgment. He combined radical instincts with a desire to be an important player near the heart of political and economic power. This ambiguous stance was reflected in the biography of his grandfather on his mother's side. Paul Janson was a champion of the underprivileged who entered parliament in 1877 for the Liberal party, but who lived in a chateau thanks to the income he made at the Brussels Bar.

Paul's father had acquired enduring family renown by being an active participant in the 1789 French Revolution. The convulsions emanating from this seismic event gave rise to the creation of Belgium. The new state was an international design meant to check French ambitions, first in union with the Netherlands, then from 1831 as a separate entity. Societal disunity was a perennial feature. The state contained two major language groups, the Flemings and the Walloons, but there were also rivalries between Catholics and anti-clericals, and later mounting tensions between owners of capital and many of their workers. A monarch was endowed with strong powers in order to keep centrifugal tendencies in check and act as the principal symbol of national unity.

As a teenager, Spaak was caught up in the trauma of the German occupation of nearly all of Belgium after 1914, and towards the end of the war he was deported to Germany. In the 1920s, he gained the reputation of being an outspoken left-wing lawyer. He entered the leadership of the Belgian Workers Party (POB) in 1931 and in the following year he made a controversial speech, not only denouncing military service but encouraging people to sabotage any future war effort.[1] Irony abounds over his subsequent political trajectory. Elected to parliament in 1933, he became foreign minister in February 1936, in a Liberal-Socialist coalition headed by his uncle Paul-Émile Janson. His earlier incendiary declaration forgotten, he promoted Belgian re-armament in the face of the threat from Hitler's Germany. He also believed there was no longer any point in relying on Anglo-French security guarantees enshrined in the Locarno Treaty of 1925. What he described as an 'independent line' in foreign policy was followed up to the moment of the German invasion on May 10, 1940. His stance then contradicted his future adherence to collective security as a means of preserving Belgian sovereignty.[2] In his memoirs, he asserted that 'if we had adhered to an open alliance with Britain and France, we would have been beaten in 1940 and Belgium's destruction and occupation would have followed. We were right to try and avoid this fate'.[3]

Spaak did not remain impervious to the nationalist spirit that had been convulsing Europe, one increasingly impatient with parliamentary conventions. In one speech made in 1938, he endorsed a 'socialisme nationale' which was a rejection of Marxism and its international focus rather than a repudiation of democracy.[4] For some years, he had been an ally of Hendrik de Man, possibly the most controversial figure ever produced by the Belgian Left. A capable Flemish intellectual, he had sprung to fame in 1933 by drawing up a 'Labor Plan' meant to confront the acute challenges produced by the post-1929 economic slump. It proposed a radical reconstruction of Belgium's economic structure with banking and finance becoming largely subject to state control. His ultimate goals were far more sweeping. Orthodox parliamentary rule was played out, in his view, a tool of vested interests that was unable to offer a way out of the crisis of the 1930s. He soon joined the government after rising high in the POB. What his preferred 'third way' involved only became clear in 1940, when he hailed the levelling of economic frontiers in a Europe now united by arms.[5] But by then, he had been side-lined by the party apparatus, which feared losing out if his blueprint of 'authoritarian democracy' was implemented.

Spaak also kept his distance as his political career flourished. On 15 May 1938, he became Prime Minister. He stood down after nine months due to controversy arising from the pardon given to a World War I collaborator. A mob besieged his home, attacking him upon his arrival. The incident showed the volatility of the period, as a highly visible pro-fascist Rexist Party squared up against a growing communist party, both with their bases in Spaak's Wallonia.

More than ever, it was a time when the balancing role of the monarch was needed. In 1934, Leopold III had succeeded his father Albert I, a symbol of national resistance as a result of remaining in the pocket of unconquered Belgian territory until Germany's defeat in 1918. In May 1940, the second German invasion produced a breach between the government and the king which would not be healed and in which Spaak would play a pivotal role.

On 28 May 1940, with the country on the point of succumbing to the German invasion, Leopold decided to end hostilities. He believed further resistance was futile and 'wished to share the fate of his soldiers and his people in order to maintain morale and to lessen their suffering'.[6] There was consternation in the government over his unwillingness to go into exile like other monarchs whose countries the German *Wehrmacht* had overrun. Following attacks on Belgian refugees in France, who heard the Prime Minister, Paul Reynaud denounce Leopold as 'the traitor king', the Belgian government, whose members were in Paris, in turn issued a furious public denunciation.[7]

Spaak later observed:

> 'The King was a hard-working and thoughtful man...He could not understand that his function as Head of State took precedence over that of Supreme Commander…A little flexibility would have been his salvation. One reason for his obstinacy was his conviction that he could see things more clearly than his ministers'.[8]

Leopold made the surrender a purely military act and offered himself as a prisoner. He did not seek to form a puppet administration and held aloof from de Man (who saw the Nazis, however crude, as harbingers of a new and superior Europe).[9] The kaleidoscopic nature of events led the Belgian government, when in exile in London, to soften its approach towards the king. In a broadcast Spaak made in November 1941, he implored Belgians to 'close your ranks round the prisoner King....In refusing to cooperate…with the occupying power…the King is an example to his people'.[10] But his tone changed as the war swung against Germany, and Britain actively promoted resistance in occupied Europe. At the end of 1942, the government asked him to lead active resistance and, less than a year before the liberation of Belgium in September 1944, to publicly condemn collaborators.[11]

In July 1945, Spaak travelled to Switzerland, where Leopold was then living, to urge Leopold to abdicate, promising that the government would say that he had not betrayed his country. There was no demand for a republic. But the atmosphere had been transformed by the collapse of the fascist powers. The King's singular stance now discredited him in the eyes of a large and vocal minority of Belgians.

Leopold would have been able to point to Spaak's own irresolution in the critical year of 1940. Doubting Britain's ability to hold out, and stuck in un-occupied France, months elapsed during which he and his cabinet colleagues equivocated about what steps to take. What he described as his 'faint-heartedness' then made him doubt his ability to resume a front rank role in Belgian politics.[12]

On 10 May 1940, as Hitler's tanks rolled into Belgium, Spaak's reaction had been one of defiance when, as foreign minister, he received the German ambassador. He refused to allow him to read out his statement and denounced Berlin's 'criminal aggression'.[13] Not long after, he and other ministers were evacuated from Dunkirk on a British warship. But their stay in Britain was short, as it seemed unlikely Britain could hold out. He was in Paris by the end of May and as France hurtled to military defeat, he and the cabinet moved first to Limoges and then to Vichy where Marshal Philippe Petain's government was established. In mid-June, Spaak refused an offer from the British to be evacuated by air to Britain along with other ministers. He was disparaging to his colleagues about British prospects.[14] There was a groundswell of opinion among their ranks to work for the reconstruction of Belgium. Spaak has related that the Government hoped to arrange a peace treaty, enabling some degree of independence.[15] Luckily for them, Leopold refused to respond to their overtures during 'a momentary weakening' (the words of Hubert Pierlot, the Prime Minister) that in fact lasted around six weeks.[16]

Pierlot and Spaak left Vichy on 28 August 1940, after mulling over reports that Britain's doom might not be imminent after all. After a hazardous escape, involving a gruelling clandestine journey across the Iberian Peninsula, they arrived in Britain on 22 October 1940.

In retrospect, it is possible to argue that Belgium was not as scarred by the German occupation as France or, for that matter, the Netherlands. But efforts at post-war reconstruction were undermined by divisions over the fate of Leopold, who was keen to end his Swiss exile and re-assume his kingly duties. He refused either to express regret for his wartime role or step down. On 12 March 1950, a referendum was held to answer the question, 'Do you agree that the King should resume his exercise of his constitutional powers?' The result showed the country to be split on linguistic, class and religious grounds. 57.68 percent of those voting supported the proposition, while 42.32 percent were opposed. In Flanders the pro-Leopold vote was 72 percent. But Wallonia voted against Leopold by 58 percent, and Brussels voted against him by 52 percent.[17]

With the left and the Liberals boycotting the vote, on 20 July 1950, a majority of parliamentarians, (Catholics to the fore) voted to end the regency and allow Leopold's return. Within 48 hours, he was back, but his call for unity and forgiveness was angrily spurned by many Belgians. Spaak was apocalyptic about what could ensue. Out of office at this point, he wrote: Was it really necessary that 'blood should flow and the most cruel of civil wars should be unleashed' to make the government see reason.[18]

He led demonstrators to the royal palace on 27 July, amidst cries of 'Leopold to the gallows'.[19] Strikes erupted, and violence flared between non-striking Catholic union members and striking Socialists. On 31 July, 100,000 demonstrators marched on the capital from Wallonia. They broke through roadblocks, and the country seemed on the verge of a disastrous fracture. But that evening Leopold finally conceded, stepping down in favour of his son Baudouin.

A searing national quarrel, that highlighted Belgium's territorial and linguistic divisions, impaired national cohesion and contributed to renewed outbreaks of internal strife during the second half of the 20th century. But Belgium avoided becoming a failed state. What was seen as the imperative of European unity by Spaak and others, would replace the diminished monarchy as the force preserving Belgian cohesion.

Spaak would occupy the offices of prime minister and foreign minister intermittently from 1945 to 1966. But he was scaling down his commitment to national affairs. Instead, his energies were channelled into the movement for European political and economic convergence, whose moving spirit was the French financier, Jean Monnet. Spaak had first met him in Washington DC in 1940. Monnet, then aged 52, had been immersed in the world of Anglo-Saxon high finance for many years, seeking to be of service to France. As the United States once again became embroiled in European affairs after its entry into the world conflict at the end of 1941, he enlisted the backing of leading financiers, law-makers and later soldiers, for what he claimed was his goal of a Europe that resembled, far more closely than before, the political model of a United States of Europe.[20]

Spaak was busy aligning Belgium with the United States in the emerging global power struggle with the Soviet Union, which became known as the Cold War. His international stature was bound to benefit from his success in steering most of the Belgian political elite, including his own left-leaning party, the POB, into the pro-American camp.[21] As the only prominent left-wing figure among the founding fathers of what eventually became the European Union (EU), he was indispensable for the mission of reassurance meant to allay working-class fears that this was not yet another form of capitalist exploitation. In 1948, he was elected president of the Organization for European Economic Cooperation (OEEC), a strictly inter-governmental initiative meant to coordinate US Marshall Aid for Europe.

The OEEC was damned in the eyes of Monnet, who had set his sights on creating a large-scale *supranational* European organization: 'it's only a watered-down British approach to Europe'.[22] Monnet was then in charge of French post-war planning and his dream flew off the drawing board when he won the backing of six countries for a West European Coal and Steel Community (ECSC) with a supranational body to control industrial policy. The pressure imposed, particularly on the initially un-enthusiastic French political class, by leading US policy-makers and technocrats to get behind the initiative, was pivotal.

The ECSC came into being in 1953, and immediately Monnet sought to bring into being a European Defence Community (EDC) with a 'European Political Community' acting as a 'common political roof' for both it and the ECSC. He enlisted Spaak to be the chief architect of this ambitious undertaking. However, he was unable to overcome deep-seated French objections to a project that would involve German re-armament. Opposition transcended left and right and was spearheaded by General Charles de Gaulle. In August 1954, at a meeting in Paris, Spaak pleaded with a sceptical French Prime Minister, Pierre Mendes-France to back the defence initiative: 'what matters is the integration of Europe. EDC is only the first step in that direction, but if there is no EDC, then everything falls to the ground'.[23] Later in that year, the French national assembly voted it down. Monnet resigned as president of the ECSC. The use of 'Federal' and 'European government', terms previously used by Monnet to give integration a high profile, was discontinued. It would be Spaak who urged Monnet to conceal the project's political goals and to proclaim instead economic cooperation as the central purpose.[24]

Spaak was the crucial front man for the now more circumspect quest to build a post-national Europe. His energy, deviousness, resilience, and skills at chairing big events, and lobbying behind the scenes, were blessed with success at Messina in 1955. Agreement was hammered out in this Italian city for a customs union or Common Market that would formally come into being with the signing by the six founding nations of the Treaty of Rome on 25 March 1957. Just weeks beforehand, he had dropped his circumspection to describe it as 'the most important event in the history of Europe since the French Revolution'. Nevertheless, on the surface the ambitions of the founders were played down and, on Spaak's advice, the phrase, the United States of Europe was struck out. He was careful instead to emphasise an 'economic community'.[25]

Almost completely struck from the record too is the fact that the architects of the emerging European polity believed that its greatness in historical terms was bound up with including Africa in the enterprise. Spaak declared in February 1957: 'Would it not be a success, if we could realize the dream of Eurafrica, which, after the reunion in Paris, seems able to become reality?'[26] There were no dissenters among the founders of today's EU about the need to harness the resources of Africa to turn Europe into a geopolitical force able to hold its own, both against the Soviet Union and the United States. Robert Schuman, whose candidacy for sainthood is at the time of writing being considered by the Vatican, spoke in 1957 about 'the institution of a true community between the peoples of Europe and of Africa'.[27] In his eyes, economics would be at the centre of the pluri-continental compact that would be shaped by 'reciprocity' and common interests.

In successfully overruling sceptics in his own cabinet about the Eurafrica concept, West Germany's Chancellor Adenauer, placed emphasis on the economic advantages for the new European order; the minutes summarised his feelings in this way: 'just think of the Sahara with its oil and uranium deposits. Equatorial Africa also constitutes a significant reserve'.[28]

But a French Algeria in the EEC would prove a mirage. The scale of the nationalist uprising against French rule led France to withdraw completely and, in 1962, grant independence to local rulers who made the new Algerian state a hub for anti-colonial sentiment across Africa. Ironically, it was an avowed French nationalist, Charles de Gaulle, ruler of France from 1958 to 1969, who presided over this *volte-face*. Spaak was perplexed and unhappy by the consequences of his return to power: 'he restored peace in Algeria but achieved this by doing the opposite of what he had promised…'[29] He talked frankly in his memoirs of de Gaulle being 'the most dangerous adversary of the two ideals for which I have fought for nearly a quarter of a century: the Atlantic Alliance and European unity'.[30] De Gaulle impeded further pro-integration moves in the EEC through the 1960s, and in 1967, NATO's headquarters were forced to move to Brussels after he pulled France out of the military wing of the alliance.

The absence of a common European front meant that the 'neo-imperial' ambitions of the EU's founding fathers vanished into the sands. Within three years of Spaak unfurling his grandiloquent dream for Eurafrica, Belgium had granted independence to the Congo, its huge central African possession. Having been secretary general of NATO since 1957, would have enabled him to grasp the depth of US opposition to the nascent EU retaining sovereignty and economic power in large parts of Africa.

Belgium had a sizeable population in Katanga, the mineral rich province in the south of the Congo, as well as a large air base. There was important support within the political elite for a secession bid by Katanga, which was a serious possibility until the mid-1960s. Unlike other prominent figures, such as King Baudouin and Gaston Eyskens, prime minister as the crisis erupted, Spaak was desperate to avoid a break with international opinion.[31] He had not, however, reverted to being an anti-colonialist, as shown by his sympathy for the Portuguese case for retaining a direct presence in Africa (one that would continue until 1975).[32] But he may have believed opinion in Belgium was too divided over the colonial issue, and the United States too powerful for Belgium to dare go it alone. Thus, in August 1960, he turned down the overture from the King to quit NATO and head a national unity government.[33]

He did quit his NATO position early in 1961 and, soon back as foreign minister, he scaled down covert Belgian involvement in the Katangan secession.[34] After the death of the UN secretary general Dag Hammarskjold, in a mysterious plane crash in the Congo in September 1961, the cost of defying the United Nations may have seemed too high a price to pay.

By the time he announced his retirement from politics in 1966, Belgian policy in Africa was broadly aligned with that of the United States, which was opposed to secession attempts in decolonising Africa.[35] Various Belgian economic and financial interests had lost out. But Spaak, having described the Congo crisis as the most difficult one that he had had to face in his public career, was not among the losers.[36]

In 1968, after a fitful stability had descended on the Congo, which was embarking on a lengthy period of dictatorial rule under Joseph Mobutu, Spaak visited the country as a representative of the International Telegraph and Telephone Company (ITT). The American company's European headquarters were in Brussels, and he was a member of its board. A Pathé newsreel film exists, showing him and his delegation being received by Mobutu, who decorates him with the National Order of the Leopard.[37]

Spaak was the first, but by no means the last, of the top decision-makers at the heart of the European project to plunge into business. The well-endowed lobbies established in Brussels by major corporations as the EU's regulatory powers increased, produced a symbiotic relationship between powerful multi-nationals and the rule-makers in this expanding bureaucratic leviathan. Thus, the move by top commissioners into business roles was hardly an unusual process.

Spaak had exercised, with energy and aplomb, a bewildering number of roles in a forty-year career in public affairs. He seemed an indestructible cork, capable of remaining afloat in the roughest of seas. From *enfant terrible* of Belgian socialism to proponent of neutralism in the age of Nazi power, to champion of Atlanticist defence against the Soviet Cold War danger, to ebullient sentinel of the new post-national Europe, to cheerleader for a post-colonial but still European-influenced Africa - arguably no other figure on the European stage in the decades of his ascendancy had been as versatile. And he was not finished yet.

In 1971, to the surprise of many, he emerged from political retirement and was re-elected to parliament. It was not, however, for the Belgian Socialists (POB). Ties had been severed in 1966 when the party refused to back Brussels as the site for NATO's headquarters.[38] He stood instead as an independent aligned to the Front Democratique des Francophones (FDF) which sprang up to defend the interests of previously ascendant francophones in Belgian society and politics. From the 1950s onwards, an increasing share of the leading roles within the state was assumed by Flemish speakers. They tended to be bilingual (many also speaking English) and displayed managerial capabilities and technocratic abilities, which were less obvious among francophones.[39] Spaak was a monoglot and he identified with francophone frustrations. The country had been convulsed in the 1960s by inter-communal friction centering on what the language policy should be in educational institutions and localities, and a language frontier was established to contain strife. At the height of the royal crisis in 1950, Spaak had told the congress of the POB that 'we can unleash all sorts of actions throughout the country, economic, political social, even in the field of relations between Walloon and Fleming…'[40] So in this power struggle he had not been averse to using the ethnic weapon to achieve his ends.

Despite his attempt to bury political nationalism, he was now heard to argue that community issues were central concerns.41 A stubborn pride, bound up with his own not inconsiderable ego, took precedence over internationalist causes, ones seeking to relegate various particularisms, that he had championed. But any temptation to dismiss him as a heretic should be avoided. Spaak is perhaps the first example of a capable politician who found the agenda of European unification too constricting. He died suddenly on 31 July 1972, but the Spaak name continued to reverberate in Belgian politics.

Tragically, his son Fernand Spaak met a violent and premature end in 1981. He was killed by his wife on account of his infidelities with both sexes. At the time, he was chief-of-staff to Gaston Thorn, the president of the European Commission, having occupied the same position under Jean Monnet for much of the 1950s.[42]

Paul-Henri's daughter Antoinette Spaak inherited his parliamentary seat and indeed led the FDF to important successes in a career that stretched into this century. (She died in 2020 aged 92). She combined a strong attachment to regionalism with a European outlook. Both she and her father were happy to promote a form of identity politics that did not clash with, or threaten, the viability of a supranational project, as states based on national sovereignty did. The career of this political magnate illustrates how ambitious Europhiles have been prepared to exploit local sentiments to prevail in politics. It is likely to be a recurring trait in the EU for as long as the entity remains in existence.

---

[1] J.H. Huizinga, *Mr Europe, A Political Biography of Paul-Henri Spaak,* London: Weidenfeld & Nicolson, 1961, p. 230.
[2] See Stephen George, 'Paul-Henri Spaak and a Paradox in Belgian Foreign Policy', British Journal of International Studies, Vol. 1, No. 3, 1975, p. 255.
[3] Paul-Henri Spaak, *The Continuing Battle: Memoirs of a European 1936-1966,* London: Weidenfeld & Nicolson, 1971, p. 10.
[4] Martin Conway, 'The Extreme Right in Inter-War Francophone Belgium: Explanations of a Failure', *European History Quarterly,* Vol. 26, No. 2, 1996, p. 286.
[5] Peter Dodge, *Beyond Marxism: The Faith and Works of Hendrik de Man,* The Hague: Martinus Nijhoff, p. 197.
[6] E. Ramón Arango, *Leopold III and the Belgian Royal Question,* Baltimore: Johns Hopkins University Press, 1963, p. 3.
[7] Huizinga, *Mr Europe,* p. p. 139-41.
[8] Spaak, *The Continuing Battle*, p.p. 18, 20.
[9] Arango, *Leopold III,* p. 110.
[10] Huizinga, *Mr Europe,* p. 175.
[11] Huizinga, *Mr Europe,* p.p. 179-80.
[12] Spaak, The Continuing Battle, p.p. 50, 90-1.
[13] Huizinga, Mr Europe, p.p. 112-13.
[14] Huizinga, *Mr Europe,* p. 160.
[15] Huizinga, *Mr Europe*, p.p. 159, 163.
[16] Huizinga, *Mr Europe,* p. 163.
[17]Arango, *Leopold III,* p.p. 190-1.
[18] Huizinga, *Mr Europe,* p. 220.

[19] Arango, Leopold III, p. 200.
[20] Keith Middlelmas, Orchestrating Europe, the Informal Politics of the European Union, London: Fontana Press, 1995, p. 10.
[21] See Maarten Van Alstein, 'From Enigma to Enemy: Paul-Henri Spaak, the Belgian Diplomatic Elite, and the Soviet Union, 1944–1945', *Journal of Cold War Studies*, Vol. 13, No. 3, Summer 2011.
[22] Christopher Booker and Richard North, *The Great Deception*, London: Bloomsbury, 2016 edition, p. 53.
[23] Booker and North, *The Great Deception*, p. 81.
[24] Tom Gallagher, *Europe's Path to Crisis*, Manchester: Manchester University Press, 2014, p. 50.
[25] Booker and North, *The Great Deception*, p. 85.
[26] Peo Hansen and Stefan Jonssen, 'Imperial Origins of European Integration and the Case of Eurafrica: A Reply to Gary Marks', *Journal of Common Market Studies*, Vol. 50, No. 6, 2012, p. 1028.
[27] Hansen and Stefan Jonssen, 'Imperial Origins', p. 1036.
[28] Hansen and Stefan Jonssen, 'Imperial Origins', p. 1032.
[29] Spaak, The Continuing Battle, p. 310.
[30] Spaak, The Continuing Battle, p. 305.
[31] Guy Vanthemske, La Belgique et le Congo (1885-1980), L'Impact de la colonie sur le métropole, Brussels: le Cri editions, 2010, p.p. 97, 137.
[32] Franco Nogueira, *Salazar, Vol. 5: A Resistência, 1958-64*, Coimbra (Portugal): Livraria Civilização Editora, 1984, p.p. 322, 601.
[33] Vanthemske, La Belgique et le Congo, p. 97.
[34] Vanthemske, La Belgique et le Congo, p.117.
[35] Oliver Boehme, 'The Involvement of the Belgian Central Bank in the Katanga Secession, 1960-1963', *African Economic History*, No. 33 (2005), p. 21.
[36] Nogueira, *Salazar - Vol. 5*, p. 567.
[37] https://www.britishpathe.com/asset/214909/, accessed 25 October 2022.
[38] Spaak, *The Continuing Battle*, p.p. 492-3.
[39] Martin Conway, *The Sorrows of Belgium*, Oxford: Oxford Uni. Press, 2012, p. 382.
[40] Huizinga, *Mr Europe*, p. 220.
[41] Fabien Conord, 'Paul-Henri Spaak: héraut ou soliste du socialisme belge?', *Annales canadiennes d'histoire / Canadian Journal of History*, Vol. 49, No. 1, 2014, p.p. 24 9.
[42] Michael Bloch, Closet Queens, London: Little Brown, 2015, p. 92.

CHAPTER 5: GIULIO ANDREOTTI

1919-2013

Over many years, Giulio Andreotti used his talents as an organizer, negotiator and intriguer, to keep in being, a political system that increasingly worked only for those close to the actual wielders of power. Perhaps he could claim particular justification for being a political chameleon who preferred to operate in the shadows through deal-making and byzantine manoeuvres. He drew attention in 1994 to 'the precarious nature of the Italian state, whose unification "was only achieved a hundred and thirty years ago, after the country had been split for more than four centuries into many separate States"'.[1] When he entered politics, the country was suffering the effects of a highly intrusive but incompetent dictatorship which produced great hardships for many citizens. Italy soon succumbed to successive military defeats that led to occupation and destructive fighting up and down the peninsula. There was no sense of relief or outbreak of reconciliation after the collapse of the fascist state. The end of the Mussolini era left a deeply fractured country, polarised into hostile ideological camps. Throughout Andreotti's marathon political career, national life never ceased to be intensely politicised. The penchant for intrigue and infighting, not only between, but within, political camps, left ambitious reform projects stillborn. The climate of partisanship meant that disreputable practices which choked national development, failed to be properly rooted out.

Andreotti's sense of cold realism and lack of illusions about mankind's character traits enabled him to navigate the treacherous waters of Italian politics, usually with ease. Eventually, this Catholic politician's acceptance of divorce and other social changes showed that he was no ultramontane standing firm against any and all social change. But, at heart, he was essentially short-term in his outlook. A flawed political system based on manipulating the state to make it a source of patronage rather than an engine of development, suited his devious style of politics. He never showed any appetite for cleaning it up or embarking on renewal. Perhaps, in the cynical world of politics, he had closed himself off from genuine reformers. Certainly, he had no illusion that any actions he endorsed were likely to herald a new and better world. As one obituarist observed: in his eyes 'people were fallible and corrupt, flawed and sinful, and one had to accept them as they were. They might be changed by divine intervention, but not by human intercession'.[2]

People tainted by their deeds and character were ubiquitous, and his conclusion seems to have been that little could be done without them. He thus chose to cooperate with scurrilous figures and leave himself open to serious allegations of colluding in assassinations or turning a blind eye to them. Ultimately, no figure at the top of European democratic politics, from 1945 onwards, spent such a lengthy period warding off serious criminal charges.

Throughout his legal tribulations, he remained composed. 'To give 24 years to a man who is over 80 is almost like wishing him a long life' was his remark in 2002, after the court of appeal sentenced him to 24 years in jail for having ordered the murder of a journalist (only for the court of cassation, the country's court of last resort, to overturn the sentence verdict the following year).[3]

Andreotti was an unusual Italian politician who scorned melodrama. His energies were focused on acquiring and retaining power. He knew how to use public money to bolster his position, but amassing wealth for himself or his family was not a priority. Well into his eighties, the light of ambition burned undimmed. He was either prime minister or a senior minister for more than half the lifetime of the First Italian Republic (1946-1992), present in all but six of the 45 governments that were in office during this period. He deservedly figures in any ledger accounting for European political Machiavellianism in this time period. But it is difficult to conclusively assert that he was instrumental in ensuring that Italy was ill-governed and prone to periodic societal traumas. In the thirty years since he vacated the political stage, Italy has continued to be afflicted by structural problems that were a feature of the Andreotti years (not a few of which preceded them). He was adroit in wielding power, arranging political compromises, and deploying Italian influence in international affairs. But despite his commitment to a European identity perhaps supplanting an Italian one, he never showed any enthusiasm for the EU's desire for prudent economic house-keeping to take root in Italy. In his absence, lesser figures might have stirred up fewer controversies, but his successors have struggled to prevent tensions over ideology, money and territory tearing Italy apart.

In his heyday, Giulio Andreotti was dubbed 'the Foreign Minister of the Vatican'.[4] He was close to at least two popes. A brilliant student who had been born into strongly Catholic family, in 1921, at two years of age, he lost his father, a schoolteacher, when he succumbed to his war wounds. As a student in the late 1930s, he became active in the Federation of Catholic University Students (FUCI). In 1942, he succeeded Aldo Moro (with whom his political career would later be intertwined) as its head.[5] At this time, he became a familiar presence in the Vatican due to his role in the nascent Christian Democratic movement. He was also using its library to complete a thesis on 'The Personality of the Criminal in Church Law'.

Alcide de Gasperi, the veteran conservative foe of Benito Mussolini, who would lead Italy on the path away from fascism as Prime Minister from 1945 to 1953, had been a library cataloguer in the Vatican for many years after being released from a fascist prison. Andreotti became his protégé, de Gasperi once remarking that 'he...can do anything'.[6] Aged 27, he would be elected to parliament in 1946, the start of a lifetime tenure spanning seven decades. In the following year, as the Christian Democrats (DC) began to outstrip the Italian Communist Party (PCI) in the battle for the control of Italy, he became a junior minister in the prime minister's office. In this role, he had more real power —and patronage—than some members of the cabinet, with a remit that included sport, culture and health.[7]

His visibility and influence arose, not because of any concrete policy accomplishments but, as a result of being a discreet and effective servant for an ageing political master. In 1948, the DC won a decisive electoral majority which resulted in the communists being denied any real power for the next thirty years. Soon, some of the main political struggles would be between the factions in the Christian Democrats. Neither charisma nor prowess in the policy field were the key ingredients required for success. Instead, what counted was the ability to wield influence in the state bureaucracy and be effective in rewarding prominent allies and more humble supporters. Andreotti gifted with immense patience, single-mindedness and ruthlessness when called for, was well able to thrive in this byzantine political world.

The politician had come of age during the pontificate of Pius XII (1939-58) who was deeply averse to innovation. Andreotti established a web of connections in the centralised civil service imposed by the Savoy dynasty from Piedmont when they became rulers of a unified Italy after 1870. The Savoys were rejected by most Italians in a referendum followed by the proclamation of the Italian First Republic in 1946. But the labyrinthine bureaucracy carried on, largely unaltered despite the disruptive fascist decades.

Marshall Aid from the USA began to increase the depleted state coffers. The economy picked up speed less due to the exploits of the state and more to the dynamism of parts of the now unshackled private economy and the unleashing of creative energies in society, notably in regions north of Rome. The state, by contrast, became absorbed in the patron-client arrangements that would define the Christian Democrats.[8] Spending decisions, even for massive projects such as the building of Fumicino airport in Rome, Andreotti's urban fiefdom, became too often enmeshed with the awarding of electoral favours.

Andreotti was already starting to be seen as a politician to watch when he became minister of defence in 1957, aged only 38. He held the post for the next six years, some of the most nerve-wracking ones in the Cold War. Italy was on the front line. Across the Adriatic lay communist Yugoslavia. It was semi-detached from Moscow yet ties with Italy were strained. A territorial dispute brought both countries near to serious conflict, over the city of Trieste, in 1954.

Buffeted by internal squabbles and often unimpressive in the discharge of its governing duties, the DC looked for legitimacy by promoting itself as the sentinel best placed to guard Italy against the communist danger. Having joined NATO upon its formation in 1949, the defence ministry was a big-spending department. After decades of denial, it emerged in 1990, that a clandestine network of anti-Communist paramilitaries, known as operation Gladio, had been set up in 1958, to combat the threat of Communist subversion and invasion and had never been disbanded.[9]

Andreotti's tenure in office also saw the mysterious death of Italy's most remarkable post-1945 entrepreneur, Enrico Mattei. Until the 1962 air disaster which claimed his life, he had been the most dynamic of the new breed of capitalists, seen as responsible for what was starting to be described as Italy's 'economic miracle'. Mattei, however, operated within the parameters of the state. This autocratic and unconventional figure single-handedly turned around Mussolini's failing state oil corporation, ENI, which he had been ordered to disband.[10] He made it a highly-effective energy giant able to compete with the US energy sector.[11] He obtained better terms in some cases from Middle East suppliers than the big cartels and was unafraid to strike deals with Soviet proxies.[12] He kept down fuel costs for Italian consumers, boosting the explosion in car ownership.

A defence ministry report released five months after his death in 1962, concluded that it had been a tragic air accident. Andreotti oversaw and approved the report.[13] Finally, after years of controversy, the Mafia informer Tommaso Buscetta announced, in 1994, that Mattei had been killed by the Sicilian mafia as a favour to its friends in the US business community. The Italian daily *La Stampa,* released the details of a judicial enquiry in 1997, which found that the wounds to his body clearly indicated that he had been killed by a bomb on board his private aircraft and not, as previously asserted, as a result of an accident caused by bad weather.[14]

Possible culprits were legion, ranging from the mafia to the CIA, and French right-wing extremists angered by Mattei positioning himself as a champion of the Algerian fighters for independence.[15] Inevitably, Andreotti's name was on the list. Ironically, Mattei had prepared the ground for Andreotti's later forays into the politics of the Middle East where he made overtures to various regimes that were viewed with extreme disfavour by the USA. He was able to flout several geopolitical red lines laid down by the US State Department and the CIA, thanks to the clientelistic networks built up by Mattei.[16]

The mafia appear to have been the likeliest culprits responsible for Mattei's violent demise. The *Cosa Nostra* would go on to eliminate equally important figures who were deemed to pose a mortal threat to its illicit activities. General Carlo Alberto dalla Chiesa, the head of the state's anti-terrorist drive was killed in 1982, as were two judges investigating the mafia, Giovanni Falcone and Paolo Borsellino, exactly a decade later and within weeks of each other.

In 2003, the appeals court in Palermo found that Andreotti had an 'authentic, stable and friendly openness towards mafiosi'. But the court ruled that these relations had not continued after 1980 and that the offence had thus fallen under the statute of limitations. A final appeals court judgement in 2004, upheld this view.[17] Up to the first half of Andreotti's career, the mafia's territorial scale and ambitions may have lacked the scope they would acquire later in the decade when Palermo could be described by a British historian as 'probably the world's chief centre for the distribution of heroin'.[18] There may well have been a feeling in influential quarters that the gravity of the Cold War confrontation excused having such tainted allies.

The second-in-command of Andreotti's faction in the DC, Salvo Lima, was a seedy figure who a parliamentary commission posthumously found had been enmeshed in the mafia. In 1992, he was shot dead by a mafia hitman when his usefulness to the mob appeared to be coming to an end. Much later, a journalist asked Andreotti whether the revelations that had spilled out about some of his lieutenant's activities had not given him cause to think that he was indirectly dealing with the mafia. His answer indicates the ability of this normally alert and wily figure to banish from his mind certain uncomfortable thoughts:

> 'But Lima never spoke to me about these things...A lot of people in Sicily have links with the mafia. That isn't just true of the Christian Democrats, but of others. It may be that there are periods in which it

> counts for more and for less. But the power of the mafia is a power that exists. It's not that it can be ignored or underestimated'.[19]

Andreotti's imperturbable facade rarely wavered when confronted with evidence of the mafia's reach extending deep into the heart of political power. Upon his death in 2013, defenders like Silvio Berlusconi claimed that he had been the victim of a relentless campaign of vilification from the political left, which would have included radical journalists, sensationalist television pundits and single-minded crusading prosecutors.[20] But it remains striking that his name was linked to successive murky episodes and that he was under investigation and in court on numerous occasions.

Perhaps he had convinced himself that the character of Italy and the times it was living through, meant that compromises with figures who would have been seen as un-frequentable in many other places were unavoidable.[21] The compromises that this sinuous figure agreed to included ones with the communist PCI, enabling the party to begin to enjoy access to state funds and, more widely, the spoils of office, hitherto the monopoly of the DC and smaller allies. The cautious Andreotti won round both the Vatican and the USA for his cautious opening during his premiership in 1972-73. It was a supremely Machiavellian manoeuvre on his part. Badly affected by the global oil crisis, Italy plunged into austerity in the mid-1970s and thanks to Andreotti, the PCI ended up being implicated in in an unavoidable policy, to the chagrin of many of its supporters.[22]

Thanks to Andreotti being seen as a reliable anti-communist bulwark, Italy got the financial loans through the good offices of the USA, which were vital to relieve the country's economic plight in the mid-1970s.[23] He cemented ties with Henry Kissinger as US policy-makers fretted about Italy's direction and prospects. In 1979, Italy would become the first European ally to host US missiles as part of a modernisation of NATO's nuclear forces.[24]

But the absence of solid or durable reforms, was leading to a build-up of discontent in the 1970s. Italy's abrupt and often messy transition from a rural society to a leading industrial nation was scarred by violence from both the far-left and the far-right, in what became known as the *Anni di Piombo* (years of lead) spanning the late 1970s and early 1980s. Numerous bombings, targeted killings, kidnappings and disappearances marked this fraught period. The most sensational occurrence was the seizure of the leading Christian Democrat, Aldo Moro, by the Red Brigades on 16 March 1978. Andreotti was in the spotlight as he was Prime Minister. After five weeks in captivity and numerous letters to the government written by him under duress, Moro was executed. Andreotti was assailed by much of the media for refusing to do a deal to secure the release of his colleague. But his unyielding approach commanded widespread backing in the political establishment (including the PCI).[25]

The political centre, represented by the DC, had shown itself enfeebled even before this crisis. Andreotti resigned in 1979, by which time the crisis of authority had led to the selection of a Head of State from the Socialists and a government headed by the first non-DC figure since 1945. He was back in office in 1983, appointed foreign minister, a post he would hold until 1987. The Prime Minister was Bettino Craxi, the forceful and highly pragmatic leader of the Socialist party. Andreotti wasn't the only DC notable content with this arrangement. Craxi faithfully adhered to the rules of the political class that rewarded the circles of power close to the state. Andreotti, for his part, was content to plunge into international relations. His tireless networking and occasional bold initiatives arguably gave Italy a higher profile on the global scene that at any point in the post-war era.

He increased his political capital in Washington by refusing to waver in the face of sizeable opposition to the deployment of new NATO missile systems in Europe. He also had no problem about supporting the process of East-West *détente* which gathered pace with Mikhail Gorbachev's assumption of power in the Soviet Union. He also stepped up dialogue with Yassar Arafat's Palestine Liberation Organisation (PLO), refused to treat him as a pariah, and took some credit for the softening of his position on Israel.[26] He regularly insisted that Italy, as a strategically-placed Mediterranean country, should constantly seek interlocutors in the Middle East. He wished to strengthen ties with the Arab world when Italy's senior ally, the US, preferred to maintain its reliance on Israel as a key ally in western Asia. He avoided a break with Washington by supporting NATO airstrikes on Libya in 1986, following a terrorist attack in Berlin attributed to its regime. But he kept open communications with the leader, Colonel Muammar Gaddafi, arguing that Italy had a duty to maintain an indispensable balance of peace and cooperation in the regions of the Near East and North Africa.[27] The extent of their correspondence was surprising when later published.[28]

In 1997, he was frank about his ties with a regime that had long been a disruptive force, promoting violence from Ireland to the Philippines. His remarks to an Irish journalist might be seen as prophetic in some quarters, given the fate of Libya after the removal of Gaddafi in 2011:

> 'Obviously, Gaddafi has things to answer for and he's certainly no Queen Victoria. I've met him often, he's a very difficult person, he makes the most terrible statements...but I am sure that he's not mad and I'm sure that you have to talk to him.'
>
> 'If Gaddafi were to fall, what sort of regime would you have in his place? There has to be a big risk of Islamic fundamentalists taking over Libya and that could mean starting a whole fundamentalist wave all the way across North Africa, through Tunisia and into Egypt'.[29]

As one of the six founders of the Common Market, Italy only acquired prominence in the integration process during Andreotti's time as foreign minister. In June 1985, with Italy the holder of the European Presidency, he and Craxi, through arguably doubtful procedural manoeuvres, called a majority vote on the convening of an inter-governmental conference, something supposedly ruled out under rules enshrined in the Luxembourg compromise of 1966.[30] This crucial ploy enabled the opening up of free markets, a central feature of the Single European Act which was being decided upon, to be shaped by the European Commission whose power over national members thus grew enormously. This successful power play by Euro centralisers, would pave the way for the Maastricht Treaty which created the European Union in 1992.

Andreotti would show Thatcher that the doleful epithet ascribed to Italy of being 'the sick man of Europe', failed to be an accurate image, at least in the diplomatic sphere. He had made his attachment to the principle of a federal Europe clear already and Margaret Thatcher should have been on her guard. But neither the champion of an inter-governmental Europe, nor her advisers, seem to have anticipated that this gnomish figure with his large, stuck-out ears and hunched back, could play such a revolutionary role in the integration process. He used the skills which had given him the nickname of 'the fox' at home to build a coalition across the then ten-strong community which managed to isolate her. Later, in her memoirs she would ruefully refer to him as person who had 'a positive aversion to principles' after another summit collision in 1990, where his Machiavellian skills were more than a match for her combative spirit.[31] He, in his turn, praised her intelligence but complained of her 'authoritarian disposition'.[32]

Andreotti was a decided exponent of radicalism and innovation to forge a European polity while seeming to prefer immobilism in Italy itself. In 2011, near the end of Andreotti's life, a European Union armed with important political powers would be able to intervene decisively in Italian finance and governance, unseating one prime minister, Silvio Berlusconi, and replacing him with an unelected technocrat Mario Monti. This was by no means the most disruptive or damaging outcome for Italy of a process which led to the impetuous creation of a single Euro currency, one that Italy's weak finances meant it was ill-suited to join. Her rulers worked to build a leviathan of European power while neglecting to ensure that Italy could stand up for itself when France and Germany wished to protect their interests with the onset of a crisis of unprecedented financial magnitude in 2008.

Future-orientated in key foreign policy matters, Andreotti seemed wedded to inertia in the domestic political arena. Italy was the chief violator of EU rules during his last and longest period as prime minister, stretching from 1987 to 1992. It seemed to occur to few of the Europhile figures in the elite that the increased leverage of the EU in state financial matters could destabilise the Italian way of handling national public finances. The electoral prospects of those at the top of an increasingly wobbly party system were bound up with continued heavy deficit spending. Pensions were being paid to one-fifth of the total population by the end of the 1980s.[33] Andreotti seems to have been unmoved by the anger, and even disgust, which much of Italian society was displaying towards the political system in the 1980s. Perhaps the fact that it first took the form of a territorial protest movement in the economically important but politically weak north of Italy, left this sardonic Roman unmoved. Instead of an effort to clean up abuses and reform outworn practices, he and his confederates in the DC and the other governing parties, tinkered with the rules of the game to entrench their influence.

The ability of leading figures in public life to systematically flout laws governing bribery and corruption ended at the start of the 1990s. Magistrates and prosecutors, enjoying huge popular support, grew bolder in their investigations. Brazen mafia executions and laws emanating from Brussels promoting market policies and incurring severe penalties for the illicit use of state money, weakened the grip of political barons.[34] In Andreotti's own view, the fall of communism and the ending of the Cold War, decisively speeded up the collapse of the political status quo.[35] But it was the Socialists whose power base dissolved first. The t*angentopoli* ('bribesville') scandal, involving bribes to politicians for state contracts, erupted in Milan in 1992, and very soon the other four parties, which had ruled in tandem for many years, were engulfed in similar scandals across Italy. The meltdown of the party system meant that that the votes were lacking for what many assumed would be the end point of Andreotti's career, his elevation to the Italian presidency. However, in 1990, he was made a senator for life by President Francesco Cossiga. It meant that he continued in parliament until his death, aged 94, in May 2013.

Andreotti remained visible not just on account of enjoying this sinecure. He paid visits to pariah Middle Eastern countries, like Libya and Iran (as well as the Gaza strip), where he was received with great pomp. A welter of books and articles flowed from his pen. He gave interviews and a film was made about his 1991-2 trial for alleged mafia involvement, that won a top prize at the Cannes film festival. He briefly lost his temper at its unflattering portrayal but soon regained his composure and said that it was aesthetically remarkable.[36]

While other chieftains of the First Republic were jailed, fled into exile or vanished into obscurity, Andreotti could be spotted attending the early mass at his local church on a daily basis, as he had done for decades. He was a benefactor to the poor and was known to be considerate to his staff.[37] It adds to the riddle of a man whose influence in ensuring that post-fascist Italy failed to become a respected, stable democracy, is widely considered to be far from negligible.

---

[1] Binoy Kampmark, 'The Death of Il Divo', *Counterpunch*, 8 May 2013, accessed 25 October 2022. https://www.counterpunch.org/2013/05/08/the-death-of-il-divo/, accessed 25 October 2022.
[2] Donald Sassoon, 'Obituary of Giulio Andreotti', *Guardian*, 6 May 2013.
[3] Sassoon, 'Obituary'.
[4] Marcello Sorgi, 'Addio ad Andreotti, l'uomo simbolo', *La Stampa*, 7 May 2013.
[5] António Versori, 'Bettino Craxi and Giulio Andreotti', in Mark Gilbert, Erik Jones and Gianfranco Pasquino, *The Oxford Handbook of Italian Politics*, Oxford: Oxford University Press, 2015, p. 379.
[6] John Hooper, 'Prince of darkness', *Guardian*, 20 February 2009.
[7] Versori, 'Bettino Craxi and…'.
[8] Mark Gilbert, 'Warriors of the New Pontida', *Political Quarterly*, Vol. 64, No. 1, 1993, p. 101.
[9] Emma Wallis, 'Death of Il Divo: Italy's powerful Giulio Andreotti dies at age 94', *Deutsche Welle*, 6 May 2013.
[10] Denis Mack Smith, *Modern Italy, A Political History*, New Haven and London: Yale University Press, 1997, p. 429.
[11] See Leonardo Maugeri, L'arma del petrolio: Questione petrolifera globale, guerra fredda e politica italiana nella vicenda di Enrico Mattei, Florence: Loggia dè Lanzi, 1994.
[12] Andrew Gumbel, 'Autopsy may solve deadly mystery of the Mattei affair', *Independent*, 28 August 1997.
[13] See Salvatore Brancate, Enrico Mattei? Un pescatore di trote, lunga intervista a Graziana Verzotto, Palermo: Ila Palma, 1997.
[14] Gumbel, 'Autopsy'.
[15] Marta Musso, 'The Transmediterranean gas pipeline: a political history', in Les Routes de Petról/Oil Routes, edited by Alain Beltran, Frankfurt am Main: Peter Lang, 2015, p. 3.
[16] Gumbel, 'Autopsy'.
[17] Robert Graham, 'Giulio Andreotti, Italian statesman', *Financial Times*, 6 May 2013.
[18] Mack Smith, *Italy*, p. 463.
[19] Hooper, 'Prince of darkness'.
[20] Wallis, 'Death of Il Divo'.
[21] Marcello Sorgi, 'Addio ad Andreotti', *La Stampa*, 7 May 2013, https://www.lastampa.it/politica/2013/05/07/news/addio-ad-andreotti-l-uomo-simbolo-1.36091511, accessed 31 January 2022.
[22] Obituary, Giulio Andreotti, *Daily Telegraph*, 6 May 2013.
[23] Silvio Pons, 'Cold War Republic: The 'External Constraint' in Italy during the 1970s', in A. Varsori and B. Zaccaria (eds.), Italy in the International System from Détente to the End of the Cold War, Security, Conflict and Cooperation in the Contemporary World, London: Palgrave, 2016, p. 50.
[24] 'Obituary, Richard Gardner', *New York Times*, 2 March 2019.

---

[25] Versori, 'Bettino Craxi and…', p. 536.
[26] Giulio Andreotti, 'Foreign Policy in the Italian Democracy', *Political Science Quarterly,* Vol. 109, No. 3, 1994, p. 535.
[27] Andreotti, 'Foreign Policy', p. 536.
[28] M. Bucarelli and L. Micheletta, *Andreotti and Gaddafi. Letters and documents 1983-2006,* Rome: Editions of History and Literature, 2019.
[29] 'The trials and tribulations of Giulio Andreotti', *Irish Times,* 6 August 1997. https://www.irishtimes.com/news/the-trials-and-tribulations-of-giulio-andreotti-1.94452, accessed 26 March 2022.
[30] A. Varsori, 'Italian Foreign Policy in the 1980s: From Enthusiasm to Disillusion', A. Varsori and B. Zaccaria (eds.), Italy in the International System from Détente to the End of the Cold War, Security, Conflict and Cooperation in the Contemporary World, London: Palgrave, 2016, p. 4.
[31] Tom Dawson, 'Il Divo', *List Films,* 19 March 2009, https://film.list.co.uk/article/16596-il-divo/, accessed 11 March 2022.
[32] See Antonio Varsori, 'Giulio Andreotti, Margaret Thatcher e le relazioni italo-britanniche negli anni Ottanta, *Ventunesimo Secolo,* Vol. 19, No. 2, 2020.
[33] Mack Smith, Italy, p. 493.
[34] Versori, 'Bettino Craxi and…', p. 326.
[35] 'The trials and tribulations of Giulio Andreotti', *Irish Times,* 6 August 1997.
[36] Sassoon, 'Obituary'.
[37] 'For whom the bell tolls; Giulio Andreotti', *Economist,* 11 May 2013.

PART 2
CHAPTER 6: FRANCO-GERMAN LEADERS

Grandstanding and Platitudes

Franco-German political and military elites preserved deep-seated mutual antagonism between 1870 and 1945. The remark of the Catholic French politician Georges Bidault, made in 1946, that: 'the separation of the Ruhr and Rhineland from Germany is the only way to keep Germany from its national industry—war.', was far from atypical.[1] He was then foreign minister in a government led by Charles de Gaulle. The 'liberator of France' himself had stated two years earlier, that he considered it essential for the security of France that the Ruhr basin and land on the left side of the river Rhine be taken out of any future German state that was allowed to exist.[2]

Yet a growing convergence of interests would soon bury this debilitating enmity. In its place, a Franco-German alliance grew up that would be at the centre of decision-making in the European era of shared sovereignty, one that would culminate in the creation of the European Union in 1993. The friendships between Franco-German political heavyweights, from Adenauer and de Gaulle to Helmut Schmidt and Giscard d'Estaing and on to Helmut Kohl and Jacques Delors, are well-known and have been woven into the story of European convergence. Yet, with the exception of the 1992 Maastricht Treaty, it is striking how little of real substance or lasting consequence emerged from this informal alliance, certainly nothing that could be said to have transformed the destiny of Europe. The careers of the four figures examined in this section suggest that what drove this bilateral friendship was a set of national interests that were seen as mutually compatible. Certainly, on the French side there was no underlying desire to submerge nationhood within a new European political order. After the unification of Germany in 1990 this soon also became the standpoint in Berlin.

Intellectuals have often been more extravagant in their political dreams than politicians. In May 2003, Jürgen Habermas and Jacques Derrida published a manifesto entitled: 'February 5, or What Binds Europeans Together: A Plea for a Common Foreign Policy, Beginning in the Core of Europe'.[3]

February 15, 2003, had been a day of big demonstrations in various European capitals, protesting the launch of the second Iraq war. The manifesto did not prove to be the catalyst for the vaulting hopes of these high-profile thinkers. But it did show how distrust, if not visceral dislike of America, was one of the few powerful bonding agents that existed in European politics.

This is somewhat ironic: of all the Allied states, it had been the United States which had stood out for rehabilitating Germany and not imposing a punitive peace. But generous-spirited benefactors are not always appreciated. Arguably, resentment towards the guarantor of the post-1945 security order in Europe, and impatience with its perceived meddling, has underpinned Franco-German cooperation over a considerable period. The commercial advantages which both countries have been able to derive from a European Union whose expanding powers they have very much shaped, has also been crucial. But common mercantile interests, intertwined with anti-Americanism, have been insufficient to provide the basis for a new post-national European order.

Leadership, first in West and then united Germany, has usually been stronger and more consequential than in France, despite the highly presidential nature of the post-1958 Fifth Republic. There have been a series of dominating Chancellors, at best purposeful and long-term in focus, at worst parochial, self-centred and impulsive. Perhaps some of the most fateful decisions in modern European government were made by three successive chancellors. Helmut Kohl's decision to press ahead with creating the single currency in the absence of a European exchequer, springs to mind. So does Gerhard Schröder's decision to forge an energy alliance with Vladimir Putin, and Angela Merkel's decision to embrace the Green energy agenda, thus doubling-down on dependence on Russian gas and oil. Her policy moves eroded the sense of solidarity and inter-dependence that had bound together major Western nations, as indeed did decisions emanating from US presidents Obama and Trump. Merkel and her defenders sought to argue that Germany's energy stance and increasingly close trading links with Russia and China were occurring in a neutral framework beyond politics and bound up with technology, trade and concern for the planet. But the idea that such decisions had no political ramifications was fiercely contested by others.

Adenauer, the first leader of the Federal German Republic (FDR) was perhaps not the most suitable national pedagogue for a new democratic era. He may have rejected the militarisation of Germany (viewing it as a boon that the US would pay for German defence for well over half-a-century), but he was autocratic and strong-willed. He relied on lawyers and civil servants, some of whom were tainted with a Nazi past, as trusted lieutenants rather than colleagues in his own Christian Democratic Union (CDU).[4] But much of his claim to greatness lay in burying perhaps the most destructive national rivalry modern Europe had ever seen. Between November 1958 and November 1963, he and de Gaulle, met on fifteen occasions, had one hundred hours of talks, and wrote to each other over forty times.[5] Reconciliation was perhaps assured because of Adenauer's willingness to allow France to use the then European Economic Community for national purposes. There is no sign that, while downplaying German nationalism, he saw any contradiction in sponsoring nationalist behaviour by France in what was supposedly a project meant to relegate the national principle to an unimportant place in European affairs. De Gaulle refused to hide the fact that European institutions were 'the means for France to recover what she ceased to be after Waterloo: first in the world'.[6]

Well-placed French firms benefited from a European project tilted towards French interests. But the national economy was unable to conquer historically poor productivity, resulting in a weak *franc* and frequent devaluations. Elite German *schadenfreude* led de Gaulle to resist German pressure for a further devaluation at the end of 1968, his last major act. It prompted his most faithful collaborator, Michel Debré, to observe in his memoirs: 'I know the Germans sufficiently to be aware that they abuse their power as soon as they are in a position to do so.'[7]

It is often overlooked that there was an outspoken proponent of 'German Gaullism' who was prominent at this time, the Bavarian politician Franz-Josef Strauss. He wrote in 1966, that 'the United States of Europe, with their own nuclear deterrent, must be in a position to protect themselves in order to achieve an equal partnership with the United States of America'.[8]

Helmut Schmidt, the Social Democrat Party (SPD) figure who was chancellor from 1974 to 1982, entered the role also appearing somewhat detached towards the cause of European unity. A British Foreign Office assessment of 1974 included this observation:

> 'Schmidt...is certainly not likely to push the Federal Government in the direction of a more forward Western European policy... He is not so much anti-European as agnostic about it. He is sceptical about the Community's ability to provide solutions for the immediate problems confronting Europe.'[9]

Schmidt will be remembered for trying to secure European monetary stability during the turbulent 1970s, by promoting the Exchange Rate Mechanism (ERM) along with Valéry Giscard d'Estaing of France. Their plan for a currency linkage between the two lead EU states possessing contrasting economies, was hatched by a small group of advisers and was not placed before public opinion for consideration.[10] Launched in 1979, even as it offered a boost for backers of political union, the effort to fix exchange rates largely proved unsuccessful.[11] Nevertheless, the momentum now behind monetary union institutionalized Germany's economic dominance in Europe; as the economist Thomas Szász observed, monetary arrangements are built on power relationships.[12]

The Franco-German relationship grew to be at the centre of Schmidt's political strategy, not least due to poor relations with the US during the 1977-81 presidency of Jimmy Carter. Schmidt was ready to defy the

Americans over nuclear power sales and responses to Soviet aggression. One analyst reckons that he liked the Soviet leaders Brezhnev and Gromyko 'almost to the same extent that he disliked Mr. Carter and [his chief aide] Mr. Brzezinski.'[13] But his anti-communism was unbending as, according to the journalist Jim Hoagland, 'he recognized the threat that the Soviet deployment of SS-20 missiles posed for Europe before any other Western leader.' He wrote in 1990: 'Without Schmidt's persistence, there almost certainly would not have been a NATO decision to deploy intermediate range nuclear missiles in Europe as a counter to the Soviet build-up.'[14]

Helmut Kohl, Chancellor from 1984 to 1998, was the driving force behind momentous events that swiftly followed the retreat of Soviet power from lands in east-Central Europe under its control. It has been reckoned that without his boldness, 'the integration of central and large parts of Eastern Europe into the free world might not have happened.'[15]

Having won Mikhail Gorbachev's assent, he exported the Deutschmark to the German Democratic Republic (GDR) and absorbed the ex-communist satellite into the Federal Republic. Integration would be quick and relatively painless, he predicted.[16] It wasn't. Nevertheless, 'the international suspicion that something is inherently wrong with the Germans also seems to have largely dissipated' thanks to the seeming resolution of the German Question. Nazism had finally been overcome, in Kohl's mind, 'thus paving the way for the emergence of a morally superior state.'[17]

Kohl then turned to the wider European Union. The 'crowning theory' that he insisted upon was that the enactment of monetary union would foster the political unity needed to make the former work.[18] Initially this was not his view. At a meeting with Mitterrand in 1989, he angrily snapped at him:

> 'It [the single currency] poses a heap of problems for me, my majority is reluctant, the business community doesn't want it, the time is not right'.[19]

But increasingly, the sense that the hands of history were on his shoulders made him consider that the single currency could positively transform

Europe. Shortly after becoming chancellor in 1982, he had told Mitterrand that he would make every effort to prevent a Bismarckian German state from reappearing, but in the early 1980s, his style was increasingly didactic but perhaps without the shrewdness that had characterised the first architect of German reunification.[20]

By abolishing the Deutschmark, he claimed to be sacrificing German interests on the altar of European unity. However, at the same time he insisted on Bundesbank terms for monetary union which created a built-in advantage for productive economies like Germany in comparison with consumer-orientated ones, especially in Mediterranean Europe. He admitted afterwards that 'in the case of the euro, I was like a dictator'.[21] So overwhelming was his dominance of his parliamentary forces and indeed the country, where the CDU and CSU controlled two-thirds of the Bundestag in the early 1990s, that it was futile to block his wishes. Many involved in the negotiations for the Maastricht Treaty of 1992 were surprised when he defied public opinion and his own business community and agreed on a launch date for the Euro.[22] He then, unwisely, used his prestige to insist that Italy be allowed to join the Eurozone, even though it failed to fulfil the entry terms.[23] His successor Schröder was content to allow Greece in too, a few years after the 1999 launch of the single currency. These two steps, pressurising the newly-set-up European Central Bank (ECB) into allowing a low interest rate to be set in order to allow Germany to cope with the challenge of reunification, and endangering the health of the experiment by ushering in unsuitable members, would cost the European project dear. The Eurozone had been set up as a half-finished monetary union, one which ruled out fiscal support by one member state for another. Kohl had hurtled down a Panglossian path in order to alleviate French fears of a revival of German power. Embedding a reunified Germany firmly within a revived and more closely integrated European Union, seemed to be the painless formula. It wasn't.

In 1998, Kohl was swept away by scandal and despite his achievements, has failed to establish a secure place in the pantheon of German post-war leaders comparable to Schmidt or Willy Brandt, the architect of the *Ostpolitik* strategy designed to ease tension with the Soviet bloc and forge cooperative economic ties.

By the turn-of-the-century, the limits of Franco-German engagement were becoming clear. France was failing to supply pro-integration champions. Much of the French elite 'wanted the EU to be the power that France could no longer be—but declined to surrender to the EU portions of sovereignty necessary to give the EU powers of swift decision…'[24]

On the French side, there was no lack of resourceful figures keen to leverage influence for personal advantage as 'left' and 'right' labels grew increasingly opaque and meaningless. A new caste of leaders emerged who were by no means confined to France and who saw themselves as part of money-focussed and deal-making world elites. Dominique Strauss-Kahn (DSK), the rising star of the French socialists in the early 2000s, perhaps fitted especially well into this category. He had prepared France for entry into the Eurozone and was described as someone who 'appeals to the left and right of the governing spectrum.' In 1999, he resigned as France's finance minister after being put under investigation in what would be the first of several sex scandals.[25]

In 2007, when the job of managing-director of the International Monetary Fund (IMF) opened up unexpectedly that year, President Nicholas Sarkozy strongly endorsed him for the post, in what was widely seen as a move to get a rival out of the way.[26] When the Greek debt crisis erupted in 2009, DSK found himself a central figure. Along with the leaders of France and Germany, he agreed to a debt relief package whose most obvious beneficiaries were the West European banks which had lent heavily to Greece. The IMF was discarding its most sacred rule – never lend to a bankrupt government until its debt has had a 'haircut' – (been restructured). The Fund, in a 2016 report, admitted that it had gone badly astray in its handling of the Greek crisis.'[27]

By then, DSK had vanished into private life, having been forced to step down from the IMF in 2011, due to being caught up in another sex scandal.[28] In the meantime, the deflationary package imposed by the Europeans on the IMF board (in conjunction with the ECB and France and Germany) had thrown Greece into years of depression.[29] The intention was to rescue a dysfunctional currency union by making Greece the scapegoat for its poor management. Greece no longer had the fiscal levers—its own currency or ability to adjust its interest rates—to navigate out of trouble.

A mass fire sale of Greek assets without any stimulus or relief meant the second decade of the 21st century was a lost one for Greece.[30]

Nicholas Sarkozy, France's President from 2007 to 2012, claimed publicly that France and Germany made up a 'privileged' economic partnership.[31] But Germany was pulling away from France, whose goods were increasingly uncompetitive on the world market, leading to de-industrialisation as well as feeding social divisions and a sense of gloom at home.[32] Leading politicians in both countries had fewer inhibitions than before about displaying a mercantile streak. At home, they increasingly ruled over a political void in which political life was in retreat, as shown by declining party memberships and electoral turnouts.[33] France made no objections to Berlin's gas pipeline deal with Russia even though it violated EU energy laws.[34] Both states were content to preside over a closer economic orientation towards China and Russia, even though no clearcut benefit for their countries or indeed the EU was obvious. This was hardly a Franco-German trait alone. In Britain, Prime Minister David Cameron, and his chief ally George Osborne, ignored the warning signs about the return to single-ruler autocracy in China with growing Maoist elements. Osborne insisted as late as 2015, that 'China can count on Britain to be its best partner in the West.'[35] Yet this would soon turn out to be Germany, which was poised to overtake the USA to become China's biggest trading partner, accounting for nearly ten percent of Germany's foreign trade.[36]

By now, with war raging in Ukraine, the Atlanticist section of public opinion in Germany was aghast that decision-makers had stoked Putin's neo-imperialism by becoming so dependent on his energy products for German industrial production. The newspaper *Die Welt* called Germany's relationship of economic dependency towards Russia the 'greatest and most dangerous miscalculation in the history of the Federal Republic'.[37]

With China showing an increasingly bellicose attitude towards Taiwan in 2022, there was little expectation that Germany would show solidarity with the world's first and only primarily Chinese democracy if it was seized by Xi Jinping's forces. Chancellor Scholz dodged questions about how Berlin would respond, making it plain that only token sanctions were likely following an invasion.[38] His stance was perhaps not entirely removed from that of his predecessor Helmut Schmidt. He had grown up in the Third Reich, 'he was disillusioned, displayed a cynical attitude; rejected political visions and advocated pragmatism.'[39] Late in his life, he had described Putin's 2014 seizure of Crimea as 'completely understandable'.[40]

Schmidt had been seared by experiences of dictatorship and war. Kohl, a decade or so younger, had been caught up in the collapse of the Third Reich in 1945. They were by no means politicians who lacked exposure to the rawness of the human condition. Yet each opened German doors to China, starting in the 1970s, without making their cooperation conditional on the communist state retreating from its totalitarian past. Schmidt was sceptical that China could ever evolve in a democratic direction. Kohl was the first western leader to make overtures to Beijing after the1989 Tiananmen massacre, when he visited a base of the People's Liberation Army. Schröder was the first EU leader to call for an end to the Western arms embargo on China.[41]

International bodies, ranging from the World Trade Organization (to which China was admitted in 2001) to the World Economic Forum (WEF), with its annual gatherings in Davos, Switzerland, increasingly became the arenas where thrusting, career-minded politicians light on ideology, gathered. This was true as much for European politicians on the conservative wing of politics as those on the left. Figures such as François Fillon, Macron's unsuccessful challenger in 2017, and Armin Laschet to whom Merkel passed the mantle of CDU leader in 2021, only for him to be buried in a landslide electoral defeat, were happy to personally identify with Russian interests.[42]

In neither France nor Germany, have parties which grew far closer to lobbyists, banks, and other corporate firms, than to their own voting base, found it easy to thrive. Indeed, in 2017, the two main pillars of the French left and centre-right, the Socialists and Gaullists, suffered an electoral meltdown from which they have yet to recover. In 2021, for the first time ever, the CDU and SPD total vote share dropped below 50 percent. It was a pyrrhic victory for the SPD's Scholz. But he was soon unable to cast off controversy. Without charges ensuing, prosecutors searched his emails in 2022, as part of a corruption investigation into how a bank based in Hamburg managed to avoid paying huge amounts of tax when he had been the city's mayor.[43] He went out on a limb, opposed by most in his own coalition and in the major Euro-Atlantic capitals, by giving a Chinese firm a big economic stake in the port of Hamburg, by which time it was clear that all business in China was subordinate politically to a regime felt by many to be undergoing re-Maoisation.

Germany never faltered in declaring its European loyalties, even as it became ever clearer that economic interests eclipsed political alliances and strategic undertakings. Similarly, during Macron's first presidential term, the need for a 'sovereign Europe' was never far from his lips, even though he strove to reinforce bilateral ties with Russia which, under Putin, was menacing a growing number of pro-Western states. He rebuffed the German proposal that France allow the EU to replace it at the UN Security Council, while Merkel in her turn rejected the longstanding French desire for the states benefiting from the Euro to financially aid the unsuccessful ones.[44] Accompanied by EU Commission head Ursula von der Leyen on his visit to China in April 2023, Macron rejected her fidelity to Euro-Atlantic solidarity in security matters and loudly insisted that France must put its own geo-political interests first. It was merely the most brazen display of a long-term reflex.

These leaders saw themselves increasingly detached from party and country. Schröder was quick to adopt the 'Third Way' formulas dreamed up by Anthony Giddens, the sociologist who, for some years, provided Tony Blair's intellectual underpinning. It was a formula for global cooperation in which the nation-state was allotted a subsidiary role. Giscard d'Estaing also was keen for the role, not just of the international statesman, but the wise elder ushering Europe along a transformational path. To varying degrees, Mitterrand and Merkel displayed similar commitments but their careers ultimately remained shaped by the vagaries of electoral politics in France and Germany respectively.

The annual Franco-German ministerial council is supposed to signify a unique partnership. Its abrupt postponement, in October 2022, was a sign that the bilateral relationship was failing to hold up in the crisis conditions which Europe found itself in.[45] Macron was peeved at the unwillingness of Germany to agree to the pooling of EU debt and by its launching of a massive economic stimulus package, even at the risk of distorting the internal market.[46] Germany, after Merkel, 'brutally detached itself' from a partner with whom it increasingly diverged.[47] Berlin displayed fewer misgivings than ever about setting aside the coordination of major policies at a European level to pursue, instead, a mercantilist relationship with China that was at the expense of fellow EU members and Western allies.

What has been termed 'the Franco-German strategic vacuum' extended into 2023, over Germany's refusal to allow its Leopard tanks to be sent to assist Ukraine in its efforts to repel a Russian invasion. Chancellor Scholz's stance (from which he was prevailed upon to retreat) was seen as the most momentous security decision taken by Germany since its unification three decades earlier.[48]

Thanks to the burgeoning European project, both France and Germany found a means of containing mutual suspicions and rivalries, but only for divergent economic cycles and interests, and the sloppiness and selfishness of their project management, to give rise to a different set of tensions—ones which defy easy resolution.

---

[1] F. Roy Willis, *France, Germany and the New Europe*, Stanford: Stanford University Press, 1968, p. 80.
[2] Ronald Irving, *Adenauer*, London: Pearson, 2002, p.p. 108-9.
[3] Laqueur, *After the Fall*, p. 79.
[4] Williams, *Adenauer*, p.p. 386-9.
[5] Mark Gilbert, *European Integration: A Concise History*, Plymouth, UK: Rowman & Littlefield, 2011, p. 76.
[6] Ashoka Mody, *Euro Tragedy, A Drama in Nine Acts*, Oxford: Oxford University Press, 2018, p. 31.
[7] Quoted in André Szász, *The Road to European Monetary Union*, New York: St Martin's Press, 1999, p. 25.
[8] See Mathias Haeussler, A 'Cold War European'? Helmut Schmidt and European integration, c.1945–1982, *Cold War History*, Vol. 15, No. 4, 2015, p. 434.
[9] Haeussler, A 'Cold War European', p. 428.
[10] Mody, *Euro Tragedy*, p. 58.
[11] Mody, *Euro Tragedy*, p. 59.
[12] Szász, *The Road to…*, p. 214.
[13] Bogdan Denitch, 'When the wall stood still', *New York Times*, 8 April 1990.
[14] Jim Hoagland, 'Helmut Schmidt, Germany and the World', *Washington Post*, 18 February 1990.

---

[15] Daniel Johnson, 'Germany's Crisis of Conscience', *The Critic*, June 2022, https://thecritic.co.uk/issues/june-2022/germanys-crisis-of-conscience/, accessed 11 July 2022.
[16] Carol J. Williams, 'Obituary: Helmut Kohl', *Los Angeles Times*, 17 June 2017.
[17] See Christian Wicke, 'In Memory of the "Two Helmuts": The Lives, Legacies, and Historical Impact of Helmut Schmidt and Helmut Kohl', *Central European History*, Vol. 51, No. 2, 2018, p. 295.
[18] Clay Clemens, 'In Memory of the "Two Helmuts"', p. 290.
[19] Elizabeth Guigou, *Une femme au coeur de l'état*, Paris: Fayard, 2000, p.p. 77-8.
[20] Mody, *Euro Tragedy*, p. 66.
[21] Mody, *Euro Tragedy*, p. 82.
[22] Mody, *Euro Tragedy*, p. 94.
[23] See Gallagher, *Europe's Path*, p.p. 20-1.
[24] Julius Friend, *Unequal Partners: French-German Relations, 1950-1990*, Washington DC: Praeger 1991, p. 93.
[25] David Gauthier-Villars, 'The Arrest of Dominique Strauss-Kahn: Controversy Dogged Leader', *Wall Street Journal*, Asia, 17 May 2011.
[26] Yanis Varoufakis, *Adults in the Room*, London: Bodley Head, 2017, p. 26.
[27] *The IMF and the Crises in Greece, Ireland, and Portugal*, Washington DC: Independent Evaluation Office of the International Monetary Fund, 2016, https://ieo.imf.org/en/our-work/Evaluations/Completed/2016-0728-the-imf-and-the-crises-in-greece-ireland-and-portugal.
[28] Steve Erlanger, 'Strauss-Kahn Concedes "Error" in Sexual Encounter With Maid', *New York Times*, 19 September 2011.
[29] Ambrose Evans Pritchard, 'IMF admits disastrous love affair with the euro and apologises for the immolation of Greece', *Daily Telegraph*, 29 July 2016.
[30] See also Ashoka Mody, 'The IMF abetted the European Union's subversion of Greek democracy', *Open Democracy*, 1 September 2018, https://www.opendemocracy.net/en/can-europe-make-it/imf-abetted-european-union-s-subversion-of-greek-democracy/.
[31] Open Europe, 'Je t'aime...moi non plus', 21 January 2011.
[32] See Granville, *What Ails*.
[33] See Peter Mair, Ruling the Void, The Hollowing of Western Democracy, London: Verso, 2013.
[34] Ambrose Evans-Pritchard, 'Germany must choose whether it is with the West or with China: it cannot have it both ways', *Daily Telegraph*, 4 November 2022.
[35] George Osborne, 'Why Britain and China should stick together', Spectator, 22 September 2015.
[36] Matthew Karnitschnig, Why Germany won't get tough on Beijing — even if it invades Taiwan', PolitocoEU, 12 August 2022, https://www.politico.eu/article/why-germany-wont-get-tough-on-beijing-even-if-it-invades-taiwan.
[37] Ambrose Evans Pritchard, 'Olaf Scholz must choose between an energy embargo on Russia, or a moral embargo on Germany', *Daily Telegraph* ,15 April 2022.
[38] Karnitschnig, 'Why Germany'.
[39] Andreas Fulda, 'With their cynical approach to the People's Republic of China', @AMFulda, 26 July 2021, https://threadreaderapp.com/thread/1419586679212490767.html.

[40] Derek Scally, 'Schmidt attacks western sanctions on Russia as "nonsense"', *Irish Times*, 29 March 2014.
[41] Fulda, 'With their cynical approach.'
[42] Charles Bremner, 'Fillon 'made €50,000' from Putin link, *Times*, 22 March 2017; Editorial Board, 'Pro-Putin Laschet is a disastrous choice for Germany and the West', *Reaction*, 22 January 2021, https://reaction.life/pro-putin-laschet-is-a-disastrous-choice-for-germany-and-the-west/.
[43] Jorg Luyken, 'Olaf Scholz embroiled in bank's alleged tax fraud as prosecutors search his emails', *Times*, 9 August 2022.
[44] Granville, *What Ails*, p. 102.
[45] See Sylvie Kaufmann, 'En bouleversant les équilibres en Europe, la guerre en Ukraine déstabilise aussi la relation franco-allemande', *Le Monde*, 19 October 2022, accessed 27 October 2022.
[46] Hans von der Burchard, 'Franco-German tiff threatens to knock EU off balance', PoliticoEU, 19 October 2022, https://www.politico.eu/article/france-and-germany-postpone-bilateral-summit-until-january/
[47] Daniel Johnson, 'How France became trapped in a spiral of chaos and decline', *Sunday Telegraph*, 6 November 2022.
[48] @FrançoisHeisbourg, 20 January 2023.

CHAPTER 7: VALÉRY GISCARD D'ESTAING

1926-2021

No other leader of post-war France was as committed to deepening the process of European integration as much as Valéry Giscard d'Estaing. He acted as if France were naturally the paramount western European power, and like other French leaders, treated the EU as a means of projecting its own national influence. But he was also able to articulate a pro-integration message with some conviction. However, he failed to convert the bulk of the French electorate to what was essentially a technocratic and top-down European project and was often highly evasive about its implications.

His role in exposing the weakness of Gaullism as a personal political cause whose energy quickly sagged with the departure of its founder, was a crucial one for the long-term evolution of French politics. His economic record as a promoter of a form of capitalism underpinned by firm state oversight, in no small measure contributed to him winning the French presidency in 1974. Sporadic populist gestures could not conceal his haughty manner and his liking for the trappings of office. He won a reputation for modernisation and reform, but his aloof, managerial approach left too many people behind, especially the young.

Nearly thirty years out of power deepened his absorption with European affairs and intensifying global economic cooperation. Chosen as the Convenor for a European Constitution in 2003, he was wily and determined to impose his will, while over-estimating his power to regiment diverse interests. He failed to produce a package able to persuade

French voters that it was right to cede yet more powers to the EU to enable it to fulfil global ambitions. Referendum defeats in two of the founders of the original Common Market shook the entire Union and exposed the gap between the people and the Brussels elite.

He was born in 1926, in the western German city of Coblenz where his father was serving as inspector of finances with the French occupation authorities. From a moneyed, conservative family in the Auvergne, his father was a strong supporter of the Vichy government and was decorated by Marshal Pétain. In 1944, the young Giscard declared his support for the exiled De Gaulle. His military role is cloudy, but after a few months he had become a brigadier and had acquired the Croix de Guerre.[1]

In 1956, Giscard entered Parliament through the 'family seat' on the right-wing independents list, held until then by his maternal grandfather. A brilliant elite education enabled him to be seen 'as the cleverest young man in France'. He was an effective finance minister for nine years. He could present his budget each year virtually without notes and was often formidable in television debates.

Despite carefully-chosen gestures to demonstrate that he was not lacking the common touch, especially after reaching the Presidency in 1974, it was not hard to portray him as too-clever-by-half. His tendency to get under some people's skin was a political impediment. He lacked the easy assurance and capacity for self-mockery of another right-wing liberal, Italy's Silvio Berlusconi. The Italian also proved more successful in getting out of scrapes far worse than any Giscard ever got entangled in.

De Gaulle never had any doubts about Giscard's ability; along with Georges Pompidou, he was the only person the general addressed with the words 'when you are president of France'.[2] But he also mistrusted this capable figure, whose family political roots lay in the liberal right that never assimilated itself to Gaullism.

Throughout his career, a series of internecine party struggles played out that Giscard was either victim or perpetrator of. Pushed out of the cabinet in 1966, he later opposed de Gaulle's unsuccessful referendum on administrative reforms which led to the president's resignation in 1969.

Later, he became the driving force behind the Union pour la Démocratie Française (UDF), the federation of non-Gaullist parties on the centre-right of French politics. For much of the 1960s and 1970s, he was the chief overseer and planner for the French economy.

'National champions' were identified and backed in electronics, nuclear energy, rail and aviation to enable France to shine in competitive world markets. He drew praise for presiding over an expansion of nuclear energy that supplied France with abundant, cheap electricity. Along with West Germany, he had a crucial role in creating the 1972 fixed-exchange-rate arrangement that evolved in 1979 into the European Monetary System, the forerunner of the Euro currency finalised in 1999.

The death of President Georges Pompidou, in May 1974, opened up a vacuum, which the right-wing liberal possessed the skill and luck to fill. He positioned himself as an exponent of liberal reform in a country which has oscillated between radicalism and reaction.[3] Bernard-Henri Lévy, long France's best-known public intellectual, referred to him as 'the man to whom French women owe so much'.[4]

Alterations in the status of women were a landmark of Giscard's single-term presidency, arguably surpassing his much-touted contribution to European integration. Key reference points of his seven-year tenure, between 1974 and 1981, include the legalisation of abortion, the reinstatement of divorce by mutual consent, and free contraception. A centrist, Giscard was also the first president to hand women full ministerial portfolios, and he appointed the very first secretary of state... for "the condition of women".[5] These measures weakened his standing on the French right, but also exposed the limits of social conservatism in France.

Giscard's progressive instincts can be overplayed, however. He refused to abolish the death penalty, and ten years before his death, he told journalists that he would probably have maintained the death penalty if re-elected'.[6]

On architectural matters, he opposed novelty. An early decision was to halt schemes to build skyscrapers and office towers in Paris. He also contemplated cancelling the Pompidou arts centre, that his predecessor had approved, in a bid to appease the radical spirit of 1968. Its shocking novelty led *Le Figaro* newspaper to conclude that 'Paris has its own Loch Ness monster'.[7]

Traditionally restive and unsettled France had a centralised political system whose ruler (until 2007) was only required to seek electoral validation every seven years. Accordingly, it was prudent for Giscard, at least initially, to make his presidency seem a humanising one. He wanted to appear at ease with social change. Communication specialists occupied a central place during his presidency, seeking to convey the image of 'the Citizen President' but ultimately to no avail.[8] The bid to appear less remote than his predecessors did not prosper, however. He soon proved to be an autocrat who interfered in areas normally left to the prime minister.

He ran up against the energetic holder of this role, Jacques Chirac, whom the President soon viewed as a potential usurper. Chirac was mishandled, and during a cabinet meeting in August 1976, much taken up with the President's account of his hunting exploits on a visit to Gabon, as the guest of its dictatorial ruler Omar Bongo, he walked out on Giscard. (He was the first Fifth Republic prime minister to walk out rather than wait to be sacked.) Months later he founded the Rassemblement pour la République (RPR) and in 1977, when the mayoralty of Paris was restored for the first time since the Paris Commune of 1871, he was elected to the position.

Giscard was an upholder of 'mondialism', an approach in international relations which gives France considerable freedom of action, even as part of the Western alliance. But, particularly in relation to the Middle East, initiatives meant to project French influence were not always sure-footed. A nuclear reactor was sold to Iraq in 1975, 'for peaceful purposes', which Israel duly bombed.[9] The Iranian cleric Ruhollah Khomenei was allowed to set up his headquarters-in-exile on the outskirts of Paris and Giscard returned him to Paris, in an Air France jet upon the overthrow of the Shah Reza Pahlavi in 1978.

In a decade of burgeoning oil prices, the search for fresh supplies was already an abiding preoccupation. This led to Giscard's administration falling for a costly hoax.

The head of Elf, the state-owned oil company, was allowed to sign a 400-million-franc contract for one year's exclusive use of Project Delta, a supposedly revolutionary invention for detecting oil deposits from the air. A penniless Belgian count and an Italian, claiming to be a professor of nuclear physics, came up with a 'miracle discovery', an airborne black box which promised wonderful results. Their breakthrough turned out to be no more than a clever assemblage of dials and wires but, by now, another 300 million had been handed over. The brilliant fraud only came to light after Giscard's time as president and it failed to reach court despite the vast sums involved.[10] *At* the height of the controversy, Giscard warned of 'the shameful risk of the abasement of France' if the issue was dwelled upon.[11]

Giscard was a modest forerunner of European leaders, like Boris Johnson, who poured far vaster sums into alternative energy technology when the science was even more phantasmagorical. In order to bury the affair, he even warned that he 'possessed confidential files on certain political personalities in power that could ruin their careers'.[12]

With Russia, he had a track record of influence-seeking and attempted conciliation which produced few concrete results. Receiving Leonid Brezhnev in Paris at the end of 1974, he told him that absolute freedom of the press was not necessarily a good thing because it 'sometimes led to excesses, even to abuses'.13 Later, he gave the car-obsessed Leonid Brezhnev a red sports model.14 After the 1979 Russian invasion of Afghanistan, and without informing France's allies, he flew to Warsaw for the first talks between a Western leader and President Brezhnev.15 He returned home saying that the Russians were about to pull back, which turned out to be false. Perhaps the kindest way of looking at Giscard's courting of Brezhnev was that he 'was a great believer in the power of personal relationships to influence the course of history'.16 Certainly, with many French intellectuals dropping their illusions about the Soviet system, after the revelations from Aleksandr Solzhenitsyn, his courting of the Soviets seemed a naive caprice.

Giscard was more assured in his handling of European integration. The period from de Gaulle's row with the EEC in 1965 to the mid-1980s, was one lacking in decisive steps involving the dilution of national sovereignty. Franco-German cooperation remained the pivot, enabling past divisions to be overcome and French influence in the Brussels institutions to be safeguarded and prolonged. When Giscard took office, this crucial partnership seemed to be in trouble. West Germany appeared to be heading off in an independent direction. Due to the success of Chancellor Willy Brandt's Ostpolitik in the early 1970s, there were worrying signs that the relationship with Moscow was acquiring undue importance in Bonn. Equilibrium was restored when Helmut Schmidt became Chancellor in 1974. They met frequently and spoke in English without interpreters. With West German backing, Giscard was also the founder of the annual summits of the world's leading economic powers, which became known as the Group of Seven (G-7).

Giscard was assiduous in cultivating global figures, in the hope that personal chemistry could further his ideas for French centrality in a still-tense bipolar world. Close ties with Gerald Ford, Henry Kissinger and Klaus Schwab of the World Economic Forum, resulted. But one international relationship cost him ill and may have played the key role in ending his role at the top of French politics, aged only 56. This was his friendship with Jean-Bedel Bokassa, the brutal and increasingly idiosyncratic ruler of the Central African Republic. Giscard chose this poor, landlocked country for his first visit as president to Africa. Later, he was the first head of state to congratulate him on his becoming emperor. He was accused of accepting a gift of diamonds from Bokassa, valued at about a quarter of a million US dollars. Riots in Bangui, the capital city, were suppressed with great cruelty in April 1979, and about a hundred children were massacred on the orders of Bokassa, who many believe participated in the killings.[17]

Giscard helped engineer a coup in September 1979, after Bokassa's excesses started to tarnish his own image. However, he was allowed to flee to France with looted millions from the national treasury. One month later, *Le Canard enchaîné* broke the story of the diamonds, which he had accepted in 1973 but not declared. The political magazine claimed to have the documents to prove it, and Giscard's explanations for what had happened were thought by many to be laboured and evasive.[18]

Giscard was fortunate that a long-running scandal concerning the wartime role of Maurice Papon, the budget minister during the final three years of his presidency, only erupted after he had left office. He had been responsible for anti-Semitic measures in the Bordeaux region under Vichy. After the war, he had a successful thirty-year political career, easily slipping into the machinery of the post-war state. He was prefect in Corsica and Algeria, then Paris police chief under President Charles de Gaulle in 1958, holding the post until 1967. As Algeria's tensions spilled into France, his tenure as police chief was marked by Arab demonstrations in October 1961, during which beatings carried out by police under his orders resulted in dozens of Algerians' bodies being fished out of the River Seine.[19]

'There are no crises of conscience when one obeys the orders of the French state' Papon would say once he was in the dock.[20] But his day of reckoning was long postponed as he was thrice-elected a Gaullist deputy after 1968, before serving under Giscard's last Prime Minister Raymond Barre. Giscard's successor Mitterrand admitted that he had intervened to stall investigations coming to court.[21] On 6 May 1981, *Le Canard enchaîné* published an article, 'Papon, aide de camps. Quand un ministre de Giscard faisait déporter des juifs' ('Papon, official of the camps: When one of Giscard's ministers deported the Jews'). But no accusations at burying his past were levelled at Giscard. Papon's trial in 1997-98, was the longest in French history. Although found guilty of complicity, and sentenced to ten years in prison, (of which he served three), the court absolved him of guilt in the deaths of the deportees rounded up by him, most of whom perished at Auschwitz.

Raymond Barre deft stewardship of the economy as prime minister in the late 1970s, shielded France from the worst of the global economic downturn, but he and Giscard got little credit. The President was insufficiently trusted by other chieftains on the centre-right to see off the perennial challenger François Mitterrand, who defeated him by 3.5 per percentage points in 1981. A period in the political doldrums followed. But in 1982, along with ex-US President Gerald Ford and Henry Kissinger, he became involved in cooperative elite initiatives on the world stage to promote economic convergence in the capitalist West. Over time, he became the chief pro-integration EU voice in France, after Jacques Delors. He shelved his belief in an inter-governmental European project in favour of forms of central direction where French influence and the partnership with Germany (united in 1989) could be embedded.

It took almost a decade before his erstwhile rival Chirac, President of France from 1995 to 2007, adopted his world view. They both endorsed the Maastricht Treaty, drawn up at the end of 1991 in the Dutch town of that name. This watershed agreement re-worked the supra-national and inter-governmental balance in favour of greater central direction over a broader policy range. Sensitive policy areas like justice, policing, and immigration were now subject to common EU standards, overseen by the bureaucracy in Brussels.

By his late seventies, Giscard had acquired the reputation of a sophisticated sage on the future of Europe, even though arguably his push for monetary union back in the 1970s had unleashed developments which weakened the prospects for European unity.[22] Thanks to the backing of Chirac, in 2002, Giscard was appointed to preside over a European Convention. The initiative had come from Belgium, which had long sought to subsume its own state failures with outspoken commitment for accelerating EU integration. Giscard was supposed to preside over a process meant to tidy up the EU's complex constitutional order. Almost two decades of treaty making would be formalised in an EU Constitution, which would define the EU's competencies. The selection process, which restored the role of Giscard as a potential history-maker after two decades in the political slow-lane, was opaque. One hundred and two delegates gathered in Brussels on 28 February 2002, to see how he meant to handle his weighty responsibility. It was immediately made clear that the agenda was to be controlled by a thirteen-member Praesidium chosen by himself. He ensured that French would be the working language. He also raised eyebrows by demanding a salary equivalent to that of the EU Commission chief.[23]

The British MEP Daniel Hannan, later recalled: 'I made the mistake of asking the former French president...whether, if his aim were truly to reconnect Europe to its peoples, it made sense for him to commandeer the grandest hotel suite in Brussels, with a commensurate salary and expenses. His reply—"one must be comfortable"—made me feel suitably small. But it was also the authentic voice of the EU élite—pompous, *de haut en bas*, lacking in self-awareness…'[24]

It soon became clear that his aim was for the European Council to supersede the Commission and be the seedbed for a future government of Europe. His preference would have been no surprise to any who recalled that he had been the one who had introduced the Council as a pillar in the architecture of the EU, by holding regular summit meetings of its national leaders from the mid-1970s onwards. Delegates, by no means hostile to the EU's post-national direction, expressed unhappiness a year later when Giscard unveiled his reform proposals. They were seen as an attempt to entrench (and indeed expand) the power of the main national drivers, France and Germany, at the heart of EU affairs. The former Irish Prime Minister John Bruton, a member of the praesidium, spoke out strongly against Giscard d'Estaing's view that member states should be excluded or downgraded to being associate members, if they didn't ratify the constitution.[25]

A particular thorn in Giscard's side was Gisela Stuart, a British Labour MP, who had been appointed as a delegate by Tony Blair, perhaps in the expectation that her German upbringing would make her a vigorous exponent of faster and deeper integration. She was initially hopeful that the Convention would result in the EU becoming more open and accountable. But she was disillusioned by what she came to see as a manipulative exercise under an inflexible chairman who was pushing the agenda of unrepresentative elites aiming to strengthen their grip even further at the expense of democracy. She wrote in 2003:

> 'Not once, in the sixteen months that I spent on the Convention, did representatives question whether deeper integration is what the people of Europe want...whether it provides the best basis for a sustainable structure for an expanding Union…'[26]

In the end, Giscard's wish for a cohesive, federal Europe with its own president and foreign minister, an effective but secondary Commission, a powerful parliament, and the same legal rights, entitlements and taxes across the EU, was dashed. National interests, in the by now fifteen-member EU, diluted his vision. A disconsolate Giscard was heard to murmur on 5 June 2003, 'I feel the federation slipping away'.[27]

His influence on the substance of the draft Constitution would be limited.[28] Nevertheless, he backed the document that was signed by EU leaders in Rome on 29 October 2004. A referendum then took place in several countries, including France, for its ratification. Giscard was probably wise to keep a low profile. A mood of resentment against remote governance soon dominated the campaign. Given the widespread sense of alienation, towards the énarques in the Paris ministries, there was insufficient appetite to be directed by an even remoter set of rulers in Brussels or Berlin.[29] The vainglorious Giscard was not the man to puncture this discontent. After the rejection by the French electorate on 24 May 2005, he made the rather acid declaration: 'the rejection of the constitutional treaty by voters in France was a mistake that should be corrected'.[30] There was no change of heart from him or EU decision-makers that might have led to a less centralised alternative. His view of the voters as inconvenient obstacles was confirmed when the text was revamped and re-named the Lisbon Treaty rather than the European Constitution.

By now, in the autumn of his years, Giscard was disconsolate, as the EU was bogged down in disputes over how to handle the near melt-down of the Euro currency, whose crisis overshadowed the last decade of his life. In a 2014 book, *Europa: The Last Chance for Europe,* he called for a rebooting of the European project, with the 'urgent' construction of a 'strong and federated' entity of 12 European nations that would include the six founding members plus six more recent recruits (but with Britain conspicuously excluded).[31]

He had already confessed that he had been seriously mistaken to champion the entry of Greece into the EU in 1980, when clearly it wasn't ready to cope with the challenges. ('To be perfectly frank, it was a mistake to admit Greece...Greece is basically an Oriental country').[32] But he showed no inclination to criticise the misuse of EU financial institutions by EU powerholders in response to the deep-seated financial crisis in Greece that erupted after 2008.

Until the emergence of Emmanuel Macron, he was the most notable achiever who belonged to a high bureaucratic caste, which governed France in a centralist and didactic manner. The French revolution had merely replaced the décor of a Paris-dominated France, ensuring that the authoritarian direction of the state was upgraded and imposed on the whole nation. Giscard strove to ensure that the French centralising ethos also became the guiding principle of the EU, albeit with mixed results. He was conservative and even aristocratic in his tastes and bearing. Yet he was content, as so many other outwardly conservative contemporaries were, to embrace what was essentially a technocratic and socialist project because of the opportunities that it offered to wield power and influence.

He died, aged 94, on 2 December 2020, having succumbed to coronavirus. Appropriately, there were fulsome tributes from the leaders of France and Germany, whose leadership role in Europe he had promoted with the greatest consistency. 'Re-imagine Europe' is a foundation dedicated to the memory of 'a man whose belief in Europe and whose need to keep up with the times have become founding principles for the way we work'.[33] Currently, its strategic director is one of his children, Olivia Giscard d'Estaing, a former investment banker and asset manager.

Giscard was too aloof to be an effective promoter of a European community spirit. He left behind no Eurocentric party to pursue his elevated hopes. Far more people now exist who are keen to lift the citizens of the 28-member European Union from old habits and thinking. But, except in a few places like the Netherlands, overtly federalist parties are conspicuous by their absence. The post-national cause is overwhelmingly elitist in aims and composition and it is unlikely to decisively advance, as long as meaningful power continues to be invested in electoral democracy.

---

[1] Kim Willsher, 'Obituary', *Guardian,* 7 December 2020.

[2] David Buchan, 'Obituary: Giscard d'Estaing', *Financial Times*, 2 December 2020.

[3] Flora Lewis, 'Giscard, in interview, stresses his belief in "liberal reform"', *New York Times*, 28 July 1975.

[4] Benjamin Dodman, 'Giscard grasped the mood of the 70s, but French women won their own rights', *France 24,* December 2020.

[5] Dodman, 'Giscard grasped', p. 2.
[6] Willsher, 'Obituary', p. 1.
[7] Chris Foges, *Le Figaro*, 21 December 2021. https://www.telegraph.co.uk/art/architecture/like-loch-ness-monster-richard-rogerss-pompidou-centre-shocked/, accessed 20 February 2022.
[8] Jean-Louis Thiébault, 'Variations in presidential leadership in France', *French Politics*, Vol. 14, No. 4, 2016, p. 522.
[9] Brian Moynahan, *The French Century*, Paris, Flammarion, 2007, p. 425.
[10] Moynahan, *The French Century*, p. 426-7; Le Monde television, 'L'Extravagante Affaire des avions renifleurs', *Le Monde*, 24 March 2012, https://www.lemonde.fr/vous/article/2012/03/24/l-extravagante-affaire-des-avions-renifleurs_1675067_3238.html, accessed 20 February 2022.
[11] https://fr.wikipedia.org/wiki/Affaire_des_Avions_renifleurs, accessed 20 February 2022.
[12] Marci McDonald, 'Sniffing out a cover-up', *Macleans*, 6 February 1984, https://archive.macleans.ca/article/1984/2/6/sniffing-out-a-coverup, accessed 20 February 2022.
[13] Nicolas Badalassi, '"Neither too much nor too little" France, the USSR and the Helsinki CSCE', *Cold War History*, Vol. 18, No. 1, 2018, p. 11.
[14] Moynahan, *The French Century*, p. 425.
[15] Telegraph Obituaries, 'Valéry Giscard d'Estaing, obituary', Daily Telegraph, 3 December 2021.
[16] Buchan, 'Obituary'.
[17] Jonathan Power, 'Giscard and the story of his diamonds ', *The Citizen*, Dar es Salaam, 16 December 2020.
[18] Telegraph Obituaries, 'Valéry'.
[19] 'Obituary', Maurice Papon, French official convicted for Vichy role', *Los Angeles Times*, 18 February 2007.
[20] Moynahan, *The French Century*, p. 429.
[21] South Florida Sun-Sentinel, 18 February 2007.
[22] See Mody, *Euro Tragedy*, p.p. 110-11.
[23] Michael O'Neill, The Struggle for the EU Constitution: A Past and Future History, London: Routledge, 2009, p. 94.
[24] Daniel Hannan, 'Imperial, out-of-touch Giscard d'Estaing embodied the pompous EU elite', *Daily Telegraph*, 6 December 2002.
[25] 'Sign or Sinks says Giscard', *Sunday Business Post*, 26 October 2002.
[26] Gisela Stuart, *The Making of Europe's Constitution*, London: Fabian Society, 2004, p. 3.
[27] 'Giscard's dream blown away', *Sunday Business Post*, 8 June 2003.
[28] Mareike Kleine, 'Leadership in the European Convention', *Journal of European Public Policy*, Vol. 14, No. 8, 2007, p. 1243.
[29] Daniel Hannan, 'Non-sense', *Spectator*, 23 April 2005.
[30] Buchan, 'Obituary'.
[31] Jacopo Barigazzi, 'Valéry Giscard d'Estaing: Towards a Smaller Europe', *PoliticoEU*, 10 April 2018, https://www.politico.eu/article/valery-giscard-destaing-toward-a-smaller-europe/, accessed 20 February 2022.
[32] Maurice Weiss, 'Interview with Helmut Schmidt and Valéry Giscard d'Estaing', *Der Spiegel Online*, 11 September 2012.
[33] https://reimagine-europa.eu/, accessed 20 February 2022.

CHAPTER 8: FRANÇOIS MITTERRAND

1916-1996

Under François Mitterrand, a French Head of State with important executive powers who ruled from 1981 to 1995, the privileging of personalities and influential cliques deepened, as ideology and class receded as markers in politics. He is recalled as someone who gave responsibility to people according to their fidelity towards him, instead of according to their real capacities'.[1] As a young man, he had been downbeat about France's prospects, and it was a pessimism he never shook off. Wielding power was a holding operation, and with such an approach to occupying high office, it is hardly a surprise that a coherent reform agenda failed to get off the ground.

No other self-proclaimed French socialist ruled for as long as he had. But it is not a harsh verdict to say that he lacked a vision of where he wanted to take France. He has been described as 'an elusive shape-shifter whose goals remained unknown even to his closest aides'.[2] A long exposure to the vicissitudes of politics perhaps bred in him a caution about promoting major transformations in the condition of the nation. He went through a series of political incarnations. In the 1930s, he started out as a right-wing traditionalist. He was a centrist politician after 1945, a firmly pro-colonial minister in the 1950s, a proponent of a break with the 5th Republic in 1968, a socialist opposition leader in the 1970s, an often regal-sounding French President from 1981, and finally a leading backer of European integration.

Once at the pinnacle of the nation, he often adopted a high moral tone, but in reality, nepotism and an air of laxity towards dubious people increasingly marked out his political reign. The reputation of the political world was at a low ebb when he bowed out, and arguably it has never recovered. Friendship was more important than ideology or ideas. A bureaucratic upper middle-class (always a sizeable presence in France) undoubtedly grew in scope and importance under him. The working-class, by contrast, was left behind and the concerns of industrial workers and public employees who, in 1977, comprised 44 percent of the population, never appeared to be central ones for Mitterrand.

The Socialist Party (PS) lacked both solid convictions and competent leaders able to put aside rivalries. It was soon weighed down by political and financial scandals and fell increasingly under the sway of a technocratic leadership fixated by career ambitions and latterly, bureaucratic aspirations at the European level. During the Mitterrand era, the PS faced successive electoral defeats and internal crises. Ironically, the need for the President to share power with the centre-right enabled the 5th Republic to finally appear consolidated in the 1980s. Meanwhile, it took another twenty years for the once more bedraggled, parliamentary left to retreat to the margins of politics, where a politically-orphaned Mitterrand had found it in the 1960s.

Mitterrand was born in 1916, to a Catholic, middle-class family in a part of south-west France where most of the traditional commercial elite had Protestant Huguenot roots. Pursuing his academic studies in Paris in the second half of the 1930s, he belonged firmly on the political right. His political journey in the 1930s has been summed up in this way: he 'was a member of the far-Right, but his enthusiasm, which is part of extremism, was checked by his Catholic commitment, and by his intellectual ambivalence'.[3] His pre-war contemporaries who knew him then, recall that he showed no enthusiasm for the Popular Front elected to office in 1936, but then, and later, was much interested in the French reactionary Charles Maurras.[4] Later, he carefully 'retouched' the history of this time and the Vichy period (1940-44), when a puppet regime ruled in the part of France initially left unoccupied by the Germans.[5] In 1940, he had been a sergeant in an infantry regiment, was wounded, then captured, only to escape from captivity in Germany after several attempts. He worked for the Vichy regime. But his job didn't implicate him in acts of racial or political persecution. He received a decoration from the Pétain regime, as late as 1943, when its end was approaching. By that year, he had joined the Resistance, where he displayed courage and organizing ability. That November, he secretly left France to meet Charles de Gaulle in Algiers. A brother-in-law of de Gaulle, in a television interview, claimed that he saw Mitterrand as an *arriviste* and was suspicious of the ambivalence he displayed in the war years.[6] Mitterrand reciprocated, repulsing a bid by de Gaulle to control Resistance networks like his, that would be a springboard into politics. Eventually, he would cast himself as the anti-de Gaulle of French politics.[7]

Determined to follow his own star, he was never a team player, but from his time in a prisoner-of-war camp he was an effective networker.[8] 'The Sphinx' became a nickname that never left him. He once boasted that his closest friends knew only 30 percent of his thinking.[9] His political career began in earnest in 1946, when he won a seat for the Rassemblement des Gauches Républicaines, an assortment of centrist notables who had been involved in the resistance and were firmly anti-communist. He served in no less than eleven governments during the Fourth Republic (1944-1958). He showed organizing ability, coolness under pressure, and a stubborn adherence to whatever policy he believed in. As justice minister (1956-57), he displayed no qualms about endorsing a repressive policy in the increasingly bloody war with anti-colonial insurgents that was tearing Algeria apart.[10] He advised President René Coty to reject appeals for clemency in the great majority of cases involving indigenous Algerians who had been condemned to death.[11] Not since 1831, had there been a justice minister who had presided over as many executions as Mitterrand.

A series of colonial wars drained France of wealth, prestige and human lives, as well as poisoning civil-military relations. In 1958, the parliamentary republic effectively collapsed, and with de Gaulle as the driver of events, was replaced by a presidential Fifth Republic. For years afterwards, Mitterrand branded it as 'a coup d'etat' hatched by his old adversary.[12] Now, as part of a discredited and defunct regime, he was on the rocks politically, aged only 42, required henceforth to position himself firmly on the French left in order to cling to the hope that his fortunes would recover.

His personal life was also in flux. He was married to Danielle Gouze, who came from a family of atheistic schoolteachers and freemasons and was always well to the left of her husband. She discovered him to be a Don Juan who was highly flexible in personal relations as well as political ties.[13] In 1957, he met Anne Pingeot, a curator at the Louvre, with whom he had a daughter in 1974. Later, he tolerated his wife's affair with a live-in-lover considerably her junior, who often made a third party at their breakfast table. Upon Mitterrand's death in 1996, he would be attended at his graveside by both his wife and legitimate sons and by his mistress and illegitimate daughter.[14]

In 1959, Mitterrand staged an assassination attempt on himself as a way of boosting his image on the Left, where he felt his best hopes of a career now lay. It seemed bogus to many at the time and landed him in hot water. But the true facts only emerged shortly before Mitterrand's death, when a far-right former deputy and later plotter against de Gaulle, revealed that the incident was entirely fake and that he had been the bogus assassin.[15] It was the first true insight into his character for many people: 'he was secretive, reckless and ready to consort with shady operators'.[16]

He proved resilient despite other miscalculations that would disfigure his future political career. An unshakeable belief in his own destiny was always a great advantage. Two decades of adversity lay ahead, however, with only fleeting glimpses of the promised land. In 1965, standing in the presidential election for a small left-wing force, he succeeded in being a magnet for many distanced from de Gaulle and Gaullism. Jean Monnet was so annoyed with de Gaulle's goading of the prototype EU that he endorsed his candidacy. But he also secured the backing of René Bousquet, the chief of police under Vichy. The *Dépeche du Midi* newspaper which he controlled was, according to Mitterrand, one of the few dailies 'favourable to us during the Gaullist period...I wrote editorials in it'.[17] Much to his chagrin, de Gaulle was forced into a run-off where Mitterrand made a strong showing (with 45 percent of the vote).

During the tumultuous May 1968 events, Mitterrand publicly urged de Gaulle to capitulate 'before the rising force of an angry people'.[18] However, his gamble that 1968 might be another year of revolution like 1830 or 1848 fell flat. Within days, nearly a million people marched up the Champs Elysée to the Arc de Triomphe chanting 'Mitterrand charlatan, Mitterrand to the gallows, Mitterrand you failed'.[19] Later in 1968, this wave of French moderation triumphed in elections, but Mitterrand's luck held. Representing a safe seat, he clung on while many of his rivals on the left were consigned to what would prove permanent oblivion.

Finally, in 1971, an alliance with disparate factions on the non-revolutionary left enabled him to become leader of a re-organized Socialist party (PS). He showed great tactical flair and accomplished the unlikely feat of convincing many activists that despite his baggage, the left could rule under his guidance. It required oratory where he insisted: 'Whoever does not consent to the break with the established order, with capitalism, cannot be a member of the Parti Socialiste'.[20] Pierre Mauroy, one of his few working-class lieutenants, and Prime Minister from 1981 to 1983, reflected that: 'He came to socialism when he was over fifty. He intellectualised his way there. It took him ten years of hard reading'.[21]

To succeed in the long march to power, he would need to lure five million communist voters, and by various stratagems, turn them into an electoral prop of his own party. The realisation of this scheme was perhaps his greatest political accomplishment. With communist backing, he narrowly beat Valéry Giscard d'Estaing in the May 1981 presidential election. Gaullism had grown insipid, the general's heirs being afraid of embracing an overt conservative identity because of France's political culture.

One-third of his first ministerial team were teachers and it took little persuasion for them to embark on policies to expand the power of the state and boost productivity at a time when much of the West was mired in recession. Almost $20 billion poured out of France in May 1981 alone, once the new course was apparent.[22] In banking, insurance and industry, workers got a fifth week of paid holiday, the retirement age was lowered from sixty-five to sixty, and a massive civil service recruitment drive occurred.[23] In theory, higher wages would stimulate greater consumer spending, creating more jobs as production rose to meet demand. But the fresh consumer spending sucked in imports, which sparked a balance of payments crisis. Planning was soon jettisoned, and the free market re-embraced. Stringent budget cuts in 1983 meant 'effectively asking voters to return the presents they had just received'.[24]

In June 1983, he admitted mistakes and declared: 'perhaps we were dreaming in 1981'.[25] Six months later, he remarked: the French are beginning to understand' [that] 'it is the firm that creates wealth...[and] employment'. The writer Brian Moynahan observed: 'it was of course Mitterrand who was slow to understand wealth creation' or understand the workings of the economy.[26] Later, he would struggle when debating with his chief conservative rival, Jacques Chirac, on economic questions.[27]

Ultimately, persistently high levels of unemployment during most of his presidency, produced a rupture between his party and the French working-class. He gave far too much ammunition to far-right opponents who painted the ruling left as the embodiment of political dishonesty and sleaze. He failed to discourage the view that 'the only cause in which he ever deeply believed was himself'.[28] Increasingly, in the 1980s, he was seen to preside over often distrustful factions backed by an unstable voting base. This was no substitute for a strong working-class presence, which increasingly a new hard-line challenger, the *Front National*, could claim to have in different parts of the country.

Mitterrand probably deserves credit for embarking upon decentralisation measures. But he was far more at home with a planned, centralized society in which he could insert favourites and protégès. Donors able to meet the demands of party finance, as well as media consultants, were far more important than trade-union leaders. France was one of the earliest places where the political left fell under the influence of media, educational and even financial interests, who were more interested in social engineering (around approved globalist norms) than in unglamorous but necessary tasks of social and economic reform.

Mitterrand was an ambitious, but essentially old school, politician whose exposure to the treacherous politics of the 1930s and 1940s, perhaps inoculated him against a belief in a markedly ideological agenda. It meant that he was willing to share power with apparent enemies in an uneasy 'cohabitation'.

In 1986, the Gaullist Jacques Chirac, crushed the left in parliamentary elections. Under the subsequent compromise, Mitterrand retained control over France's foreign policy. But domestic policy would be the province of Chirac and his team. Mitterrand's show of flexibility towards rivals helped to consolidate the Fifth Republic. It was in contrast to his hostility towards perceived Socialist rivals, especially Michel Rocard.

He had cordial relations with Margaret Thatcher, the premier figure of European conservatism in the 1980s. At the outset of the Falklands crisis in April 1982, he telephoned her to assure her of French diplomatic support in her bid to expel Argentinian forces from the British South Atlantic territory.[29] By contrast, European Socialist solidarity meant little to Mitterrand, as shown by his reluctance to endorse the EU accession bid of Felipe González, the left-wing Prime Minister of newly democratic Spain (before his southern neighbour joined in 1986). His unwillingness to see a reduction in subsidies going to the French agricultural sector, eclipsed any concern he may have had of an authoritarian comeback in Madrid.[30]

Perhaps his dealings with the French Communists gave him an insight into the decline of Soviet power. On several occasions in 1981, he told German officials that Moscow would no longer be able to dominate its satellite countries. He was in advance of his time with such forecasts.[31] Soon after, he showed solidarity with his Atlantic partners by being prepared to go before the Bundestag to rally a sceptical German public opinion and urge acceptance of the deployment of Cruise and Pershing missiles. He stated:

> '[It is] our conviction that nuclear weapons, as the instrument of deterrence, are, whether one likes it or not, the guarantee of peace from the moment... Anyone who gambles on "decoupling" the European and American continents would, in our view, be calling into question... the maintenance of peace'.[32]

Mitterrand's pro-nuclear stance was more driven by French interests than by Euro-Atlantic concerns, especially as defined by the United States, a country whose hegemony he had no wish to reinforce. He showed the lengths he was prepared to go in order to uphold French nuclear interests when, on 10 July 1985, the Rainbow Warrior, a vessel docked in Auckland, New Zealand and preparing to protest against French nuclear testing in the South Pacific, was blown up. The scandal led to the resignation of the defence minister Charles Hernu, a former minor Petainist official whom Mitterrand had known for decades.[33] Twenty years later, it was revealed by the head of the secret service at the time, that Mitterrand had personally authorised the mission to stop the ship, without knowing (or perhaps caring) how it would be done.[34]

Mitterrand's presidency was more imperial than republican. He sought to enshrine a cultivated, dignified and resolute France prepared to defend its interests in a turbulent world. An effort was made to try and win over citizens who disliked the corrupt side of his regime, by depicting it as an expression of French grandeur and civilization that was above politics. The arts budget was dramatically increased: Mitterrand raided public coffers to build monuments to his long rule: a crystal pyramid in the courtyard of the Louvre, a national library, a new opera house, a celebrated Grande Arche, several of which proved to be poorly built.

In order to achieve re-election in 1988, he strove to stand above party and project, the image of a national father figure. There was no proper programme, no socialist banners, no collective spirit, just a personal plebiscite.[35] He was helped by a centre-right unable to paper over its own divisions. But low political moves were an essential part of his survival plan.

For the 1986 legislative elections he had changed the two-round majority voting system to proportional representation, ostensibly in the interests of widening democracy. However, Mitterrand's ulterior motive was to boost parliamentary representation of the *National Front (FN)* and sow division in the traditional Gaullist right. This wasn't such an outlandish move, at least in the French context. Mitterrand and others had continuous links with individuals who had dubious Vichy records. All post-war governments sought to brush events in the war years well under the carpet and not probe too deeply into anyone's activities from 1940 to 1944.[36] One of his Prime Ministers, Pierre Bérégovoy, told a journalist: 'We have every interest in pushing the National Front. It keeps the Right from being elected. The stronger it is, the harder we'll be to beat. It's a historic chance for the Socialists'.[37]

A crowded political centre and the electoral collapse of the Communists created a vacuum, which was duly filled by the FN.[38] In 1995, 46 percent of Jean Marie Le Pen's voters were workers or employees.[39] The new liberal progressivism of the Socialists, based on tinkering with social values and norms in order to validate various academic theories, left many struggling French citizens unimpressed. The exploits and antics of political entrepreneurs with a sense of entitlement could (and increasingly did) alienate less exalted folk.

Mitterrand's electoral alchemy weakened (perhaps fatally) the ability of the Left-Right polarity to define and shape political life. France paved the way for the emergence of a new dualism in Europe between populism emphasising national themes and a cosmopolitanism which downplayed the nation and placed growing emphasis instead on individuals and their role in an increasingly globalised world.[40] France may come to be seen as the birthplace of a replacement to the Left-Right binary divide. Populism versus cosmopolitanism, that is based around acceleration of European integration, has spread beyond France as a defining framework for politics. But whereas in post-1945 Europe, left and right gradually came to co-exist, populism is viewed as heretical and dangerous by Euro-minded elites who are regarded in like manner by those whose reference point is the nation.

Jacques Attali was Mitterrand's chief ideas man, encouraging him to experiment and innovate. He was an effortlessly self-promoting guru, given ample funding to implement some of his futuristic notions.[41] His office was literally beside Mr. Mitterrand's in the Elysée Palace and virtually all visitors passed through it to get to the president, which meant he chatted with most of them as they waited to see Mr. Mitterrand.

He told one American journalist in 2000: 'You know for years I was more powerful than the prime minister…I was the closest adviser to the president'.[42] One of his many books was a set of diaries covering the Mitterrand years, which biographers of Mitterrand are very reticent about quoting due to perceived inaccuracies.[43]

Attali grew up in Algeria in the 1940s and early 1950s, but his absorption with cutting edge technology, and how it could burnish the image of the man whom he served as counsellor, meant he had little time to think of practical solutions to integrate the growing population of Mahgrebi descent. A combination of exclusionary labour laws, an enclave religious identity, prejudice from parts of society, and poor educational opportunities kept many (not all) at the margins of society. The lack of upward mobility meant that disaffection slowly spread, as growing numbers fell under the sway of clerics preaching a message of radical disengagement.[44]

Irrespective of their background, Mitterrand showed little interest in the declining fortunes of his fellow citizens: 'We have tried everything we could to fight back unemployment,' he said. 'There is nothing else we can do'.[45] This was far from being the case. He preferred relying on companies enmeshed with the state, even when the pressures to try something new seemed irresistible. A meeting with Apple Macintosh innovator Steve Jobs, arranged by those who wished France's nascent computer industry to learn from his company, got nowhere.[46] It would have been far from ignominious if his standing had been eroded by the economic inertia of his Presidency. But, increasingly, it wasn't just policy drift but moral disarray which overshadowed his last term.

He displayed few qualms about endorsing unsavoury regimes in post-colonial Africa that might perpetuate French power or influence, no matter how corrupt or repressive they might be. He appointed as his 'official counsellor for Africa' his own son Jean-Christophe who was later found guilty of tax evasion and given a suspended jail sentence. In Rwanda, he and his entourage displayed palpable lack of concern about the racist and genocidal trajectory of the Hutu government in this ethnically-riven state.[47] In 2021, long after one of the continent's grimmest tragedies had unfolded there in 1994, a successor Emmanuel Macron attended a ceremony in the country where he acknowledged grave French mistakes in its response to the attempted genocide of the Tutsi minority.[48] (The remark that: 'In such countries, genocide is not too important…' has been attributed to Mitterrand).[49]

He has been described as 'a man fascinated by highway robbers, excited by... those opposed to society, more interested in hooligans with a good gift of the gab than in competent, well-bred *énarques*' (graduates from elite institutions).[50] The friendship that did most to discredit him was the one that lasted for many decades with René Bousquet, the collaborationist Vichy police chief in 1942-3. The son of a radical socialist notary, he was responsible in large part for the mass round-up of Jews in Paris in July

1942. He was convicted in 1949 of collaboration, and then pardoned because he had given important help to the Resistance. In 1983, the Nazi hunter Serge Klarsfeld produced evidence of his role in the 1942 deportations. Mitterrand admitted that he had sought to discourage his prosecution acting, he claimed, in order 'to avoid reigniting national divisions'.[51] He continued to see Bousquet right up until 1986. He even said to a later foreign minister Roland Dumas, that 'Had it not been for the war, he would have been a minister, maybe Prime Minister'.[52] Instead, he would be assassinated in 1993, shortly before he was due to stand trial, accused of crimes against humanity.[53]

It also came to light while he was still alive that Mitterrand had sent a wreath to Pétain's grave each year from 1987 to the early 1990s.[54] He cooperated with Pierre Péan, a historian exploring his formative years, explaining that 'when you are young it is difficult to choose...I managed to come out all right. It is unfair to judge people by mistakes that can be explained by the atmosphere of the times'.[55]

Prime Minister from 1988 to 1991, Michel Rocard, created a stir in 1998 by stating 'my real problem was that Mitterrand was not an honest man...he let people he liked get away with a lot of things, sometimes too much, on condition of...even sometimes financial complicity'.[56] One of Rocard's successors, Pierre Bérégovoy, killed himself in 1993 after details of an interest-free loan that he had received from a close friend (and fellow prisoner-of-war) of Mitterrand's, Patrice Pelat emerged.[57] In 1982, Pelat is alleged to have sold his business to a recently-nationalised electricity company, at a price well above its true value thanks to pressure exerted by Mitterrand.[58] He had been indicted for corruption when he died in 1989. Mitterrand's sports minister, a self-made millionaire named Bernard Tapie, was later imprisoned for fixing a football match and evading taxes. He enjoyed the President's backing even when the scandals were out in the open.[59]

The dramatic events surrounding the abrupt ending of the Cold War, the reunification of Germany and the collapse of the Soviet Union, occurred quite early in Mitterrand's second term. Along with cultural matters, foreign affairs were chiefly absorbing his interests by now. Dexterity was lacking in his handling of the German reunification process and in his reaction to the failed coup against the Soviet reformer Mikhail Gorbachev, mounted in August 1991.[60] Approaching the close of his presidency, the prostate cancer which had been diagnosed as early as 1981, and which had been kept in remission through the 1980s, was beginning to sap his strength and render him enfeebled, but it wasn't until he had been operated on, in September 1992, that news of his condition reached the public.

In the numerous books published about the momentous territorial changes in Europe at the end of the 1980s, Mitterrand does not emerge as a pivotal figure. His priority was to promote a fixed exchange rate within the EU in order to protect the struggling French economy from further difficulties. Germany's Chancellor Kohl initially reflected the views of the financial and political establishment and was sceptical if not dismissive of the idea. But as he grew into the role of 'imperial chancellor', after having overseen German unification, he increasingly warmed to the idea.[61] By now, in public, the two men were firm exponents of European integration. Mitterrand preferred a confederal approach, in which governments of the major member states retained primacy in the new order. However, he felt that the pace of the integration journey needed to speed up in order for a much larger Germany to be locked into the post-national European agenda. In 1993, he announced that he would not appoint anyone as Premier who wasn't committed to a close Franco-German relationship.[62] The formation of Eurocorps, a 35,000 strong Franco-German corps announced in 1992, with a European mission, had been announced the year before. But he was disinclined to see European military power being used to try and end the post-1991 conflict in Yugoslavia. By the time he made a dramatic dash to the besieged city of Sarajevo on 28 June 1994, (on the occasion of the 80th anniversary of the assassination there of Archduke Franz Ferdinand) the war was mainly being directed against civilians. The sufferings of the population were slightly eased. But the *coup de theâtre* was widely seen as a substitute for more forceful action.[63]

Demoralisation about the impotence of the EU in the face of the eruption of violent ethnic hatreds, in what by now was the former Yugoslavia, perhaps made it harder for Mitterrand to convince French voters to arm the European institutions with sweeping new powers. On 6 September 1991, when put to a referendum, the Maastricht Treaty passed with a bare

51.05 percent of votes, mainly the better-educated and more successful part of the electorate. Many French citizens were beginning to transfer their contempt for 'politicians' at home to the decision-makers in Brussels. It was not difficult for Eurosceptics of various hues to describe the project of 'more Europe' as a rich person's affair that had little in it for them. Among a cynical public, there may not have been undue surprise when Roland Dumas, a close ally and former foreign minister, said in June 2001 that, in 1994, his boss had approved illegal payments worth $15million to help Chancellor Helmut Kohl's Christian Democrats win an election 'because he considered that they were useful for France'.[64]

Mitterrand told the French people, in his last New Year's Eve address on December 31st, 1994, 'I believe in the powers of the spirit, and I shall never leave you'.[65] But, by their voting habits and what they told pollsters, large swathes of voters were swiftly abandoning his brand of empty and platitudinous politics. At elite level, the Fifth Republic may have become consolidated under Mitterrand, but a growing crisis of confidence was being displayed towards the institutions due to the behaviour of many of his appointees. They behaved like a separate caste, uninterested in the condition of ordinary citizens, despite being elected under emancipatory slogans. A crisis of legitimacy grew up in a political order where rival parties alternated in office but chose to act as a political class united in defence of caste privileges.

Mitterrand may have dabbled with extremist ideas in his youth, but the most lasting damage was caused when, as an ageing president, his cynical manoeuvring brought the politics of entrenched selfishness back in from the cold.

---

[1] Franz-Olivier Giesbert, *François Mitterrand ou la tentation de l'hístoire*, Paris: Seuil, 1977, p. 57.
[2] Yascha Munck, 'Book Review: "A Taste For Intrigue"', *Wall Street Journal*, 9 May 2014.
[3] Claire Andrieu, 'Managing Memory: National and Personal Identity at Stake in the Mitterrand Affair', *French Politics and Society*, Vol. 14, No. 2, 1996, p. 19.

[4] John Laughland, *The Death of Politics: France Under Mitterrand*, London: Michael Joseph, 1994, p.p. 205-7.
[5] Julius W. Friend, The Long Presidency, France in the Mitterrand Years, 1981-1995, Oxford and Boulder: Westview Press, 1998, p. 9.
[6] Laughland, *The Death of Politics*, p. 216.
[7] Julius W. Friend, 'François Mitterrand: All Sins Forgiven?', *French Politics and Society*, Vol.14, No. 1, 1996, p. 34.
[8] David Hanley, 'A Taste for Intrigue: The Multiple Lives of François Mitterrand', *Modern and Contemporary France*, Vol. 23, No. 1, 2015, p. 129.
[9] Yascha Mounk, 'A Taste for Intrigue', *Wall Street Journal*, 9 May 2014.
[10] John Lichfield, 'General accuses Mitterrand of condoning torture and killings', *Independent*, (London), 3 May 2001.
[11] Philip Short, *Mitterrand, A Study in Ambiguity*, London: The Bodley Head, 2013, p. 183.
[12] See François Mitterrand, *Le coup d'état permanent*, Paris: Plon, 1964.
[13] Short, *Mitterrand*, p. 116.
[14] Philippe Marlière, 'Republican King', *London Review of Books*, Vol. 36, No. 8, 17 April 2013.
[15] See Robert Pesque, Mon vrai-faux attentat contre Mitterrand: La vérité sur l'affaire de l'Observatoire, Paris: Michel Lafon, 1995.
[16] Marlière, 'Republican King'.
[17] Ronald Tiersky, *François Mitterrand, a Very French President*, Rowman & Littelfield, Lanham, Md, 2003, p. 358.
[18] Short, *Mitterrand*, p. 252.
[19] Short, *Mitterrand*, p. 255.
[20] Marlière, 'Republican King'.
[21] Moynahan, *The French Century*, p. 433.
[22] Moynahan, *The French Century*, p. 432.
[23] Friend, The Long Presidency, p. 30.
[24] Yascha Mounk,, 'Book Review'.
[25] Friend, The Long Presidency, p. 45.
[26] Moynahan, *The French Century*, p. 434.
[27] Friend, The Long Presidency, p. 18.
[28] Stanley Hoffmann, 'A Symposium on Mitterrand's Past', French Politics and Society, Vol. 13, No. 1, winter 1995, p. 8.
[29] Charles Moore, *Margaret Thatcher, the Authorised Biography: Vol. 1*, London: Penguin, 2014, p. 678; Friend, The Long Presidency, p.p. 229-30.
[30] See Judt, *Postwar*, p. 527.
[31] Frederike Schotters, 'Mitterrand's Europe: functions and limits of 'European solidarity' in French policy during the 1980s', *European Review of History: Revue européenne d'histoire*, Vol. 24, No. 6, 2017, p. 978.
[32] Schotters, 'Mitterrand's Europe', p. 979.
[33] Sam White, 'Mitterrand's fatal cover up', *Spectator*, 28 September 1985. John Laughland, 'Past imperfect', Spectator, 26 June 1993.
[34] Short, Mitterrand, p.p. 407-09.
[35] Short, *Mitterrand*, p. 459.

[36] Paul Webster, 'Paris refuses to be moved by the Jewish ghosts of the Velodrome: President Mitterrand will not make amends for the Vichy regime', *Guardian*, 17 July 1992.
[37] Friend, The Long Presidency, p. 86.
[38] James Markham, 'Au Revoir to Ideology', *New York Times*, 28 February 1988.
[39] Friend, *The Long Presidency*, p. 154.
[40] See Pierre Manent, 'Populist Demagogy and the Fanaticism of the Center', *American Affairs*, Vol. 1, No. 2, Summer 2017.
[41] Diana Geddes, 'Populist Demagogy and the Fanaticism of the Center, The High-flyer Takes Wing', *Spectato*r, 16 June 1990.
[42] Kevin J. Delaney, 'Second Life: Ultimate Political Insider Jacques Attali Emerges as a Savvy Web Entrepreneur', *Wall Street Journal*, 13 November 2000.
[43] See Friend, *The Long Presidenc*y, p. 282, note 5.
[44] See Andrew Hussey, The French Intifada, the Long War Between France and its Arabs, London: Granta, 2015.
[45] Marlière, 'Republican King'.
[46] Granville, *What Ails*, p. 50.
[47]Charles Bremner, 'Mitterrand's son is guilty of £400,000 tax evasion', *Times*, 9 December 2004.
[48] Kim Willsher, 'France is not complicit in Rwanda genocide says Macron commission', *Guardia*n, 26 March 2021.
[49] Philip Gourevitch in "Reversing the Reversals of War," *New Yorke*r, 26 April 1999.
[50] Friend, *The Long Presidency*, p. 256.
[51] See Hugh McDonnell, 'François Mitterrand and the gray zone of Vichy', French Politics, Culture & Society, Vol. 37, No. 2, Summer 2019, p.p. 90-2. also, Tiersky, François Mitterrand, p.p. 352-8.
[52] Short, *Mitterrand*, p. 535.
[53] Douglas Johnson, 'Obituary: René Bousquet', *Independen*t, 9 June 1993.
[54] Tiersky, François Mitterrand, p. 357; Pierre Péan, *Une Jeunesse française: François Mitterrand, 1934-47*, Paris: Fayard, 1994.
[55] Tiersky, *François Mitterrand*, p. 357.
[56] Crispian Balmer, *National Post*, (Canada), 21 November 1998.
[57] Friend, The Long Presidency, p. 40.
[58] Friend, 'François Mitterrand: All Sins', p. 33.
[59] Friend, *The Long Presidency*, p.p. 149, 256.
[60] Friend, *The Long Presidency*, p. 264.
[61] Mody, *Euro Tragedy*, p.p. 94-95.
[62] Gallagher, *Europe's Path*, p. 79.
[63] Tom Gallagher, *The Balkans After The Cold War*, London: Routledge, 2003, p. 93.
[64] John Lichfield, 'Jailed Dumas drags more minister into bribes scandal', *Independen*t, 19 June 2001, Moynahan, p. 442.
[65] 'The monarch of Modern France', *Irish Time*s, 13 August 2005.

CHAPTER 9: GERHARD SCHRÖDER

1944-

Germany was easily the greatest West European beneficiary of the peaceful ending of the Cold War. Not only did a forty-year era of territorial partition come to an end, but it ceased to be one of the likeliest arenas for the emergence of a Third World war. Moreover, due to its newly-acquired demographic weight and enduring economic strength, it enjoyed increasingly uncontested primacy within the European Union.

Hitherto, the West German republic, with its capital in Bonn from 1949 to 1990, had gone to determined lengths to mask its strength and live down a calamitous past. It had rarely asserted its power over other nations, allowing France to be the *de facto* national driver of the integration project. Soon, it dropped its bashfulness and expressed views that were still clothed in pro-European sentiment, but usually driven by specific German interests. At a rhetorical level, it saw no reason why the federal structures, which had seemingly worked so well for post-Hitlerian Germany, could not be the basis for an eventual pan-European state. The creation of a single European currency, the Euro, would probably not have occurred in 1999, without active German sponsorship.

The speedy reunification of Germany was anticipated by few analysts before 1989 and very few forecast that the rhetoric of European integration would mask policies that enshrined German economic nationalism. The single currency was used by Germany to consolidate its industrial hegemony in Europe. When flaws in the design and implementation of the Euro plunged the European financial order into a crisis after 2008,

Germany ensured that, throughout the various bids to rescue the project, the core interests of its bankers and manufacturers were never lost sight of.

Gerhard Schröder was Chancellor of Germany when the Euro was launched in 1999. A decade later, he had become the highly visible mascot for the most glaring example of German exceptionalism – the energy alliance between Germany and the Russia of Vladimir Putin. He was the amply-rewarded front man, given influential positions in the politically-managed Russian energy business. He showed disdain for critics of his collusion, or indeed his declared friendship, with an autocrat who was increasingly oppressive at home and warlike in the vicinity of Russia.

The smugness of a talented and self-important lawyer who, as Chancellor, showed that he was hardly wedded to coherent or fixed left-wing principles, was perhaps no great surprise to those alert to the shift in the ethical foundation of European politics. Shape-shifting politicians, increasingly unfazed about displaying strong appetites for wealth and influence after holding senior office, were becoming increasingly numerous. Schröder's identification with a coercive ruler was an indication that the rules of politics were not changing under the German ascendancy of the EU. Peaceful, legalistic procedures were not driving out a 'might is right' mentality in European affairs. The controversial political theorist Carl Schmitt's assertion that warlike aggression was likely to be hard to displace from politics, seemed to be amply vindicated by events in the Schröder era.[1]

It was striking that he avoided any sanction from his own party or the German state for becoming an unabashed apologist for the leader of a resource-rich state, increasingly contemptuous of norms and conventions thought necessary for the maintenance of peace in Europe. His Social Democratic Party (SPD) still wished to see power transfer from national members to centralising EU institutions, in which German influence would be hard to check. Yet it did not seem to think that, for this journey to succeed, it needed to avoid compromising entanglements with a dictator, especially one who increasingly had only contempt for the ethos of peace and mutual cooperation that was supposedly the bedrock of the EU system.

Schröder remained a spectral presence in European politics. He was the best-known Kremlin backer or *Putinversteher* (Putin whisperer). The iron clad consensus about the importance of the energy alliance with Russia meant that he could not easily be banished. Six months after Russia invaded Ukraine and with Schröder defiantly stating about his friendship with Putin that 'I don't do *'Mea Culpa'*, the SPD found that insufficient grounds existed to expel him from the party.

At least, his self-sufficiency enables him to stand out from the clubbable and networking swarm of European politicians who scrambled to acquire power and influence in the final decades of the 20th century. He had a strong urge to succeed on his own terms and for most of his time in the public eye he has been seen as a loner. Indeed, his friendship with Vladimir Putin, while gaining him opprobrium, never seems to have dented his self-belief.

It is likely that his humble origins and tough early life nurtured the sense of defiance which has been a trademark of Schröder through his public life. He was born in the small north German town of Mossenburg on 7 April 1944. Days earlier, his father had been killed as the Wehrmacht retreated from Romania. In order to support a family of five children, his mother cleaned barracks for the British forces occupying north Germany. Schröder worked in the fields and, at the age of 14, he abandoned his schooling to sell crockery as a door-to-door salesman. The urge towards self-improvement meant that he paid for night courses in order to finish high school.

It has been claimed that he often told his mother, 'One day I'll take you away from all this in a Mercedes'.[2] But his route to fame and fortune lay through left-wing politics. He studied law at Gottingen University and joined the Yusos, the youth branch of the Social Democratic Party (SPD). He was then nineteen, and just four years earlier, the SPD had abandoned the class war and dropped Marxism from its statutes. In the mid-1970s, he became the party youth leader in the district of Hanover in the state of Lower Saxony, which would be his political power base. In 1978, he became the SPD's *nationwide* youth leader. By now, armed with a law degree, he was a practising lawyer. In his best-known case, he defended a Red Army Faction terrorist Horst Mahler in a parole hearing.[3] By 1978, he was a leading far-left spokesman for the SPD, organizing protests in his region against the deployment of NATO missiles in Germany.

But his dalliance with the far-left was short lived. Once installed as national youth leader, he executed the first of several U-turns in his political career. In his memoirs, the former party chairman, Hans-Jochen Vogel, accused Schröder of using the SPD as a trampoline for his own career leaps.[4]

What seemed to some like Schröder's irresistible rise was halted in June 1986 when he appeared poised to win the regional election in Lower Saxony. An SPD victory would have allowed the party to gain control of the upper house in the Bundestag. Four years into his chancellorship, Helmut Kohl of the CDU would have been forced out. 'I assume I'll win,' the then 42-year-old Schröder confidently declared on television. 'And that will be the end of Helmut Kohl'.[5]

The CDU was engaged in expanding the nuclear power industry. The Chernobyl nuclear disaster had occurred a few months earlier. Schröder was reaching out to the rising Green party, not least owing to his marriage to Hiltrud Schwetje, an environmentalist, vegetarian, and animal-rights proponent. The pair were described at that time as 'the German equivalent of the Clintons, a political power couple who were young, attractive, and on the move'.[6] But the electorate was still not persuaded of the dangers of nuclear energy. The CDU retained power.

Schröder's turn to run Lower Saxony came in 1990, and he was Minister-President until 1998. In that year's federal election, he was the candidate for chancellor at the head of an electoral alliance between the SPD and the Green Party. He was distrusted by many party regulars because he found it hard to conceal his enjoyment of the good life, through ties with firms like Volkswagen, a major employer in his region.[7] But he was respected for his prowess on the campaign trail and his effectiveness on television. His side won a 21-seat majority. But he enjoyed no political honeymoon. NATO's armed offensive in the spring of 1999, against Serbia, following the Milošević regime's decision to deport much of the Albanian population from the disputed province of Kosovo, caused strains in the coalition. 1999 was also the year of the launch of the single currency. In opposition, he had called the Euro 'a sickly premature baby', but once in power, he threw his weight behind the inclusion of Greece in the Eurozone. One of his senior advisers, Wolfgang Nowak, recalled in 2011: 'We were told by Gerhard Schröder that he would make an "honest" currency out of the Euro. But his first official act was to admit Greece, a country that had been blatantly falsifying budget figures'.[8]

At home, his rule was dogged by opposition to his pro-business policies. Schröder was embarking on cutting social welfare benefits and labour costs in order to make German industry more competitive. It led to Oskar Lafontaine, hitherto his closest political ally, walking out of the government in 1999, and soon after, quitting the SPD itself. Party membership began to haemorrhage as Schröder was branded 'the comrade of the bosses'.[9] Leading one of the most unpopular post-war governments, he presided over the loss of successive regional elections. His ailing and unhappy party seemed destined for a drubbing in the 2002 federal election. But he hung on, assisted by a lacklustre conservative challenger and by his energetic response to catastrophic floods which struck North Germany at the height of the electoral campaign. His refusal to endorse the US-led invasion of Iraq, and his insistence that he was 'the peace Chancellor', also came to his aid. But uproar over his ongoing austerity measures continued unabated. It led to his resignation as party leader in 2004, and the calling of early federal elections on 18 September 2005, after further steep electoral losses. The Nobel laureate Gunter Grass spoke up for him on the campaign trail. He pointed out that Merkel would have led Germany into the Iraq quagmire and claimed that Schröder represented a 'tradition of tolerance going back to the European enlightenment'.[10] The result was a near dead-heat. The slim advantage enjoyed by the CDU enabled it to head a grand coalition with the SPD, which retained the majority of cabinet seats.

Schröder chose this moment to announce his departure from German politics. But it was hardly a retreat from the limelight. As chancellor, he had insisted on retaining control of relations with Russia and, just days before leaving the post, he would embark on what would be the most durable alliance of his entire political career. He joined the board of Nord Stream, the company building the pipeline under the Baltic Sea to enable gas from Russia to reach Germany directly. He now became the key salesman for, and defender of, the European Union's growing dependence on Russian energy products. Arguably, thanks in no small measure to Schröder's leverage, Russia, by 2021, found itself in the powerful position of supplying about 20 percent of Europe's oil, 40 percent of its gas, and 20 percent of its coal.[11] For many years, the bilateral deal evoked more controversy abroad than in Germany. Editorials in the US press slammed his decision to embark on a strategic partnership with Russia's President Putin who had imprisoned the leading figure in the energy sector, Mikhail Khodorkovsky two years earlier and ordered the seizure of his assets. The ruthless move was just the prelude for ever bolder crackdowns on opposition as Russia returned to dictatorial control, this time under a venal form of state capitalism. Schröder had no hesitation in calling Putin 'a flawless democrat' in 2004, as the jails started to fill with enemies, those who did not reach premature ends as a result of mysterious accidents or murder.[12] This was also the year when Putin took a Cossack choir to Hanover to celebrate Schröder's 60th birthday.

It is doubtful if Schröder pondered deeply about how his alliance with Putin would be viewed at home. He was a lone wolf who had turned against various allies whom he had cultivated on the way to the top. Two alpha male politicians were bonding, joined together by commerce and the opportunity to mock the sensibilities of bourgeois European politics.

Schröder took the measure of the German political establishment. However much he was disliked for his conduct, its luminaries seemed unlikely to sanction him. He was well aware of how deep the conciliatory attitude towards the Soviet Union and its kleptocratic successor ran in Berlin. Willy Brandt's *Ostpolitik* initiative in the early 1970s, that succeeded in de-escalating East-West tensions for a time, continued to be romanticised.

To the consternation of many leaders in former Warsaw Pact countries which had escaped Soviet control and had joined the Euro-Atlantic order buttressed by NATO and the EU, Germany failed to acknowledge that indulgence towards an aggressive Russia imperilled the European peace. The mantra of German foreign policy remained that 'there can be no security in Europe without Russia or against it'.[13] In the teeth of scepticism,

German officialdom insisted that the special relationship with Russia helped maintain continental harmony. This cliché appeared to be a blank cheque for escalating Russian misbehaviour, while criticism was silenced thanks to the rewards flowing to numerous German clients of Russia.

Far from Schröder ending up a pariah in the SPD, he won over others in the party to his stance on Russia. Three of Merkel's foreign ministers during her 16-year chancellorship were SPD politicians. One of them, Frank-Walter Steinmeier was a protégè who had been unenthusiastic about the rapid dismantling of East Germany back in 1989.[14] He later complained in 2016, that the holding of military exercises by NATO on its eastern flank was 'sabre-rattling and war-mongering'.[15]

In 2006, the then President of Estonia, Toomas Hendrik Ilves privately coined the term *Schröderizatsiya* to signify the corruption of politics in West Europe through the influence of Russian money and state power. Fifteen years later, when he revealed that the neologism had been devised by him, he stated clearly that it meant 'the corruption of a political elite by another country' and that he had Germany in mind.[16]

Ilves's strictures elicited a non-response from Germany. The opinion of the lands, which had obtained independence after long years languishing in the Soviet sphere, simply counted for very little in Berlin. Certainly, while he was formulating Russian policy as Chancellor, Schröder never took into consideration the views of these countries. The narrow self-absorption of the German elite made the European unity aspirations of many within it seem rather disingenuous. 'Germany is an industry association pretending to be a state', was the disparaging view of a Czech security official after the war in Ukraine erupted.[17]

The cognitive dissonance of perhaps most in the German political class, was shown by their failure to recognise that a special energy partnership between Russia and Germany made Ukraine, Poland and the Baltic States far less secure. As long as gas from the Siberian oil fields crossed the territory of Ukraine, it was less easy for Russia to behave aggressively towards it. But once the Nord Stream pipeline was operational, it did not take long before Putin started to wield his big stick. Threats and intimidation quickly escalated into audacious land grabs. Crimea was seized in 2014 and insurgencies were mounted in Eastern Ukraine. Germany refused to confront the fact that Nord Stream increased its own vulnerability to economic blackmail by Russia. The pipeline was of primarily geopolitical, and not economic, importance to this country, whose leadership was in the grip of neo-imperialist thinking.

Even when regular Russian troops, such as the BUK anti-aircraft unit operating in eastern Ukraine, shot down (probably accidentally) Malaysian Airlines flight MH17 on 17 July 2014, the outrage failed to convince Chancellor Angela Merkel that Germany's access to cheap energy was being obtained at the price of its own standing as a responsible actor in the field of European security.[18] A massive Russian hacking attack on the Bundestag in 2017 incurred no reaction from her. No senior figure was prepared to publicly disavow the undertaking, of by now President Steinmeier, that Germany will never participate in a war against Russia. It seemed to imply that Germany would remain impassive, however provocative the actions of Russia's leader became. Such a level of detachment seemed to be implying a special German exemption from NATO's Article 5 commitment of mutual assistance and begged the question of where the country's ultimate loyalties lay.[19]

Schröder was in no danger of facing isolation, even as his partner Putin left increasingly bloody footprints within Russia or in neighbouring countries which he was determined to suborn. A biography, that perhaps could only have appeared after the disintegration of the Russo-German energy compact, found that he was very much *persona grata* in German governing circles.

Reinhard Silberberg, Germany's permanent representative to the European Union in Brussels, gave him dinner in the Belgian capital in 2016, along with Matthias Warnig, a former East German Stasi officer who had gone on to be a leading player in Nord Stream.[20] This was not long after a laudatory biography had appeared by well-known historian Gregor Schöllgen who concluded that, 'There is no question that this man's place in the history books is certain'.[21]

The state-owned Russian oil giant Rosneft had been placed on the European Union's sanction list for its involvement in the seizure of

Crimea. But the appointment of Schröder as chairman of its board of directors in 2017, failed to produce an outcry in Berlin. 'It's my life and it's me who decides what to do with it, and not the German press,' he defiantly stated when the news broke.[22] Merkel responded using similar phraseology when President Trump complained that Germany had become an economic captive of Russia: we 'can make our own policies and make our own decisions'.[23]

In a 2017 interview with a German newspaper, Schröder applauded the Russian leader for his 'rational behaviour,' and added, 'Compared with the US president, we should be glad to have Putin'.[24] These views did not prevent him being invited to campaign on behalf of the SPD in that year's Bundestag election. Martin Schulz, the party's candidate for Chancellor, pursued an anti-American line. He complained that the US call for countries like Germany to raise their defence spending was ridiculous. Schröder, for his part, said it was unthinkable to imagine that territorial aggression could occur in Europe.[25]

Schröder never allowed himself to be closely quizzed about the basis of his friendship with a leader who springs from the *siloviki*, the ruthless Russian security establishment. It is only possible to speculate whether he has latent admiration for the way that he rules his country and tries to impose his will on different parts of the world.

Schröder invariably contended that his involvement in the energy sector should be seen as strictly a private business undertaking. This was the position which his successor Olaf Scholz was still enunciating in early 2022, on the advice of Jens Plötner, his main national security adviser. [26] Schröder himself occasionally let his guard slip. In 2007, when Putin reacted fiercely to the removal of a Soviet-era war memorial, from the centre of the Estonian capital Tallinn to a military cemetery, he sprang to the Kremlin's defence, slamming Estonia for contradicting 'every form of civilised behaviour'.[27] In May 2020, he was calling for economic sanctions against both Russia and China to be lifted. In an article on his blog, he trundled out clichés, like the importance of reconciliation, without pausing to reflect what meaning bilateral harmony would have if Germany's eastern partner behaved abominably to other countries, including ones that were allies of Germany.[28]

A few months later, in September 2020, he insisted there were 'no proven facts' that Russia was behind the poisoning of leading Russian opposition activist Alexei Navalny — although Germany's military laboratory had announced that the samples taken from his blood confirmed the presence of a nerve agent from the banned Novichok poison. In response, Navalny branded him as Putin's 'errand boy' and Schröder responded with a threat that he would sue the paper that published the interview with him, for libel.[29]

Norbert Röttgen, a prominent CDU parliamentarian, was by now ready to criticise Schröder's Russian role.[30] In 2019, Merkel successfully lobbied for a restoration of Russian voting rights in the Council of Europe, a prestigious human rights organization, despite no change in the developments that had led to its suspension in the first place: Putin's assault on Ukraine.[31]

On 24 February 2022, Russia finally discarded all remaining pretence about its determination to extinguish Ukrainian independence and launched its invasion. The ending of an epoch of wishful thinking was already confirmed by Christoph Heusgen, Merkel's foreign policy adviser from 2005 until 2017, when he stated on 22 February that they had underestimated Putin's sheer brutality.[32] Until the very last minute, Chancellor Olaf Scholz had refused to send defensive weapons to Ukraine. He also prevented allies such as the Baltic States from supplying Kyiv with German-made arms. The UK's Royal Air Force was also banned from crossing German airspace to supply anti-tank missiles.[33] On the day the war started, the finance minister Christian Lindner is reported to have told the Ukrainian ambassador in Berlin that there would be no point in Berlin sending weapons to Ukraine or shutting Russia out of SWIFT, the international payment system, because his country only 'has a few hours' of sovereignty left.[34]

However, Scholz, just weeks into his role, had already reassured Putin, in pre-invasion discussions, that Germany would continue to oppose Ukraine joining NATO. Contacts between the German leader and Schröder continued. He was easy to find as he retained his own private office in the Bundestag, a perk given to all former chancellors.

As the Russian leader's stance became increasingly confrontational, Schröder refrained from imparting any moral advice. Instead, in a January 2022 podcast, he slammed Ukrainian criticism of Germany's refusal to supply the country with weapons, as 'really outrageous'.[35] At the start of February, it was announced that he was due to replace Timur Kulibayev, the son-in-law of Kazakhstan's former long-serving president Nursultan Nazarbayev, on the board of Russian energy giant Gazprom.[36] The news did not dissuade Scholz from seeking the advice of his former party leader on the eve of trips he was due to pay to both Moscow and Kyiv. Murmurs in the CDU, criticising the Chancellor for his ties with Schröder, could be heard. But Armin Laschet, a heavyweight figure in the CDU, remained on good terms with Schröder.[37]

Within days of the Russian invasion, a special session of the Bundestag was convened on 27 February, in which Scholz spoke of 'a change in the history of our continent'.[38] Steps to reduce reliance on Russian energy supplies were later set out.[39] Military aid for Ukraine was promised, though the authorities there grew exasperated about both its quality and the slowness of its arrival.[40] The recently-completed Nord Stream 2 pipeline, had already been frozen by Berlin on 22 February.

In this maelstrom of events, little was heard from Schröder. He suffered a reputational hit as the city of Hanover announced that he was no longer an honorary citizen. The team which had run his office in the Bundestag for several decades, quit. In vain, Scholz implored him to renounce his posts in the Russian energy world. On returning from a visit to Moscow in the summer of 2022, he stated that Germany must strike a deal with Putin to avoid an energy crisis and Ukraine should give up its claim to Crimea.[41] By now, Russia was on the military defensive after its initial plans to decapitate the government of Ukraine and occupy Kiev, had collapsed.[42]

To no small degree, Schröder's influence as the eternal go-between smoothing contacts between the Berlin elite and his friend in the Kremlin had helped shape both the energy and foreign policies of Germany. Once in semi-official disgrace, it was still possible to detect his influence. For a long time, Germany refused to slap a ban on imports of Russian oil and gas. With world energy prices soaring, it meant that the country was sending €800 million a day to Russia, vital revenue enabling it to prosecute what was a very costly war for Russia. Obviously, Scholz was not entirely isolated as other European states relied on Russian gas. He argued in 2022, that an immediate ban would cause great economic and social harm.[43] But Germany was also a wealthy country with one of the lowest levels of debt in the world. Far more drastic belt-tightening had been required of Greece to preserve the European financial system a decade earlier.

Germany may be at a crossroads. The Ukraine crisis is forcing it to decide whether its geo-strategic interests can be placed apart from those of the rest of Europe, as they have arguably been since Schröder's role as a transnational energy baron began. Wolfgang Ischinger, perhaps Germany's most eminent security expert and for many years chairman of the prestigious Munich Security Conference, was in no doubt about what needs to be done. On 28 March, he expressed his worry about 'loss of trust in Germany by important NATO and EU partners'. He saw 'trustworthiness as the single biggest postwar German asset' and went on to say: 'Once lost, trust is very hard to rebuild. This is why I joined [the] call to shut down oil/gas imports from Russia now, even if it will hurt a lot.'[44]

Germany has gradually moved along this path. It is a repudiation of Schröder's record as a power-broker. Viewed as an indecent operator traducing his democratic principles to consort with a murderous dictator by some, others will view the 79-year-old as an exacting but indispensable intermediary between the two lead nations in post-Cold War Europe. Latitude towards him may still even be found in important Euro-Atlantic power centres. The United States has slapped sanctions on far less important figures who cooperated with the Kremlin under Putin. But Schröder has been left untouched. Perhaps he is seen in diplomatic and intelligence circles as a figure who, however tarnished, could still utilise his links with whoever rules in the Kremlin to de-escalate a crisis of frightening dimensions. It would be the ultimate deal-making situation for a supple and cunning lawyer with forty years of experience as a fixer at the heart of German politics and Eurasian business.

It is bound to be disquieting in the eyes of many, that it is a competent, and widely-endorsed politician, belonging to a party that has been one of the architects of European integration, who went rogue in this way. He allied with a Russian strongman whose leading allies were, by the close of 2022, using chilling rhetoric that would not have been out-of-place in the Third Reich during its cruellest phases. Schröder's refusal to break with a blood-stained leader, and the lack of response from his colleagues, raises deeply troubling questions about the ethical foundations of modern European politics.

---

[1] See Stefan Auer, *European Disunion: Democracy, Sovereignty and the Politics of Emergency*, London: Hurst Publishers, 2022 for a deeper discussion of Schmitt's relevance to contemporary EU politics.
[2] Imre Karacs, '"Bosses Comrade" for Chancellor', *Independent*, 27 September 1998, https://www.independent.co.uk/news/german-elections-bosses-comrade-for-chancellor-1201127.html,
accessed 17 February 2022.
[3] 'Gerhard Schroeder', Encyclopedia.com, 11 May 2018, https://www.encyclopedia.com/people/history/german-history-biographies/gerhard-schroder, accessed 17 February 2022.
[4] Oliver Gill, 'How Gerhard Schröder led Germany into a love affair with Putin', *Daily Telegraph*, 12 March 2022.
[5] Gill, 'How Gerhard Schröder'.
[6] https://www.encyclopedia.com/people/history/german-history-biographies/gerhard-schroder.
[7] Imre Karacs, 'Profile Gerhard Schröder: The third way to oblivion', *Independent*, 4 September 1999.
[8] Wolfgang Nowak, 'Germans don't want a Europe of broken promises and big bailouts', *Daily Telegraph*, 6 September 2011.
[9] Karacs, 'Profile Gerhard Schröder'.
[10] Luke Harding, 'Germans set to give Merkel grudging win', *Guardian*, 18 September 2005.
[11] Michael Schellenberger, 'The West's Green Delusions Empowered Putin', *Bari Weiss Substack*, 24 March 2022, https://bariweiss.substack.com/p/the-wests-green-delusions-empowered, accessed 26 March 2022.
[12] Schroeder's Gazprom Job', *Wall Street Journal*, 12 December 2005.
[13] Jeremy Stern, 'Ukraine's Brave Stand Against Putin Upends Germany's Pro-Russia Policy', *Tablet Magazine*, 1 March 2022, https://www.tabletmag.com/sections/news/articles/ukraines-brave-stand-against-putin-upends-germanys-pro-russia-policy, accessed 6 March 2022.
[14] Reinhard Bingener'Russland und die SPD: Die Moskau-Connection', *Frankfurter Allgemeine Zeitung*, 13 March 2023, https://www.msn.com/de-de/nachrichten/politik/russland-und-die-spd-die-moskau-connection/ar-AA18zjYy, accessed 23 March 2023.
[15] Matthew Karnitschnig, 'Putin's Useful German Idiots', *PoliticoEU*, 28 March 2022, https://www.politico.eu/article/putin-merkel-germany-scholz-foreign-policy-ukraine-war-invasion-nord-stream-2/,

accessed 28 March 2022.
[16] Toomas Hendrik Ilves, 'Alexei Navalny and the West's Schröderizatsiya', *CEPA*, 5 October 2021, https://cepa.org/alexei-navalny-and-the-wests-schroderizatsiya/, accessed 26 February 2022.
[17] Jakub Janda, 25 October 2022, Twitter, @JakubJanda.
[18] Andreas Umland, 'How Germany's Nord Stream Pipes Promote War in Europe', *Euractiv*, 21 January 2022, https://www.euractiv.com/section/global-europe/opinion/how-germanys-nord-stream-pipes-promote-war-in-europe/, accessed 27 February 2022.
[19] Stern, 'Ukraine's Brave Stand'.
[20] Bingener, 'Russland und die SPD'.
[21] Gregor Schöllgen, *Gerhard Schröder Die Biografie*, Munich: Deutsche Verlags-Anstalt, 2015. For the source of the quote, see Bingener, 'Russland und die SPD'.
[22] 'Putin and Schröder: A special German-Russian friendship under attack', *Deutsche Welle*, 31 January 2022, https://www.dw.com/en/putin-and-schr%C3%B6der-a-special-german-russian-friendship-under-attack/a-55219973, accessed 27 February 2022.
[23] Shellenberger, 'The West's Green'.
[24] 'Putin and Schröder'.
[25] See Reinhard Bingener and Markus Wehner, *Die Moskau-Connection Das Schröder-Netzwerk und Deutschlands Weg in die Abhängigkeit*, chapter 6, Munich: C.H. beck Verlag, 2023.
[26] Karnitschnig, 'Putin's Useful German'.
[27] 'How to fight back', *Economist*, 10 May 2007.
[28] Gill, 'How Gerhard Schröder'.
[29] 'Putin and Schröder'.
[30] Nastassia Astrasheuskaya and Guy Chazan, 'Former German Chancellor Gerhard Schröder Nominated to Join Gazprom Board', *Financial Times*, 4 February 2022.
[31] Stern, 'Ukraine's Brave Stand'.
[32] Wolfgang Münchau, 'Decades of foreign policy undone', *Eurointelligence*, 23 February 2022.
[33] Daniel Johnson, 'How Olaf Scholz gave Vladimir Putin the green light to invade Ukraine', *Daily Telegraph*, 26 February 2022.
[34] Karnitschnig, 'Putin's Useful German'.
[35] Laurenz Gercke, 'Ex-German Chancellor Gerhard Schröder mocked for Ukraine comments', *PoliticoEU*, 28 January 2022, https://www.politico.eu/article/germany-ex-chancellor-gerhard-schroder-mocked-for-sucking-up-to-putin/, accessed 3 March 2022.
[36] Astrasheuskaya and Guy Chazan, 'Former German'.
[37] Münchau, 'Decades of foreign'.
[38] Wolfgang Münchau, 'Germany's attitude to Russia is changing. Does it go far enough?', *Spectator*, 5 March 2022, https://www.spectator.co.uk/article/germanys-attitude-to-russia-is-changing-does-it-go-far-enough, accessed 6 March 2022.
[39] Julian Lee, 'Germany Is Trying to Pivot From Russian Oil. It'll Struggle', *Bloomberg News*, 27 March 2022, https://www.bloomberg.com/opinion/articles/2022-03-27/ukraine-war-germany-is-trying-to-pivot-from-russian-oil-it-ll-struggle?srnd=premium-europe, accessed 2 April 2022.
[40] Henry Bodkin and Jorg Luyken, 'Tensions rise as Germany fail to deliver weapons promised to Ukraine', *Daily Telegraph*, 21 March 2022,

https://www.telegraph.co.uk/world-news/2022/03/19/tensions-rise-germany-fails-deliver-weapons-promised-ukraine/, accessed 22 March 2022.
[41] James Warrington and Giulia Bottaro, 'Germany must strike Putin energy deal and Ukraine should give up Crimea', *Daily Telegraph*, 3 August 2022.
[42] 'German ex-chancellor Schroeder spoke with Putin for hours on Thurs night', *Reuters*, 19 March 2022, https://www.reuters.com/world/europe/german-ex-chancellor-schroeder-spoke-putin-hours-thurs-night-newspaper-2022-03-12/, accessed 15 March 2022.
[43] Matthew Lynn, 'Germany can afford to ban Russian gas completely, why hasn't it?', *Daily Telegraph*, 25 March 2022, https://www.telegraph.co.uk/business/2022/03/25/germany-can-afford-ban-russian-gas-completely-hasnt/, accessed 26 March 2022.
[44] @Ischinger, Twitter, 28 March 2022.

CHAPTER 10: ANGELA MERKEL

1954-

Various Europeans who grew up under communism found themselves unexpectedly thrust into leadership positions upon the arrival of democracy after 1989. Their performances naturally varied, but none would have as much staying-power as Angela Merkel. The remarkable thing is that, until well into her thirties, she had displayed no interest in politics and, indeed, when the Berlin Wall fell in 1989, her response was a nonchalant one. But once she drifted into the politics of the newly unified Germany, she proved a master practitioner, outsmarting and side-lining far bigger people. Her self-control, taciturnity, and deceptively homely manner concealed a ruthlessness that enabled her to become Chancellor of Germany within fifteen years. Another sixteen as the leader of the country with the largest population in Europe, and the fourth largest economy in the world, followed. This was a period of prolonged crisis in the political economy of Europe, impacting terribly on southern countries. In the east, a Russia increasingly contemptuous of international norms, steadily menaced peace and security in much of its neighbourhood. But despite enjoying pre-eminence among European leaders, her response to the challenges shaking post-Cold War Europe was often a timorous and transactional one. Under her, Berlin became known as 'a city where issuing sonorous proclamations of "responsibility" and the "lessons of history" is often assumed to be the same thing as actually acting on them'.[1]

She was a pro-market centrist committed to Germany's long-term international partnerships who otherwise displayed few strong beliefs. She strove to ensure that German interests were never lost sight of, as more power accrued to EU institutions. Her relations with an assertive and unpredictable Russia were ultimately shaped and driven by commercial considerations rather than the need to be a reliable guardian of democratic Europe.

She stuck to established routines even as cracks grew more visible in the early twenty-first century European edifice. Avoiding unnecessary risks or the need for change, either at home or in the wider global framework, became dominant reflexes. She only broke with caution with her scrapping of nuclear energy or abrupt decision to allow entry to one million refugees from the Middle East in 2015, if she thought it kept her in step with public opinion. Her level of popularity remained high because she was seen as keeping uncertainty and danger at bay in an increasingly unpredictable world. But her political vehicle, the Christian Democratic Union (CDU) grew steadily weaker as her reign lengthened.

She was a skilled political manager whose chief priority too often seemed to be the preservation of her own ascendancy, rather than using her leverage and power to secure long-term improvements in the condition of Germany or enable it to handle responsibility at the European level. A mood of self-satisfaction and complacency prevailed for much of her years at the top with little serious debate encouraged within her party or the wider society about options for the future. Merkel obstinately clung to an economic model based on exporting high-end industrial goods to China and importing cheap gas from Russia. This was despite the internal and external behaviour of both states demonstrating to clearer-eyed analysts that it was a reckless short-term expedient that exposed Germany and much of the rest of Europe to growing dangers.

The sense that history had been put on hold during her ascendancy vanished within months of her retirement with Russia's invasion of Ukraine in 2022. Her record, particularly at the international level, was promptly subjected to a level of scrutiny and often scorn, which it had rarely received during many years when she was seen as a dependable helms-woman imbued with a strong, if rather undefinable, moral authority.

Several paradoxical features stand out from Angela Merkel's 35 years of existence in the communist world. Angela Kasner, as she was then called, was born in Hamburg in 1954, but moved east a few weeks later when her father, a Lutheran pastor, took up a post in the Soviet-controlled East Germany (Deutsch Demokratische Republik: DDR) on the other side of the border. This move occurred just as large numbers of Germans were heading in the opposite direction to seek a better and freer life in West Germany.

She grew up in an unusual environment, in a seminary north of Berlin. This was alongside trainee pastors and disabled residents who were being taught to farm. Because of her father's job, her family acquired two cars and were allowed books and travel opportunities denied to other East Germans. Horst Kasner belonged to a group of ministers prepared to co-operate with the communist authorities.[2]

Her father had been instrumental in the creation of a separate Protestant church in the GDR—allowing GDR officials to keep a closer watch on its members. Joachim Gauck, a former East German pastor and dissident, who, in 2012, was elected President of Germany, once told a colleague that people in the pre-1989 Lutheran Church distanced themselves from Kasner, a member of the regime-controlled Federation of Evangelical Pastors.[3]

Later critics of Merkel have speculated that her DDR background influenced her decision-making in relation to Russia and other matters, but without any evidence being offered. She was a member of the *Freie Deutsche Jugend* (FDJ, (Free German Youth), but this was typical for her generation. She neither joined the East German peace movement nor the opposition groups that began to emerge in the eighties. But nor did she display any sympathy or support for the East German system.[4]

Her choice of theoretical physics as a profession, points to her having scant political interests. She later claimed she wanted to avoid a university subject or profession involving state indoctrination. She was a diligent student with a remarkable work ethic, studying at Karl Marx University in Leipzig before getting a doctorate in quantum chemistry. Earlier, at the age of 15, she had won a trip to Moscow as a prize for her performance in East Germany's national Russian-language competition'.[5] Eight years later, in 1977, she married a fellow scientist, Ulrich Merkel. The marriage didn't succeed, but she retained his name.[6]

Not only her numbness to politics, but her down-to-earth manner was on display in the way she passed 9 November 1989, when the Berlin Wall fell. It was a Thursday, the day that Merkel used to go to a sauna with a friend: 'Even though she was aware of the famous press conference at which the allowance to travel to West Germany had been made public, she did not alter her routine. After she had left the sauna, she heard that the borders had been opened. Thus, instead of having a beer with her friend, she visited West Berlin. She returned to East Berlin not too late, though, because she had to get up early the next morning, as she later recalled'.[7]

Amid the chaos of East Germany's final days, she landed a job as spokeswoman for its last prime minister, Lothar de Maizière. She proved sufficiently capable in this role for Helmut Kohl, the Chancellor of the newly reunited Germany, to appoint her as his Minister for Women in 1991. By now, she was a member of the Bundestag for a north-eastern coastal constituency (which she would represent for the next 31 years). Gunther Krause, then probably the most influential East German figure in the CDU, had taken her under his wing.

With his help, she was placed on the CDU party list in Mecklenburg-West Pomerania and became a candidate in a district in the same state. She learned how to organise political majorities, win debates, and 'sit out' political controversies until they faded away, (a speciality of Kohl's).[8] To the avuncular Kohl, she was little more than a political mascot, his *mädchen.* As a divorced and childless Protestant woman with no children (who remarried in 1998), she did not fit well into the party culture of the CDU, which was dominated by Catholic male politicians, often lawyers, from the south and west of the country. She mattered, however, because unlike many aspirant politicians from the DDR, she had no embarrassing skeletons in her closet. She also showed that she was no pushover, despite lacking a significant power-base inside the CDU. After a few years, she helped overthrow her original patron, Krause. Later, in 1999, she launched an audacious bid to supplant Kohl after he admitted breaking strict rules governing the financing of parties. His 'girl' promptly wrote a press article stating that 'We who now have responsibility for the Party, and not so much Helmut Kohl, will decide how to approach the new era'.[9] It was a gamble, but it paid off and by 2000 she had been elected head of the CDU. She won widespread support as a kind of 'Trümmerfrau', 'an icon of the post-war period in which women uncomplainingly cleaned up the ruins of war in order to help rebuild the country'.[10] Afterwards, Kohl told a friend that championing her had been the biggest mistake of his life: 'I brought my killer, I put the snake on my arm.'[11]

Prominent women had long been absent from German politics and Merkel had sense enough not to overplay her hand. She stood aside to allow Manfred Stoiber, the leader of the CDU's powerful sister party, the Christian Social Union (CSU) in Bavaria, to be the candidate for Chancellor in the 2002 Bundestag elections. After his defeat, nobody could out rank her, and potential rivals, such as Friedrich Merz (who eventually succeeded her as leader decades later), were encouraged to find other careers.

She was elected chancellor by the Bundestag on 22 November 2005, but this was only after a poor performance in the elections which had taken place in September, giving the CDU a very slim lead but no majority to govern alone. She managed to unite the party and bargained effectively with the Social Democrats (SPD) for a so called 'grand coalition' government.

Merkel's elevation came hard on the heels of the rejection of a proposed European constitution by French and Dutch voters in referenda held earlier in 2005. It could have been an opportunity for her to confront some of the major defects in the EU. Not least of these was that countries with incompatible economic needs had been placed in the currency union launched in 1999. If one Eurozone member got into difficulties, then it would be hard to prevent contagion spreading, because of the absence of a central lender able to rescue the stricken nation. But 'Merkel never wanted to open up fundamental issues in the EU and she was not interested in profound reforms'.[12] Instead, the European Constitution was rebranded as the Lisbon Treaty and passed in 2009. Not only did it increase the German voting weight in the EU institutions, but it gave the European Court of Justice jurisdiction over all areas of EU law for the first time, upgrading it from an economic tribunal into a supreme court'.[13]

Her predecessors, Kohl and Schröder, had allowed Italy, and later Greece, to join the single currency even though they did not fulfil the criteria for being viable members with sound finances. It was a political decision, Kohn feeling 'the weight of history' on his shoulders.[14] Merkel's response was equally political when, in the wake of a financial crisis that erupted in the United States in 2009, lending dried up, sending interest rates on government debt soaring and a hugely overdrawn Greece was plunged into crisis. Initially, the Greek crisis was played down by her as a local difficulty which Greece would have to manage. In March 2010, she ruled out the possibility of Greece being bailed out financially as this violated the 1992 Maastricht treaty which laid down the rules for the Euro. But by May, she was prepared to ignore EU statutes and break these rules once it became clear that banks in the creditor nations which had heavily invested in Greece, would suffer huge losses.[15] Accordingly, Greece was provided with a loan under punitive terms that triggered a deep recession, with the Greek economy shrinking by 21 percent over the next four years, and the political system destabilised. As the crisis spread across the Mediterranean from Iberia to Cyprus, the same harsh formula was repeated. The debtor states, not the creditor ones, in the Eurozone were required to carry out massive cuts which weakened their economies and produced intensifying social misery. Germany was able to impose its will through its control of key bodies in the EU apparatus, not least the European Central Bank (ECB). During 2011, Merkel publicly berated the Mediterranean states for being addicted to vacations and early retirement, unlike Germany, despite OECD statistics revealing that no foundation existed for her claim.[16] The progressive weakening of these countries, as capital flowed out of them, was allowed to continue until mid-2012 before the acuteness of the financial crisis in Spain and Italy forced a re-think: 'only then did she agree to let the ECB assume its role as lender of last resort. It took direct intervention by Barack Obama to extract this concession'.[17] 'Real leadership,' wrote economic analysts Professors Matthias Matthijs and Daniel Kelemen, 'would have required acknowledging and addressing the structural roots of the eurozone woes'.[18]

Historian Timothy Garton Ash contended that 'the chancellor has an extraordinary power to lead, and she missed that chance and let the narrative of the idle, corrupt south, preying on the virtuous north, become established in German public opinion and politics'.[19] Attending Kohl's 80th birthday celebration in 2010, Merkel listened to criticism from her predecessor, for not doing enough to help Greece. He complained about 'people who act as though Greece does not matter'.[20]

It would have been less costly for EU states, less time-consuming, and less damaging for the social and economic fabric of Greece, if the country had been offered 'a safe and supported path out of the euro zone. That is the course of action that Finance Minister Wolfgang Schäuble has supported internally for years'.[21] Instead, Merkel clung to a moralising discourse which produced years of crisis at the top of European institutions and dashed belief in further ambitious steps to merge economic and financial institutions within the Eurozone. It was only during the 2020-21 Covid pandemic that she approved the creation of financial instruments that let the EU issue jointly guaranteed debt, and dispense some of the cash as grants, rather than yet more loans on distressed countries.[22] Following the Russian attack on Ukraine, the immense sacrifices Germany demanded of other countries during the European debt crisis and the ruling elite's extreme reluctance to impose far smaller costs on itself despite the undeniable irresponsibility of energy policies emboldening a dictatorial Russia, were recalled in many quarters.

Growing Russian unpredictability would be a headache for Merkel throughout her chancellorship. She preferred to confront it with minimalist measures. Her election programme in 2005, used blunt language to distance itself from the SPD's policy, towards Russia and China, one 'bereft of principles'. It backed strong ties with Russia – but not at the expense of its neighbours.[23] However, in coalition with the SPD, Merkel stood over almost identical policies. The Nord Stream pipeline begun under her predecessor as chancellor, Gerhard Schröder, continued to be built. It allowed Russian gas to flow directly to Germany, making a mockery of EU coordination in energy policy. In terms of the CDU, Merkel was hardly out on a limb in shutting her eyes to the lawless and aggressive nature of Russia. Before Vladimir Putin had taken charge in 1999, Kohl had pushed successfully for Russia's admission to the Council of Europe in 1996. He simply brushed aside evidence that Moscow's brutal intervention in Chechnya and its deep human rights shortcomings meant that it fell well short of the standards needed for membership.[24] By 2005, her first year in office, Merkel needn't have probed deeply to see that in Russia, an arbitrary and kleptocratic form of governance was becoming entrenched. The rule of law was increasingly flimsy, as shown by weakening of property rights and civil society. The over five-fold increase in German exports to Russia from 2000 to 2011 meant, however, that there were well-placed lobbies strongly inclined to close their eyes to the predatory nature of Putin's Russia.[25] Their mantra was often *Wandel durch Handel*: change through trade. Deepening economic ties with democracies were bound to smooth the rough edges of the autocracy, a refrain which continued to be asserted even as the evidence for it proved increasingly non-existent.

With her East German background and the command of Russian she had acquired at school, Merkel was in a fairly good position to read the then chameleon-like Russian President's intentions. While on a state visit to Germany in September 2001, he had delivered a speech in Berlin in which he depicted Russia as 'a friendly-minded European country' whose 'main goal is a stable peace on this continent'. The Bundestag was addressed 'in the language of Goethe, Schiller, and Kant'. Putin praised democracy and denounced totalitarianism, receiving an ovation from an audience that included Merkel. But afterwards, Merkel told a colleague: 'This is typical K.G.B. talk. Never trust this guy'.[26]

To the consternation of the Baltic States and Poland, Merkel appeared ready to cast aside her responsibilities as head of the lead nation in shaping Western policy towards Russia. She turned a deaf ear to their warnings that the Nord Steam pipeline gave an increasingly anti-Western Russia a growing hold over the energy security of new EU member states. At the opening ceremony in November 2011, she insisted that Nord Stream was a 'commercial project' only and praised Russia as an 'outstanding partner for Europe's energy supply'.[27] (By coincidence, the pipeline emerges from the Baltic Sea close to Greifswald in her electoral district).

There were occasional moments when Germany put aside a transactional interpretation of the bilateral relationship. Thus, the role it played in securing the release from prison in 2013 of the former oil mogul Mikhail Khodorkovsky, was an indication that human rights issues had not completely been lost sight of. Similarly, in 2020, prompt action by Merkel helped save the life of the opposition leader Alexei Navalny after he was poisoned by a nerve agent while on an internal Russian flight. Merkel said that the crime committed against him violated the 'basic values and basic rights' that Germany and its allies upheld.[28]

Such gestures aside, Merkel initiated no moves to better prepare the West to stand up to an increasingly bellicose Russia which had invaded Georgia in 2008 and would occupy parts of Ukraine six years later. Another coalition with the SPD, inaugurated in 2013, repeated the tired formula that 'security in and for Europe can only be achieved with, not against Russia'.[29] A modernisation of defences along NATO's eastern flank were not considered.[30] Frank-Walter Steinmeier, Gerhard Schröder's Chief of Staff, and President of Germany from 2017, was an enthusiastic proponent of the 'common spaces' idea with Russia as foreign minister in Merkel's third government. He was also known for naive statements on the rule of law in Russia.[31] This might have been a worthy attempt at Germany seeking to exercise soft power, but as the German security expert Wolfgang Ischinger later noted, '...soft power without hard power is like a football team without a goalkeeper'.[32]

Germany had been running down its armed forces for years. It spent little more than one percent on defence which meant that the German armed forces effectively abandoned their role as the core land defence component of NATO.[33] Ursula von der Leyen, before becoming head of the European Commission in 2019, had been Germany's defence minister for six years. There was no effort by either her or Merkel, who had taken the CDU well to the left, to challenge marked pacifist tendencies in public opinion and make the case for fresh investment in defence.

If strong figures had remained in the CDU, able to make the case for not neglecting Germany's Euro-Atlantic security responsibilities as the post-Cold-War order came under assault in different ways, Merkel might have been pressurised into ending Germany's chronic military weakness. But her authority was, after only a few years as Chancellor, unquestioned in the CDU. She could easily ignore Kohl who, in a book of interviews called *Aus Sorge um Europa* published in 2011, slammed her for tearing down 'his' Europe, turning her back on nuclear energy, getting too close to Putin, and mishandling the Eurozone crisis.[34]

Her outlook on the post-Cold War security architecture, developed in the 1990s, was not a heretical one. She supported George Bush's invasion of Iraq and on its eve, published an article in the *Washington Post* of 20 February 2003, titled 'Schroeder doesn't speak for all Germans'. She bonded with Barack Obama around liberal Atlanticist principles, didn't make an issue of it when the bugging of her private mobile phone by the American intelligence service emerged, and never broke with his outspoken successor as US President, Donald Trump, despite colossal divergences in outlook.

Merkel was an assured tactician, quietly adjusting policies to suit day-to-day requirements and calmly responding to sudden crises (remaining in regular telephone contact with Putin through her years in power). Vacillation characterised her rule in different ways. Inertia when confronted with major challenges may have stemmed from her growing reliance on detailed briefings on public attitudes on various issues. She sat on the fence before adopting a policy position. So ingrained was this tendency, that in 2015, the *Langenscheidt* dictionary's word of the year was *merkeln*: 'to Merkel' is 'defined as "to do nothing, make no decisions, issue no statements"'.[35]

But delay and dither could be punctuated by sudden rash departures, ones producing fateful consequences. One was her abrupt decision, in the wake of the 2011 Fukushima Daiichi nuclear disaster in Japan, to close eight of Germany's 17 nuclear plants. This move led on to the policy of *Energiewende*, the "energy transition" aimed at phasing out all nuclear power plants by 2022 and a sharp shift towards decarbonising the economy.[36] She turned against nuclear energy on the basis of one incident, in a country vulnerable to natural disasters, but declined to take on the coal lobby, as a result of which, German carbon emissions per capita soon far exceeded those of Britain and France.

Coherent long-term planning on energy was hard to detect. It was also conspicuous by its absence in the digital economy. By 2022, Germany had only the 34th fastest average internet connection speed of the 38 most industrialised nations.[37] Merkel seemed numb to the challenges of the digital age. As cars metamorphosed into computers on wheels, a manufacturing rival like South Korea made the digital switch, but German companies like VW, Daimler, and BMW didn't and, by 2021, Tesla was worth three times as much as the three combined.[38]

It has been argued that 'successive Merkel governments were slavishly beholden to the car industry. This compliance helped to bring about the *Dieselgate* scandal, which arose upon it being revealed that Volkswagen was installing software that enabled its cars to cheat during emissions testing. German regulators overlooked the scandal, which was broken by the US authorities. Merkel's response to the fiasco revealed a deep anti-entrepreneurial streak: the carmakers received massive cash subsidies from the state rather than being forced to clean up their act and become more competitive.[39] (Hungary is the location of major German car manufacturers, who benefit from cheap local labour. It has sometimes been argued that Merkel's reluctance to move against its prime minister Viktor Orbán, for his prickly stance on various issues, stems from the importance of this investment for the German economy).

For many years, sharp examination of Merkel's policy record was avoided and indeed could appear at times to be heresy, given her reputation as a bulwark of stability. But as her rule neared its end and it became impossible to conceal various mistakes, the taboo was increasingly broken. In June 2021, Wolfgang Münchau begged the rhetorical question: why did the leader of a rich country like Germany fail to invest in new technologies? Why did she refuse to lay solid foundations for the euro area? Why did she do business with Putin and make her country dependent on Russia's natural resources? Why did she agree to climate change targets and then fail to implement them?'[40]

His explanation was the primacy that Merkel had built up at home and the lack of opportunity to challenge her agenda. Her record might have come under critical scrutiny far sooner if the quality of reporting on German affairs, particularly in Britain and America, had been higher. But instead, it had a reverential quality right up until her departure from office. Columnists in the left-wing press and the corporate media burnished her image as the regal stateswoman of Europe.[41] Germany's apparent stability was embodied in the country's unruffled leader.

The veteran British journalist John Kampfner had a book published in 2020 called *Why the Germans Do it Better: Notes from a Grown-Up Country* in which he contrasted febrile, immature Britain with a serious and adult Germany. He was in no doubt that: 'Much of contemporary Germany's resilience has been wrapped up in the personality of one woman, Angela Merkel'.[42]

The numerous British commentators, who were post-national in outlook, saw her as the doughty champion of post-Cold War global liberalism. They often viewed her as an idealist, when in fact defending the German national interest was her abiding preoccupation. They usually fought shy of exploring how a German mercantilist policy designed to underpin the interests of German firms and financial institutions in EU policy-making was at the centre of her internationalist stance. It was only the outbreak of war in Ukraine in 2022, which led to any deep-seated exploration of how German hunger for Russian gas had helped entrench a regime in Moscow that was increasingly hostile to Western democratic values. It only became acceptable in the mainstream media to explore Germany's role in strengthening a predatory Russian order once Putin's army fell on Ukraine in 2022.

Hagiography on behalf of Angela Merkel briefly stalled in late 2015 when, without consulting EU partners, she opened the borders for Middle Eastern refugees, a million of whom eventually settled in Germany. It was a completely unexpected decision. A few months before, an encounter with Reem Sahwil, a 14-year-old Palestinian refugee who spoke flawless German, was filmed on television. When the girl expressed her fear that her family would be deported, Merkel told her that if everyone like her stayed, thousands of other refugees from the Middle East and Africa would flood into Germany, something the country couldn't cope with. When Sahwil began to cry, Merkel said: 'But you've done really well for yourself. Let me give you a stroke' which she proceeded to do.[43]

But she abruptly reversed her stance when opinion polls indicated that most Germans favoured a compassionate response to multitudes of

Syrians who were heading towards Germany. The borders were opened and soon she was shooting selfies with young Syrian men. But attitudes changed after reports of mass assaults on women at New Year celebrations in Germany, involving some of these refugees. The CDU began to suffer in the polls. Very quickly, Merkel reversed gears and placed restrictions on further entry. Ultimately, her refugee policy was more successful in dividing Europe than in alleviating the humanitarian crisis.[44]

During the presidency of Donald Trump, it was no surprise that Merkel was seen as a substitute leader of the free world. She was much in demand as a speaker able to offer a degree of moral purpose in an increasingly strained Western political order. She placed continuing faith in the concept of global government, best exemplified by a European project transferring powers and competencies towards a post-national centre. Few commentators probed that Germany was the one country which defied gravity and managed to ensure its national priorities shaped the European agenda in key respects. German dominance of European policy-making was something that at the end of the Cold War had been feared in different quarters. But when it transpired, it acquired a benign dimension, given the respect German leadership under Merkel was held in.

Only in a few quarters did the decision to press ahead with a second gas pipeline, between Germany and a Russia which had been fighting a war in eastern Ukraine since 2014 through proxies, indicate that she might have lost the feel for important underlying realities. Polling actually showed that society was becoming far more wary of Putin's Russia than many in the German elite were. In March 2015, an Allensbach opinion poll pointed to the German public's clear position on who was primarily responsible for the conflict in Ukraine. Fifty-five percent of respondents blamed Russia, while only 20 percent blamed Ukraine. Only eight percent of respondents said they had a positive view of Putin, down from 43 percent in 2001. But only three percent opposed Nord Stream 2.[45]

In 2017, a sharp decline in Merkel's electoral potency was evident. The CDU/CSU suffered an electoral loss of 8.6 percent, while the right-wing *Alternative für Deutschland* (AfD) gained almost the same amount. This anti-system party would soon have a foothold in all 16 regional parliaments. Sharing power with it was anathema, so once again she turned to a grand coalition with the SPD, which had also made big losses, an alliance that it took six months to hammer together.[46]

In a speech to CDU MPs in 2018, she compared the darkening global horizon to the period preceding the Thirty Years' War (which ravaged what is today Germany) and warned of the complacency that long years of peace can induce.[47] Yet she had spent 16 years refusing to restore the health of the euro by embarking on a fiscal union on workable foundations, preferring instead fiscal surveillance by Germany and other creditor nations in the Eurozone over the indebted ones.[48] She also showed insouciance about the danger that Britain might quit the European Union, which happened after 52 percent of voters endorsed the idea in a referendum held on 23 June 2016. She had been unbending after Prime Minister David Cameron asked for her support in his quest to make Britain exempt from elements of the EU's expanding bureaucracy. Earlier, in 2014, she had installed arch-integrationist Jean-Claude Juncker as EU Commission chief, against British objections. This violated the Brussels convention that no major state is ever overruled on this key post.[49]

She also brushed aside warnings from Poland's former foreign and defence minister, Radek Sikorski and others, who claimed that the privileged energy partnership with Russia revealed a side to post-1945 Germany that was selfish and parochial.[50] He caustically observed that Germans, 'for the first time in history found themselves surrounded by exclusively friendly states. And they didn't feel our pain of being a flank country, of being on the edge of the world of democracy, rule of law and security'.[51] Heiko Maas of the SPD, foreign minister from 2017 to 2021, was especially unapologetic about criticism towards his country's energy pact with Russia, whether it came from the USA, the European Parliament (which condemned Nord Stream 2 by 433 votes to 105 in December 2018), or from East European states.[52]

Perhaps no other figure on the centre-right of European politicians was as capable of smoothly transacting political business with the left, as Merkel was. In 2022, the former leader of the far-left Die Linke Gregor Gysi even suggested that Merkel should be sent to Moscow to negotiate a ceasefire with Putin.[53]

In 2018, Merkel announced that she would not be standing for a fifth term as chancellor. Her party had run out of ideas and drive as it became increasingly indistinguishable from the moderate wing of the SPD. One journalist remarked that 'she never became mentally a part of the CDU. She is strange to everything in the Party. It is only a function of her power, nothing else'.[54]

By contrast, her working relations with a varying cast of SPD figures usually proceeded smoothly. Steinmeier, Olaf Scholz and others displayed scant concern about Germany having acquired a Russian-dominated energy sector and could be relied on to turn a blind eye to Putin's excesses, or those of minions such as Aleksander Lukashenko in Belarus.[55]

John Kornblum, a former U.S. Ambassador to Germany, remarked in the middle of her rule that: 'If you cross her, you end up dead. There's nothing cushy about her. There's a whole list of alpha males who thought they would get her out of the way, and they're all now in other walks of life'.[56] Her designated female successor, Annegret Kramp-Karrenbauer (AKK) fell victim to this ruthlessness after she dared to try to distance the party from Merkel's refugee policy. Merkel helped drive her out as CDU leader in February 2020.[57] The substitute she foisted on to the party was 'the gaffe-prone and uninspiring Armin Laschet. He was one of the most unabashed defenders of the energy alliance with Putin in German politics. Gerhard Schröder's assertion made in 2020 that 'Russia is an important partner for Europe, not only for political reasons. We need the mineral resources that the country has in large quantities', could just as easily have come from this drab regional worthy, given his track-record.[58]

Merkel was bowing out as chancellor, the only one since 1949 to have done so voluntarily. Her decision to foist a figure like Laschet on the electorate is an indication that she did not anticipate that allowing the Russian dictatorship to exercise domination over the German energy sector might lead to worse destabilization in East-Central Europe. Nor it seems did the administration of President Joseph Biden in the USA. In July 2021, it unexpectedly agreed to end longstanding US opposition to the Nord Steam 2 project. Its completion had been delayed by up to a year, and at least $1 billion added to the cost, after several key participants pulled out after being threatened with sanctions by the previous administration. US acquiescence occurred without any recognizable benefit in exchange: Merkel had neither promised increased engagement for NATO nor more caution about its deepening economic ties with China.[59]

Under Laschet, the CDU fell an astonishing 8.9 percentage points to obtain only 24 percent of the vote in the Bundestag election held in September 2021, easily its worst post-war result. Until the Russian invasion of Ukraine in February 2022, it would have been reasonable to expect Merkel to have been anticipating a long goodbye of prestigious events on the international stage befitting her stateswoman-like position. But overnight, her record as a maintainer of European peace seemed devalued if not obsolete. She contented herself with a statement four days after the attack that:

> 'There is no justification for this blatant breach of international law. This war of aggression by Russia marks a profound turning point in the history of Europe after the end of the cold war'.[60]

AKK, once Merkel's heir apparent, was far more direct and delivered her own mea culpa: 'I'm so angry at ourselves for our historical failure. After Georgia, Crimea and Donbas, we have not prepared anything that would have really deterred Putin. We have forgotten the lesson... that negotiation always comes first, but we have to be militarily strong enough to make non-negotiation not an option for the other side'.[61]

Within hours of the invasion, the head of the German army, General Alfons Mais, revealed the poor state his political masters had left the Bundeswehr in: 'the army that I have the privilege to lead, is more or less stripped bare. The options that we can offer politicians to support the [NATO] Alliance are extremely limited'.[62] Foreign minister Annalena Baerbockt from the Green Party, who had refused to sell arms to Ukraine in February 2022, was stating in late March, that the time had arrived for 'post-pacifism'. On 27 February, German Chancellor Olaf Scholz announced a shift in German defence and energy policies in response to

Russia's action in Ukraine. He promised that Germany would become Europe's biggest defence spender and that immediate measures would be taken to reduce its energy dependence on Russia. Sweeping sanctions on Russia would be imposed. But they would stop short of energy imports, which Germany would continue to purchase.[63]

Perhaps with the limits of the German response in mind, Ukraine's President Volodymyr Zelensky was blunt when he addressed the Bundestag by video link from his war-torn country on 17 March: He accused Germany of sacrificing Ukraine to protect its own business interests, saying:

> 'We see how many links your companies still have with Russia, with a country that uses them, and those of other countries, to finance the war…We warned you. We told you Nord Stream was a preparation for war. We were answered, it's a question of business. It's business, business, business.'[64]

Central figures in the relationship with Russia, such as President Steinmeier, went on record to say that: '[T]he way I clung to Nord Stream 2 was clearly a mistake'.[65] As for Merkel, she was invited by Zelensky to visit the ravaged town of Bucha 'to see what the policy of 14 years of concessions to Russia has led to'.[66] Instead, she retreated into silence as the war in Ukraine raged. She was assailed for her mercantilism by the influential George Soros and for her 'feckless reliance on Russian gas' by Nobel laureate for economics Paul Krugman.[67] The conservative daily *Die Welt* hoped for 'a reversal of Merkel's policies of guaranteeing peace and freedom through treaties with despots'.[68]

Three months into the war, a German commentator argued that 'Merkel is starting to look like a Tony Blair figure, lauded in power but whose legacy quickly collapses after leaving office'.[69] She was accused of de facto taking Germany out of NATO, overseeing the collapse of the German military, while allowing the Kremlin to buy (or at least rent) a good part of Berlin's elites.[70] In June 2022, she publicly stated that she had always understood the threat from Putin and was aware that he wanted to destroy Europe. In light of this, she was criticised for failing to 'explain the danger to

Germans and Europeans. By not communicating, she left the continent unprepared'.[71]

Robert Habeck, the economy minister from late 2021, expressed his incredulity upon discovering that Merkel had made no contingency plans in the event of Putin halting energy supplies to Germany.[72] She remained tight-lipped in 2022, when Nord Stream was sabotaged in late September, after leaks developed in the gas pipeline following an attack widely thought to be from an underwater drone. Putin had already substantially halted the gas flow to Germany. Such an end to an economic investment which, in key respects, defined Merkel's chancellorship is ironic given how so much diplomatic capital was used up (and valuable bilateral relationships were tarnished) in order for it to come to fruition.

It is likely that a self-contained Merkel will mount a strong defence of her record in forthcoming memoirs. Perhaps by the time of their appearance, any temptation to make her a sole scapegoat will recede given the realisation that the naivete, self-righteousness, and blindness which led to one of Europe's worst post-war disasters, extended far beyond any single individual. Successive leaders in democratic Germany have preferred to avoid fundamental problems, emphasising instead constraints that impede them from making a constructive response. It is a posture of 'evading the appearance of agency or responsibility'.[73] Still fully on display under her successor Olaf Scholz, it was perhaps under Merkel that this purposeful inaction produced the most harm for Germany and Europe. Merkel's Germany was happy to reap the economic benefits of European integration and peace, but it steadfastly refused to pay the cost required to maintain it.

---

[1] Jeremy Cliffe, 'Germany has become the roadblock at the heart of Europe', *New Statesman*, 21 January 2023, https://www.newstatesman.com/quickfire/2023/01/germany-ukraine-tanks-roadblock-europe, accessed 21 January 2023.

[2] Luke Harding, 'East German past of iron lady revealed', *Observer*, 26 June 2005, https://www.theguardian.com/world/2005/jun/26/books.germany, accessed 11 March 2022.

---

[3] George Packer, 'The Quiet German', *New Yorker*, 1 December 2014, https://www.newyorker.com/magazine/2014/12/01/quiet-german, accessed 11 March 2022.
[4] Werner Reutter, 'Who's afraid of Angela Merkel?', *International Journal*, Vol. 61, No. 1, 2005-6, p.p. 216-18.
[5] Jeremy Cliffe, 'A fatal attraction', *New Statesman*, 27 July 2022.
[6] Dominic Sandbrook, 'Auf Wiedersehen to Angela Merkel', *Daily Mail*, 24 September 2021.
[7] Reutter, 'Who's afraid', p.p. 218-19.
[8] See Mark M. Thompson and Ludmilla Lennartz, 'The Making of Chancellor Merkel', *German Politics*, Vol. 15, No. 1, 2007, p. 105.
[9] Packer, 'The Quiet German'.
[10] See Thompson and Lennartz, 'The Making', p. 106.
[11] Packer, 'The Quiet German'.
[12] Bojan Pancevski, Germany's Scholz vows to overhaul economy as next chancellor', *Wall Street Journal*, 24 November 2021.
[13] Ambrose Evans-Pritchard, 'Angela Merkel's disastrous legacy is Brexit and a broken EU', *Daily Telegraph*, 19 January 2021.
[14] Sven Bőll, Christian Reiermann, Michael Sauga and Klaus Wiegrefe, 'Euro struggles can be traced to origins of common currency', *Der Spiegel Online*, 7-8 May 2012, accessed 17 March 2022.
[15] Open Europe, 'They said it wouldn't happen', 11 May 2010, https://openeuropeblog.blogspot.com/2010/05/they-said-it-wouldnt-happen.html, accessed 5 March 2022.
[16] Charlotte McDonald, 'Are the Greeks the hardest workers in Europe'. *BBC News*, 26 February 2012, accessed 19 February 2022.
[17] Evans-Pritchard, 'Angela Merkel's disastrous'.
[18] Sandbrook, 'Auf Wiedersehen'.
[19] Timothy Garton Ash, 'The fateful chancellor', *New Statesman*, 15 September 2021.
[20] Marcus Walker and Matthew Karnitschnig, 'Zeal and Angst: Germany Torn over Role in Europe', *Wall Street Journal*, 8 May 2010.
[21] Peter Müller and René Pfister, 'How Merkel failed Greece and Europe', *Der Spiegel Online*, 3 July 2015, accessed 11 March 2022.
[22] 'The mess Merkel leaves behind', *Economist*, 25 September 2021.
[23] John Lough, *Germany's Russia Problem: the struggle for balance in Europe*, Manchester: Manchester University Press, 2021, p. 133.
[24] Lough, Germany's Russia, p. 115.
[25] Lough, Germany's Russia, p. 145.
[26] Packer, 'The Quiet German'.
[27] Lough, Germany's Russia, p. 143.
[28] Guy Chezan and Mark Seddon, 'Merkel demands Kremlin explanation as Navalny poisoning confirmed', *Irish Times*, 2 September 2020.
[29] Lough, Germany's Russia, p. 143-44.
[30] Andrew Michta, 'Decision Point: Renewed Transatlanticism or a Post-American Europe?', *American Interest*, 9 July 2020, https://www.the-american-interest.com/2020/07/09/renewed-transatlanticism-or-a-post-american-europe/, accessed 4 March 2022.

[31] Lough, Germany's Russia, p. 131.
[32] Lough, Germany's Russia, p. 2-3.
[33] Julian Lindley-French, 'Putin's great illusion', *The Lindley-French Analysis,* 28 February 2022.
[34] The book is reviewed by János Martonyi in 'Helmut Kohl: man of Germany and Europe', *Hungarian Review,* 13 September 2015, https://hungarianreview.com/article/20150911_helmut_kohl_man_of_germany_and_europe/, accessed 24 March 2022.
[35] Wolfgang Streeck, 'Angela Merkel's empty leadership', *UnHer*d, 23 December 2021, accessed 29 December 2021.
[36] Binoy Kampmark, 'Auf Wiedersehen Mutti: How Angela Merkel's centrist policies shaped Germany and Europe', *The Conversation*, 25 January 2021, accessed 29 December 2021.
[37] Sandbrook, 'Auf Wiedersehen'.
[38] Evans-Pritchard, 'Angela Merkel's disastrous'.
[39] Maurice Frank, 'Angela Merkel was no saint', *UnHerd,* 6 December 2021, accessed 29 December 2021.
[40] Wolfgang Münchau, 'Overrated - now fading', *Eurointelligence,* 26 June 2021, https://www.eurointelligence.com/column/merkel, accessed 29 December 2021.
[41] Matthew Karnitschnig, 'Busting the Merkel Myth', *PoliticoEU,* 2 December 2021, https://www.politico.eu/article/angela-merkel-busting-the-myth-german-chancellor-legacy, accessed 29 December 2021.
[42] Aris Roussinos, 'British Centrists' Deluded Worship of Germany', *UnHerd,* 18 December 2020, accessed 29 December 2021.
[43] Frank, 'Angela Merkel', *UnHerd,* 6 December 2021.
[44] Karnitschnig, 'Busting the Merkel Myth'.
[45] Lough, Germany's Russia, p. 214.
[46] Katja Hoyer, 'When will Germany grow up?' UnHerd, 18 February 2021, https://unherd.com/2021/02/when-will-germany-grow-up/, accessed 29 December 2021.
[47] 'Merkel vergleicht Syrien-Konflikt mit Dreißigjährigem Krieg', Handesblatt, 14 May 2018.
[48] Evans-Pritchard, 'Angela Merkel's disastrous'.
[49] Evans-Pritchard, 'Angela Merkel's disastrous'.
[50] Bojan Pancevski and Joe Wallace, 'With Nord Steam 2 Freeze, Germany Takes First Step to Cut Russian Gas Reliance', *Wall Street Journal*, 23 February 2022.
[51] Stuart Lua, '"We told you so"!: how the West didn't listen to the countries that know Russia best', PoliticoEU, 9 March 2022, accessed 11 March 2022.
[52] Soeren Kern, 'Biden Administration "Surrenders" to Germany on Russian Gas Pipeline', Gatestone Institute, 4 August 2021, https://www.gatestoneinstitute.org/17603/germany-russia-nord-stream-biden-administration, accessed 29 December 2021.
[53] Jőrg Luyken, 'The AfD's unlikely conversion to Merkelism', Spectator Online, 18 September 2022, https://www.spectator.co.uk/article/the-afd-s-unlikely-conversion-to-merkelism, accessed 30 September 2022.
[54] Packer, 'The Quiet German'.

[55] 'Clouds over Merkel's legacy as Russian invasion lays flaws bare', AFP, 12 March 2022, https://www.france24.com/en/live-news/20220312-clouds-over-merkel-s-legacy-as-russian-invasion-lays-flaws-bare, accessed 14 March 2022.
[56] Packer, 'The Quiet German'.
[57] See Wolfgang Streeck, 'Plus Ça Change', *New Left Review*, No. 131, September/October 2021.
[58] Oliver Gill, 'How Gerhard Schröder led Germany into a love affair with Putin', *Daily Telegraph*, 17 March 2022.
[59] Kern, 'Biden Administration'.
[60] Philip Oltermann, 'Germany agonises over Merkel legacy', *Observer*, 5 March 2022.
[61] Daniel Johnson, 'How Olaf Scholz gave Vladimir Putin the green light to invade', *Daily Telegraph*, 26 February 2022.
[62] Soeren Kern, 'Germany, in Historic Reversal, Abandons Pro-Putin Russia Policy', *Gatestone Institute*, 1 March 2022, accessed 2 March 2022.
[63] Kern, 'Germany, in Historic'.
[64] Justin Huggler, 'Volodymyr Zelensky condemns Germany for financing Russian invasion of Ukraine', *Daily Telegraph*, 17 March 2022.
[65] Oliver Moody, 'Merkel's toxic legacy': Germany nears a reckoning over ties to Russia', *Times*, 7 April 2022.
[66] Justin Huggler, 'How the Ukraine war exposed the dark side of Angela Merkel's legacy', *Daily Telegraph*, 9 April 2022.
[67] Christopher Williams, 'George Soros warns Ukraine conflict risks sparking Third World War', *Daily Telegraph*, 24 May 2022. Paul Krugman, 'How Germany became Putin's enabler', *New York Times*, 7 April 2022.
[68] John MacDougall, 'Clouds over Merkel's legacy as Russian invasion lays flaws bare', *Agence France Presse* (AFP), 12 March 2022, https://www.france24.com/en/live-news/20220312-clouds-over-merkel-s-legacy-as-russian-invasion-lays-flaws-bare, accessed 14 March 2022.
[69] Sabine Beppler-Spahl, 'The scapegoating of Angela Merkel', *Spiked Online*, 11 April 2022, https://www.spiked-online.com/2022/04/11/the-scapegoating-of-angela-merkel/, accessed 2 May 2022.
[70] John Schindler, historian, @20committee, Twitter, 18 February 2022.
[71] Andreas Kluth, 'Merkel Will Enter History as the Neville Chamberlain of Our Time', *Bloomberg*, 9 June 2022, https://www.bloomberg.com/opinion/articles/2022-06-09/angela-merkel-s-appeasement-of-vladimir-putin-has-reshaped-her-legacy, accessed 10 June 2022.
[72] Guy Chazan, 'Robert Habeck was Germany's most popular politician. Then he took office', *Financial Times*, 12 January 2023.
[73] Constanze Stelzenmüller, 'Merkel's lack of regrets illustrates the fallacies of Germany's Russia policy', *Bloomberg*, 21 June 2022, https://www.brookings.edu/blog/order-from-chaos/2022/06/21/merkels-lack-of-regrets-illustrates-the-fallacies-of-germanys-russia-policy/, accessed 23 June 2022.

PART 3
CHAPTER 11: PIRATES OF THE MEDITERRANEAN

Southern Europe merits a section on its own, something which is denied the larger Scandinavian landmass. The redoubtable Kekkonen of Finland is one of the twenty figures profiled, but the individuals who influenced Scandinavian politics generally were temperate, predictable and consensual in their approach to party management and their national responsibilities. Admittedly, there were figures like Denmark's Uffe Elleman-Jensen, Sweden's Olof Palme and his successor as Prime Minister Fredrik Reinfeldt, whose zeal for taking bold international stances or opening their countries to much accelerated immigration, marked them out as contentious. They have been followed by Mette Frederiksen, Denmark's Prime Minister since 2015, who is best known for the opposite, an unsentimental and hardnosed stance on immigration. It has made her Europe's most successful Social Democrat. Not long before her re-election in late 2022, Denmark signed an agreement with Rwanda that would allow this African country to be a processing centre for asylum seekers wishing to live in Denmark.[1]

Such assertive types were rare in Scandinavia, whereas in Europe's south they have been easy to spot. But the welfare of the nation is not always closest to their hearts. A proprietorial attitude to the state, shading over into alleged malfeasance, has characterised each of the figures profiled here. Only one, Milo Djukanović has arguably left his country in a better condition than he found it.

Long-term handicaps have made it difficult for the Mediterranean South to evolve towards a Scandinavian ideal of consensus-orientated politics focused less on personalities, factions, and ideologies and more on implementing policies that prove of tangible national benefit.

Periodically, fierce struggles have erupted over scarce resources and limited positions to fill in the apparatus of state. Partisanship has spilled over from the political arena into wider society. Two of the countries that feature in this section have had civil wars in modern times, and afterwards, both Andreas Papandreou and Pedro Sanchez have displayed not a little of the intransigence that marked their countries descent into tragic discord. Memories of foreign domination or interference in internal politics still prove unsettling. Territorial challenges to the integrity of the state and its boundaries surfaced with contrasting intensity and duration in Spain and Italy.

More positively, each of these South European countries have produced reformers with an agenda of modernisation and a disinclination to treat the state as a semi-personal fiefdom: Alcide de Gasperi in Italy who presided over the early post-fascist years of economic recovery; Spain's Felipe Gonzalez who was a pivotal figure in the hazardous transition from Spain's military backed dictatorship to a pluralist civilian regime; Constantin Karamanlis of Greece who was an anchor of moderation in turbulent years from the mid-1950s to mid-1980s; and Portugal's Anibal Cavaco e Silva whose 1986-95 premiership saw economic liberalisation and development after years of polarising rule, first from the right and then the left. But arguably none of these estimable figures was able to leave an enduring mark on institutions or political practices.

National bureaucracies continued to be overly politicised.[2] Strong regulatory bodies able to prevent banks indulging in hazardous practices were often conspicuous by their absence. Italy excepted, most of these countries were ushered into a powerful European decision-making entity not long after the close of dictatorial rule. They were in receipt of substantial transfer of funds from the EU, which were earmarked for infrastructure. Such transfers were described as the means to bring about the convergence of the members of the EU, both old and new, in terms of productivity and living standards. Such a gradual transformation was seen as a prerequisite for creating a common economic and social framework, out of which a politically integrated Europe could emerge.

The 1999 launch of a single currency was hailed as a crucial driver in this journey towards unity. However, political torpor and the prevalence of a group think mentality within elite ranks across the Mediterranean (despite the persistence of power struggles over resources), meant that there was no hard-headed evaluation of the impact of the Euro currency on national economies. The prediction of the well-known economist Alan Walters, made in 1986, that a single currency, with its single monetary policy and uniform fiscal policy, would amplify differences between the stronger and weaker member nations, was disregarded.[3] Nicholas Kaldor, the Anglo-Hungarian economist, had warned as early as 1971, as the first proposals for a Europe-wide money arrangement were being canvassed, 'not only that such a currency would be economically inefficient but that it would undermine the political unity it was intended to promote'.[4] The currency of a monetary zone with economically diverse members would be valued at a rate beneficial for some but disadvantageous for others.

For a decade after 1999, the banks of strongly performing countries channelled investment into ones with weaker economic profiles, characterised by low productivity, high rates of debt and steep inflation. Economic growth stalled in Southern Europe once the arrival of the Euro accentuated the tendency of national economies to be geared towards consumption rather than productivity.

Political leaders ignored the danger signs (if they were even aware of them). The pious hopes that ruling elites would be prudent house-keepers in order to avoid economic shocks, proved to be fanciful. After 2008, 'the eurozone's combination of high government-debt burdens, banking fragility, and low growth' offered the classic conditions for the collapse of investor confidence that plunged the region into crisis.[5] German fund managers, keen to invest capital flows that were the fruit of recurring trade surpluses, had sought easy and quick profits by crowding into what seemed like the perennially sunlit South European investment market.

Germany's iron control of the EU's economic machinery meant that austerity was imposed on the stricken 'Club Mediterranean countries', the term for them used by the British financial journalist Ambrose Evans Pritchard.[6] Recalcitrant national leaders like Berlusconi and Giorgios Papandreou were pressurised into quitting by using market mechanisms or else by means of warning of the dire consequences that could result in defying the ECB's formula for managing the crisis - with the interests of banks that had made unwise investments kept firmly in mind.

The quality of governance and effectiveness of national institutions tumbled in the countries most affected by the Eurozone crisis, perhaps only Spain defying the trend. It had enjoyed some of the best years of its troubled modern history in the decades before the appearance of the Euro. Arguably, the Franco regime in Spain had displayed a modernisation urge after1960 as strong as that seen in democratic Italy. The post-authoritarian political system that emerged with the dictator's death in 1975, was more disposed to consensus and pact-making among different political contenders than equivalents in Greece or Portugal. A corps of neutral officials existed which, under the restored constitutional monarchy, guided the country through different challenging episodes.[7] The bail-out funds eventually released by Chancellor Merkel were used more effectively by Spain in the mid-noughties than elsewhere, and the condition of troubled banks improved.[8] However, an alarmingly high youth unemployment rate of 18 percent refused to budge.

In Italy and Greece, youth unemployment also soared during the decade when Germany imposed its deflationary preferences on the Club Med countries. Especially for those with advanced qualifications, there was a flight abroad in search of better prospects. It meant that in this economically stricken part of Europe, the constituency for political and economic renewal actively diminished.

In Italy, the left was enmeshed with ailing financial institutions, such as Italy's oldest bank, the scandal-ridden Banca Monte dei Paschi di Siena (MPS).[9] It meant that it struggled to act as a credible alternative for the populist showman Berlusconi. A series of leaders in the Democratic Party quickly came and went. Under local government fixers, the non-communist left had been discredited by municipal corruption scandals. Thirty years later, with former communists increasingly to the fore, the promotion of different forms of identity politics preoccupied the left and damaged its appeal. A quirky New Age force, the 5-Star movement, did well in the 2013 and 2018 parliamentary elections. Elections in the autumn of 2022 pushed to the forefront a conservative right-wing coalition headed by Giorgia Meloni of the Fratelli d'Italia (Brothers of Italy) which had surpassed the populist Lega and Berlusconi's Forza Italia. Despite lacking any pro-Putin ties and being Atlanticist in her pronouncements, much of the international media greeted the replacement of an un-elected emergency administration under former ECB chief Mário Draghi with an elected one under her, with grave foreboding.

Perhaps the only thing that can be said with any certainty is that opportunist fixers, promiscuous in their allegiances and driven by the search for sinecures, will continue to be a central element in Italian politics. Careerists ready to adjust their positions on everything, from the war in Ukraine to Net Zero, are unlikely to provide active defiance to EU policies still beholden to German interests. In 2022, Polish Prime Minister Mateusz Morawiecki said the threat of imperialism in the EU needed to be fought like Russian imperialism and that the EU, instead of being democratic, resembled an oligarchy, with Germany and France wielding the real power.[10] Such a readiness to defy a European status-quo, whose decisions have marginalised and impoverished much of Southern Europe, has numerous adherents in the region. But it evaporates in the world of deal-making politics.

The fate of Greece after 2009 does not give grounds for hope that political renewal will occur, thrusting better quality elected representatives to the forefront. The scale of the austerity between 2009 and 2014 saw raised taxes and reduced state expenditure, equivalent to a reduction of 15 percent in GDP.[11] It led to a completely new political force, the far-left Syriza, winning power in 2016. Against a background in which nearly half of all Greeks between the ages of eighteen and thirty-five said their parents supported them financially, the new government pleaded in vain with Berlin for a relaxation in austerity.[12] Ashoka Mody, then an official with the IMF, closely involved with the bailout strategies of the time, endorsed this call. He believes that 'reduced austerity would have given the Greek economy breathing room to grow over time, [and] the government would have become more capable of repaying its creditors'.[13] EU decision-makers disagreed. Instead, the advice offered by Jeroen Disselbloem, the Dutch Labour Party minister, who was head of the Eurozone group of finance ministers, showed the immense gulf that had opened up between northern and Southern Europe irrespective of party allegiances: 'You cannot spend all the money on women and drinks and then ask for help'.[14] By 2022, more than one-third of Greece's population was living in poverty and a wage of 800 euros a month after tax was common.[15]

Spain was the Club Med country most prepared to stand up to pressure from EU power-holders. A conservative administration under Prime Minister Mariano Rajoy guided the country out of serious recession before its parliamentary defeat in 2018. A Socialist-communist coalition under the brash and sometime confrontational Pedro Sanchez, who was very much in the tradition of Craxi and Papandreou, has been propped up by separatist parties mainly from Catalonia. In 2017, several of them had staged a rebellion in a failed attempt to secede from Spain. This is a dramatic *volte-face*, since Felipe Gonzalez, the most successful-ever leader of Spain's Socialist Workers Party (PSOE) as well as being a key architect of Spain's democratic transition, had been an implacable foe of militant separatism. Death squads had even been sanctioned by his government in the late 1980s in order to try and crush a campaign of murder and kidnapping in the Basque Country. By contrast, Sanchez amnestied leaders of the 2017 rebellion in 2021 and, in the following year, he agreed to the demand of his Catalan allies that the teaching in Spanish in state schools in the region be discontinued, despite the strong demand for it. The contrasting stances of the two former socialist leaders, one of working-class origins, the other the son of a high-ranking state bureaucrat, shows how far the need to make identity politics the centre of the left's appeal, has advanced in just a few decades.

Increasingly multi-racial, Portugal still retains a degree of cultural homogeneity, and it offers some other contrasts with the Club Med countries with which it is invariably bracketed. Through a decade of economic crisis and austerity, governmental stability has been the norm. From 2015, the Socialist Party (PS) has acquired increasing dominance of national affairs. Its readiness to break a long-held convention and rule with the backing of Marxist-Leninist and Trotskyite parties, enabled it to form a government even though well-behind the centre-right in terms of seats. By the time it won an overall majority from nervous voters at the end of the Covid pandemic in January 2022, it was building a concentration of power extending from local government to some of the major state institutions and not excluding the shrinking number of major private firms. It possesses a key political weapon which helps to explain its hegemony: the control of transfer funds from Brussels, which are needed to maintain public services in the face of declining productivity. Much of the funding is allocated in order to reinforce relations of dependency in an ageing population, with only lip-service paid for the need for economic reform and the introduction of efficient technologies.

Prime Minister António Costa, in office since 2015 (between 2017 and 2021 in alliance with the far-left), insists that the state has to be the motor of economic development. However, the bureaucracy is a byword for inefficiency and nepotism. Only around 45 percent of the Portuguese population between the ages of 25 and 64 have completed the final years of high school education, a lower rate than for all OECD countries other than Mexico and Turkey. In Poland and the Czech Republic, for example, the completion rate is 90 percent.[16] These two central European countries have recently overtaken Portugal in economic terms. Nearly forty years of EU membership have witnessed a decline of private industry, agriculture and fishing – once important mainstays of the economy.

In 1995, Portuguese GDP corresponded to 81 percent of the European average, but by 2023, this is projected to fall to 77.6 percent (despite the later inclusion of EU members which initially were far poorer than Portugal).[17] The public sector employs 15.2 percent of those in work.[18] Many branches of the state increasingly appear to be adjuncts of the ruling Socialists, rather than independent entities removed from politics.[19] The President, Marcelo Rebelo de Sousa, is drawn from the opposition but at times has appeared an accessory of the politically adroit Costa. Under him, criticism of the nepotism associated with periods of left-wing rule is discouraged and even a former governor of the national bank is being pursued in the courts for making awkward revelations felt to be injurious to Costa.[20] In December 2022, he was weakened by the eruption of what was deemed in the media as a major scandal. In March of that year, business manager Alexandra Reis had quit a position in the re-nationalised state airline TAP with a half-million euro pay-off. She was quickly appointed to run the air-traffic control system. A media outcry then ensued within days of her being appointed to the government as treasury minister. It turned out that the wife of her boss, the finance minister, had been a close colleague in TAP (though no wrong-doing is suspected or has been proved). One commentator referred to 'a government of friends, brothers, children, husbands, wives and old colleagues who intersect in the Council of Ministers, regulatory agencies, state-owned companies, city councils, directorates-general; always the same people, naming each other, hopping tirelessly between places in the sphere of the State'.[21] Sinecures for insiders while tax-payers shouldered a burden made worse by high inflation (and young people emigrated in droves due to the lack of jobs), deepened resentment towards the status quo that seemed weighted in favour of insiders. Portugal seemed to be enmeshed in a velvet autocracy, unable to renew itself by recruiting competent people outside its own narrow ranks. The experience of other South European countries would suggest that a turbulent future may await Portugal unless competent alternative leaders emerge (as happened during the last period of systemic crisis in the 1970s).

Stagnant Portugal's stability is now utterly bound up with the smooth continuation of the semi-state EU entity. This looks rather less of a foregone conclusion than it did before the Covid pandemic and the outbreak of a war in Ukraine, which imperils the flow of energy that powers the industry of the main EU paymaster, Germany. Such vulnerability to sudden geopolitical shocks is not the whole story across Southern Europe. Montenegro has been included because it has shown itself adaptable in the face of recurring crises over a lengthy period. Even as 4.6 million people have left the six Western Balkan countries between 1990 and 2019, which amounts to 25 percent of the population, an artful and tough-minded leader, Milo Djukanović, has increased state capacity.[22] If a misgoverned Western Europe faces some of the acute uncertainty which overwhelmed Tito's Yugoslavia in the 1980s, it is quite possible that desperate populations will place their hopes in local or regional leaders who show evidence of being able to carry out some of the functions that once resided in central states. The career of Djukanović, rather than the far better known, and still notorious, Slobodan Milošević, might therefore be the more appropriate one to dwell on.

---

[1] Sune Engel Rasmussen, 'Denmark Prime Minister Poised for Re-Election Amid Surging Inflation, War in Ukraine', *Wall Street Journal*, 1 November 2022.
[2] Dimitri A Sotiropoulos, 'Southern European Public Bureaucracies in Comparative Perspective', *West European Politics*, Vol. 27, No. 3, 2004, p.p. 405-422.
[3] Mody, *Euro Tragedy*, p.p. 173-4.
[4] Christopher Caldwell, 'Let the Whorehouse Burn', *Weekly Standard*, Vol 3, No. 46, 13 August 2018.
[5] Mody, *Euro Tragedy*, p. 393.
[6] Ambrose Evans Pritchard, 'Olaf Scholz must choose between an energy embargo on Russia, or a moral embargo on Germany', *Daily Telegraph*, 15 April 2022.
[7] See Sotiropoulos, 'Southern European'.
[8] Mody, *Euro Tragedy*, p. 393.
[9] Mody, *Euro Tragedy*, p. 369.
[10] 'Poland says Berlin and Paris running EU as an 'oligarchy', *Deutsche Welle*, 16 August 2022, https://www.dw.com/en/poland-says-berlin-and-paris-running-eu-as-an-oligarchy/a-62828931, accessed 4 October 2022.
[11] Mody, *Euro Tragedy*, p. 413.
[12] Mody, *Euro Tragedy*, p.p. 420-21.
[13] Mody, *Euro Tragedy*, p. 414.
[14] Mody, *Euro Tragedy*, p. 430.
[15] James Jeffrey, 'Greece's beauty masks untold poverty', *Spectator*, 18 February 2022.
[16] Mody, *Euro Tragedy*, p. 410.
[17] Luís Rosa 'As vitórias de Cavaco e o poder absoluto', *Observador*, (Lisbon), 6 June 2022, accessed 2 October 2022.
[18] Luís Rosa 'O ogoverno dos funcionários públicos', *Observador*, (Lisbon), 23 August 2021, accessed 2 October 2022.
[19] Luís Rosa 'Um governo ao serviço do partido', *Observador*, (Lisbon), 28 March 2022, accessed 2 October 2022.
[20] Helena Matos, 'Precisa-se manual de boas maneiras para criticar o PS de forma correcta', *Observador*, 21 November 2022, https://observador.pt/opiniao/precisa-se-manual-de-boas-maneiras-para-criticar-o-ps-de-forma-correcta/, accessed 21 November 2022.
[21] João Miguel Tavares, 'O prognatismo mandibular do Governo de António Costa', *Publico*, (Lisbon), 30 December 2022.
[22] Afisa Latić supplied these figures, @Nafisa_Latic

CHAPTER 12: ANDREAS PAPANDREOU

1919-1996

In mid-twentieth century Greece, major fault-lines over ideology and the role of proud and acquisitive institutions, such as the military and the monarchy, as well as the corrosive impact of invasion and occupation, impeded the modernisation of the state and the emergence of a stable democracy. National life remained polarised and unsettled even as stark divisions over the nature of political power receded elsewhere. The 1946-49 civil war between communists and their opponents, ongoing cleavages and rivalries, and then a harsh seven-year military dictatorship (1967-74) imposed by a far-right military faction, disfigured Greece. For almost the next half-century, its politics were marked by partisanship, excess, and unwise decision-making, punctuated by periods of fleeting consensus and stability.

Three generations of one family, the Papandreous, were never far from many of these dramas. George Papandreou (1888-1968) was a traditional purveyor of patronage politics who was on the liberal side of Greek politics. He was Prime Minister periodically in the mid-1960s before the military takeover. That fateful event was facilitated by infighting and intrigue between different vested interests, with the United States finding it hard to remain detached because of Greece's strategic importance during the Cold War. By the time the colonels regime was toppled in 1974, due to its brutality and incompetence, another Papandreou, Andreas (1919-1996), son of George, was poised to begin a tumultuous two decades as the leader of the Pan-Hellenic Socialist Movement (Pasok).

He was an arch-manipulator. His raucous and untidy style of politics bore more relation to populist but non-fascist figures in Latin America, the Middle East or pre-1945 Europe, than to a contemporary social democrat or even a Greek political boss of earlier vintage. The political time frame Greece belonged to suggested that he was an earthy and unruly chieftain presiding over a messy process of democratisation. However, his political style, straight out of a *telenovela* set in Latin America, was a convenient facade which concealed the concentration of power in few hands, the entrenchment of vested interests, and the use of public resources for informal ends. Papandreou differed from 'third way socialists', who were his contemporaries in Europe, by his refusal to conciliate and recruit opposition interests in order to legitimise a system that benefited privileged insiders rather than the citizenry in general. The wider society, although left empty-handed in policy terms in many respects, played a periodic role in the drama of the Papandreou years. Six parliamentary elections were held during his period in, or close to, office and the public were able to play the role of props, either as fervent admirers or else bitter critics of this resourceful firebrand. When death removed him from politics in 1996, it soon became noticeable that Greek politics rapidly reverted to the European norm, influenced by the bureaucratic and technocratic direction being offered by the European Union which Greece had joined in 1981. Politics grew increasingly formulaic and managerial as media and business interests, as well as a class of professionals whose income was largely derived from involvement in politics, prevailed. Privileged insiders allied to various interest groups, filled positions as parties alternated in office. Connections mattered far more than qualifications, a syndrome which was becoming ingrained in other European democracies as the reach of the state lengthened.

Arguably, Andreas Papandreou had been a path breaker, at least in cementing the role of insiders who used nepotism and networking to scale the political heights. Belonging to a high-status political family proved incredibly useful in the tumultuous second quarter of the last century when he came of age. His father was able to extricate him from the secret police of the Metaxas dictatorship in 1939 and send him to the USA to study economics at Harvard. He was released from US army service in July 1944 to be part of the Greek delegation at the founding conference of the United

Nations at Bretton Woods. In 1958, he brought his American wife and four children back to Greece where the then Prime Minister, Constantin Karamanlis, acceded to a request from his father to make available state resources for him to found an economic research institute.[1]

Andreas Papandreou was naturally drawn to the transactional form of politics where connections could be made and exploited for fruitful ends. In 1963, by now a parliamentary deputy for the Centre Union (CEU) with his father running Greece, he remarked: ‘Greece is probably the only country in the world where the prime minister has a son who is an American. And for God’s sake, let’s exploit it'.[2]

Yet he was already emerging as a vocal foe of US-style capitalism and Washington’s policies in Vietnam and the Eastern Mediterranean, especially regarding Cyprus and later Israel. Indeed, in the closing decades of the Cold War, he pursued a fiery anti-Americanism that earned him the reputation as a charismatic nationalist well able to sway the large swathe of a public increasingly resentful of foreign interference in Greek affairs.

Until the descent of the United States into its own frenzied political strife in the second and third decades of the present century, it was hard to classify the maverick Papandreou. But arguably he acquired unconscious emulators on the left of US politics who are building their reputation on strident definitions of identity politics and the need to erase a history of past exploitation and humiliation for what they see as victimised categories in American society.

Papandreou’s ill-defined radical rhetoric and idiosyncratic conduct that occasionally grabbed world headlines, helped conceal the fact that ultimately his intention was to confine power and advantage to the ruling few. Only his extravagant style may have distinguished him from colourless left-wing apparatchiks in West European governing ranks, some of whom were seeking to whittle away checks and balances and maximise their political advantages. Institutions such as parliament, political parties, state regulators, media, and bodies with a civic vocation, were less and less able to restrain figures wielding executive power. Papandreou’s reliance on informal mechanisms, coteries of personal loyalists and economic allies, in order to discharge state business, the way he preferred, was not hidden as it was in other EU states. One of his mistakes was to make little attempt to conceal his enjoyment of power and its trappings. His erratic way of handling the economy, expanding the bureaucracy and raising finance, plunged the state into crisis and ultimately led to Papandreou facing very serious criminal charges. His rule was a poor advertisement for the democratic wave which was supposedly transforming much of southern Europe as the twentieth century drew to a close.

The vitality of dynastic politics in Greece meant that it was not hard for one of Andreas Papandreou's children, Giorgios (1951–), to embark on a successful political career in his turn. He emphasised similar themes of economic and social justice to his father when he became leader of Pasok in 2004 but his style was different. He was a more collegiate and less abrasive figure. His restrained manner was more in keeping with the bearing of contemporaries on the European left in their governing roles. He also had lengthy experience in government which his father had lacked before reaching the summit of politics. But Giorgios' stint as prime minister was brief, lasting from 2009 to 2011. Chronic mishandling of the economy, which was by no means all the fault of Pasok, plunged the country into a deep economic crisis. The European currency, the Euro, whose rules Greece was ill-suited to comply with, placed the country at the centre of an enduring Europe-wide financial crisis.

At one of its key moments, in 2011, Giorgios was prepared to revert to the demagogic practices of his father by holding a referendum in order to increase his leverage, as fellow EU leaders demanded stringent austerity. But these senior EU decision-makers were more than a match for him. The assertion of nationalism collapsed and soon he was out of office and gone from the helm of Pasok. He, like his father, talked the language of personal dignity and national freedom but during their periods of influence and power they arguably produced the opposite. Greeks grew reliant on institutions like the sprawling state bureaucracy, as well as the media and white-collar trade-unions. These bodies, as well as overtly political forces, encouraged a spirit of dependence and weakened a sense of personal responsibility. Community and civic identification eroded in the face of surging materialism and a sense of entitlement, which Andreas in particular, encouraged with his profligate spending policies. Thus, a society which had grown disorientated and fragmented, was ill-placed to resist the harshest austerity measures seen anywhere in post-1945 democratic Europe.

The Greek exposure to the vagaries of *personalised* politics (thriving on the right as well as the left during the country's supposed march to modernity) produced a national calamity which, in social and economic terms, may take years for the country to recover from. It was all a far cry from PASOK, in its early 'anti-imperialist' phase, when it rejected Greece's Cold War orientation while advocating economic 'self-management' and the 'socialisation' of the means of production.[3] In 1974, Andreas and close associates set up a new socialist political force which they refused to describe as a party in order to underscore its radical intent. It was meant to satisfy the hunger for change and had as central demands, full equality before the law, democratization, political participation, social justice and cultural modernisation.[4] A wave of enthusiasm enabled activists and believers to form local cells, even in the country's most remote areas.[5]

Upon Pasok's formation, there was a consensus about ensuring that it should ditch traditional patronage practices and be a democratically-run mass party. But by 1981 when, after 3 elections, Papandreou was able to form a government, such hopes lay in ruins. He resisted pressures to ensure, that during candidate selection, preference should be given to dedicated activists rather than notables. Forty of the 75 members of the party's first Central Committee had been purged by 1977.[6] A forceful Papandreou ensured that a leader-dominated party emerged. Office-holders in his father's old Centre Union enjoyed preference when parliamentary candidates were being elected. They were accustomed to deferring to a chief and instinctively sensed that the party's ideology was largely decorative.[7]

With pliable associates, Papandreou embarked upon upgrading Greece's traditional form of clientelism, where a patron offered favours to supporters in return for loyalty and backing, to something far more ambitious. Greece had joined the EU on the eve of his initial electoral victory which meant that the 1980s were a decade when, thanks to funding from Brussels, the state was in a position to grow rapidly. Public appointments were used to buttress the party's influence within the central and local bureaucracies. Allies, friends and close family members were able to wield patronage in this era of plenty. The case of Dimitra Liani, a woman almost half his age, whom Papandreou took up with late in his career is a case in point. Margaret Papandreou, his wife of over thirty years, helped Dimitra become a member of her husband's private entourage on Olympic Airways in 1985. She even used her influence to land this enterprising younger woman her own chat show on television. She had turned a blind eye to frequent infidelities by her husband that included an illegitimate daughter in Sweden where the family was in exile before 1974. 'Eventually he returns to me,' Margaret Papandreou used to tell close friends. One justification her estranged husband had for the marital break was that she was an unsatisfactory homemaker, complaining that 'she had never even cooked me an egg'.[8]

Papandreou was essentially an old-fashioned magnate with pre-modern tastes in relationships who camouflaged himself as a progressive moderniser. His immense self-belief and skill as a manipulator enabled him to transcend manifold public and private contradictions in his life to keep the party office-seekers loyal to him personally.[9] He convinced old-guard figures and younger careerists that democratic procedures were unnecessarily time-consuming and that his charisma was the party's best asset. Nearly fifteen years were required to elapse before his attempts to treat the state almost as a private fiefdom encountered major opposition. In 1988, Dimitris Halikias, the governor of the Bank of Greece, conducted an investigation which revealed that Papandreou and numerous appointees were deeply implicated in a financial scandal, involving the embezzlement of $300 million, masterminded by a Greek businessman George Koskotas. He was later imprisoned for 25 years, others close to Papandreou (including two finance ministers) received lesser sentences, and he himself was acquitted by eight votes to seven, after a nine-month trial that took place in parliament.[10]

This reputational meltdown was the culmination of increasingly erratic decision-making. Between 1980 and 2004, the Greek public sector expanded so remarkably that it came close to equalling the eurozone average. By 2009, some 850,000 people were employed in the public sector in a country of just under 11 million people.[11]

One analyst described the major missteps that paved the way for eventual fiscal disaster:

> 'A generous wages policy (especially in 1981–1983), the increase in the number of civil servants...indirect nationalization of firms in difficulty, the upgrading of pensions (and rise in the number of beneficiaries, particularly among farmers), high expenditure in the defence sector and, last but not least, Pasok's manifest failure to curb major tax fraud—all dramatically deepened the public deficit and national debt. Social spending climbed during these years, rising from 11.5 percent of GDP in 1980 to 17. 9 percent in 1985'.[12]

A culture of non- respect for rules plagued Pasok from the senior level (ministers, central party bureaucracy, MPs) downwards. High-ranking salaried officials in the bureaucracy, and especially in public enterprises, enjoyed many privileges (high salaries, bonuses, bogus overtime, pension rights) while a much larger group of employees had to be content with far more modest pay.[13] The right to strike was effectively withheld from much of the labour force, thanks to legislation that made it almost impossible to exercise.[14] Meanwhile, the unemployed enjoyed very limited protection, producing 'a deep chasm—one of the deepest in Europe—between insiders and outsiders in the labour market'.[15]

The underdog mentality cultivated by Papandreou, who initially styled himself as the head of a liberation movement, was deceptive. Its discourse may have extolled the dispossessed, but the main beneficiaries of his rule were mobilised groups such as white-collar trade unions, bureaucrats, favoured business groups, and consultants who were unqualified office-seekers.[16]

Pasok's bid to erect a durable power-base by carrying out a thorough colonization of the state bureaucracy, as well as the party's deepening relationship with business interests, which often shared its complacency about financial probity, occurred as its public relations machine noisily proclaimed its radical social credentials. Breakthroughs undoubtedly occurred in a few areas (such as amnesties for those on the losing side in the civil-war) with middle-class citizens often being the primary gainers. Margaret Papandreou and several friends formed the Union of Greek Women early in Pasok's tenure and this socialist feminist group accomplished changes in the civil code, especially the family law section, legalizing civil marriage, eliminating the dowry, enabling women to be heads of household.[17] Informal criteria, such as her proximity to the leader, ensured this breakthrough occurred. All too often, as his years in office lengthened, Papandreou's patronage or protection was, however, extended for dubious reasons. Towards the end of his rule, when a cabinet meeting was discussing corruption charges against a Pasok figure heading a public utility, Papandreou said, "I understand that he wanted to offer himself a small present, but not 500 million!"[18]

Much of Papandreou's attention was taken up with asserting an independent foreign policy that would single Greece out as nobody's puppet. In 1981, he told the London *Times* that he was not prepared to accept, as a permanent arrangement, the existence of the two blocs, NATO and the Warsaw Pact.[19] Much invective was generated against the emotionally-charged issue of US military bases but the number of visits by US warships actually increased after 1981. The US diplomat Monteagle Sterns, who had disparaged Papandreou in a profile sent to the US State Department in 1974, was insouciant about the intent behind his rhetoric when he returned as ambassador in the early 1980s.[20] In 1985, when he was threatening to ban NATO ships carrying nuclear weapons, a British diplomat reported that Papandreou's chief motivation was 'to give his supporters the impression of activity'.[21]

Geopolitical realities meant that embracing neutrality was never a serious option for Greece. In 1984, his government announced that the primary concern of its new defence doctrine was deterring Turkey.[22] Greece remained committed to reliance on the EU for strengthening its economy and improving social conditions. Papandreou could cause occasional scenes at EU summits, but most EU colleagues viewed them as a political act meant to burnish his nationalist credentials at home. Similar latitude was usually shown to his strongly pro-Palestinian stance in the Arab-Israeli dispute. In some EU quarters, his closeness to the Romanian dictator Nicolae Ceauşescu, his backing for the Soviet-inspired crackdown against the Solidarity movement in Poland, and his defence of the shooting down of the Korean Air Lines Boeing 747 by the Soviets were, however, viewed with less indulgence.[23]

Ephemeral stunts such as 'the Five Continent Initiative' for Peace and Disarmament in 1984 involved much junketing and posturing. But the amount of media coverage given to Papandreou's grandstanding as a foe of American imperialism undoubtedly went down well among nationalistic Greeks. His misconduct and mounting policy failures did not result in his outright political rejection, partly because he was able to exploit suspicion of the West within Greek public opinion in the immediate wake of the Cold War.

The tide started to go out in earnest for Papandreou in 1988 when Theodor Stathis resigned as minister of defence procurements on 14 December. His exit was accompanied by an eight-page letter that denounced a series of scandals and deplored the government 'associating with crooks and con men' who embezzled public funds.[24] As the first cracks appeared in Pasok's edifice, it lost its majority in elections held in June 1990. But the drop in support was far less than many might have expected for a party reeling from such grave accusations. Insufficient numbers of voters were convinced of Papandreou's involvement in the Koskotas Affair. Its conservative rival, New Democracy (ND), was only able to rule in coalition with the communists. Such an unexpected denouement led to a much-needed reduction in the political temperature. Pasok's strategy of polarisation, in order to strengthen the loyalty of its base, had arguably damaged social relations. In the countryside, supporters of the two main parties conducted their important social rituals in separate 'blue' and 'green' coffee-shops.[25]

It took three parliamentary elections in under one year before the parliamentary logjam could be broken and ND was able to form a government with a working majority. In office from April 1990 to October 1993, Constantin Mitsotakis was unable to serve a full term due to elite disagreements emanating from the strong feelings in Greece over NATO attempts to end the wars in the former Yugoslavia. Pasok won a comfortable majority but the last two years in office of Papandreou made a mockery of the claim that he was 'the people's guy in power'.[26] The evidence quickly mounted that he was little more than an observer in the unfurling of day-to-day policy.[27] His wife Dimitra and her entourage shared power in uneasy proximity with Pasok regulars. By the mid-1990s, the conflict in the western Balkans was reaching a climax and inflammatory statements emanated from Papandreou's office. He saw the crisis in Yugoslavia, in simple terms, as one nurtured by 'two old friends from the Second World War: Germany and the Vatican'.[28] There is strong evidence for the claim that the Athens government alerted Serbian nationalists (with whom ties were close) about NATO plans to take armed action against them.[29]

By now, Papandreou's health was precarious, and he was forced to resign on 15 January 1996, when it was clear that he could no longer discharge his duties. Dimitra and her *camarilla* who included two Orthodox priests, an astrologer, as well as members of Athenian high society, had been in the driving seat when regional stability was needed more than ever, as NATO got involved in its first military conflict since its inception.[30] (The situation was not unlike the last stint in power of Argentina's Juan Peron in 1972-73 when he was manipulated by unscrupulous elements in league with his wife).

The deeply irresponsible way that power had been exercised, finally sparked a backlash in Pasok. Prime Minister Kostas Simitis from 1996 to 2003, largely ditched noisy populism and made a show of modernising the administration. Giorgios Papandreou, son of Andreas, and party leader from 2004 to 2012, continued along this path but it was largely tinkering. In 2022, the only Pasok deputy left in the European Parliament, Eva Kaili, found herself at the centre of a major bribery scandal which led to her detention and soon rocked the EU institutions to their foundations. In the meantime, the economy of Greece had been ravaged as a result of the ill-advised step taken to join the Euro, and the Papandreou clan's power had turned to dust.

It may well require a psychological study to explore why Andreas Papandreou was so capricious, boxing himself into a corner by his self-indulgent behaviour and provoking recurring crises. It is surely also worth asking why those able to restrain him chose not to do so, or left it too late, before trying.

It may be relatively easy to discern why there was compliance from power-brokers in Pasok: too many were able to benefit from his informal exercise of power in which much state money went into wasteful bureaucratic sinecures or else drained away into the pockets of well-placed clients of Pasok. It takes slightly more effort to explain the patience of the electorate with an irresponsible leader who failed to produce the improvements in the apparatus of state which could undoubtedly have made a real difference to the living conditions of a multitude of Greeks. Andreas Papandreou was at his most inventive and artistic in offering a rousing spectacle based around colourful nationalism. It was able to dull the critical faculties of many Greeks, only for them to turn away completely from Pasok after 2010, by which time Greece was mired in fresh divisions and grinding economic hardship.

The explanation for the patience of his colleagues in EU institutions and powerful national governments is perhaps the chief mystery. Papandreou damaged the image of the EU as an entity opposed to belligerent nationalism. His record during the crisis and violent break-up of Yugoslavia, arguably emboldened some of the most intransigent forces in the conflict from 1989 to 1995 and undercut EU efforts to search for a peaceful resolution of disputes. Later, as the project for European integration lost much of its allure and the internal politics of major players like France began to seem as conflictual as Greece's had been, some leaders emulated his demagogic style, so perhaps it is wrong to see Papandreou as such an outlier in the story of post-national European politics.

---

[1] Vassilis Fouskas, 'The making of a Greek Democrat and a Political Maverick', *Political Quarterly*, Vol. 84, No. 2 July 2013, p.p. 295-6.
[2] Jonathan Swarts, 'Andreas Papandreou, The Making of a Greek Democrat and a Political Maverick, *Mediterranean Quarterly*, Vol. 24, No. 3, 2013, p.p. 131-2.

---

[3] Anna Bosco and Susannah Verney, 'Polarisation in Southern Europe: Elites, Party Conflicts and Negative Partisanship', *South European Society and Politics*, Vol. 25, No. 3-4, 2020, p. 266.
[4] Gerassimos Moschonas, 'Superficial Social Democracy: PASOK, the State and the Shipwreck of the Greek Economy', in M. Fulla, M. Lazar (eds.), *European Socialists and the State in the Twentieth and Twenty-First Centuries*, London: Palgrave, 2020, p. 380.
[5] Takis S. Pappas, 'Patrons against partisans: The Politics of Patronage in Mass Ideological Parties', *Party Politics*, Vol 15, No. 3, 2009, p. 320.
[6] Pappas, 'Patrons against', p. 330.
[7] Pappas, 'Patrons against', p.p. 321-22.
[8] For the information in this paragraph, Andrew Gumbel, 'Profile: Dimitra Papandreou: Naked lust for power', *Independent*, 5 November 1995.
[9] Pappas, 'Patrons against', p. 326.
[10] Kevin Featherstone, 'The 'party-state' in Greece and the fall of Papandreou', *West European Politics*, Vol. 13, No. 1, 1990, p.p. 103-5. George Kassimeris, 'Greek Everyman: Andreas Papandreou at 100', Political Quarterly, Vol. 90, No. 2, 2019, p. 306.
[11] Nicolaos Zahariadis, 'Greece's Debt Crisis: A Tragedy of European Proportions', *Mediterranean Quarterly*, Vol. 24, No. 1, 2010, p. 39.
[12] Moschonas, 'Superficial Social', p. 383.
[13] Moschonas, 'Superficial Social', p. 391.
[14] Michalis Spourdalakis, *The Rise of the Greek Socialist Party*, London: Routledge, 1988, p. 230-32.
[15] Moschonas, 'Superficial Social', p. 393.
[16] See Richard Clogg, *Greece 1981-89: The Populist Decade*, London: Palgrave 1993.
[17] Kathleen Hendrix, 'After a Greek Tragedy: Her Life as a Political Wife Over, Margaret Papandreou Bounces Back to Lifelong Causes', *Los Angeles Times*, 3 August 1989.
[18] Mario Modano, 'Scandals Stain Socialist Regime', *Toronto Star*, 14 January 1989.
[19] Eirini Karamouzi and Dionysios Chourchoulis, 'Troublemaker or Peacemaker? Andreas Papandreou, the Euromissile Crisis, and the policy of peace', 1981–86, *Cold War History*, Vol. 19, No. 1, 2019, p. 44.
[20] 'Greek Political Leadership—Andreas Papandreou', Telegram From the Embassy in Greece to the Department of State, 20 November 1974, *Foreign Relations of the United States, 1969–1976, Volume XXX, Greece; Cyprus; Turkey, 1973–1976*, https://history.state.gov/historicaldocuments/frus1969-76v30/d30.
[21] Karamouzi and Chourchoulis, 'Troublemaker', p.p. 53-4.
[22] Andreas Stergiou & Christos Kollias, 'Between pragmatism and rhetoric: a critical assessment of Greece's defence and foreign policy in the 1980s in light of new primary sources', *Southeast European and Black Sea Studies*, Vol. 18, No. 4, 2018, p. 561.
[23] Stergiou & Kollias, 'Between pragmatism', p. 558.
[24] Dina Kyriakidou, 'Roasting Papandreou: Greek Satirists Ridicule Premier's Love Life', *Washington Post*, 7 February 1989.
[25] Bosco and Verney, 'Polarisation in', p. 267.
[26] Thomas Landon, 'The Papandreou family: Protagonists in Greece's Fate', *New York Times*, 13 July 2011.
[27] Kassimeris, 'Greek Everyman'.
[28] Takis Michas, *Unholy Alliance: Greece and Milošević's Serbia*, Austin, TX: A & M University Press, 2002, p. 35.
[29] Michas, *Unholy Alliance*, p. 39.
[30] Gumbel, 'Profile: Dimitra'.

CHAPTER 13: SILVIO BERLUSCONI

1936-2023

Silvio Berlusconi celebrated his 86th birthday on 29 September 2022, four days after the victory of the political centre-right in the Italian general election. Although he had only entered electoral politics when in his fifties, he had been a prominent figure in Italian public life for much longer. As a larger-than-life media tycoon, he exemplified the switch from a capitalist world absorbed with making things to one seeking vast profits from conjuring up images that diverted minds and dulled or debauched the senses.

He was the first ambitious and opinionated billionaire in a major democracy to plunge into politics and attempt to re-shape the narrative in fundamental respects. Others, from Elon Musk to George Soros and Bill Gates have, to some degree, followed in his footsteps, with mixed results. Their ability to acquire political influence coincided with the failure of mainstream political forces on both sides of the Atlantic to provide credible leaders able to confront growing turbulence with effective policies or, at least, reassuring stances.

He headed the first populist movement to enjoy qualified success in Italy in diluting the power of entrenched party political interests. His *Forza Italia* claimed to be liberating the citizen from the depredations of a parasitical elite.

Few of his bold promises to free Italians from the dead hand of the party-state were realised. But he remained an irrepressible, if increasingly frivolous, figure on the political scene for three decades. He was hated by the political left for his success in popularising free market ideals and for defying its efforts to banish him from public life.

Personal defects blunted the force of his attempt to enable business practices to elbow aside bureaucratic norms in national politics. His abrasiveness was eclipsed by his propensity for scandal and, more seriously, the shallowness of his commitment to institutional change. Nevertheless, the failure of established forces in politics to master a fissiparous political situation, kept him in contention long after most politicians retire or die. At the start of 2022, he was judged to have an outside chance of being elected President of Italy and styled himself as the pro-European conscience of this centre-right formation.

At its head is Giorgia Meloni, a 45-year-old pro-family traditionalist, offering a brand of prudent conservatism that was rarely on offer in Italy, even during the decades of Christian Democratic (DC) rule. Berlusconi has outlived pious DC corruption, stillborn efforts of the post-communist left to entrench itself, and noisy populist uprisings ranging from Mateo Renzi's Tuscan Blairism to the New Age agitation of Beppe Grillo and his Five Star movement.

Once a disruptor, Berlusconi had become a pillar of the status quo. He claimed to be the voice of liberalism, despite over a decade of often close association with Vladimir Putin. He summed up the promiscuity of the post-manufacturing capitalist class, often ready to strike up alliances with forces from Black Lives Matter to Xi's China, which nowadays seems to possess only impatience and disdain for the framework of liberal order which enabled capitalism to endure.

Chameleon-like, he was keen, even in his ninth decade, to seize whatever political marketing opportunity was going. In this respect, he merits comparison with Macron and to a lesser extent Johnson. There is ample evidence that this trio lack a vision or concrete agenda beyond their own self-promotion. Accumulated wealth and ownership of television channels enabled him to retain influence. It is now narrowly-focused and, among the young, he possessed little or no standing. Today in Italy, they are most likely to abstain from voting, with the politically-minded disproportionately backing the right. However, thanks to cultural changes which Berlusconi was often at the heart of, as well as economic constraints, the under-35s comprised only 21 percent of the electorate in 2022, having been 35 percent in 1983. His vehicle received a meagre seven percent of the vote in the general election held in September 2022. He tried to make trouble for Meloni, sworn in as Prime Minister on 20 October, making inflammatory comments about Ukraine having started the war engulfing part of its own country.[1] But Meloni was more than a match for someone who was shifted off to be President of the Senate.

Silvio Berlusconi was born in 1936 and grew up in a time of upheaval. Mussolini's fascist regime, war, invasion and occupation, widespread destruction and the danger from a powerful home grown communist movement, overshadowed his formative years. He was a precocious youth who grew up in a tight-knit and supportive family. His middle-class parents initially enjoyed a modest lifestyle but his father, in the banking business, retired as managing director of the Banca Rasini, a small but important Milanese bank. Academically able and socially extrovert, imbued with musical talents, he was a cruise ship singer in early youth before graduating from law school in Milan with excellent grades.

Shortly afterwards, in 1961, he cut his first property deal. He soon emerged as an innovative property developer. Between 1972 and 1979, he constructed the Milano Due residential complex in Segrate, a town in the outskirts of his home city. It was acclaimed for its futuristic architecture and imaginative walkways. In recognition, Berlusconi was knighted (made a *Cavaliere del Lavoro)* by President Giovanni Leone in 1977.[2]

In 1973, he formed the first Italian private television channel, which expanded into a nationwide network of local TV stations. Millions bored with the stodgy fare of state television (RAI), became converts to Berlusconi's potent mix of variety and quiz shows, tacky comedies, and Hollywood blockbusters.[3] An alliance with the then Prime Minister, (also from Milan) Bettino Craxi, proved invaluable. When judges in various cities attempted to shut down his channels, Craxi simply issued a decree placing them on a legal footing. It was later found that Berlusconi's media group funnelled close to 21 billion lire (around $17m) into Craxi's secret offshore bank accounts.[4]

Berlusconi would have learned much earlier in his business career that cultivating strong ties with influential political figures was necessary for his enterprises to enjoy spectacular growth. From the early 1970s, the Sicilian, Marcello Dell'Utri, was his right-hand-man in different ventures and later the driving force behind the creation of his political vehicle Forza Italia.[5] Berlusconi has insisted that a fortune that would eclipse that of the Agnelli family, the owners of Fiat, was obtained by hard-work and risk-taking. But various writers have speculated that the meteoric nature of his economic rise could only have occurred through backing from interests that preferred to remain hidden. He was one of numerous influential figures enrolled into the P-2 masonic lodge, which was long implicated in political plotting and economic corruption. President Sandro Pertini declared it illegal in the early 1980s, its grand master Licio Gelli being arrested in Switzerland and convicted of serious crimes.[6]

In 1978, Berlusconi's economic interests were so vast and disparate that he placed them in a holding company called Fininvest. It went on to include not just property but businesses stretching from insurance, banking, and advertising to film production, publishing, football and television channels. It was probably in 1986 that he became a trademark figure in Italian society. In that year, he bought AC Milan football club, saving it from bankruptcy. He then won over many Italians by pouring money into it. By 1994, AC Milan had won both the Italian league and the European Cup three times and the Intercontinental Cup twice. Four years before, his second marriage had been a notable social occasion. One of his best men was Craxi and a decade later, at the start of 2000, he would attend the, by now disgraced, politician's funeral in Tunisia where he had fled into exile. The normally ebullient figure was described as standing 'back from the grave, praying and weeping. 'I don't want to speak,' he said. 'He was a friend for 20 years'.[7]

The downfall of Craxi, as the *tangentopoli* scandal of illegal bribes was uncovered, had preoccupied the Berlusconi family. His brother and business partner Paolo was arrested and sentenced to a prison term in 1994 (and again in 2013).[8]

Berlusconi chose the moment that the Italian party system was in meltdown, with the Christian Democrats and Socialists disintegrating and the Communists dissolving and regrouping, for a bold new departure. He took to the field of politics as a player. A party that was very much his brainchild, Forza Italia (Go For It Italy) had been formally set up in December 1993. On 26 January 1994, he announced that he would be leading an accessible and different political force ready to serve all Italians who shared moderate, anti-communist, pro-market views.[9] Inevitably, there was no lack of commentators ready to claim that his real motive was to protect his business interests. It was a time of unprecedented electoral flux. The *Toghe Rosse* (Red Cloaks), as Italy's often leftward-leaning prosecuting judges are nicknamed, had long been investigating his business affairs. In the mid-1990s, they now enjoyed unparalleled popular esteem as they uncovered corruption rackets involving venal politicians and collaborators in business and the local administration. The worst suspicions of Italians about how misgoverned their country had been for a long time, were now confirmed.

Berlusconi may have decided that it was now imperative to get ahead of the field and transfer his entrepreneurial flair to the political arena. His vehicle Forza Italia lacked a coherent conservative strategy, and Berlusconi never acquired one in subsequent decades. It was a bundle of platitudes and shibboleths cleverly converted into a slick and seductive political marketing strategy. His political views were explained in his dramatic speech of 26 January 1994:

> 'We believe in business, in competition, in progress, in efficiency, in the free market and in social equity, which comes from justice and liberty...a society where instead of class envy and class warfare there is generosity and hard work'.[10]

Berlusconi had shown already that he hardly lacked crucial attributes often seen as necessary to thrive in politics. He was gregarious, thick-skinned, resilient, glib as well as ruthless whenever his own interests were threatened. Once he tasted power, he lost no time in placing on the statute books, laws which have been labelled 'personal laws'.[11] They allowed the decriminalisation of false accounting, permitted trials to be transferred to other locations and law, and reduced the stature of limitations for certain crimes.[12]

But first the Italian voters needed to be informed about his political offer and convinced that it was worth trying out. Accordingly, his television channels were put to work in order to provide a constant bombardment of information about Forza Italia.[13] From the outset, he stressed the need for a direct partnership between him, as the moderniser and crusader against base politics, and the citizen voters.

He used his marketing empire to ascertain the inclinations and preferences of the voters, through an extensive battery of surveys. He cleverly exploited the anti-political mood which had become entrenched after 54 governments in forty years, with often little to show for their time in power. No effort was made to repackage himself as a serious and sober statesman-in-the-making. Instead, an essential element of his appeal was his opulent lifestyle, described as 'part-Dallas, part-Mediterranean chic'.[14] Many viewed it as the height of tasteless vulgarity, but his egotism, showmanship, and combativeness, for at least fifteen years, proved alluring in a Mediterranean society where spectacle and bravado had never lost their roles in politics.

Massimo D'Alema, a dominant figure on the restructuring political left during the early Berlusconi years, was convinced that his rise confirmed the natural irresponsibility of Italian society.[15] Berlusconi showed his political agility by hammering out an alliance with the territorial and populist Northern League (LN) and the former fascists and nationalist conservatives gathered in the National Alliance (AN). With Forza Italia being the principal point of reference, it was called the Pole of Freedom in the restive north and Pole of Good Governance in the south and the islands, which traditionally looked to Rome.

The electoral formula proved a winning one. Armed with a parliamentary majority, Berlusconi became Prime Minister in May 1995. But his government lasted a bare seven months due to tensions between the regionalist Lega and the AN that favoured a strong central state. The persistence of these tensions enabled the political left to rule from 1996 to 2000. But conflict and instability in turn beset various governments composed of former communists, socialists, a few Christian democrats and others. When elections became due in May 2001, Berlusconi's patience at re-uniting his centre-right forces paid off. He reinforced his longstanding claim that five years under it showed that the left did not believe in the market, nor in private initiative, nor in profits, nor in the individual.[16] He projected himself as someone whose successful career well-equipped him to raise the living standards of Italians. He promised to lower taxation; modernise the state administration; provide public works for the southern poor; establish greater security in the cities; stamp out illegal immigration; reform the judicial system and, not least, 'put an end to the prying and punitive actions of excessively independent magistrates'.[17]

Berlusconi's media empire was invaluable in securing him a definitive victory in May 2001, the start of five unbroken years in office. Housewives were avid consumers of his programmes. No less than 44.8 percent of a group who were a significant social category (given the low percentages of female employees in Italy), voted not just for the centre-right but specifically for Forza Italia. Young people also proved a strong base of support: 'his television was full of young people, his party was a young one, he made them dream of success'. He also made an overt pitch to religious Italy, particularly via the promotion on television of 'charismatic figures, such as Padre Pio, the Capuchin friar believed by many to have been endowed with miraculous powers'.[18]

His second government may have lasted a full term, but it proved to be an acute disappointment. Five years in office showed that Berlusconi had no coherent programme that he was prepared to dedicate his energies to realising. He attracted wider scrutiny, not for pioneering badly-needed reforms, but on account of melodramatic and self-indulgent gestures. These ensured that his long-promised attempt to replace a parliamentary system with a directly-elected presidential one, in which an executive had a mandate to govern, was as far away as ever from being secured.

Within weeks of taking office, his authoritarian proclivities seemed to be confirmed at the July 2001 G8 summit in Genoa, when the police raided the dormitory where protesters were resting and badly assaulted them. (In 2010, a court in Genoa condemned 15 officials for their role in this matter).[19] In July 2003, when speaking at the European Parliament, he recommended to the German MEP, Martin Schulz, the leader of the Socialists in the chamber, that he should take a film role as a concentration camp guard: 'you would be perfect'.[20] A duel with the well-known *Economist* magazine, which wrote frequent editorials on organized crime, corruption and powerful political forces in Italy, brought him much unwelcome publicity after he sued the magazine.[21] In 2001, as he was returning to power, it had placed on its cover the accusation that Berlusconi was 'unfit' to hold office.[22]

Whittling down the powers of the judiciary became his preoccupation, and much of the legislation passed was designed to prevent Berlusconi and his allies from being prosecuted.[23] The dean of Italian political science, Giovanni Sartori, himself no radical, argued that Berlusconi is simply interested in doing what he wants. His book on the era described a 'Sultanate', in which Berlusconi rules 'over a paper party [that is] literally prostrate at his feet. He nominates whatever ministers he wants, fires whom he wants, as if they were his service staff'.[24]

Berlusconi had promised in 2001, that if his contract to improve Italian personal and political circumstances failed to obtain tangible results, he would retreat from the political fray. An ambitious project for strengthening prime ministerial powers and reducing other branches' prerogatives failed in a 2006 referendum. His attention was too often diverted to his own mounting legal problems and attempts to fend off persistent allegations of conflicts of interest between his public and private roles. He neglected to devote the time and care needed to weave together the different interests inside his unwieldy alliance.[25] He put short-term personal goals above any long-term systemic goals involving the restructuring of the Italian political system.[26] In 2005, he scrapped the partial first-past-the-post system, secured via referendum a decade earlier by reformers outside parliament, in favour of a hybrid one that he hoped would enable him to fend off his leftist foes.[27]

He went down to electoral defeat in 2006. His promise to reduce the burden of the state on the individual Italian earner showed no sign of being realised. In the decade to 2010, when he had mostly been in charge, the overall tax burden in Italy increased from 41.5 to 42.5 percent, whereas the average EU17 tax rate fell from 40.9 to 39.0 percent.[28]

Berlusconi's defeat had been a narrow one. The victorious Olive Tree coalition, the latest incarnation of a centre-left struggling to re-invent itself, was beset with factional and personal rivalries. It had no new political project and was dominated by professional politicians who often had no occupational alternatives.[29] Berlusconi's political vehicle faced drawbacks of a different nature. Forza Italia was dominated by lawyers, publicists and senior employees. But even after its 2006 defeat, it remained by far the most sizeable Italian party, having polled more than 9 million votes, 23 percent of the national vote. The abundant shortcomings of the left enabled Berlusconi to be reconfirmed in office with a comfortable majority after snap elections were held in April 2008. But he had lost much of his glamour, and his authority was not what it had been within the centre-right.

His lawyers continued to absorb much of his attention. As someone worth £8 billion in 2004, he struggled to fight off investigations over conflicts of interest. Berlusconi joked that he had become prime minister in his spare time.[30] But some allies didn't find the affair that he was embroiled in with Noemi Letizia, an 18-year-old Neapolitan would-be TV star, such a laughing matter. Two years later, in February 2011, it became far more serious when he was charged with paying for sex with a nightclub dancer when she was one year below the legal 18 years age-limit for providing sexual services.[31] These trysts were yet another factor enabling him to be seen as a uniquely idiosyncratic head of an important European country.

Politically weakened and facing growing defections from allies, he was driven from office in 2011. His fourth government had coincided with growing economic troubles for Italy. When the left had been in charge in the late 1990s, the country had been shuffled into the single currency of the Eurozone, essentially by concealing its massive debt level.[32] Even before the Euro entered into crisis, due to the debt-financing difficulties of southern European EU states, the Italian economy had been struggling. The exchange rate at which the Euro had been fixed benefited Germany and disadvantaged Italy's industrial exports. The Italian economy would be mired in stagnation, hardly growing much during the first two decades of the 21st century. Berlusconi was no admirer of the European Union. It was full of the types of bureaucrats, accountants, and policy wonks whom he had frequently tangled with at home. Italy's parlous finances prompted him to enter into discussions with several other states about pulling out of the Euro and restoring the lira in order to revive competitiveness. But the European Central Bank, in charge of EU monetary policy, was determined to foil such a move. Mário Draghi, the new head of the ECB and his predecessor Jean-Claude Trichet, wrote a letter to Berlusconi in August 2011 demanding sweeping cuts to public expenditure. In doing so, they were violating the mandate of the bank.[33] Their intrigues against the government in Rome caused Italian debt yields to soar and in November 2011, Berlusconi was, in effect, sacked by President Giorgio Napolitano, quickly replaced as Prime Minister by Mário Monti, a former European Commissioner.[34]

The Economist roundly applauded Angela Merkel for helping to 'get rid of clowns ... like Berlusconi'.[35] It was also the revenge of the old political class which Berlusconi had long railed against, Napolitano, having been a veteran Communist party figure before 1989. There was no wellspring of patriotic protest at home about a transnational stitch-up because Berlusconi's halo by now was deeply tarnished. He had been less concerned with accomplishing the triumph of free market ideas than with ensuring that his own business interests enjoyed state protection.

His political career entered a cul-de-sac due to mounting legal troubles. By 2016, seven convictions had been annulled under Italy's statute of limitations, there had been nine not guilty verdicts, thirty-five charges dropped, and several other cases were ongoing.[36]

But in July 2013, a serious setback occurred when he was definitively sentenced to four years' imprisonment for fraud and embezzlement. Berlusconi was never incarcerated. He served less than one year of the sentence, which was in any case transmuted into social work; he spent much of it playing the piano in an old people's home.[37] Nevertheless, he had to surrender his passport and he was debarred from holding public office for six years. (He was also obliged to renounce his knighthood).[38]

His party, from 2009 re-named the People of Freedom (PdL), obtained 29.1 percent of the vote (along with smaller allies) in the 2013 parliamentary election. But Berlusconi was unable to play a directing role while being debarred from public office and its fortunes declined. A new populist challenger, the Five Star Movement (5MS), ate into its support. This eclectic party, described as 'a primal scream' against the party establishment, in time revealed itself to be an alternative left force strongly focused on the environment, but it won over young voters who might previously have endorsed Berlusconi.[39]

He was effectively out of politics until 2018, when this time the northern Lega party overtook the restored Forza Italia and he faced an even stiffer challenge, especially in his southern strongholds from a relatively new and overtly conservative formation, the Brothers of Italy (Fratelli d'Italia) led by Giorgia Meloni.

During these years in the political wilderness, he continued to make headlines due to his friendship with Vladimir Putin. He called him the 'Numero Uno' of world leaders as he invaded and threatened neighbours and menaced allies of Italy, such as Britain.[40] He visited the Russian leader in Crimea in 2015, after he had seized it from Ukraine. In 2013, at the height of his trial over what was known as the 'bunga bunga' party sex scandal, Putin had earlier said: 'Berlusconi faces trial for bedding women. If he was gay, no one would ever lay a finger on him'.[41] Once the Kremlin strongman was well into the confrontational phase of his rule, Berlusconi displayed little reticence about lavishing fulsome praise on him. In 2015, he declared:

> 'Vladimir is the exact opposite of the image portrayed of him in the western media. He is a really sensitive person, a man of profound feelings, always respectful of others. He is very gentle, a man with a delicate sensibility.'

His voice rising, Mr Berlusconi went on to say that he was 'in total disagreement' with sanctions on Russia for its annexation of Crimea and its role in the war in eastern Ukraine'.[42]

Forty-five days after Putin launched a full-scale invasion of Ukraine, shocking the world with atrocities committed against many thousands of civilians, Berlusconi appeared to have a change of heart. On 9 April 2022 he declared that he was 'deeply disappointed and saddened' by Putin's behaviour: 'I knew him for twenty years and he always seemed to me to be a democrat and a man of peace'.[43]

Some were bound to wonder about his sincerity: in 2008, at a joint press conference with Putin in Sardinia, Berlusconi made a gesture imitating a gunman shooting toward a Russian journalist who had asked a question about Putin's personal relationships. Nobody in the room said a single word.[44]

A brief last hurrah occurred in January 2022, when, at 85, Berlusconi sought to become the President of Italy. He got to within fifty votes of being chosen by the Italian parliament. But the contest was deadlocked, and the incumbent Sergio Mattarella was talked into accepting a second term.[45]

After over 25 years as a player, the political scene was little different in key respects than how it had been when he crashed into politics in the mid-1990s. Gianfranco Pasquino wrote of 'party fragmentation, divided and contentious coalitions, cumbersome policy-making processes, and weak political and governmental leadership' and this was also the disheartening context in which he stepped aside.[46] The Italian left panicked, but Berlusconi turned out to be an idiosyncratic and self-indulgent presence who ensured that any revolution in governance was postponed indefinitely.

An increasingly frail Berlusconi died on 12 June 2023. Predictable expressions of glee emanated from quarters, mainly on the left, who regarded him as being a ghastly corrupt figure, a blight on politics who was as near to fascism as made no difference. But there was plenty of affection too, even on the left. It is easy to forget that it was Italy's best-known socialist, Bettino Craxi, godfather to two of his children, who used the discretionary power of the state to enable his media empire to take off in the 1980s. 'For me, he was a leader whom I found capable, shrewd and, most important, true to his word', declared Tony Blair, Britain's longest serving left-wing party Prime Minister.[47] European left-wing forces not in the grip of ideology could work with figures like Berlusconi.

In a drab and sectarian age, he cut a political dash and is likely to be seen as an energetic and resourceful man of multi-faceted talents. He had failed to alter the political system in any meaningful way despite being a strong regular vote winner. Thanks to poses, stunts, images, outbursts and non-stop drama associated with his time in politics, he is likely to be a reference point for an entire era. But at least in politics, he left nothing that was tangible and durable behind him. He is likely to remain a period piece, illuminating the unsatisfactory Italian post-Cold War era.

---

[1] Nick Squires, 'Vodka sent by Putin to Berlusconi as a birthday present breached EU sanctions', Daily Telegraph, 20 October 2022.
[2] Mark Donovan and Mark Gilbert, 'Silvio Berlusconi and Romano Prodi', in Mark Gilbert, Erik Jones and Gianfranco Pasquino, *The Oxford Handbook of Italian Politics,* Oxford: Oxford University Press, 2015, p. 396.
[3] Donovan and Gilbert, 'Silvio Berlusconi', p. 397.
[4] 'An Italian Story', *Economist*, 28 April 2001, https://www.economist.com/special/2001/04/26/an-italian-story, accessed 6 February 2022.
[5] Donovan and Gilbert, 'Silvio Berlusconi', p. 396.
[6] Mack Smith, *Modern Italy*, p.p. 468, 487.
[7] Jude Weber, 'Craxi funeral mixes tears and insults', *National Post,* (Toronto) 22 January 2000.
[8] 'Silvio Berlusconi Court sentences former leader to jail', *BBC News,* 7 March 2013, https://www.bbc.co.uk/news/av/world-europe-21701022, Mack Smith, *Modern Italy,* p. 487.
[9] Gianfranco Pasquino, 'The Five Faces of Silvio Berlusconi: The Knight of Anti-politics', in *Modern Italy,* Vol. 12, No. 1, 2007, p. 40.
[10] Rosemary Righter, 'Beyond Bunga', *Times Literary Supplement,* 29 January 2016.
[11] See Felicia Allum, 'Silvio Berlusconi and his "toxic" touch', Representation, Vol. 4, No. 3, 2011, p. 291.85.
[12] Allum, 'Silvio Berlusconi', p. 287.
[13] Pasquino, 'The Five Faces', p. 40.
[14] Paul Ginsborg, 'The Patrimonial Ambitions of Silvio Berlusconi', *New Left Review,* Vol. 21, May-June 2003, p. 36.
[15] Ginsborg, 'The Patrimonial', p.p. 26-7.
[16] Donovan and Gilbert, 'Silvio Berlusconi', p. 397.
[17] Ginsborg 'The Patrimonial', p. 280.
[18] Ginsborg 'The Patrimonial', p. 29.
[19] Allum, 'Silvio Berlusconi', p. 285.
[20] Allum, 'Silvio Berlusconi', p. 288.
[21] Federico Varese, 'Messages from the Mafia', *London Review of Books*, Vol. 27, No. 1, 6 January 2005.
[22] 'Why Silvio Berlusconi is Unfit to Lead Italy,' *Economist,* 28 April 2001.
[23] Giovanni Sartori, *Il Sultanato*, Rome-Bari: Laterza, 2009, p.p. 21-33.

[24] John Lloyd, 'When in Rome', *Financial Times*, 5 September 2009.
[25] See Kurt Weyland, 'How Populism Dies: Political Weaknesses of Personalistic Plebiscitarian Leadership', *Political Science Quarterly*, Vol. 137, No. 1, Spring 2022.
[26] Pasquino, 'The Five Faces', p. 54.
[27] Righter, 'Beyond Bunga'.
[28] Donovan and Gilbert, 'Silvio Berlusconi', p. 402.
[29] Pasquino, 'The Five Faces', p. 52.
[30] Alan Friedman, 'Silvio Berlusconi and Vladimir Putin: the odd couple', *Financial Times*, 2 October 2015.
[31] John Hooper, 'Silvio Berlusconi to face trial accused of paying for sex with teenager', *Guardian*, 15 February 2001.
[32] Gallagher, *Europe's Path*, p.p. 20-21.
[33] Anderson, Ever Closer Union?, p. 174.
[34] Ambrose Evans Pritchard, 'The great Euro putsch rolls on as two democracies fall', *Daily Telegraph*, 13 November 2011.
[35] Editorial, 'One woman to rule them all', *Economist*, 12 September 2013.
[36] Righter, 'Beyond Bunga'.
[37] Nicholas Farrell, 'Can anyone beat Berlusconi to the Italian presidency?', *Spectator*, 15 January 2022.
[38] Donovan and Gilbert, 'Silvio Berlusconi', p. 405.
[39] Tim Gwynn Jones, 'The lipstick walks', *Twenty-Four Two*, 23 July 2022, https://twentyfourtwo.substack.com/p/the-lipstick-walks
[40] Friedman, 'Silvio Berlusconi'.
[41] 'Berlusconi and Putin: an enduring love', *The Local* (Rome), 20 June 2015, https://www.thelocal.it/20150611/berlusconi-and-putin-an-enduring-love/, accessed 30 May 2022.
[42] Friedman, 'Silvio Berlusconi'.
[43] *G4Media* (Bucharest), 10 April 2022, https://www.g4media.ro/silvio-berlusconi-se-declara-dezamagit-de-prietenul-sau-vladimir-putin-mi-s-a-parut-intotdeauna-un-democrat-si-un-om-al-pacii.html, accessed 30 May 2022
[44] 'Berlusconi hosts Putin in Sardinia', *Times of Malta*, 19 April 2008, https://timesofmalta.com/articles/view/berlusconi-hosts-putin-in-sardinia.204731, accessed 30 May 2022.
[45] Farrell, 'Can anyone'.
[46] Pasquino, 'The Five Faces', p. 47.
[47] *Daily Telegraph*, 12 June 2023.

CHAPTER 14: MILO DJUKANOVIĆ

1962-

The dexterity and cool nerves of Milo Djukanović confirms some stereotypes indelibly linked with the Balkan peninsula, but also explodes others. He has dominated the politics of Montenegro for over three decades, and often party and state seem to have been merged in his person. Where he deviated from the norm was by decisively spurning the politics of ethnic antagonism that has long hung over the region like an ugly cloud.

Having started out as a local protégé of the most notorious proponent of ethnic strife in South-Eastern-Europe, Slobodan Milošević, he gradually broke away from him through the 1990s. Montenegro's freedom of action within the Yugoslav federation, every other republic having left, was painstakingly acquired. This high wire act was a hazardous undertaking. Montenegro was split between fervent adherents of Serbia and others who preferred local self-rule, especially with Serbia fast becoming an international pariah in the 1990s. There was no guarantee that Djukanović could avoid falling off this tightrope. He was identifying with the often fickle and divided Western powers and reaching out to distrusted Muslim and Catholic minorities in a land that was over 80 percent Orthodox in religious affiliation. He took in large numbers of refugees, faced down outraged militants in his own Democratic Socialist Party (DSP), the former League of Communists, and met the US President in 1999 just after NATO air power had been used against Milošević.

In 2006, the pinnacle of his career occurred when he restored the independent status of Montenegro, after having been part of a monarchical, and later communist, Yugoslav state since 1918. Exactly a decade later, the strategically-placed Adriatic country became the 29th member of NATO. He rejected socialism for capitalism, single party rule for at least a modicum of democracy, and ethnic supremacy for minority rights. But his rule was opaque, his family prospered mightily and control of the levers of the state meant no transfer of power occurred for nearly a third of a century. As a Balkan ruler, he may be the figure who most resembles Marshall Iosip Broz Tito, the architect of communist Yugoslavia. Both were master tacticians, good at arranging advantageous foreign alliances and unafraid to enjoy the finer things of life. Resentment towards his style of rule, viewed as increasingly high-handed and acquisitive, resulted in the DSP losing office in 2020 but with Djukanović remaining in effective charge as president.

This reverse occurred as geopolitical turbulence in the region returned, with the West struggling to maintain its commitment to ensuring a fitful stability, and not only Russia but Turkey also vying to take its place. Djukanović is a resourceful and talented politician who has confronted challenges which most politicians rarely have to face. His greatest achievement was to keep tragedy at bay in his small and vulnerable country during the murderous 1990s.

Djukanović was just 27 when he emerged from the obscurity of the gritty industrial town of Nikšić in 1989. Until then, his existence had been uneventful. Tall and athletic, he had excelled at basketball, besides showing an early interest in politics. He was the son of a judge and public affairs were likely to have been a subject around the dinner table. For the previous forty years there had been only one party, the League of Communists. But that was about the change. The ambitious communist banker Slobodan Milošević was taking advantage of the power vacuum that had opened up after Tito's death in 1980 to recentralise power. He set out to revive the previously taboo subject of Serbian nationalism in order to try and make the multi-ethnic Yugoslav polity more receptive to Serbian interests. He thought he could get away with this bold exploit thanks to the nerve centre of the state being the main Serbian city, Belgrade. Both Serbs and Montenegrins predominated in the army, the media would soon be in his grasp, and he was busy removing old guard communists still committed to 'brotherhood and unity'. When the cynically-named 'anti-bureaucratic revolution' reached Podgorica, Djukanović was one of a trio of enforcers who carried out the orders from Belgrade. Along with the secret police, they organized workers to demand the ousting of the old guard. With Miloșević's backing, he became Prime Minister of Montenegro in February 1991, at the age of only 29.

What kind of inheritance was it? Yugoslavia was just months from dissolving into violent acrimony. Serbian hardliners were determined to use force to expand their territorial holdings. Implacable resistance was being planned by Croatian nationalists. The republic of Slovenia was on the verge of breaking away. Macedonia and Bosnia, very mixed ethnically, desperately hoped to escape any resulting conflagration, one ultimately successfully, the other most tragically not.

Soon Montenegro would be the only republic prepared to remain in Federal Yugoslavia, along with Serbia, which held down the overwhelmingly Albanian province of Kosovo. It is unlikely that the new Yugoslav strongman paid much attention to Montenegro, from which he could expect only acquiescence in what proved to be a strategy of conquest as wars erupted first in Croatia in 1991 and then with devastating intensity in Bosnia-Herzegovina in 1992.

But watchful observers might have been able to observe early flickers of discontent in Montenegro, where identification with the Serbian cause was often combined with resentment about being taken for granted and used by the Serbian older cousin. No war fever was noticeable. 5,000 demonstrators at a Podgorica rally in June 1991 proclaimed, 'Heroism today is to avoid war'.[1] Many young men sought to avoid the military draft, Djukanović threatening harsh punishment of deserters in October 1991.[2] The next month, Montenegrin forces played a prominent role in the attack on the Croatian city of Dubrovnik, a few miles up the coast. For many foreigners, this architectural jewel was Yugoslavia's best known city. Massive shelling led to seven Baroque palaces being destroyed. Overall, 55.9 percent of buildings were damaged. On 14 January 1992, 104 Nobel Prize laureates published a full-page advertisement in the New York

Times urging the world to stop the unrestrained destruction by the Yugoslav army (JNA).[3]

Eight years later, in June 2000, Djukanović met with Croatian President Stipe Mesić and apologised for Montenegro's role in the attack. His small Adriatic territory was still part of the Federal Republic of Yugoslavia (FRY), but much had happened in the meantime. Perhaps one sobering event had been the imposition of sweeping United Nations sanctions in May 1992. Montenegro was now essentially isolated and an international pariah alongside Serbia. For an alert and street-wise politician, it no longer looked as if Milošević's land grab and crackdown on minorities was going to be an easy path to victory. There was going to be no quick and permanent land grab given the international hostility that was being whipped up. The price of colluding in barbaric methods was quite likely to be a steep one. Acting as Milošević's understudy, and parroting rhetoric emphasising historical wrongs and a sense of victimhood, increasingly looked as if it might backfire. The Serbian strongman had a formidable apparatus of power, but Djukanović may have imperceptibly come to see him as an engine of destruction who might easily bring down any and all who became tools in his various power plays.

Milošević's rule was personal and idiosyncratic. Sir Ivor Roberts, Britain's ambassador to Yugoslavia, as his power disintegrated, is just one of those who spotted how much he was under the influence of his wife Mira Marcović 'whom many Montenegrins and Serbs regard as a low-wattage Stalinist shrew' (the impression conveyed by a US journalist Blaine Harden).[4] Djukanović finally decided to signal his disenchantment with his mentor in 1997. Writing in the influential Belgrade publication *Vreme,* he unambiguously asserted that Milošević was 'a man of obsolete political ideas, lacking the ability to form a strategic vision of the problems this country is facing, surrounded by unsuitable individuals who are following the time-tested method of many authoritarian regimes'.[5]

The first wave of demonstrations, which would eventually drive him from power in 2001, were already occurring in Belgrade in 1997. Perhaps a more significant influence on Djukanović's evolving thinking was the Dayton peace agreement of 1995 which involved Milošević making significant concessions to a US-backed consortium of powers armed with a United Nations mandate to solve the conflict in Bosnia. The West needed to reach out to him but, from 1995, he looked increasingly to be on the way down, a transitory figure regarded by many decision-makers in Western capitals as a mendacious butcher. But his regime retained an ability to strike out not only at ethnic foes, but at disloyal allies who dared to break ranks. Mysterious assassinations occurred in Belgrade in the last years of the 1990s as Djukanović insulated himself against his old patron.

The Montenegrin's first move was to cover his local political flank. He succeeded in retaining control of the Democratic Socialist Party (DSP) and holding out against Serb-orientated former allies. He ran for president in 1997 and made up for their loss of support by reaching out to the republic's minorities, the Muslim and ethnic Albanians who, in total, made up 22 percent of the population. Some of their leaders would soon be included in his government. But first he had to win and then be inaugurated as President. In January 1998, on the eve of the inauguration, a 10,000-strong crowd, many armed, led by his old comrade and now bitter rival Momir Bulatović, stormed the presidency building with automatic weapons and Molotov cocktails:

> 'Someone tossed a hand grenade at the entrance. Among the wounded were 37 members of Djukanović's police force; four were hurt seriously. But the police did not shoot back. They drove the crowd away with tear gas and stun grenades, and the police chose not to arrest any of the demonstrators'.[6]

Djukanović declared later that the JNA had been looking for an excuse to intervene in Montenegro. A well-trained police force had been quietly built up which was prepared to stand by him even in adversity. Its loyalty was reinforced by the fact that it was paid well and on time. Unlike in Serbia where pensions and salaries were many months in arrears at this time, in Montenegro they were paid far more promptly to citizens. This ensured the loyalty of many who might have reserve or feel some distaste for his voyage away from age-old pro-Serb verities. In her war of words with her husband's mutinous satrap on the Adriatic coast, Mira Marcović denounced him as a smuggler in power. This was by no means a far-fetched accusation. A US journalist not ill-disposed to the boss of Montenegro wrote in 1999:

> 'For a number of years, around 2 o'clock every morning, several giant Russian-made transport planes landed at the airport on the edge of the capital. The planes brought in American and European cigarettes, which were trucked to the coast and smuggled by boat to Italy. Djukanović's Government imposed a "transit fee," which, according to Branko Perović, the Foreign Minister, added about $30 million a year to the republic's coffers. That's not a lot of money by European standards, but with an annual budget of just $270 million, the Montenegro Government was relying on smuggling for more than 10 percent of its revenue'.[7]

Djukanović's brazen revenue-raising gambit was not damaging at home. A local human rights lawyer, elected to the Yugoslav parliament, declared in the 1990s, that 'Everyone in Montenegro thought that finally there was someone in Government who knew how to create money'.[8] The Italian authorities were not so agreeable, and for some years criminal charges hung over him for alleged smuggling involvement.[9] But it was the Americans who increasingly counted in the region, after years in which European powers had dithered while parts of the Balkans burned. Washington's verdict was summed up by the remark of an unnamed US official. 'It was cigarettes. It wasn't drugs or arms'.[10] In other words, the smuggling was a necessary evil in a volatile region and, warts and all, Montenegro's plucky leader still deserved to be supported.

During the January 1998 showdown, the US special envoy to the Balkans, Robert Gelbard, had strongly condemned the behaviour of Bulatović and warned Milošević to ditch any idea of regime change in Montenegro.[11] As if to reinforce the point, Milošević was plainly told by the US envoy in the spring of 1998, that he should not rule out NATO use of force against him if repressive actions in Kosovo weren't halted.[12]

On 28 March 1999, NATO launched aerial bombing, first against Serbian military targets and then against key civil infrastructure, as Milošević gave orders for the wholesale deportation of Albanians in Kosovo. The NATO offensive would last until early June 1999 and undoubtedly was the most pivotal moment in Djukanović's political career. At the outset, he had refused to obey an order from Belgrade to declare a state of emergency. Large numbers of Albanian refugees were welcomed and around 120,000 in total would be taken in from various conflict zones during the 1990s.[13] In response, the US government gave financial aid to this pro-Western corner of Yugoslavia, $15 million being a first instalment in the spring of 1999. US Secretary of State Madeleine Albright endorsed the view of one of her officials, who described Djukanović as 'a stable and rational politician' in a region beset by zealous nationalism. She believed he had 'a critical role to play in building democracy in Yugoslavia'.[14] But there was no guarantee that even in his strongly fortified Presidential Building, he could emerge unscathed in a trial of strength with Milošević. The JNA in Montenegro was around 10,000 strong. With Serbian cities under heavy bombardment, it would not have been out of character for the beleaguered Serbian leader to use this moment to settle accounts with him.

It was never a foregone conclusion that the military showdown would end in NATO's favour, but a ceasefire was declared on 3 June 1999 and Djukanović emerged as one of the beneficiaries of this outcome. His gamble in aligning with the West seemed to have paid off and in mid-June 1999 he had a meeting with US President Bill Clinton who was attending the G-7 summit in Slovenia. The tall, neatly-suited and self-confident Montenegrin towered over Clinton. Having made a positive impression on various US diplomats, it is likely that the US President was relieved to meet a relatively straightforward Balkan political figure who did not dwell on history but seemed in tune with US hopes for the region. The United States was not a major obstacle in Montenegro's quest for statehood. But several European NATO members stood in its way, believing that Serbia remained a key state in the Balkans and that the separation from Montenegro would prevent it enjoying future stability. But with Milošević swept from power in 2001, it was hard even for NATO's Secretary-General, Javier Solana of Spain, to impede Djukanović.

An independence referendum, held in Montenegro on 21 May 2006, approved full statehood by 55.5 percent of voters, narrowly passing the 55 percent threshold. Parliament then declared independence on June 3. By now, Djukanović was one of the best-known Balkan leaders. He pressed home his advantage by seeking membership of various Euro-Atlantic bodies, not least the European Union and NATO. Results were mixed. Montenegro began the EU accession process in 2007, against a background of a fast-growing economy. But membership hopes were dashed by the recession getting underway in 2008, which hit Montenegro hard and froze most accession bids. After a 2010 meeting in Washington with US Secretary of State Hillary Clinton, her husband, now a private citizen, paid a visit to Montenegro in 2011 as the guest of Djukanović's closest economic ally, Dusko Knezević.

The ties built up over nearly two decades between senior US policy-makers and Djukanović helped squash whatever resistance there was in Western Europe about admitting Montenegro to NATO. Accordingly, on 5 June 2017, it became the 29th member of the defence alliance. Its main value to NATO planners was the strategic position it occupies in the western Balkans. The region had failed to acquire enduring stability for many reasons, but differences over the future of Bosnia, and Serbian anger over the loss of Kosovo, counted high among them. NATO has no base in Montenegro, and Italy and Greece provide it with air defence. Nevertheless, Russian anger was undisguised. Foreign minister Sergei Lavrov had declared in 2014 that the expansion of NATO into the former Yugoslavia was a provocation.[15]

It remains unclear whether the foiled, clumsily-mounted attempt of armed Russian nationalists to kill Djukanović on the eve of elections in October 2016, was a response hatched at some level within the Russian state. It was variously described as a Balkan comic opera plot or something more sinister meant to wrong-foot the West in what had been a corner of the Balkans where many retaining a Serbian outlook still cherished past links with Russia.[16]

Djukanović was in the habit of switching from the roles of prime minister to president and back during his more than twenty years at the helm. He was a smooth operator, ruthless when required behind-the-scenes but permitting regular elections where the opposition failed to win, due as much to its own defects as to machinations by the ruling DSP. He had several able lieutenants capable of filling the vacuum if he was unexpectedly removed from political life. But the evidence mounted that he sought to exercise control, not so much through a political force, but through the force of family influence. His sister, brother, son and nephew variously exercised positions of influence in the legal field, banking, the energy sector, and tourism (an increasingly vital earner for the country).[17]

Perhaps Djukanović's most glaring error was to accept a massive Chinese loan in order to build a motorway from landlocked Serbia to the port of Bar on the Adriatic coast. The terms of the loan were onerous and, by the end of 2021, Montenegro needed the assistance of the EU and Western investment banks in order to meet exacting interest payments.[18] The government in Podgorica now handling this massive headache was a coalition of disparate forces united by their desire to break Djukanović's grip on power.

Ironically, it was his mishandling of a religious issue that resulted in a major reverse for him. President for the third time (since 2017), he signed into law, in 2019, a parliamentary act which passed into state hands properties that the Serbian orthodox church has been using for at least a century. Historically, the church had been a major force in Montenegro, which had been ruled as an ecclesiastical principality from 1516 until 1852. On news of the property grab, there was huge uproar.

To add to his discomfiture, relations had broken down with his longstanding business ally Dusko Knezević. From London, where he had repaired after the authorities had opened a criminal investigation into his activities, he published articles and released videos claiming to show that Djukanović had been at the pinnacle of a kleptocratic system.[19] Large-scale protests erupted in early 2019, which were dwarfed by a more serious challenge at the end of the year from the Serbian church. The popular uproar contributed to the DSP being turfed out of office after thirty years, in the autumn of 2019. Until succumbing to Covid in 2020, Bishop Amfilohije Radović, a long-term foe of Djukanović, spearheaded the popular upsurge designed to cancel the expropriations. Three years later, on 2 April 2023, he went down to an emphatic defeat in the presidential election to a 36-year-old economist, Jakov Milatović, whose anti-corruption manifesto proved alluring to most voters.[20]

It remains to be seen whether time has also run out for Montenegro's now beleaguered strongman. In recent memory, only Marshal Tito has had a longer continuous stretch of power in South-East-Europe. Djukanović can be viewed from various perspectives—perhaps as a Renaissance prince, resourceful and ruthless with a smooth demeanour, or else as a European version of a durable post-colonial African leader, with a growing tendency to allow power to go to his head, or finally, as an adaptable survivor from the age of communism, with the skills to construct a hybrid regime, and profit from the need for Western powers to find local allies, as they keep a wary eye on a perennially unsettled part of Europe.

Who knows, it might well be that the leader of this small Balkan state is the contemporary European leader who most faithfully follows Machiavelli's route-map for acquiring and holding power.

---

[1] Gallagher, The Balkans after the Cold War, p. 64.
[2] Wikipedia, 'Siege of Dubrovnik', https://en.wikipedia.org/wiki/Siege_of_Dubrovnik, accessed 25 March 2022.
[3] Wikipedia, 'Siege of Dubrovnik'.
[4] Ivor Roberts, 'Milošević was a pyromaniac and a firefighter', *LSE blog*, 17 March 2017, accessed 19 April 2022. https://blogs.lse.ac.uk/europpblog/2017/03/17/roberts-milosevic-was-a-pyromaniac-and-a-firefighter/; the quote is from Blaine Harden, 'Playing chicken with Milošević', *New York Times Magazine*, 25 April 1999.
[5] Kenneth Morrison, *Montenegro: A Modern History*, London: I.B. Tauris, 2008, p. 71.
[6] Harden, 'Playing chicken'.
[7] Harden, 'Playing chicken'.
[8] Harden, 'Playing chicken'.
[9] Norman Davies, Vanished Kingdoms, The History of Half-forgotten Europe, London: Penguin, 2012, p. 582.
[10] William Booth and Steve Mufson, 'Montenegro's Leader Caught in the Middle As Friend of the U.S', *Washington Post*, 14 May 1999.
[11] *BBC World News*, 15 January 1998.
[12] Eric Moskowitz and Jeffrey S. Lantis, 'Conflict in the Balkans', in Fateful Decisions: Inside the National Security Council, editors, Karl F. Inderfurth and Loch K. Johnson, New York and Oxford: Oxford University Press, 2004, p.256.
[13] Ivor Roberts, 'Better days in the Balkans', *The Tablet*, 21 March 2019.
[14] Booth and Mufson, 'Montenegro's Leader'.
[15] Ivana Gardasevi, 'Russia and Montenegro: How and Why a Centuries Old Relationship Ruptured', *Quarterly Journal*, Vol. 17, No. 1, 2018, p. 69.
[16] Katie Foster, 'Russians, accused of organizing a plot to assassinate a European leader', Independent, 7 November 2016; Gordon N. Bardos, 'Montenegro's corrupt party of socialists is killing the country', *National Interest*, 28 January 2020,

https://nationalinterest.org/feature/montenegros-corrupt-party-socialists-killing-country-117821, accessed 19 April 2022.
[17] Marc Santora, 'Balkan spring turns to summer, and hopes for change diminish', *New York Times*, 1 June 2019.
[18] Nikola Dordevi, 'Montenegro narrowly avoids Chinese debt trap, for now', *Emerging Europe*, 9 August 2021, https://emerging-europe.com/news/montenegro-narrowly-avoids-chinese-debt-trap-for-now/, accessed 17 April 2022.
[19] Ivor Roberts, 'Time for Europe's longest-serving ruler to go', *PoliticoEU*, 22 February 2019, https://www.politico.eu/article/time-for-europes-longest-serving-ruler-to-go/, accessed 23 April 2022.
[20] Jean-Baptiste Chastand, 'In Montenegro, President Milo Djukanovic suffers a resounding defeat after 30 years in power', *Le Monde*, 3 April 2023.

CHAPTER 15: PEDRO SÁNCHEZ

1972-

After the successful implantation of democracy with a mixed capitalist system in West Germany, the transition to democracy in Spain was perhaps the most encouraging political development witnessed in Cold War Europe, at least during its later phase. Forty years later, the political stage in Spain is no longer dominated by pragmatists and consensus seekers as it was in the 1970s and 1980s. Instead, Spain is polarised on territorial, cultural and economic issues and the moderate ground has shrunk considerably.

Pedro Sánchez, who heads the Spanish Socialist Workers Party (PSOE) and has been Prime Minister since 2018, is the brash and imperturbable pilot in a gathering political storm. A master of political marketing, ideologically he stands for little except for a belief in a global political order where networks of middle-class progressives can compete for influence in trans-national institutions. So far, radical alliances with the far-left and separatists have been seen by him as the best means to stay in office. He angers liberal, conservative and also dissident socialist opponents by displaying a proprietorial approach to the state and allowing his fringe allies to increasingly influence its workings. His power base is not his party, which has fared poorly in national and regional elections, but a range of forces which benefit from state patronage (particularly the media). Sánchez is a political entrepreneur who has been adept at diverting attention from a deepening economic crisis by promoting disputes over the social and cultural direction of Spanish society. While promoting a series of corrosive binary disputes over issues ranging from religious schools, euthanasia, and the future of the monarchy, he has shown conspicuous enjoyment in the exercise of power and its trappings. Divisions among his opponents have kept him on top. But it is an open question how Spain can easily move on from his calculated revival of old antagonisms and the relish he has shown for pursuing cultural conflicts that have undermined stability in democracies that are on a much stronger footing than the one in Spain.

A constant trademark of the Sánchez era has been his trenchant discourse against the legacy of the Franco regime. Spanish politicians raise the issue of the civil war which brought him to power with far more frequency than was the case thirty years ago.[1] Legislation effectively outlawing any positive evaluation of the late dictator has been drawn up. Yet it is not surprising that the Socialist leader rarely dwells on his family's circumstances in this controversial phase of Spanish history.

Both of his parents pursued successful careers in the lower reaches of the administrative elite which sprang up in the second half of the dictatorship. A regime slowly shedding its harshest features had created a large state-led economy and a range of social services. His father in time switched from a position in the culture ministry to the world of business, where he was the owner of a successful light industrial firm, his mother remaining a bureaucrat in the social welfare system.

Spain witnessed major changes in the structure of society in the late 20th century, the reduction in size of the industrial working-class standing out. The expansion in size of the bureaucratic elite (especially due to the creation of 19 autonomous regions and communities after 1978) would enable it to become a fulcrum of power where national resources were concentrated. When in power, PSOE would increasingly reflect the priorities of the bureaucratic state and so (to a lesser extent) would its chief rival, the centre-right Popular Party (PP). Accordingly, it may not have been unusual for Sánchez, lacking any organic links with the working-class, to have risen to the top of the party at a very young age.

He was self-confident, fluent and capable of acquiring a string of qualifications in the social sciences and humanities. Opportunities to travel and mix in liberal circles in other countries, not unnaturally, made him a ready exponent of the post-national ideas for organizing the political and economic affairs of the West, which are often known as globalism. His embrace of cosmopolitan assumptions and values meant that he had few inhibitions about baiting political conservatives, who remain stronger in the Spanish middle-class than in other countries. His self-belief and his disinclination to hide his enjoyment of the trappings of office, enable him to be compared with Tony Blair, Emmanuel Macron and Gerhard Schröder, dynamic figures who sprang from the European left and whose joint motto could easily be: 'I did it my way'.

Politicians with Sánchez's penchant for self-aggrandisement were not fashionable in the first two decades of Spain's democratic rule. Following the competitive election held in 1977, Spain became famous for the implementation of the politics of consensus, in which all significant national players opted for negotiation and dialogue rather than confrontation and the encouragement of partisan fury. The major figures at the centre of the political transition, the ex-Francoist Adolfo Suarez, the socialist Felipe Gonzalez, and the communist Santiago Carrillo, usually bent over backwards to be conciliatory and pragmatic in their public roles. There had been enormous pessimism among observers and practitioners of Spanish politics about the ability of a democratic system to sink durable roots in a country which had been a byword for political strife over most of the previous 175 years. The coup attempt on 23 February 1981, mounted by Colonel António Tejero showed the vulnerability of the political system, as would the more enduring threat posed by insurrectionary separatism.

A pugnacious and perhaps naturally adversarial politician like Sánchez was perhaps fortunate in the timing of his entry into active politics. When he was elected to Madrid's city council in 2004, a return to polarisation was already becoming noticeable. The conservative prime minister, José Maria Aznar divided public opinion and the political world by participating in the US-led invasion and occupation of Iraq in 2003. Back in government from 2004 to 2011, PSOE swung left under José Luís Zapatero. Lacking a governing majority, he reached out to the successor of the communist party, the ultra-left-Green alliance IU-ICV, as well as to pro-separatists of the left in Catalonia. Zapatero also sought to mobilise support by politicising the long dormant civil-war, which the first wave of democratic rulers had resolved must not be turned into a political weapon, due to the possible harm caused to a far from consolidated democracy.[2]

Sánchez (born in 1972) spent his twenties honing his political skills, expanding his *résumé*, and working as a political consultant and adviser in Brussels, and in Sarajevo (as part of the shaky United Nations-led peace process in Bosnia). Such a trajectory was far from unusual in turn-of-a-century European social democracy as middle-class technocrats absorbed with process and regulatory frameworks, rather than concrete improvements to society, became steadily more prominent.

Just turned 41, and lacking any administrative experience, Sánchez was pitched into the leadership of PSOE in 2014. A vacuum had opened up owing to the unpopularity of Zapatero and many of his ministers, who were struggling to deal with an intensifying financial crisis. Riddled with debt, Spain's banks had been poorly supervised when both PSOE and the PP ruled. The resulting crisis meant a squeeze in the living standards of millions of Spaniards with a new far-left party Podemos, being able to maximise the discontent.

After losing power in 2011, PSOE was in disarray. Sánchez's energy and flair as a campaigner enabled him to snatch the leadership prize. His manifesto was rather vacuous. But he sought to appeal to the moderate base with mainstream policies as well as a commitment of unyielding opposition to the PP, in office from 2011 to 2018 with Mariano Rajoy as prime minister.

The political turbulence sweeping across much of Mediterranean Europe, as a result of the near-depression conditions arising from the long post-2008 financial crisis, put an end to the spirit of consensus. Amidst bitter recriminations over corruption and mismanagement at the top of government, two general elections were held a year apart from each other, in 2015 and 2016. Sánchez tried and failed to banish widespread scepticism about the ability of PSOE to steer the economy out of crisis. His party received the worst results in its recent history in these two contests, despite being up against an unimpressive conservative opponent. Sánchez dug in and was only prevailed upon to stand down in late 2016.

El País, the influential left-leaning newspaper, was withering in an editorial: 'the departure of... Pedro Sánchez, following the resignation of a majority of his executive committee, is essential... [He] has turned out not to be a proper leader, but rather an unscrupulous fool who does not hesitate to destroy the party that he has led with so much error, rather than admit his enormous failure'.[3]

Sánchez appeared to be the gravedigger of the Socialists, as his party narrowly avoided being overtaken in terms of popular support by the populist Podemos party in the 2016 election. But he was down but not out. Sánchez confounded many inside and outside his own party by managing a swift comeback. He campaigned against a much better-known challenger and won by cultivating grassroots support in defiance of the party bureaucracy. This was a particularly turbulent time in Spanish politics as shown several months later, in October 2017, when nationalist and far-left parties in Catalonia used their majority in the autonomous parliament, to try to break-away from Spain. PSOE opposed the secession bid but was also critical of the firm methods used by the Rajoy government to quell it.

In June 2018, Sánchez became prime minister after the PP government, now reliant on moderate Basque votes, was defeated in a vote of confidence. He was in charge of a minority government until parliamentary elections, held in April 2019, left PSOE the largest party without an overall majority. Single-party rule was now out of the question not only because of Podemos but also due to the emergence of two new parties, Vox, a firmly conservative nationalist force and Ciudadanos, an anti-separatist party advocating consensus. Lacking the votes to pass a budget, Sánchez clung to office, calling yet another election in December 2019. Ciudadanos collapsed, unable to agree a governing pact with PSOE, owing to misgivings about Sánchez, Podemos fell back, but Vox more than doubled its seats. At this point, Sánchez decided to form a coalition with Podemos and a range of pro-separatist parties, having ruled out such a formula when campaigning in 2018. He had said that, like nine percent of Spaniards, as Head of Government, I would not be able to sleep at night.[4]

Controversially, included in the new ruling alliance was Euskad Herria Bildu (Basque Country Land), widely viewed as the heir of the Herri-

Batasuna group, which had carried out numerous acts of terrorism against politicians and justice officials before the year 2000.

Sánchez was able to allay internal party critics for reaching out to fringe forces because he had returned PSOE to power after years in the wilderness. For his new allies, he appeared a credible dialogue partner because of his own social radicalism. He never showed much respect for the monarchy and was outspoken in his atheism and opposition to religious schools, making sure that no bible or crucifix were on display when he was sworn in as prime minister. Within days, he announced his intention to remove the remains of General Francisco Franco from their symbolic resting place at the Valley of the Fallen near Madrid, which was carried out in 2019.

Until his resignation in March 2021, to make an unsuccessful bid on behalf of Podemos to win the Madrid regional election, Pablo Iglesias its leader was a vice-president of Spain. The consumer affairs ministry had been created as part of a deal with the far-left IU-ICV and the post was allocated to one of its deputies, the 29-year-old Alberto Garzon, who concentrated on steps to promote an ecologically healthy diet among Spanish youth.

A thick-skinned prime minister swatted away charges that he was allowing the government, at a time of acute crisis, to be absorbed with niche causes. He worked well with each of the far-left figures in the government, including Yolanda Díaz, from the IU-ICV who soon proved to be a gifted populist in her own right. Figures this far to the left in the political spectrum had not been included in the government of a major west European democracy for many decades. Critics warned that one by-product might be an erosion in the neutrality of certain public ministries. In 2021, he floated the possibility of altering the law in areas which were felt to constrain his left nationalist allies in Catalonia and Navarre.[5] A year later, he decriminalised the law on embezzlement and, more seriously, abolished that of sedition. Most major western countries prohibit acts endangering the existence of the state, and his move put Spain well outside the mainstream.[6] These moves have received very little attention in the rest of Europe. It was only Sánchez's decision, in 2021, to pardon Catalan politicians convicted of rebellion, having previously endorsed the jail terms when handed down in 2019, which briefly caused a stir.[7]

Sánchez plunged into the culture wars with gusto. He was adept at offering proposals that deepened polarisation and drew attention away from his governing record, as when he put the Historical Memory bill before parliament, just before the Covid pandemic struck. Opponents see it as nothing less than an attempt to allow one wing of the political spectrum to decide which interpretations of the past possess legitimacy and to ensure that the education world would reflect its preferences.[8]

The strongest hostility to this cultural offensive came from Vox, which had mobilised working-class and small-town support, and was participating in several autonomous governments. The governing parties, along with media allies, denounced Vox as far-right, or indeed fascist. The left barely concealed its hope that its rise would splinter the right and keep Sánchez and his allies in power, irrespective of their economic record.

The eruption of the pandemic in early 2020 put a hold on Sánchez's more ideological plans. This two-year emergency witnessed an expansion in the size of the central state and an apparatus of advisory bodies. Spending at central government level increased by around 30 percent between 2018 and 2022, as PSOE opened up space for left-wing allies at the heart of government.[9] With 23 cabinet ministers and 33 secretaries of state, Sánchez's government was the biggest since the start of the current political system.[10] The practice did not originate with him. But Sánchez has not hesitated to concentrate EU structural funds in municipalities where PSOE governs, further raising the political temperature.[11] Controversy surrounds the fate of the €72 billion due to be provided under the EU's Recovery and Resilience plan. The Independent Audit for Spanish Fiscal responsibility, created in 2013, at the request of the EU, has expressed concerns both about the absence of transparency and a framework to ensure that the funds would be targeted at structural reforms (a primary aim of the EU Commission initiative).[12]

The impact of Covid on economic conditions was worse in Spain than in many other sizable European states. The strong economic reliance on a tourist industry, which was effectively suspended for two years, led to a sharp fall in economic activity. Between 2005 and 2022, the Spanish economy appeared to go into reverse. Despite a marked increase in population, the total labour force grew by only 400,000 in that period. The public debt grew from 42 percent to around 120 percent of GDP. Meanwhile, unemployment jumped from 8 to 16 percent in this 17-month period'.[13]

Spain suffered from adverse events, ranging from Covid to the earlier global financial crisis, which originated elsewhere. But there was no lack of analysts who claimed that the depth of the difficulties and the lack of a substantial recovery were due to the way that Spain was governed. The colonising of the state institutions by the ruling parties, the poor preparation and selection of elites, along with a wasteful and flawed education system, were seen as drivers of decline.[14]

Sánchez's swaggering demeanour rarely suggested much unease on his part about Spain's economic performance or its prospects. His powerbase was largely located in sectors of society which were able to thrive despite the darkening economic picture (with growth for 2022 slashed from 7 percent to 4.3 percent).[15] It comprised a large caste of politicians, businesspeople who traded with the branches of the state that they ran, public employees, trade-unions, and the media. The Spanish media increasingly reflected the anti-capitalist radicalism of iconoclastic Spaniards. Major titles skated over Sanchez's use of state facilities when on vacation and were prepared to promote him as an 'underdog'.[16] However, print and electronic titles and channels (much augmented by Covid financial relief from the state) were starting to be eclipsed by a plethora of rival online media outlets.

Critics, such as Joaquín Leguina, who ran the city government in Madrid from 1983 to 1995 and was head of PSOE in the capital for much of this time, have been unsparing about Sánchez. In 2021, this historic socialist described him as a vengeful individual who crushes anyone who dares to defy his systematic efforts to place radical feminism and sympathy for separatist feeling at the centre of party affairs.[17]

Ignacio Varela, who worked in the prime ministerial office of Felipe Gonzalez between 1982 and 1993 believes that PSOE's leader has acted like a taxidermist, removing the party's vital organs, leaving it in a mummified state. It is a radical makeover that has led to the party becoming his personal vehicle. He is one of many voices who believe that the longer he occupies his position, the greater will be the damage to a democratic and law-based state.[18]

The regional system of governance is a curb on his power, with foes of PSOE doing well outside areas where separatism is strong. A major reverse occurred in May 2021, when Isabel Ayuso consolidated right-wing control of Madrid, the PP more than doubling its number of seats. Another followed in June 2022, when Andalucia, long the jewel in PSOE's regional electoral crown, saw it roundly rejected for a second successive time.

Under King Felipe VI, the Crown, although lacking any executive prerogatives, also upholds a unified Spain rather than the patchwork of cultures and ethnic identities that Sánchez seems increasingly comfortable with.[19] The various state organs, from the justice system to the intelligence services, increasingly struggle to repel overt political interference. The overhaul of the intelligence service that Sánchez promoted, in spring 2022, may undermine the neutrality of one important branch of a state which has confronted repeated terrorist threats. He insists that a state with expanding powers and resources is the answer for many of Spain's problems. But at the same time, no other post-1977 prime minister has been as ready to interfere in state bodies like the Attorney General's office. Officials in different areas have been regularly removed because he claims their performance has been unsatisfactory. But critics allege that a string of dismissals occurred because of the need for a scapegoat, or because they refuse to endorse decisions which are felt to be of doubtful legality.[20]

In growing numbers, former party colleagues now openly express fears that Sanchez intends to erode or suborn constitutional procedures that were painstakingly drawn up after the dictatorship to ensure balance and consensus underpin Spanish democracy. In December 2022, six former Socialist ministers were among 300 signatories from across the party who warned about Sanchez's plans to alter Spain's constitutional framework to suit the wishes of the radical minority which sustained his government in office.[21] During the run-up to parliamentary elections announced for July 2023, Sanchez redoubled his efforts to neutralise the Constitutional Tribunal (CT). It was clearly seen by him and his far-left and nationalist allies as a force standing in the way of their vision of a Spain shaped not by consensus, but by the radical vision of a range of mobilised groups espousing differing forms of identity politics. Arguably, the Prime Minister's allies have revived the outlook that had led to the downfall of democracy in Spain in earlier historical epochs. Instead of bodies like the CT being chosen on a neutral basis and being entrusted with safeguarding the constitutional order, they argued that it was sufficient for its membership and deliberations to be determined by whoever comprised the parliamentary majority.[22]

Albert Rivera, a centrist politician who had played a determining role in foiling the secessionist bid by Catalan nationalists in 2017, issued a warning to Sanchez, in the closing days of 2022, that he was in danger of being seen as emulating the actions of Latin American demagogues like Peru's recent president, Pedro Castillo, who had attempted a 'self-coup' by dissolving the country's main political institutions. He pointed out that: 'the Constitutional Tribunal is the only containment dam that the State has to defend itself against unconstitutional laws that limit or prohibit fundamental rights or jeopardize national unity or equality among all Spaniards'.[23]

Rivera expected the EU to exercise a restraining role on Caesarist ambitions emanating from the heart of Spanish government but feared that there would still be a real possibility of Spain being mired in permanent institutional crisis, citing the example of Argentina as a real possibility.

Under Sanchez, Spain may have reverted to one of the most perilous political moments it has known since the restoration of democracy five decades ago. It is increasingly clear that he enjoys the closest affinity not with the mainstream of his own party, which has been hollowed out by him, but with parties, enjoying between 15 and 20 percent support nationwide, which regard the 1978 Constitution as a block on their radical republican and pro-separatist instincts and ambitions. Due to the alliances that he has stitched together and a growing tendency to rule by decree, bypassing parliament or allowing little time for contentious decisions to be discussed, he has turned PSOE into a confrontational force rather than the consensual one it long appeared to be.[24]

'Voters delivered a verdict on Sánchez's ideological brand of politics in regional and city elections held on 28 May 2023. Many were chiefly interested in the local record of rulers. Sánchez had famously not concerned himself with delivery and the quality of representation and it was no surprise that he and his party fared badly. Before internal critics could gather force, he called a general election for 23 July. PSOE was demoralized, while the far-left beneficiaries of his rule regrouped. The ambitious firebrand Yolanda Díaz formed a new electoral force called Sumar. Meanwhile in Brussels dazed officials suddenly found that Spain would be in no position to begin the Presidency of the European Council when its turn came on 1 July. Throughout his career Sánchez had rarely thought about anyone other than himself.

Whether in government or opposition, he is likely to remain influential. But the prospects for Spanish democratic stability are bound to be uncertain as long as personal and partisan interests predominate in a party which, for many years, was one of the lynchpins of Spanish democracy.

---

[1] Matthew Bennett, 'Los políticos españoles hablan más de la Guerra Civil en 2022 que hace 30 años', *The Spain Report*, 6 November 2022, https://thespainreport.substack.com/p/los-politicos-espanoles-hablan-mas, accessed 7 November 2022.
[2] See Stanley G. Payne, 'The Politics of Memory', *First Things*, May 2021.
[3] Editorial, *El País*, 28 September 2016.
[4] Carlos Calvete, 'The Creeping Coup D'État in Spain', *European Conservative*, 2 January 2023, https://europeanconservative.com/articles/commentary/the-creeping-coup-detat-in-spain/, accessed 3 January 2023.
[5] Sergio Aguilera, 'Sánchez se abre a modificar también la malversación: "Esperemos la tramitación"', *El Espanol*, 13 November 2022, https://www.elespanol.com/espana/20221113/sanchez-abre-modificar-malversacion-esperemos-tramitacion/718178196_0.html, accessed 14 November 2022.
[6] Calvete, 'The Creeping Coup'.
[7] Sam Jones, 'Spanish government pardons nine jailed Catalan leaders', *Guardian*, 22 June 2021.
[8] Payne, 'The Politics of Memory'.
[9] Editorial, *ABC newspaper*, 10 April 2022.
[10] Editorial, *ABC newspaper*, 10 April 2022.
[11] Carlos Calvete, 'Political Discrimination in the Spanish Government's Allocation of Funds', *European Conservative*, 6 February 2022, https://europeanconservative.com/articles/news/political-discrimination-in-the-spanish-governments-allocation-of-funds/, accessed 19 April 2022.

---

[12] Jorge Vila Lozano, 'Madrid's snap election and the Mandela effect', *New English Review*, June 2021, https://www.newenglishreview.org/articles/madrids-snap-election-and-the-mandela-effect/, accessed 16 April 2022.
[13] Jesús Cacho, 'España, veinte años perdidos', *Vozpopuli*, 24 April 2022, https://www.vozpopuli.com/opinion/espana-veinte-perdidos.html, accessed 14 May 2022.
[14] Cacho, 'España', quoting Jesús Fernández Villaverde.
[15] 'Spain "Better Prepared" for Possible Recession, Prime Minister Says', *Bloomberg News*, May 24th, 2022.
[16] See Arturo Lezcano, 'El viaje de Pedro Sánchez en su 'Peugeot' después de dimitir como secretario general', *Vanity Fair*, (Spanish edition), 5 September 2018, https://www.revistavanityfair.es/la-revista/articulos/viaje-pedro-sanchez-peugeout-moncloa/32460, accessed 26 October 2022.
[17] Esther Esteban, 'Pedro Sánchez es un vengativo, destila odio y eso no es bueno para el PSOE', *El Espanol*, 14 May 2021, https://www.elespanol.com/eldigitalcastillalamancha/20210514/leguina-esther-esteban-pedro-sanchez-no-psoe/581193429_0.html, accessed 17 May 2022.
[18] Ignacio Varela: 'Dudo que el PSOE pueda recuperarse después de pasar por las manos de Pedro Sánchez', *The Objective*, 24 April 2022, https://theobjective.com/espana/2022-04-24/ignacio-varela-entrevista-sanchez-tezanos-redondo/, accessed 17 May 2022.
[19] António Caño, 'Nuestro Rey democrático', *The Objective*, 26 December 2022, https://theobjective.com/elsubjetivo/opinion/2022-12-26/nuestro-rey-democratico/, accessed 3 January 2023.
[20] António Salvador, 'Todos los 'cadáveres' del presidente', *El Independente*, 14 May 2022, https://www.elindependiente.com/espana/2022/05/14/todos-los-cadaveres-del-presidente/, accessed 17 May 2022.
[21] Juan Fernández-Miranda and Marta Martínez, 'Exministros y exdiputados socialistas, contra el plan de Sánchez que beneficia a los condenados del "procés"', *ABC newspaper*, 12 December 2022, https://www.abc.es/espana/seis-exministros-socialistas-suman-manifiesto-plan-sanchez-20221212082352-nt.html, accessed 3 January 2023.
[22] See Jorge Vilches, 'Sánchez, a la historia de la infamia', *The Objective*, 30 November 2022, https://theobjective.com/elsubjetivo/opinion/2022-11-30/sanchez-historia-infamia/, accessed 3 January 2023.
[23] Albert Rivera, 'Las democracias también enferman', *The Objective*, 26 December 2022, https://theobjective.com/elsubjetivo/opinion/2022-12-25/las-democracias-tambien-enferman/, accessed 3 January 2023.
[24] Jorge González-Gallarza, 'The failure of Spanish democracy', *European Conservative*, 8 December 2022, https://europeanconservative.com/articles/analysis/the-failure-of-spanish-democracy/, accessed 3 January 2023.

PART 4
CHAPTER 16: ENTREPRENEURS OF ETHNICITY

Movements seeking to break up long-established states, have been the happy beneficiaries of changes in political culture and social outlook, which they usually have done little to bring about. An 'adversary culture' has sprung up (first recognised by the American political scientist Daniel Bell), that displays 'a sceptical if not cynical stance toward established institutions, traditionalist values and ways of life'.[1] At least in the affluent West, the growth of material comfort and general human well-being and security has prompted younger generations to embrace introspective causes bound up with lifestyle and personal identity. This new 'radicalism' reveals disaffection with many features of the contemporary order.

Without needing to strive as much as past generations to obtain many of the necessities of life, certain groups of voters instead base their political choices around the search for psychological well-being. The strongest passions expressed in the political arena in the first decades of the twenty-first century have often stemmed from a desire on the part of usually white middle-class radicals to assert identities bound up with perceived historical wrongs and current dangers to the planet. Often what is most clearcut is the wish to repudiate existing identities based on the nuclear family, nation, or class roles in favour of ones advanced by those who presume to speak for submerged and oppressed minorities. Various activist movements have taken the offensive against what are seen as oppressive forces of authority, whose norms, expectations, or indeed very existence, are seen as harmful and provocative. At times, identity politics can easily slide into a form of therapy in which activists transcend their unhappiness by adopting an exaggerated form of moral superiority. Manifestos are often introspective, displaying little interest in preserving or strengthening material gains for society. Instead, if political power is an objective, the priority is often to promote symbolic demands (reparations, race quotas, defunding of the police) which supposedly appeal to mobilised minorities but which often have little appeal to the wider society (including most minority members).

In Britain, Spain and Ireland, secessionist movements, with a strong performative dimension, have drawn adherents from segments of the middle-class in education, the communications industries and administration. They are often seen as embodying what, in Britain, are known as the chattering classes. Groups unsettled by the pace of economic change, or who feel that being born into wealth and privilege gives them a duty to rebel, can be drawn to these movements.

By contrast, backing is often weak or absent from productive groups at ease with the status quo or used to planning ahead for the future. State organs and the media often previously bolstered the outlook and positions of these conventional strata of society. But that is ceasing to be the case as bureaucracies have embraced the agenda of radical minorities and much of the media has chosen to try and overcome commercial decline by championing the concerns of radicalised niche groups.

Journalism was never free of strong political alignments, but they have come to dominate even conventional reporting. Causes such as Scottish Nationalism, Catalan separatism, or Irish Republicanism were once seen as impractical or anachronistic when those in charge of major nations were able to promote a widely-accepted narrative based on consensus, continuity, or the desirability of slowly-evolving change. But these movements have acquired greater credibility in the information industry as core narratives have receded and authority has fragmented. Their edginess and militancy are seen as badges of virtue in societies where the politics of class and nation have started to be superseded by activism involving taking a stand on various passionately-held contemporary causes.

It matters little if, once tasting power, the performance of these movements is dismal if not disastrous. The criterion for judging activist movements which have acquired influence or control of resources, laws or territory is more often than not the authenticity and conviction with which they pursue their mission as a vanguard for change. Their effectiveness or probity as decision-makers, guarantors of freedom, or controllers of funds, often slips into the background when evaluating their public performance.

Floundering or unbalanced minority movements in charge of a territory are essentially judged on how effective they are as impresarios of identity. Thus, there is always an incentive for them to manufacture conflict with rulers at central level or intensify existing ones. Ruling nationalists in both Catalonia and Scotland developed this type of permanent strategy of tension to a high art. Astro-turfing against a familiar foe diverted attention from administrative failings and was guaranteed to attract the attention of numerous media outlets. Many could safely be expected to frame the coverage along the lines of the nimble minority David versus the stumbling and arrogant central Goliath.

Whereas the new politics of territorial identity was full of possibility, the stances of increasingly unloved central states were defensive and destined to eventual failure. In a 2017 article, Steven Erlanger of the *New York Times* described Britain as 'undergoing a full-blown identity crisis', adding that it was 'a hollowed-out country', 'ill at ease with itself', 'deeply provincial', and engaged in a 'controlled suicide'.[2]

The British parliament was then deadlocked over how far to endorse a narrow vote in a high turnout referendum in favour of Britain leaving the European Union. This assertion of state primacy over trans-national forces had occurred in 2016, after a lengthy period in which the central state, increasingly run by cosmopolitan new elites, had downgraded national sovereignty, even frowning on patriotism as a unifying concept. It is arguably easier for secessionist movements to win arguments and thrive when the central state spurns nationhood or is incoherent in its defence. Perhaps the high-point of this trend had occurred in 2005, when Britain's then Prime Minister Tony Blair told Labour Party members: 'I hear people say we have to stop and debate globalisation. You might as well debate whether autumn should follow summer…'[3] A Labour critic of Blair later stated that, for him, 'the nation state was merely the regional administrator of a global system' requiring 'the frictionless movement of people, money, goods and services'.[4]

Blair and his party had been responsible for drawing up ambitious and arguably ill-planned forms of devolution for Scotland, Wales, London and Northern Ireland. The untidy asymmetrical process of decentralisation encouraged backing for the idea that Britain was turning into a 'mosaic society' without any clearcut or over-arching identity. Arguably, Spain under Pedro Sánchez, from 2018 has gone further, repudiating the idea that there should be parity between the identity and culture bound up with the central state and autonomous territorial formations. In a major concession to nationalist allies, the Socialist leader announced in July 2022, that Spanish would no longer be required to be taught in Catalonia's public schools.

It is not just in regions that are decentralised on an ethnic basis, where the priority is often on affirming or rewarding favoured identities, instead of, as in the past, maintaining or improving the quality of governance. But it is ruling separatists which have gone furthest with this tendency. They often dedicate their energies to acquiring hegemony over state functions, which are important for cementing identity. Education is by far the most important one, perhaps closely followed by the media. Domination of the media enables them to control the official narrative, seen as a crucial requirement if their mission is to triumph. They use these influencers of identity to try and create an 'us and them' mentality with the larger state that they wish to break away from. Curricula and programme content are used to convert youth in particular towards acquiring the same outlook and mentality of those who are already pro-separatist. The emphasis shifts from the performance of the regional state, how effective it is at delivering practical benefits to the population, and how accountable ruling Nationalists are to the intolerable nature of being trapped in an 'alien' state that disrespects local nationalists' feelings too much of the time.

Nationalists aim to force through cultural changes so that younger generation voters view territorial issues and assertions of identity as primordial ones that eclipse all others. They dwarf the efficiency, probity, and dedication to improvements of rulers as criteria when casting votes.

Technicians of power in the separatist camp see an advantage in tapping into a sense of alienation or to sensitivity to slights and criticism often felt by younger voters. They play on injured feelings and perceived lack of respect from elders or powerful groups in society. It involves the nationalists adopting an 'underdog' mentality and promoting a sense of victimhood and dispossession. This is ironic since they exercise their often extensive autonomous powers with more firmness than is often displayed by decision-makers at senior levels of the British and Spanish states. In fact, it is not an over-exaggeration to claim that at times they adopt a proprietorial attitude towards the state.

As these profiles indicate, ruling nationalists make sure that contracts are issued to the business sector as long as companies avoid criticising their record as administrators and show willingness to spring to their defence at particular moments. Ethnic parties, when in power, show no fastidiousness about using state resources to boost the finances of the movement. This can spill over into nepotism and kleptocracy. But since the funds being used belong to the 'overlord' state which the separatists are trying to secede from, such tactics are viewed as a smart way of weakening the grip of an 'alien' state authority. Nationalists, in what they see as their march towards full statehood, rarely if ever reflect on whether conduct which would soon land non-separatist opponents in difficulties, might disfigure the national liberation cause. Not only might misuse of state resources be viewed as morally questionable, but it could legitimise predatory approaches to power which could imperil the survival of a post-independence democracy.

Core supporters often show impatience with conventional democratic forms and at times wish to make it difficult for opponents to exercise their full rights. It is not unknown for rivals to face disruption and harassment from supporters of secession when seeking to campaign in elections.

Profiled here, Nicola Sturgeon and Jordi Pujol saw themselves as engaged on moral missions. Active after the ending of the Cold War, they reflected a political age when politicians representing mainstream forces adopted moralistic stances in their discourse and policy goals in order to appear *authentic*. The new morality in politics ultimately lessened the inhibitions felt by parties customarily holding office to interfere in the lives of citizens, as shown by the preoccupation with environmental safety or enforcing lifestyle changes. But nationalists had no qualms about altering state and society in order to make it more amenable to their project. In Europe, the precedents for the reinforcement of authority in education, the media, and public administration, were not always reassuring ones. In several European states in the 1930s a drive to coordinate and control all political, social, cultural, and educational institutions occurred in the name of national unity.

It means that boundaries are emphasised and reinforced. Usually, there is no room for overlapping identities, despite the fluid nature of identity, both in Pujol's Catalonia and Sturgeon's Scotland. One political opponent of the SNP wrote in 2022: 'The drive to divide is relentless, for the will of a majority can never appease the zeal of a minority. At its heart is a miserable ambition to force people to choose between identities rather than feel comfortable with them all, as most of us naturally are'.[5]

The obstacles placed in the way of inhabitants with a Spanish identity in the Basque Country or Catalonia due to homogenisation policies in areas like education and employment, have passed without much notice in much of the Western media. What local critics of Pujol and Sturgeon viewed as self-aggrandising behaviour on their part, was often seen as edgy, smart and even inspirational by media outlets free of their direct influence, but attracted to bold stances against defensive establishments in London or Madrid. Public broadcasting journalists and numerous colleagues in other networks have not usually rushed to interrogate nationalists about the viability of their state-building plans. More often than not, separatist politicians themselves treat the phase of consolidating their project, after the presumed success of their break-away efforts, as a secondary matter requiring little real preparation or expenditure of thought.

The degree of assurance (some would say self-righteousness) that separatist leaders can display means that they have learned to make light of informed criticism of their plans. The SNP was unfazed when one of its chief advisors, Professor Mark Blyth, an economist at Brown University in the USA, expressed doubts in 2022 about how Scotland would fare after being 'the first part of any advanced economy to split from its existing national base'. He criticised SNP plans for 'a complete lack of specificity' and was caustic about SNP ambitions to replicate Denmark: 'No, you wouldn't be Denmark. Denmark took 600 years to become Denmark'.[6] Undeterred, Sturgeon paid a high profile visit to its capital Copenhagen later in the year to open an unofficial embassy to the Nordic countries where any hard questions about the pitfalls of separation were brushed aside.

Separatists are usually on safer ground, engaging with cultural personalities. The list of show business figures in Scotland who strongly identify with Nicola Sturgeon eclipses what is seen in parts of Spain with vigorous separatist movements. This may be due to the fact that the separatist movement there has turned into such a *performative* one. A vast amount of time and energy is invested in events at home and abroad involving self-promotion and a relentless focus on arcane constitutional issues. The emphasis on presentation rather than delivery of policies inevitably weakens detachment and dulls perspective. A joint interview that was conducted at the Edinburgh Book Festival in 2022, with the veteran actor Brian Cox, produced revealing exchanges which suggested that Scotland's First Minister primarily regarded herself as a performer, just like him. The exchange caused a stir perhaps because it revealed the degree of self-absorption, some would say narcissism, that a nationalist leader can afford to exhibit.[7]

Sturgeon's perceived exhibitionism has arguably made her far less effective than more self-effacing nationalists elsewhere, who preferred to portray themselves on their frequent international excursions as servants of a much bigger cause. The Catalan separatist patriarch Pujol was certainly enigmatic. He sought to acquire self-rule incrementally and by stealth. He was a kind of regional equivalent of the Moses of European integration, Jean Monnet, seeking to acquire powers for apparently constructive purposes, while in reality consumed with the wish to create an entirely new political entity equipped with the powers of a nation-state. Towards that end, he established control of the education system, civic bodies and, above all, the media, to erect strong barriers with the rest of Spain. In terms of identity politics, Pujol was arguably innovative in daring to interfere with a population in ways most competitors would have shrank from doing. It merits underlining that ethnic identity politicians are bolder about carrying out social engineering designed to transform the character of their societies, in order to make them more susceptible to their new state agendas.

Despite his image of efficiency and probity, it wasn't long before he was treating the most advanced socio-economic part of a semi-federal democratic Spain as his own private plaything. This seems to be a recurring vulnerability among ethnic leaders. In Scotland, Sturgeon has shown similar possessive traits. As dedicated servants of a noble cause, the rules determining political behaviour are seen as not really applying to them.

Someone who was the antithesis of radical disruptors, ready to use daring and disruptive tactics to advance their cause, was the Head of State, Queen Elizabeth II. She died while this book was being written and the reaction to her passing showed that traditional forms of allegiance still possessed considerable staying power.

Her son, proclaimed King Charles III shortly after her death on 8 September 2022, visited each of the four nations making up the United Kingdom to allow people, unable to attend the funeral in London, to show their respects to his mother who had reigned for seventy years. Michelle O'Neill, the leader of Sinn Fein in Northern Ireland, had the presence of mind to warmly receive King Charles III when he came to Northern Ireland on 13 September 2022. Queen Elizabeth II had died in her Scottish Highland home of Balmoral five days earlier. Powerful expressions of both grief and affection were displayed along the route of the cortège taking her body from there, through parts of Scotland with contrasting profiles, to lie in state at St Giles Cathedral in Edinburgh. Symbolic public spaces frequently dominated by nationalists were instead now filled up with far greater numbers of people keen to offer their respectful farewells to a deceased sovereign of a multi-national realm. Eleven days of mourning, involving a whole sweep of society, caused a momentary reassessment to be made of the values which defined contemporary Britain. The unforced homage from millions of people seemed to suggest that the characteristics of modern society, emphasising personal preoccupations and emotions, ones which insurgent political causes had exploited, were perhaps far from all-powerful. Later, the outpouring of emotion and the sense of solidarity displayed, as huge numbers queued for many hours to file pass the late Queen's coffin in Westminster Hall in London, showed the reach of constitutional monarchy. It was one which could not be easily replicated by territorial separatism or left-wing republicanism.

There was a reverential popular response that transcended class, region, nation, occupation and even generation. It was perhaps an antidote to a sense of rootlessness and disconnection which has been encouraged or exploited by different forces in British society. Those weeks were described as 'a sort of reverse French Revolution for Republicanism in Britain'.[8]

The Queen, who had shown herself to be a temperate, dutiful, and benign figure through her seventy years on the British throne, had revealed in death that no one was more respected across the broad sweep of society. It remains to be seen if her successors will be able to preserve her standing and the legitimacy of the monarchy. Even at the height of the outpouring of affection, some British-focused voices doubted if a death, which had brought the biggest gathering of world leaders for any single event, could be of more than ephemeral significance.[9] At least, there was unprecedented discussion on what impact a constitutional monarchy has on the nature of governance. The monarchy's value was seen to rest in its ability to frustrate those in the political world who would like to wield unrestrained power. At their best, constitutional monarchs are above ideology and beyond faction. They are thus an obstacle in the way of radical-sounding movements which seek to thoroughly politicise state and society in order to impose a new order. The reaction to the death of Queen Elizabeth was thus a somewhat unexpected check on the ambitions and assumptions of purveyors of identity politics, not just in Scotland but perhaps also in other parts of Europe where they have seemed increasingly visible and entrenched.

But within weeks, Britain's public highways were the scene of continuous disruption by eco-extremists. The moderating effect of a much-respected monarch's farewell proved short lived. Elizabeth II's long reign might be seen to encompass a period of rare stability, whose roots were steadily eroded by the accumulating failures of internal statecraft and the inability to shield the country from destabilising global events. Outlandish or utopian schemes for re-organising the planet acquired numerous devotees from social groups once seen as reassuring upholders of all that made Britain a beacon of common sense in a stormy world. The initiative in middle-class Britain was leeching away from citizens and groups committed to democratic order and well-regulated private capitalism. Instead, the most persuasive and favoured middle-class voices increasingly belonged to petit-bourgeois radicals in search of a convenient enemy to rail against. Nobody from a disparaged political order seemed capable of withstanding the climate of revolt. So broken were ties between most of the political class and the wider national community that finding the formula that could rally the still moderate majority to face down radical extremes now thriving in parts of society's upper echelons, seemed an increasingly forlorn undertaking. Despite their impracticality and misconduct, much of the initiative still lay with dedicated nation-breakers.

---

[1] Matthew Goodwin, 'The Challenge facing King Charles III', *Matthew Goodwin Substack*, 20 September 2022.
[2] Steven Erlanger, 'No One Knows What Britain Is Anymore', *New York Times*, 6 November 2017.
[3] Patrick O'Flynn, 'Tony Blair is yesterday's man', *Spiked Online*, 5 July 2022, https://www.spiked-online.com/2022/07/05/tony-blair-is-yesterdays-man/, accessed 27 October 2022.
[4] Maurice Glasman, 'The Future Belongs to Blue Labour', *Spiked Online*, 5 November 2022, https://www.spiked-online.com/2022/11/05/the-future-belongs-to-blue-labour/, accessed 11 November 2022.
[5] Brian Wilson, 'Scottish nationalists brand of identity politics is based on a sinister and false premise', *Scotsman*, 20 August 2022.
[6] John Ferry, 'Star SNP economist fails to find the positive case for independence', *Spectator*, 19 August 2022.
[7] Tom Gordon, 'Sturgeon: "I can't wait until I don't give a f*** anymore"', *Herald Scotland*, 29 August 2022; Steerpike, 'Sturgeon's swipe at Scottish voters', *Spectator Online*, 30 August 2022, https://www.spectator.co.uk/article/sturgeon-s-swipe-at-scottish-voters.
[8] Effie Deans, 'Scottish nationalists refute their own argument', *Lily of St Leonards*, 18 September 2022, https://www.effiedeans.com/2022/09/scottish-nationalists-refute-their-own.html.
[9] Paul Kingsnorth, 'Can the nation survive Elizabeth', *UnHerd*, 17 September 2022, https://unherd.com/2022/09/the-queen-leaves-behind-a-wasteland/.

CHAPTER 17: JORDI PUJOL

1930 -[1]

Jordi Pujol was a shadowy political figure who wielded great influence in late 20th century Spain and might easily be seen as a meticulous architect of secession. This short, balding, unobtrusive figure would never have stood out in a crowd; *The Economist* uncharitably describing him 'in appearance rather like a pugilistic garden gnome'.[2] He was a mandarin, a master manipulator who bent powerful economic and social interests to his will, determined to construct a new nation in the Iberian Peninsula. Catalan nationalism had sprung up late in the 19th century, influenced by traditional conservative challenges to a centralised Spain and also by German romanticism. It took right- and left-wing forms during the first four turbulent decades of the 20th century. Nearly the entire time, the main objective was home rule rather than outright independence.

This canny, low-key operator played a constructive role in Spain's transition from authoritarian rule to multi-party democracy. His sagacity and talent for coalition building enabled him quickly to become the dominant force in Catalan politics from the late 1970s onwards. If he had a chief political *credo* it was that Catalonia did not belong to Spain, being (seemingly) a mature dynamic and advanced society, with the key attributes of a nation, that was trapped in a union with a 'backward' Spain.

But it is possible to claim that his authoritarian and manipulative style of rule impaired whatever chance there had been for Catalonia to flourish in the democratic era and be treated as a beacon of progress. The evidence is too plentiful that Pujol treated the first of Spain's autonomous regions to be established after General Franco's death very much as his own private fiefdom (perhaps even in ways the dictator had never done in Spain as a whole). He encouraged close family members and allies to have the same acquisitive attitude to public goods and services as he had acquired. The accounts of corruption that overshadowed his career finally resulted in both he and several of his children facing grave criminal charges.

It would be bad enough if it had only been personal failings that led Pujol to drive his homeland towards a state of political under-development. Arguably, his promotion of an exclusive form of regional separation has resulted in deeper and longer-lasting damage to Catalonia and to Spain overall. With impressive artistry he established control of the education system, civic bodies and, above all, the media, to erect strong barriers with the rest of Spain and promote an exclusive Catalan identity. It is not surprising that an unhappy polarised society grew up in which radicalised political activists, sought to secede from Spain in 2017.

Pujol was a silent witness to the turmoil. It is not clear whether he had any misgivings about how the pro-Catalan cause which he had patiently constructed—outwardly bourgeois, liberal and even Christian democrat in formation—had turned into a radically left-wing movement glorifying in direct action on the streets. There seems to be little left of Catalonia's image as a sensible pro-European stronghold of middle-class commerce and industry. Purveyors of ethnic identity rarely exhibit remorse when their agitation or covert plotting produce unhappy results. Instead of chastising himself for many decades of sowing social disharmony, perhaps Pujol may feel a quiet sense of satisfaction. Looking around at politicians who see it as their mission to manage citizens and force them to reluctantly embrace causes that are newly in fashion, he might feel that he is a pioneer in the politics of disruptive middle-class European *vanguardism*.

In terms of identity politics, Pujol was arguably innovative in doing things to a population many had reservations about. In this regard, he was an early scaled-down version of George Soros, the global political activist who has used much of his own wealth to promote social movements, some of which have a revolutionary vision for humanity. Whereas Soros has been spending chunks of his fortune in shaping the world according to his precepts, Pujol enriched himself and his family while on the ostensibly moral mission of forming the Catalonia that he believed in.

Pujol's emancipatory crusade was territorial and perhaps some historians will view it as a form of sectarian discord that has occasionally afflicted Spain since the era of the warring Islamic *taifas* over a millennium ago. In a Europe, parts of which are currently awash with radical identity politics, Pujol's role in signalling the end of the post-1945 European political consensus that lasted around three generations, deserves not to fall into obscurity.

Pujol was born into a middle-class Barcelona family in 1930. His early years coincided with the fall of the monarchy, the crisis of the second republic, the civil-war, and the repression subsequently inflicted by the victorious Spanish nationalist right on the left and pro-autonomy regional nationalists. The fact that his family allowed him to study the Catalan language clandestinely during his teenage years, indicates that it was a household which preserved a strong Catalan identity. In 1960, Pujol surreptitiously published a pamphlet against Franco. He was arrested and beaten until he divulged the name of the printer, and then given a seven-year jail sentence when he refused to repent.[3] He was released after thirty months and afterwards, he used his prestige, as someone who had suffered for his beliefs, to construct an embryo movement which would in turn create an underground Assembly for Catalonia.

Initially, he had planned to practice as a doctor. But he put aside his degree in medicine and instead entered the financial world. His specialty became commercial banking. Unlike the regime's ideological heartland of Castile, the Barcelona area had been a primary beneficiary of Franco's industrialising policies. There was local economic dynamism and Pujol's standing enabled him to become an unofficial leader for those people, in publishing, the media, and religious groups who were keen to re-establish a territorial political identity upon the recovery of political liberty.

In 1974, Pujol founded a two-pronged formation, part-liberal and part-Christian-Democrat. Called Democratic Convergence of Catalonia (CiU). The dictatorship was in the process of being dismantled and, within three years, competitive elections were held in Spain. The CiU backed the first constitutional government led by Adolfo Suarez. He was a pragmatic official in the former regime, widely held to be chiefly responsible for the unexpected success of a democratic transition.

In 1978, his plans won crucial legitimacy when Spaniards voted overwhelmingly in a referendum for a new constitution. It included provisions for a process of decentralisation, which proceeded to occur on an unplanned and incremental basis. It is perhaps no surprise that Catalonia was the first part of the Spanish territory to obtain a form of regional self-government. There was common ground among those active in politics about the desirability of political devolution. Unlike the Basque Country, violent extremism was virtually absent in Catalonia. The main opposition force in the late 1970s was the United Socialist Party of Catalonia (PSUC), a pro-communist force with an estimated 40,000 members. Pujol unsurprisingly was sought out by Suarez to be a key figure in the negotiations leading to a transfer of power. He was the unofficial spokesman for a broad spectrum of forces, which extended from Francoist mayors who had been inducted into the CiU to liberals and social democrats. His financial arm, the Banca Catalana was more than a bank and he pulled many opposition strings.[4]

Catalonia seemingly presented few headaches in a nerve-wracking process which included the seizure of the Spanish Cortes (Parliament) in Madrid on 23 February 1981, by dissident military figures. The strongest backing for the new 1978 constitution had come from the region, and in the following year a stature of autonomy was agreed. In 1979 Catalonia was recognised as a nationality with its own autonomous government (Generalitat). A veteran Catalan politician, Josep Tarradellas, who had been prominent in the 1930s when Catalonia enjoyed a period of home rule, was appointed its first head in 1979.

Aged almost 80, despite having played a pivotal role in negotiations with Madrid, he stood down a year later in favour of Pujol. His CiU had yet to acquire electoral domination but was greatly assisted by two developments. The initially much larger PSUC split over whether to embrace Eurocommunism or else stay loyal to the Soviet Union. Along with a splintered left, Pujol was assisted by the disintegration of Suarez's party, the Union of the Democratic Centre (UCD) in the early 1980s. It meant that the only place the Catalan bourgeoisie had to go was to his CiU.

The presence of the captains of industry, from Spain's most economically dynamic region, embellished the pragmatic image of Pujol and his broad front. On the surface, he seemed to be an advocate of consensus. His party was available to do political deals with the parties in Madrid when electoral majorities were hard to come by. Indeed, much later in 1993 and 1996, he received overtures from the two main political rivals on the Spanish stages on the left and the right, to join their governments, but he refused.[5]

From the outset, Pujol used his powers to promote a sense of Catalan separateness, exploiting historic differences to justify a strategy of differentiation. His stance was not a jarring one because in the early stages of the decentralisation process, artful and ambitious politicians across Spain were often emphasising each region's distinctiveness in order to amass status and power. The atmosphere was at times highly competitive because the so-called Spanish state of autonomies lacked a consistent design. The Basque Country enjoyed important autonomy in taxation, while it was in the educational and cultural fields that Catalonia acquired significant powers from the centre. This asymmetric distribution of competences meant that inter-territorial disputes and power struggles with Madrid were not infrequent. The constitution and the system of justice it laid down, however, acquired enough legitimacy to prevent such quarrels turning ugly.

But Pujol may have sensed that the post-Franco political order in Spain was a provisional one and that a real chance existed to weaken and eventually supplant the untidy framework for managing Spain's territorial interests and identities.[6] *Party* competition at the centre shaped how the decentralisation process was rolled out across Spain. Party rivalries in Catalonia itself would much later fuel a constitutional crisis in 2017, whose impact in the wider society was much less intense than in the fevered world of politics.[7]

Pujol first revealed his hand at his investiture on 5 May 1980, when he declared that 'if you vote for us, you will vote for a nationalist program, a nationalist government, and a nationalist president'.[8] A decade later, in the summer of 1990, he presented to his inner council his 'Plan 2000' that proposed to so completely saturate society with nationalist sentiment that future generations would acquire an identity very different from any found in the rest of Spain. Education was a pivotal priority, with monolingual schooling in Catalan being particularly important for his nation-building plans. His blueprint envisaged a conquest of state and society by nationalism not just through education, but also language, culture, foreign initiatives, business, the media, history, and sport. No stone was to be left unturned in the work of 'national construction'.[9] The newspaper *El Periodico* published important excerpts on 28 October 1990. The fact that there was no uproar is a testimony to Pujol's sagacity.[10] He had usually pursued his objectives noiselessly but emphatically, using his powers of patronage to try to conciliate and disarm even those who might have been expected to be alarmed on learning his ultimate objectives.[11]

By passing various laws on education, culture, and the media in the 1980s, Pujol hoped to produce a *fait accompli,* a territory ready for full statehood with the required symbols, paraphernalia, and mentality to embrace the challenge. The intention was to design a society differentiated from the rest of Spain in order to then demand treatment different from what was being received by the other communities. This goal was to be realised by manipulating myths and resentments.[12]

Placing emphasis on the claim that Catalonia was, and remained, a victim of Spain, continually hampered by an over-bearing Madrid, was his permanent refrain. There was a public challenge early on, but it came not from the parties in Madrid, but from Josep Tarradellas. In 1981, he complained to the director of the newspaper, *La Vanguardia,* that when he passed the baton of the presidency to Pujol, he planned to cheer Catalonia and Spain, but his successor rejected the formula. He denounced the formula of Hispanophobic victimhood which he saw at the heart of Pujolism: 'It is using a well-known and highly discredited trick of becoming the persecuted, the victim; and thus, we have been able to read in certain declarations that Spain persecutes us, that it boycotts us, that it cuts the Statute, and that it is carried away by antipathies towards us'.[13]

Ironically, not only were the supposedly implacable centralisers in Madrid politics slow to spot the danger signs, but they were ready to burnish his image when he faced difficulties. In 1984, he could have been placed on trial for corruption but instead that was the year when he was named ‘Spaniard of the Year’ by the newspaper *ABC*, the epitome of patriotic conservatism.[14]

In that year, Spain's attorney general filed a lawsuit against 25 former board members of Banca Catalana, including Pujol. He said there was evidence of ‘widespread irregularities’ by board members from 1974 to 1982, including ‘the falsification of documents and continued misappropriation of deposit funds'. A press campaign in Pujol’s defense arose, which may have resulted in the incipient court case going no further (but only for it to be re-activated and graver charges added over thirty years later).[15]

This episode did not result in Pujol modifying his outlook towards Spain. Catalonia, having been depicted as ‘the special victim of Franco’, was being stifled by staying part of a venal nation in decline. ‘Madrid steals from us’, was a refrain which acquired added force after the grave economic crisis which erupted in 2010. ‘Spain does not serve us, it is a state in decline, we must separate, we must move towards independence’ is how this pro-separatist outlook has been summed up.[16] Boundaries were emphasised and there was no room for overlapping identities, despite the fluid nature of identity in Catalan society. The promotion of culture belonged at the heart of state policy. But it was reduced to Catalan nationalist culture which, in particular, excluded numerous Catalans with immigrant backgrounds, mainly from poorer parts of Spain, who were drawn to the region by its favourable economic conditions.

Not only the schools, but television was also mobilised to inculcate an exclusive Catalan identity. *The Economist* in 2001 described how Pujol’s administration viewed the TV3 channel as being part of what the regional government was calling a “‘nation-building’ campaign. Characters with a Spanish identity rarely appear in its dramatic output, except in unflattering roles. It was financed by the local state, was protected from large-scale budget cuts, and for years received lavish advertising funding from companies that enjoyed close ties to the Generalitat”.[17] TV3, according to critics, renounced its role as a deliverer of news and broad opinions in favour of being a channel devoted to nationalist propaganda.[18] Certainly, during the crisis which erupted after 2015, few if any people single it out as a channel with any concern to dampen down feelings. Instead, it was widely seen as a persistent, and sometimes heated, exponent of separatist opinion.[19]

Given the turmoil and tragedy that state-sponsored ethnic exclusivism was giving rise to in the parts of the Balkans during the final decade of the twentieth century, it is surprising that Catalonia's homogenisation policies raised few eyebrows in Western media circles. Perhaps inevitably, Pujol set aside a large budget for wooing the global media. It may have ensured that little concern was expressed when the Catalan-speaking supporters of Catalonia were extolled as the true voice of a reborn nation, while Spanish-speakers were seen as an intrusion.

Such a condescending attitude was displayed in 2008 by Pujol's influential wife, Marta Ferrusola, who admitted it was 'very annoying' that Socialist José Montilla, who was president of the Generalitat between 2006 and 2010, had been born in Andalucia and hadn't changed his name to Josep.[20] Studies from this period show that nearly two-thirds of voters were identifying themselves as bi-national (nearly 40 percent feeling as Catalan as Spanish, 20 percent more Catalan than Spanish, and 6 percent more Spanish than Catalan), while about one-fourth felt only Catalan, and 5 percent only Spanish.[21] As the territorial issue increasingly unsettled Catalonia, surveys of opinion indicated that it was the political class which was in uproar, while society was less polarised. One analyst has written about surveys made by one polling company between 2010 and 2015 in which respondents are asked: 'What do you think is the most important problem of Catalonia? The larger group has responded "unemployment and job precariousness" (with a 46 percent average). "Relations Catalonia-Spain" always comes in the fourth place (with a 19 percent average), after "dissatisfaction with politics and politicians," and "the working of the economy."'[22]

During the 2017 crisis, it came as a surprise when well-attended demonstrations by Unionists or constitutionalists erupted on the streets of Barcelona, with many demonstrators showing exasperation over being branded as relics of fascism.[23] Prominent in this period was a young politician from Barcelona, Albert Rivera, son of a father from Catalonia and a mother from southern Spain, whose Ciudadanos party emerged in Catalonia and for some years had a strong nationwide presence.[24]

He and others asserted that a united Spain was a viable project, while a breakaway Catalonia doomed the society to economic hardship, intensifying political restrictions and isolation. Such a claim acquired some force because no European Union member showed any willingness to promote Catalan membership (due in no small part from fears about the encouragement that might be given to separatism elsewhere). Pujol had reached out to wealthy regions such as Baden-Wurttemburg (Germany), Rhone-Alpes (France), and Lombardy (Italy).[25] Along with Catalonia, they were seen as the 'Four Motors' which were keen to participate in the economic side of EU affairs as 'region states' detached from their wider national homelands.[26] The 'Europe of the Regions' concept eventually ran out of steam. It had some of the hallmarks of a rich man's club and highlighted the fact that the Catalan sovereignty movement emanated from the wealthier sections of Catalan society.

When asked about whether Catalonia ought to align with territories like Scotland, scene of an increasingly forceful nationalist upsurge after 2007, Pujol was unenthusiastic. Due to having a distinctive language and culture, he told the *Financial Times* in 2012, Catalonia was in a superior position and could not be seen as an ethnic cause or indeed a religious one (as he characterised 'the case of Ireland').[27]

Pujol was rather snobbish in his insistence that Catalonia enjoyed an exclusive status in the patchwork of nations and regions in contemporary Europe. Naturally, most of the time it was the rest of Spain that he held aloof from. In 1988, he turned down flat a proposal to make Barcelona the location of a well-resourced *national* theatre for all of Spain. The minister of culture in Madrid, Javier Solana, perhaps naively, assumed that Pujol would eagerly seize the opportunity to see the equivalent of Milan's La Scala being cited in Barcelona. But he detested the idea of international projection for the city that was not a fully Catalanist one.[28]

He was in no position to object when Barcelona was chosen as the venue for the 1992 Olympic Games. The initiative had come from the city's Socialist mayor Pascual Maragall and was being financed mainly by the central government. Pujol struggled to display much enthusiasm and revealingly told local athletes that: 'The important thing is not sport but the country...Sport helps the country to form itself, to organize itself, to know how to win and how to lose'. There was little doubt which 'country' he was referring to.[29]

One of his last stands in favour of regional purity concerned an attempt in 1999 to dub the most popular films into Catalan. Fines and cinema closures were threatened unless there was compliance. But the industry fought him in the courts, and he backed down. However, he continued to fight a rearguard action, demanding (unsuccessfully) in 2001, that if the characters in the screen version of *Harry Potter* did not speak Catalan, there should be no local premier, nor should the film be shown in the region.[30]

Pujol's cultural warfare rarely met with any concerted pushback from his rivals. Many failed to realise that what might be happening was 'the kidnapping of Catalonia by an ideology that made alleged oppression its flag'.[31] Barcelona managed to remain the electoral fiefdom of the PCE, the Catalan wing of the Spanish Socialist party (PSOE), under Pasqual Maragall, its mayor from 1982 to 1997. But there was no concerted effort by him to resist Pujol's bid to marginalise those with a mainly Spanish cultural formation or pressurise them to assimilate. It was only when Pujol was in retirement that a PCE colleague, Josep Borrell, published a study whose aim was to show that Catalonia was far from being economically disadvantaged by being part of Spain.[32]

As head of the Generalitat in the mid-2000s, Maragall was even prepared to back a revised Autonomy Statute which defined Catalonia as a nation.[33] Interestingly, there was an unusually high abstention rate in most Catalan regional elections and it seems to have been voters who had migrated to Catalonia who abstained.[34] The failure of non-separatists on the left to reach out to this segment of society and the growing tendency to try to court voters on soft nationalist lines later produced unfortunate consequences. There wasn't even an attempt to modify the electoral law dating from 1979, which had allowed the CiU's rural and small-town support base to be disproportionately favoured over Barcelona, in the allocation of seats.[35]

Pujol's party was only re-elected in 1999 due to this unbalanced electoral system. He was losing his leverage in Madrid politics as the conservative Popular party drew closer to having an outright majority. Arguably, his record of rule did not leave Catalonia as an attractive model for statehood. Power and revenue were dispensed in an opaque manner. Various public services were hived off to mixed public-private enterprises or to private firms, which the CiU usually had little difficulty in dominating.[36] Naturally, economic and other groups which favoured a sovereign Catalonia obtained preferment from Pujol.[37] At the end of 23 continuous years of power, Catalonia was described as 'his cork plantation, a country every corner of which he was familiar with...and one that was an extension of his office'.[38] The Generalitat seemed to some like an octopus with tentacles extending in many different directions, hoarding power at the expense of local authorities, and of course Madrid, or extending its influence deep into the worlds of commerce and finance.[39]

How much of a preoccupation accumulating and safeguarding economic wealth was for Pujol and his chief allies would emerge as they became the subject of criminal investigations. In 2012, a judicial inquiry opened into the family's financial affairs, and on 25 July 2014, he confessed to having kept a family fortune in an Andorran bank beyond the reach of the tax authorities.[40] His personal lawyer was given a five-year jail sentence in 2005.[41] On 17 July 2020, the *El País* newspaper reported:

> 'Judge José de la Mata of Spain's High Court (Audiencia Nacional) on Thursday recommended trying Pujol, his wife and their seven children for cashing in on their "position of privilege" in Catalonia's political, economic, and social life and accumulating "disproportionate" wealth, allegedly through illegal commissions that companies paid to secure government contracts and other favours. The judge's 509-page document offered evidence that "corrupt activities" were organized into a family structure headed by Pujol and his wife – who liked to call herself "the Mother Superior of the congregation" He noted that the family was unable to provide proof of the origin of their fortune'.[42]

Ironically, the title of the pamphlet that had resulted in the young Pujol's arrest in 1960, was entitled 'Oppressor, you are a Corrupter'.[43] Back in 2005, younger lieutenants of Pujol's, headed by Artur Mas, had forced him to remove his son and namesake from positions of influence, particularly in the financial side of the movement. They feared that his careless style might threaten their careers and jeopardize the future of the nationalist cause.[44] By 2014, with Mas running Catalonia, it was time for Pujol senior to be cast into political darkness.[45] Due to the gravity of the charges facing him, his successor felt obliged to withhold the positions he enjoyed in the CiU, as well as his pension. The timing of Pujol's disgrace may well have had an impact on the acute crisis which was shortly to unfold. Not only was the image of the godfather of Catalan politics tarnished. But many other figures in his circle were under official investigation. Simultaneously, Catalonia was reeling from a recession which was hammering all of Southern Europe.

Mas chose this moment of adversity to abruptly alter course. He decided to move CiU away from its pragmatic nation-building within a constitutionalist framework and towards overt militancy. In some ways, the ground had been prepared by the Socialists of the PCE, running the Generalitat from 2003 to 2010. They had formed the first coalition in post-Franco Spain involving not only the communists, but the Catalan Republican Left (ERC). With the agreement of the 2004-11 Socialist government of José Luís Zapatero, they had proposed a revised statute of autonomy designed to give the region the status of a nation, a move rejected by the constitutional court. Back in office from 2011 to 2018, the Popular Party was equally unreceptive. A period of kaleidoscopic changes occurred over the next decade, with the fortunes of various regional parties rising and falling. However, no doubt aided by an even more one-sided Catalan television and radio, a process of radicalisation was evident, particularly among young people. A spurt in support for the radical left was reflected in street militancy and in voting as regional elections occurred in 2016, 2017, 2019, and 2021. New forces such as the CUP (Popular Unity Candidacy) and later the Comités de Defensa de la República (CDR), very active in radical neighbourhoods, saw economic hardship as proof that the only way forward was the creation of a Catalan state.

In 2016, reeling from corruption scandals, the CiU dissolved itself, only for a successor party to instantaneously spring up called the Democratic Party for a European Catalonia (PdeCat). Its new leader Carles Puigdemont was handpicked by Mas, who chose this point to retreat into the background. Having earlier backed Madrid's austerity measures (that had been forced upon Spain by the EU), Mas now was prepared to endorse the view of previously left-wing rivals that economic distress could be laid at Madrid's door and Catalonia must secede. 'Subsidised Spain lives at the expense of productive Catalonia' read an electoral poster for the PdeCat in 2016.[46]

Thanks to a pro-independence majority in the Generalitat, Puigdemont announced an illegal independence referendum. It was held on 1 October 2017, amidst scenes of violent disorder as the central authorities sought to halt it. On the 27th, when the Catalan parliament declared independence, the government of Mariano Rajoy immediately invoked Article 155 of the constitution which allows the central authorities to step in if any region is flouting the constitutional order. The 1978 constitution, which 91 percent of Catalan voters endorsed in the referendum of that year, outlaws breakaway bids which would lead to citizens with a non-separatist outlook being trapped in a new state. The Generalitat was suspended for two months until fresh elections were held. They, and the next two contests, gave majorities to pro-independence parties. But most observers recognised that backers of independence in the population fell short of being a majority.

Pujol used to compare Catalonia with the Hanseatic League, and his successor Mas characterised it as 'the Holland of the South'. But from 2017, many hundreds of companies, some major undertakings intimately associated with Catalonia for generations, relocated, very often to Madrid. It represented a heavy loss to a region which, in 1992, was responsible for 25 percent of Spain's exports overall and 38 percent of its industrial exports.[47] 'There seemed not much left of Pujol's dream of Catalonia being a dynamic mercantile republic of the Mediterranean that was a front-rank player in the EU. His legacy had instead been one of overreach and conspiracy, concealed by an image of self-righteous moderation. Catalonia is now an unhappy land of discord, unable to build on its abundant advantages to be the engine of a democratic and productive Spain and a pillar of modernity in Europe. Currently, a fractious movement obsessed with territorial supremacy rather than good governance, one that is more militant and intransigent than the population as a whole, holds sway. The result is that introversion and a sectarian spirit are increasingly visible. Not even the best of its cultural icons are immune from censure and denunciation if they dare to withhold backing from maximalist separatist goals. Thus, the veteran musical artist Joan Manuel Serrat and the best-selling novelist Javier Cercas found themselves denounced by leading nationalists for offering nuanced perspectives on the ongoing crisis.[48]

Pujol has spoken little since his disgrace and perhaps he may even be untroubled that Catalonia, at least for the moment, is becoming synonymous with the ethnic trouble spots which he used to hold aloof from. Perhaps there is a reason for his stoical silence. After all, as one analyst has written, in much younger days:

> 'He had conceived a long historical process in which the Catalans would drive a train toward full national liberation that would pass through various stations, starting with autonomy, and on the way "would lose wagons," [with] groups that would not be willing to continue the journey to the end. In practice, the stations have been labelled Catalanism, nationalism, sovereigntism, and independentism'.[49]

However, in the aftermath of the Covid pandemic, and with war having erupted in Europe, the tide seemed to be running out for independence. A poll published in March 2022, found that support for secession had slumped to 38.8 percent, with 53.3 percent of inhabitants now being committed to remaining within Spain.[50]

---

[1] Thanks are due to Marcel Gascón Barberá for reading an early draft and providing bibliographical material.
[2] 'A canny Catalan', *Economist,* 25 February 1992.
[3] See Jordi Pujol, *Memorias, Vol. 1, (1930-1980),* Barcelona: Destino, 2008, p.p. 135-68 for this traumatic episode.

[4] Juan Pablo Cardenal, 'Epílogo', in Miriam Tey et al, El libro negro del nacionalismo La ideología totalitaria que ha conducido a Cataluña al desastre, Barcelona: Duesto, 2021, p. 510.
[5] Cardenal, *El libro negro*, p. 496.
[6] Josep M. Colomer, 'The venturous bid for the independence of Catalonia', *Nationalities Papers*, 2017, Vol. 45, No. 5, 2017, p. 964.
[7] Colomer, 'The venturous', p.p. 956-7.
[8] Paola la Cascio, 'El pujolismo entre gestión y cultura política. Unas notas interpretativas (19802003)', *Revista de Historia Contemporánea*, No. 31, 2020, p. 294.
[9] Gonzalo Núñes, 'Cuatro décadas de inmersión, silencio y propaganda: así se perdió Cataluña', *The Objective*, 5 January 2022, https://theobjective.com/espana/2022-01-05/cataluna-desastre/, accessed 12 May 2022.
[10] A book that describes in a vivid way the crafty methods that Pujol used to overcome opposition to his plans is Arcadi Espada's, *Contra Catalunya, Una Crónica*, Barcelona: Flor de Viento Ediciones, 1997.
[11] António Robles, 'Programa 2000: O cómo nacionalizar la mente de los catalanes', in *El libro negro*, p. 124.
[12] Alfredo Crespo Alcazár, 'Francesc de Carreras, Paciencia e independencia, La agenda oculta del nacionalismo, *El Imparcia*l, 14 September 2014, accessed 12 May 2022.
[13] Sergi Doria, 'El club de fans de Pujol', *ABC*, 12 December 2021, https://www.abc.es/espana/catalunya/abci-sergi-doria-club-fans-pujol-202112121105_noticia.html, accessed 15 May 2022.
[14] Victor Mallett, 'Lunch with the FT: Jordi Pujol', *Financial Times*, 8 June 2012.
[15] Ana Westley, 'Catalonian Leader Among 25 Charged In Bank Collapse', *Wall Street Journal*, 24 May 1984.
[16] Alcazár, 'Francesc de Carreras'.
[17] 'It isn't magic; Language in Catalonia', *Economis*t, 8 December 2001.
[18] Robles, 'Programa 2000', p. 122.
[19] Sergio Fidalgo, 'TV3: Una televisión «privada» pagada con fondos públicos', *El libro negro*, p. 194.
[20] *El Pais*, 15 March 2008.
[21] Colomer, 'The venturous', p. 955.
[22] Colomer, 'The venturous', p. 958.
[23] I observed one such gathering in Barcelona in December 2017.
[24] See Albert Rivera, 'We Catalans Owe the World an Explanation', *New York Times*, 4 December 2017.
[25] See Jordi Pujol, *Tiempos de Construir, Memorias, Vol. 2, (1980-93)*, Barcelona: Ediciones Destino, 2012, p.p. 368-78.
[26] See John Loughlin, '"Europe of the Regions" and the Federalization of Europe', *Publius*, Vol. 26, No. 4, p.p. 141–162.
[27] Mallett, 'Lunch with the FT'.
[28] Pedro Gómez Carrizo, 'Cultura española: Cancelada', in *El libro negro*, p. 219.
[29] Alan Riding, 'Barcelona Journal: Catalonia Is Pressing Ahead as Olympic 'Country', *New York Times*, 18 July 1992.
[30] 'It isn't magic'.
[31] Núñes, 'Cuatro décadas de inmersión'.

[32] Josep Borrell and Joan Llorach, *Las cuentas y los cuentos de la independencia*, Barcelona: Celesa, 2015.
[33] Eduardo López-Dóriga, 'La resistencia al nacionalismo en Cataluña', in *El libro negro*, p. 383.
[34] Colomer, 'The venturous', p. 961.
[35] Daniel Berzosa, 'Ley electoral catalana', *El libro negro*, p. 476.
[36] José Domingo, 'La Generalitat somos tú y yo', *El libro negro*, p.p. 288-9.
[37] Santiago Mondéjar, 'Las élites catalanas y sus satélites políticos', *El libro negro*, p. 360.
[38] José Alejandro Vara y Pablo Planas Periodistas, 'Pujol y la corrupción como instrumento de gobierno', *El libro negro*, p. 372.
[39] The long list of corruption scandals associated with the Catalan authorities up to 2012 are set out here. J. F. Lamata, 'Xavier Horcajo: «La familia Pujol ha manejado Cataluña como si fuera su rancho»', *Periodista Digital*, 20 November 2012, https://www.periodistadigital.com/periodismo/prensa/20121120/xavier-horcajo-familia-pujol-maneja-do-cataluna-fuera-rancho-noticia-689401411638/, accessed 14 May 2022.
[40] 'Jordi Pujol's fiscal fraud becomes a threat to the self-determination process', *Catalan news*, 28 July 2014, https://www.catalannews.com/politics/item/jordi-pujol-s-fiscal-fraud-becomes-a-threat-for-self-determination-process, accessed 10 May 2022.
[41] Lamata, 'Xavier Horcajo'.
[42] 'Ex-premier Jordi Pujol and entire family facing trial over suspect fortune, *El Pais* (English edition), 17 July 2020, https://english.elpais.com/spanish_news/2020-07-17/ex-catalan-premier-jordi-pujol-and-entire-family-facing-trial-over-suspect-fortune.html, accessed 14 May 2022.
[43] 'Vara y Planas Periodistas, 'Pujol y la corrupción', p. 366.
[44] Iñaki Ellakuría, 'Germà Gordó, el hombre cuya confesión podría acabar con los Pujol y Artur Mas', *El Mundo*, 7 November 2022, https://www.elmundo.es/cataluna/2022/11/07/6368045ee4d4d837438b45c4.html, accessed 8 November 2022.
[45] 'Former Catalan President Jordi Pujol gives up all his benefits and will face a parliamentary committee', *Catalan News*, 29 July 2014, https://www.catalannews.com/politics/item/former-catalan-president-jordi-pujol-gives-up-all-his-benefits-and-will-face-a-parliamentary-committee, accessed 12 May 2022.
[46] Rivera, 'We Catalans', *New York Times*, 4 December 2017.
[47] *Economist*, 25 September 1992.
[48] *Diário de Navarra*, 15 April 2021, https://www.diariodenavarra.es/noticias/actualidad/nacional/2021/04/15/el-secesionismo-pone-disparadero-los-intelectuales-criticos-con-proces-723481-1031.html, accessed 7 April 2022
[49] Colomer, 'The venturous', p. 964.
[50] Charles Devereux, 'Catalonia loses the hunger for independence', *Times*, 19 March 2022.

CHAPTER 18: NICOLA STURGEON

1970-

Nicola Sturgeon, who has spent at least 35 years as an activist, parliamentarian and leader of the Scottish National Party (SNP), has striven to make it a vanguard party of social change, displacing the emphasis on territorial politics. Once she took charge of Scotland's devolved government in 2014, and won a big electoral victory in 2015, the momentum behind the campaign to exit the United Kingdom (UK), gradually stalled. Instead, she became one of the most prominent figures seeking to reverse the British vote to withdraw from the EU in 2016. Her strong commitment to belonging to a transnational entity, whose smaller members exercise little real power in many key areas, may be an admission that she is at ease with internationalism, perhaps far more than nationalism.

During her years in power, it is hard to point to any pioneering initiatives from her in the field of governance preparing the country for a post-British future. Campaigns directed against London's remaining influence in Scottish affairs, have absorbed much of her time and indeed used up considerable state resources. This role as a voice of resistance fits her talents well. She is an able communicator, as was shown to effect during the Covid pandemic. Her insistence on crafting a Scottish response proved ineffective, however, as the Scottish fatality rate eclipsed that of other parts of the island. Mounting economic problems, some of which pre-dated the pandemic, make her calls for Scots to be given another chance to vote on their constitutional future, increasingly formulaic ones that struggle to resonate widely. Mounting failures on various policy fronts have clouded her record. Yet electoral success has continued. Due to the salience of constitutional politics, retention of power is not determined by strong government delivery but by the exploitation of divisions, which are increasingly akin to those once seen in neighbouring Northern Ireland.

The SNP packages itself as a resistance front against British overlordship and it has won successive elections on that basis, against a divided opposition. Sturgeon is adept at appealing to a sense of victimhood, springing from a grievance culture that has entrenched itself in flat-lining, post-industrial communities. Through skilful use of patronage, she has also acquired sway over the media and much of the professional-managerial elite. It enabled her to define the policy agenda, despite a failure to deliver tangible policy improvements in health, education, transport or policing.

What was perhaps most innovative about her role, was her success in moving her preoccupation with identity politics beyond *territory*, to include such issues as climate change and gender self-identification. She sought to build a party of radical social activists whose agenda seems better fitted for a post-national world order, and whose unconditional loyalty is to her. Splits, resignations, and a ferocious power struggle with her predecessor have, however, dogged this new political departure.

A woman hitherto often viewed as a colourless and self-absorbed politician, sought to re-invent herself as 'the mother of the nation' whose particular mission was to reach out to socially marginalised or fringe groups. But the failure to use the substantial funds at her disposal to improve economic conditions for lower-income groups and tackle soaring deaths from drug abuse, casts doubt on the extent of her radicalism. She is a polarising figure who strongly appeals to niche groups in what is a socially fragmented country, but someone who is insufficiently popular among broad sections of the populace to ensure that she can be a formidable driver for independence. Nevertheless, she has established great sway at home by centralising power and a high profile abroad by embracing fashionable causes. Her ability to dwarf her party and carve out her own distinctive profile, single her out as a resourceful politician able to project influence in an era where hyper-individualism is fashionable in much of the Western world.

Nicola Sturgeon was born to a family of skilled workers on 19 July 1970, a month after a British general election in which the SNP won 11.4 percent of

Scottish votes. She grew up in the small industrial community of Dreghorn in Ayrshire and appears to have been a studious and diffident youngster. She came of age as Scotland's low-performing heavy industry was decimated by the withdrawal of state subsidies and adverse trading conditions. The free market economic policies of Margaret Thatcher were popular in the English south, but in Scotland they united the proletarian left and much of the middle class in opposition, both wedded to state intervention or corporatist policies. As industrial Ayrshire faced decline in the 1980s, the lives of too many young people began to be consumed by drug abuse. Sturgeon, puritanical in her habits, plunged into politics. In 1986, she joined the SNP. In 1992, aged 22, she was the youngest general election candidate in Scotland.

She graduated around this time from Glasgow University with a law degree. One of her former teachers, Alistair Bonnington, recalls her as an unimpressive student. He has bemoaned the fact that, under her, 'Scotland [is] producing the lowest quality legislation in Europe'. He added: 'I seem to have failed to instil in her (Sturgeon) the most basic rules of how the institutions of government work in the free world'.[1]

As a newly-qualified lawyer, Sturgeon focused on matrimonial cases. One of her clients, a battered mother, complained to the Law Society of Scotland in 1997, because of her refusal to seek a court order against an estranged partner who was continuing to assault her. A new lawyer ensured that the abuse and stalking rapidly ceased, causing the woman (by now a grandmother) to reflect in 2021, that Sturgeon 'was focused on herself and her own career'.[2]

She had made repeated attempts to win a parliamentary seat in the 1990s. She was successful in the first election to the Scottish Parliament in 1999, when she was elected as a list member (MSP) in the multi-member Glasgow constituency, at a time when the SNP continued to lag far behind the Labour Party. But despite having been instrumental in transferring responsibility for Scotland's internal affairs from London to the new devolved parliament at Holyrood in Edinburgh, Labour's ascendancy was precarious. It lacked the internal coherence and self-confidence to make the new institutions work. It was thrown increasingly onto the defensive after Tony Blair co-sponsored the invasion of Iraq in 2003.

By now, Alex Salmond, a brash and wily leader, was in charge of the SNP. As he still sat as an MP in Westminster, Sturgeon led the party at Holyrood from the age of 34. She would have known that Salmond could be a difficult personality. Many years later, accusations of bullying were revealed in a trial, with Salmond admitting that his behaviour at times fell short of what was appropriate. Not long after the Me Too movement's appearance, Sturgeon spoke out on behalf of unnamed women in the SNP and civil service who had made formal complaints against him. But a former SNP MSP, Dorothy-Grace Elder, claimed in 2021, that she had been side-lined by Sturgeon for speaking out against male bullying in the party more than 20 years earlier. Her recollection of the politician as a driven, arrogant person who cold-shouldered those who were not deferential to her, surfaced at the height of the duel between the SNP leader and her predecessor in 2021.[3]

In 2007, the SNP was able to form a minority government at Holyrood due to Labour's deepening unpopularity. Sturgeon became deputy First Minister and minister of health. An effective partnership with Salmond sprang up. His seven years running Scotland, and throwing down regular challenges to London, enabled him to be seen as one of the most effective insurgents in modern British politics. He brought the SNP from the fringes of politics to the heart of power. It acquired growing sway over the civil service, much of the media and the third sector to a degree unusual for a ruling party in a modern democracy.[4] Sturgeon was his chief helper and she played a major role in drafting the White paper for Scottish Independence that was drawn up in 2013.[5] In 2012, David Cameron, the Prime Minister in charge of a Tory-Liberal Democrat coalition in London, had given the Scottish government permission to organize a referendum on independence. Salmond was able to choose the question for the ballot paper, the size of the electorate (Scots living in England being excluded) and the timetable for the campaign. The clever, uninhibited political agitation mounted by the SNP in the many months of campaigning before the vote was held on 18 September 2014, produced a sea change in outlook. The pro-independence 'Yes' campaign appealed to the growing social volatility visible in post-industrial areas. The culture of work, which had provided a stable underpinning for one of the world's first industrial societies, was receding in importance. So was religion. People were searching for a new moral paradigm, one with far fewer rules and obligations. The 2014 referendum was the first major contest of its type, perhaps anywhere, in which the new tools of social media played a significant role. The Yes side won over numerous male working-class voters seeking a fresh allegiance. It won 45 percent of the vote on an 85 percent turnout. But the separatist case failed to convince the 55 percent majority on crucial questions to do with economic and financial viability, currency, managing a high deficit, maintaining a central bank, and coping with a hard border with the rest of Britain (the destination of most Scottish trade).

Salmond took many, not least on his own side, by surprise when he announced his intention to stand down from his high offices as soon as it became clear that the pro-Union side had won. No contest for the succession was necessary. It was seen as a foregone conclusion that his reliable understudy would step into his shoes. On 22 November 2014, 12,000 people crowded into Scotland's main events venue, the Hydro in Glasgow, to hail the new leader. Before an adoring throng, Sturgeon asserted that 'this is a great time to be alive in Scotland. Our democracy is more vibrant than probably anywhere else in Europe'.[6] For growing admirers in the media, the SNP appeared to be a moral force capable of re-energising a listless nation. Less than a year later, she cemented her position by leading it to a colossal victory in the British general election. The SNP won 57 out of 59 seats, far more than the combined total it had achieved in the previous eighty years of its history.

But the party's epic climb only resulted in it reaching a plateau, which it continued to traverse during Sturgeon's nine years as leader. The SNP has struggled to map out distinctive ideas and policies to prepare the way for independence. Instead, there has been an undisguised preoccupation with consolidating its hold on national life. Sturgeon has built up a personal power base consisting of loyalists such as Lesley Evans, the influential and contested head of the Scottish civil service from 2015 to 2021, along with allies in the worlds of law, media, culture and the third sector[7]. Her party has become an ancillary prop rather than a key institution equipped to complete the freedom struggle. She married the party's chief executive Peter Murrell in 2010.

Salmond doesn't appear to have paused to wonder whether the anomalous combination of these two persons in charge of a state and a ruling party might not create future difficulties. Relations would soon sour, leading to a

Salmond-Sturgeon fight almost to the death. It would not be unlike the feud between Tony Blair and Gordon Brown, which contributed substantially to Labour losing its grip on power. In some respects, the SNP with its personality battle and its absorption with presentation, and expanding its influence across state and society, increasingly came to be a north British version of New Labour rather than an authentically new Scottish political force.

The SNP largely sat out the 2016 referendum on whether Britain should remain in the EU. On 23 June, the underdogs on the Leave side pulled off a victory and for the next three years, British politics centred around how complete the break with the EU could be and what chances there were of the whole thing being reversed.

The referendum had been a UK-wide undertaking, and on that basis, Sturgeon took part in several television debates in London. Afterwards, she declared that having voted against Brexit by 62 to 38 percent, Scots had a right to stay inside the EU; failing that, a second independence referendum should be held. (The SNP usually fails to point out that if Scotland had voted to leave Britain in 2014 it would have been leaving the EU whose conditions for fresh admission it would have struggled to meet, not least in economic terms).

The British capital had voted almost as strongly for Remain as had Scotland: it would be the well-spring of a fight-back to reverse the process. The institutions of the British establishment that were concentrated in London were unreconciled to the prospect of departing from the EU. Arguably, Sturgeon made a serious error by not fully aligning with the Remainers or the 'soft Brexit' camp. After the 2017 general election, the government of Theresa May only had a tiny majority and there were several close votes in the Westminster parliament involving the retention of key elements of the EU partnership, that could have been won with SNP support. The SNP, however, held aloof. It was driven, primarily, by the desire to strengthen the party's position at home and cultivate ties with anti-Brexit power centres on the continent.

Electorally, the party made no decisive advances. In the general election held in June 2017, the SNP lost 21 of its 56 Westminster seats (its vote share down by 13 percent.) Two years later, it recovered most of those seats. The urge to recover ground may explain why Sturgeon backed the pro-Brexit Prime Minister Boris Johnson's decision to call an early general election, which he could have been denied if the SNP and the Liberal Democrats had voted not to dissolve parliament. It is doubtful if Sturgeon anticipated that Johnson would obtain an 80-seat majority on 11 December 2019 and be able to take Britain out of the single market and the customs union of the EU on 31 January 2020.

She ignored the numerous SNP voters and some of her MSPs who had voted for Brexit. A poll of 1500 voters by *Survation* found 34.9 percent of those surveyed voters who had voted for the SNP in the Holyrood elections held in May 2016, then voted to leave the EU in the UK-wide June referendum.[8] Instead, she overtly appealed to middle-class Unionists disenchanted by the prospect of Brexit. But there was no decisive shift to the independence side among the Scottish electorate. Sturgeon was unable to show how Scotland could avoid considerable dislocation and economic damage if it left the UK. Too many voters were fully aware of the need for the £10-12 billion injections of funds from the UK treasury to bridge a Scottish deficit and maintain public services. There was no relish for a hard border with England, which would be hard to avoid irrespective of whether Scotland was inside the EU or not. At no time did EU decision-makers extend any assurances to the SNP notables on their frequent trips to Brussels that Scotland could expect special treatment to allow the inclusion of a country whose deficit of nine percent disqualified it for membership.

The 2016-19 years of Brexit tumult were when she honed her skills as an expert handler of the media. She became one of the best-known politicians in Britain, admired by many on the political left outside Scotland. Invariably, her invective was directed against the Conservatives who were viewed as 'the enemy' even though, in the 2017 general election, they were only eight percent behind the SNP in terms of Scottish votes. At times, it seemed that the primary purpose of the SNP was to defeat this ideological foe and encourage its ostracism in Scotland.

The SNP's cause might also have been better served if the Conservatives had been handled differently. Sturgeon could have offered May backing for her preferred anaemic form of Brexit in return for fresh decentralisation measures. It is worth noting that in contrast to regionalist and separatist parties in Spain, the SNP was by now numb about acquiring powers that made a material difference to society. It had shown a lack of expertise in using them effectively. Delays over the transfer of welfare powers to Edinburgh from London have been endless, due to Edinburgh's unpreparedness. Salmond had relied on Tory backing at Holyrood in his first years in office and perhaps he would have been more pragmatic in her place. Sturgeon insists that compared with the parties headquartered in England, the SNP is a moral force driven by the need to improve the human condition in Scotland. But her preoccupations as her years in power lengthened made it increasingly difficult to sustain this claim.

She was increasingly diverted from her stance on Brexit by a growing rift with Alex Salmond. The political world was stunned in August 2018 when it emerged he had been accused of inappropriate behaviour towards women with whom he'd worked while he was First Minster. In January 2019, he fought and won a civil case against the Scottish Government and had his £500,000 legal fees paid, after the handling of the complaints against him was judged to have been 'tainted by bias'. Days later, he was arrested and charged with 12 charges of sexual harassment and one of attempted rape, only for him to be acquitted by a jury (the majority of whom were women) at the High Court in Edinburgh in March 2020. Pressure to hold an enquiry into the administration's handling of the allegations made against Salmond proved hard to deflect. In 2021, the investigating Holyrood committee voted 5-4 to declare Sturgeon had misled parliament (but not knowingly).

I wrote at the time, that her persistent caginess about what she knew as she was questioned in the parliamentary inquiry, was a sight to behold. Phrases like 'not to my recollection', 'I don't recall', 'I have to check the detail', 'I'm not in possession of the information', 'I'm not 100 percent sure', 'I ask myself how I could have forgotten that', recurred throughout her day-long testimony on 3 March 2021. Her amnesia was contrasted by a blizzard of vivid recollections about her own feelings of sadness, dismay, grief, and sorrow about a durable political friendship having ended this way. Salmond was portrayed by her as an arrogant, self-absorbed boor who mistreated party colleagues and officials. It was never made clear why action was only taken with the upsurge of the Me Too movement in 2017.[9] But a separate inquiry by Irish barrister James Hamilton ruled also in 2021 that she didn't breach the ministerial code.

The affair gave an impression of amateurism and dishonesty, as well as a disregard for rules determining the separation of powers across the Scottish state. But nobody among the police, senior prosecutors, civil servants and special advisers, faced a day of reckoning. Alex Bell, a former strategist who worked closely with Salmond and Sturgeon during the referendum campaign, argued that 'loyalty to the first minister trumps the values of accountability and responsibility. The gang ethos prevails'.[10] By the climax of this political drama, it was starting to be clear that what was keeping Sturgeon afloat was not so much her party, but a support structure that she had built up through extensive use of patronage. It comprised the public bureaucracy (historically large in Scotland), universities, NGOs, consultancy firms and a host of ancillary services.

Salmond claimed that people close to Sturgeon had worked to destroy him by ensuring that he ended up in jail.[11] Several big names in the SNP's parliamentary ranks, such as ex-justice minister Kenny MacAskill, believed him and helped him set up a new party, Alba. It was cold-shouldered by most of the media and had poor results in early election outings. A mood of gloom was now perceptible in nationalist ranks. The self-image of the party, as a moral and civic expression of nationalism engaged in a vital and honourable battle against the age-old southern overlord, was proving much harder to sustain. It was impossible to blame the eternal villain, the British secret service, or any other malevolent London-based force. Instead, it had been the 'deep Scottish state' (very much answerable to Sturgeon) which arguably was prepared to act in an irregular manner. Troubled nationalists noted that it was the London conservative magazine, *The Spectator*, which tried to publish documents from the inquiry that cast doubt on Sturgeon's version of events.[12] This was after the Scottish media had declined, following a warning not to do so from the Crown Office, whose head, the chief prosecutor in Scotland, sits in the cabinet.

Eventually, it required an MP to use parliamentary privilege on 17 March 2021, to read out a text highly critical of the Scottish government's handling of the prosecution of Salmond. This was not a nationalist but a leading

Conservative, David Davis, who soon after wrote about 'a deficit of power and accountability in Scotland'.[13]

This was a time of disorientation for nationalists accustomed to believing that English Tories were invariably the enemy while their own leaders followed a superior ethical code. Their bewilderment hardly diminished when Sturgeon started to prioritise issues that had hitherto been peripheral in SNP thought and action, while being increasingly evasive about when another push for independence would occur.

At the start of the 2020s, Sturgeon began to make gender identification a touchstone of her radicalism. In 35 years of political activity, she had shown no interest in the issue which was gaining powerful traction on social media. Soon, no other head of government in the West was being as outspoken on such a contentious matter. There was no lack of critics in her own party, who argued that the furore was less about safeguarding the rights of genuinely trans people and more about allowing exploitative men to instantly recognise as women and obtain full access to public spaces hitherto reserved for women.[14] Sturgeon refused to engage with the concerns of former and present women parliamentarians in the SNP, like Joanna Cherry and Joan McAlpine, who fear that women's rights will suffer a massive reverse in Scotland if biological males are allowed to refute DNA and chromosomes and take their places in women's prisons, changing rooms, and sports teams. Twelve trans prisoners convicted of violence or sexual crimes had been accommodated in Scottish women's jails during 2020-1.[15]

A Gender Recognition Reform bill was passed on 22 December 2022, whose aim was to allow persons as young as sixteen to alter their genders without the need for a medical diagnosis. One year earlier, a Hate Crimes bill had passed into law which Scottish feminists and their defenders feared could lead to women facing criminal charges if they publicly declared that while gender is fluid, sex is binary.[16] This was the latest milestone indicating that the empirical dimension of public policy was in danger of being displaced by diversity, equity, and inclusion dogmas. Polls showed scant popular support for such a new departure. Perhaps for the first time since 2014, an issue emerged which prompted people from across the rigid constitutional divide to close ranks and mount a broad-based campaign to prevent women's rights from being eroded. Feminist activists have asked why Sturgeon, 'a politician who once described herself as a feminist to her fingertips – has become the face of what could be called "trans rights appeasement"'.[17] The world-acclaimed British author, J.K. Rowling, described her as 'a destroyer of women's rights' as her gender bill reached parliament, and Sturgeon riposted by suggesting that the novelist was not a real feminist like her.[18]

There was dismay at the First Minister's failure to condemn attacks on SNP politicians, such as Joanna Cherry, who had spoken up for women's rights in the new climate. Not only gender but children's sexuality became an issue receiving much greater government attention than ones directly affecting citizens reeling from neglect or botched state initiatives. A new directive issued by the government in 2022 to teachers, social workers and the police, made it clear that there was no longer an obligation for professionals to inform parents if their children were having underage sex.[19]

Rather than being a vigorous protector of the party's nationalist soul, Sturgeon seemed eager to turn it into a vanguard movement that is tireless in advocating social experimentation. It suggests that she sees her role in politics as not being to build a new state but to dismantle a social order which had a design for living, that however flawed, proved meaningful for millions down the generations. It has led to one of Scotland's best-known nationalists, Jim Sillars, saying that he can no longer vote for his party.[20]

An additional act of apostasy, indicating that Sturgeon had declared independence from some of her party's core assumptions, was her decision to withdraw support for new oil drilling off the Shetland islands. 'It's Scotland's Oil' had been the 1970s rallying cry which had fuelled the SNP's electoral breakthrough. Ensuring financial viability by exploiting hydrocarbons had been at the heart of the case for a 'Yes' vote in 2014, one which Sturgeon endlessly preached. In the early 2020s, Sturgeon insists that renewable energy is the golden elixir, even though the technology is in its infancy, and it won't be labour-intensive. Prematurely ending explorations and drilling, places up to 100,000 jobs at risk in North-East Scotland, an SNP stronghold, but Sturgeon didn't even consult with parliamentarians in the area before announcing oil was being ditched.[21] Instead, despite their minuscule support, she has moved much closer to the Scottish Green Party who formally entered her government in 2021. They are openly opposed to growth, hostile to commerce, as shown by their drive to force car users out of different urban areas and show little concern about the impact of their purist stance on the livelihoods of ordinary income earners. Sturgeon seems more at ease with them than with many in her own party. She has encouraged middle-class social activists, keen on personal experimentation and making Scotland a distinctive part of a new global order, to rise in the SNP as more conventional activists of longer vintage drift away.

The changing character of the SNP meant that talking about personal identity became an increasingly noticeable feature. She herself has stopped talking about delivering improvements, or else is content to launch initiatives about universal basic income or industrial investment banks that prove to be mere spin. Many of her own public conversations concern milestones on her own personal journey and their significance for groups in society that she particularly relates to. She has talked about the start of her struggles with menopause and how it throws up challenges that no male colleague has to deal with. She has shown an adversarial disposition to men, as when she declared: 'I often think the world would be a much better place if it was ruled by women. And it would be a much, much better place if it was ruled by menopausal women'.[22] She has complained that a 'polarised and toxic' climate, inflamed by social media, makes her feel less secure than when she first entered politics, and she worries about her safety.[23]

The United Nations-sponsored Climate (COP26) conference held in Glasgow in November 2021, was an ideal moment for her to project herself before the visiting media, despite having no formal role in organising or running the event. During the nine-day event, she posted, or retweeted, no less than 65 pictures or videos of herself on Twitter, often delivering international talking points or arranging selfies with notable guests.[24] But it was the almost two-year-long Covid pandemic which enabled her to reach out to a mass audience and be seen as playing a decisive role. She was offered a daily one-hour broadcasting slot by BBC Scotland, while the Holyrood parliament was suspended or else only met via Zoom. She was able to speak from a position of authority because the pro-Union parties voted for her emergency powers and even allowed her to 'modify or amend' any act of parliament 'without a vote' in a future health emergency.[25]

Her priority was to set apart her Covid strategy from that of England. She kept insisting on extended mask mandates, tougher social distancing measures, and longer lockdowns, even when it was clear that these measures were failing to dent a relatively high death toll in Scotland. In fact, Scottish mortality rates were higher than in England during the last half of 2021, when restrictions were greatly eased there, and society opened up. Perhaps a more far-seeing UK government, which ought to have been well aware by now that Sturgeon would be tempted to exploit an emergency for political purposes, might have been better advised at the outset to make the fight-back against the pandemic a single UK effort. So many of her executive decisions had been based on distancing Scotland ever further from the rest of the UK, that a different and more cooperative stance from her ought to have been considered unlikely.

The pandemic was a great opportunity to control as much of the citizenry's behaviour as possible, an instinct that she and her party had arguably already displayed in earlier forays into sensitive areas of social policy. In 2016, an abortive attempt to place state-appointed guardians in oversight roles over all children, only ended when the Supreme Court deemed it a threat to liberty with totalitarian features.[26] In her regular broadcast, she conveyed authority, especially to the elderly. By August 2020, she was achieving poll ratings of over 50 percent. These, however, failed to be maintained, as it was hard for her to dodge responsibility for local failures in the handling of the pandemic or justify an attitude of superiority towards England. She had opposed Britain's departure from the European Medicines Agency (EMA), widely seen as the best Covid policy decision made by Johnson's government, as it enabled a vaccine to be developed without the EMA's restrictions and delays.[27] Scotland's struggling economy also benefited from the Covid job retention (or furlough) scheme, by which the British Treasury provided Scottish firms with several billions of pounds to save jobs. Ironically, the SNP government's insistence on closing down or restricting much of the hospitality industry through lockdowns, long after these were eased or lifted in England, was seen as being particularly harmful to jobs in the service sector.[28]

The perception that vaccines devised in Britain saved lives and furlough money saved the economy, dented efforts by leading nationalists to argue that the pandemic showed the futility of remaining in a British political and economic union.[29] Sturgeon's unprecedented media exposure from 2020, the low profile of the pro-Union parties and their refusal to form an electoral pact, contributed, however, to the party winning a fourth term in charge of the Scottish government in April 2021.

Afterwards, there was no discernible rush to deal with accumulating problems, ranging from an ailing health service, mounting drug deaths, costly procurement failures, and underperforming schools.[30] Genuinely radical policies, from nationalising land to making practical inroads into poverty and deprivation, were not options for as long as Sturgeon was around, according to nationalist critics.[31] Faced with grim statistics showing that Scotland now produced some of the worst literacy and numeracy outcomes in Europe, it was announced in May 2022, that a pledge made by Sturgeon in 2015, that she wanted to be judged on her record in narrowing the education attainment gap in Scotland between better off and less well-off pupils, was to be officially scrapped.[32]

Perhaps the biggest blow to the image of the ruling nationalists being compassionate fighters for national improvement was to be found in the field of substance abuse. Drug deaths had increased annually since 2013, reaching 1,339 in 2020. Scotland had the worst record in the developed world, the death rate being 15 times worse than Germany, 35 times worse than France and three-and-a-half times the drug deaths in the UK as a whole.[33]

In 2021, it had been announced that more would be spent on the Constitution, External Affairs and Culture (peripheral areas or ones where the Scottish government had no formal powers) than on reducing drug deaths. (It included £50 million set aside for another referendum on independence). Such spending commitments prompted the observation that at Holyrood, choices are made about what will nominally advance the cause of independence rather than what will establish the economic and social circumstances that would make that aspiration possible.[34] The unglamorous job of just getting government done competently was not one which overtly motivated SNP ministers, who all stood in the shadow of the First Minister.

The party has shrunk in stature and relevance, its conferences being increasingly seen as heavily-managed events that need to be rapidly concluded. Its leader is reliant on middle managers in the civil service as well as ancillary bodies like NGOs, charities and universities, who often prove to be fumbling technocrats. Endless consultations into policy occur and initiatives are announced, like the Scottish National Investment Bank in 2020, which are supposed to define Sturgeon's rule as forward-looking. In practice, they often quickly run into trouble or disappear from view after much public money has been dispensed for creating a facade of progress. Perhaps her biggest blunder in governance was the handover of £586 million for largely non-existent jobs in 2016, to an Indian tycoon who, five years later, was being investigated by the UK audit agency.[35]

Structural change is elusive or non-existent. But an endless churn of presentations is lapped up by the deferential parts of the media, and results in mind-numbing Holyrood debates and public briefings. These rituals are presided over by Sturgeon, and her deputy, John Swinney, along with 'a tiny activist elite who are on first name terms with government ministers and backbench MSPs'.[36] Parliament is unable to hold the government to account for incompetence or sharp practice. Its committee system is much weaker than Westminster's. When examining how Holyrood's equality committee scrutinised the proposed new law, which would entitle all citizens to choose how they self-identity and be so regarded by the state, a close observer of the policy process, concluded that it was dominated by insiders: 'the...committee appears to have mostly invited their friends or at least those who support self-ID or are in some way beholden to government'.[37]

Writers and academics, such as Professor Jill Stephenson, Jamie Blackett, Neil Oliver and Alex Massie have warned about a merging of party and state in Scotland. A 2018 newspaper investigation revealed that companies working for the Scottish government risk having their contracts terminated if they are disobliging about the SNP.[38] Similar pressure has turned much of the civic/NGO sector reliant on state funding into a silent zone of compliance. To take just one example of many, in 2022, when a staffer at a major NGO wrote a critical review of how government policy impacted its operations, its new head—recruited from the civil service—insisted that it must be suppressed, otherwise funding would be lost.[39]

With London reluctant to use its powers to intervene in Scottish affairs, and Sturgeon's government receiving a large subsidy from the UK Treasury, much of which is ploughed into social engineering schemes, the critics mentioned (as well as others) fear that an incipient form of *gleichshaltung* may be occurring in Scotland. This was the process under which, after 1933, the ruling National Socialists in Germany sought to coordinate political, social, cultural and educational institutions in the name of national unity.

As local government is steadily enfeebled by successive budget cuts, along with the centralising policies of the SNP, few centres of independent thinking survive. Perhaps only the spending auditor, Stephen Boyle, is willing to stand up to the SNP juggernaut (and after causing headaches for SNP ministers his budget was slashed in 2022).[40] The former culture minister, Fiona Hyslop, has recommended that artists should have 'a common understanding of what the country wants'.[41] Academics have warned about interference with the study of history in schools.[42] Teaching materials containing pro-independence slogans and factsheets on Nicola Sturgeon have been condemned as 'so one-sided as to be seriously misleading'.[43] Neil Oliver, perhaps Scotland's best-known historian, has remarked that it is 'hard to avoid suspecting the independence-obsessed SNP is, paradoxically, really all about fostering a culture of total dependence'.[44]

The SNP's sway over the communications industry enables it to be an omniscient presence and promote a paternalistic image, whatever its shortcomings as an administrator. The Scottish government's 175 communications staff dwarf the BBC's 34 reporters in Scotland, meaning that even the publicly funded broadcasters have one person asking questions for every five who answer them. The bill for Holyrood's press officers and special advisers has increased by 50 percent since 2018, despite newspaper sales halving since the SNP came to power.[45]

Sturgeon has shrunk the Scottish political stage so that it is small, incestuous coteries of usually middle-class activists who shape state policies. The journalist, Stephen Daisley, summed up well the atmosphere, which led another journalist to describe Scotland under her as 'the wokest country in the world'.[46]

He wrote:

> 'What ails Scottish politics...is a noxious draught of constitutionalism, group think, ideological capture, impulsive lawmaking, and substandard legislative scrutiny. Scotland suffers from an incestuous political culture

in which policy is researched, lobbied for, drafted, legislated, reported on and analysed by people who all used to drink together down the student union. It is government of old uni mates, by old uni mates, for old uni mates'.[47]

The performative radicalism that this public relations machine enables Sturgeon to indulge in, conceals the fact that ill-considered policy choices have inflicted a massive budget deficit.[48] Low investment, caused in part by a tax raid on high earners, forced her to make drastic budgetary cuts in mid-2022 which make severe cutbacks in public services unavoidable. She benefited, from 2019 to 2022, from the unpopularity of a divided London government under Boris Johnson, and invariably went out of her way to avoid identifying with him on anything. At the start of the invasion of Ukraine, her position was clearly no different from his. But she had to be seen to be different, so she advocated for a 'No-fly zone over Ukraine policed by NATO'.[49]

On top of the cost of the pandemic, Ukraine was just another blow to stability. Accumulating crises suggested that the feasibility of Scottish independence depended on a pre-2014 world that is now gone. The Union was emotionally unrewarding for growing numbers of Scots, especially younger ones, but the case for Scottish independence was increasingly made without recourse to facts about how it could be sustained. By 2022, even within her own camp, there was little palpable enthusiasm for the early referendum that Sturgeon asserted was on its way.

She still offers satisfaction to many, not through accomplishments on behalf of citizens, but by laying on a non-stop drama concerning the fate of the nation. A fresh push on independence announced on 14 June 2022, was largely policy-free and contained the warning, from Sturgeon to those whom she hopes to win over, that 'independence will not guarantee a better future'.[50]

Despite a carefully-manicured image, 'she is self-absorbed' and 'remarkably uninterested in other people in real life'.[51] According to a former colleague, Jim Sillars, she is a triumph of style and presentation over substance:

> 'An articulate expounder of a brief, an effective attack dog on the opposition, but narrow, dogmatic, lacking imagination, and without that sweep of the intellect, and breadth and depth of thinking, that marks out politicians of the first rank from the rest. She is a machine politician: tomorrow's headline hunter, the pursuer of the celebratory selfie, the aficionado of political fashion— reluctant to define a woman —and incapable of thinking big. She has been a major speaker at umpteen party and other conferences over many years, but I doubt if anyone can remember even one [intervention] that contained an original idea'.[52]

Sturgeon had refused to groom a successor, but by 16 March 2023, her party was scrambling to find one. A six-week leadership contest, the first staged by the SNP in twenty years, was announced the day after she suddenly announced her resignation. In the words of the Conservative politician, Shaun Bailey, 'she had gone from superstar to nowhere' in a very short period of time.[53]

A series of misguided decisions in the previous four months, caused one veteran Scottish journalist, Andrew Nicoll, to observe that the warning all politicians go a little crazy if they hang on to power indefinitely, applied in her case.[54] She brushed aside advice that the subordinate parliament could not unilaterally call a referendum meant to take Scotland out of Britain, only to find in November 2022, that the UK Supreme Court (presided over by a Scottish judge) ruled unanimously that there was no constitutional basis for her claim. Undaunted, she then vowed to use the next UK general election as a de facto referendum on independence. On this issue, she was estranged even from party allies, who feared that an uncomprehending electorate would punish the SNP. Deaf to persuasion, she then ploughed ahead with arranging for a special conference in March 2023 to finalise the plans for this quixotic gesture.

Public opinion was further disregarded on 22 December 2022, when the Gender Recognition Reform (GRR) bill became law. It allows any man, to become a 'woman' merely by declaring themselves female and living as such for three months. Henceforth, 16-year-olds would be able to change the sex on their birth certificate without a medical diagnosis. This meant that rapists who declared themselves to be women could be housed in female prisons.

The cosy club atmosphere at Holyrood which isolated the political class from much of society was shown, when an amendment meant to prevent men convicted of sexual offences benefiting from the law, was rejected not just by the SNP, but by all other parties (excepting a majority of Conservatives). Polls soon showed that a law which enabled individuals to obtain a gender recognition certificate as early as 16, removing the need for a medical diagnosis of gender dysphoria, was massively opposed by the electorate. Even 31 percent of SNP voters endorsed the decision taken by British Prime Minister, Rishi Sunak, on 16 January 2023, to block the GRR law (the only Holyrood act where Westminster had deployed its powers to do so).[55] In the same week, the Prime Minister of New Zealand, Jacinda Ardern, made a shock announcement that she was quitting with immediate effect, saying she has 'nothing left in the tank'. The departure of a politician, often compared by admirers of both with Sturgeon, because of their determination to chart radical new political courses, raised speculation about the Scottish leader's mortality. But Sturgeon was adamant that she was going nowhere and had plenty of fuel left in her tank. She showed her combative side on 27 January 2023, by delivering a blanket criticism of opponents of GRR as 'transphobic', 'misogynist', 'homophobic' and even 'racist'.[56] Within weeks, polls were showing a sharp fall in backing for independence. One that was published on 13 February 2023, showed a bigger lead for the pro-Union side than there had been in the 2014 referendum.[57] A poll, taken between 10 and 15 February, showed that the SNP had slumped to 27 percent support, just two points behind the Labour Party.[58]

On February 15, Nicola Sturgeon called a hastily-arranged press conference to announce that it was time to 'reset the tone and tenor of our discourse' and that she was stepping down. Her statement was prolix and self-referential. 'I' 'me' my' were mentioned 153 times, but she mentioned Scotland only eleven times.[59] There was a much bigger media reaction, not just in Britain but across much of the world, to her going than had been displayed when the five British Prime Ministers who served during her period in office came and went. However, despite the way she had successfully projected her image during the agitation over Brexit, the Covid pandemic, and the crusade for a new Green technocratic order, it was hard to see how her practical legacy was any better than the leaders who came and went in London.

Even Nationalists, who offered praise for her fortitude, struggled to dwell on any positive advances in governance. There was no shortage of critics able to point to a range of failures which had worsened life experiences for Scots compared to other national groupings in the West. Among the more restrained was the London *Times,* which, in an editorial, observed that 'forced by mistakes of her own making, Ms Sturgeon has hastily abandoned a government without grip, a party without a plan, and a people failed miserably by both'.[60] The most fulsome praise came, predictably, from pillars of the London media who had gained heart from her unstinting attacks on the Conservative Party. Brian Wilson, a former Labour minister under Tony Blair, observed that 'a harsh tongue took her a long way'.[61] However, more recent Labour figures refused to endorse Wilson's view that 'she chose grievance politics over working hard to improve people's lives'.

Two past leaders of the Labour Party in Scotland, Wendy Alexander and Kezia Dugdale, issued statements of praise for her 'progressive' outlook and Liberal Democrat notables were similarly magnanimous.[62] It was a sign that much of the political class in Scotland was relaxed about major parts of her left-wing social engineering agenda: it displaced her original focus on political nationalism and enabled some Labour worthies to benefit from the patronage system erected in the diversity, inclusion and equality area.

Whoever succeeds her as SNP leader is likely to be aware that her dogmatism in pursuing some of the wider features of this progressive agenda, have saddled the party with a major credibility problem. It won't easily be forgotten that her nemesis probably turned out to be Adam Graham, a double rapist who had subsequently 'changed gender', without any surgical intervention, to become Isla Bryson. He was duly sent to a Scottish women's prison, and Sturgeon was unable to say, in increasingly uncomfortable interviews, what gender this prisoner was. The incoherence of someone rarely lost for words deepened her isolation.

Up until 2022, on average, just 30 people changed gender each year in Scotland.[63] Her desire to make Scotland a world leader in radical transgender legislation revealed her to be a zealot whose advanced ideological views had left the bulk of the population behind. Her absorption with this niche cause hurt the cause for independence. The growing band of nationalist critics scorned her for relegating it to promote her own image as a voice of international middle-class niche politics. Her readiness to impose extreme change on an unwilling population had led the author J.K. Rowling, who lives in Scotland, to take to social media in October 2022 wearing a T-shirt emblazoned with the words: 'Nicola Sturgeon, destroyer of women's rights'.[64]

Throughout 2022, there had been a steady exodus of women members from the SNP. Ash Regan, a member of her government who resigned over GRR, called for these and other members to be able to rejoin the party in order to be able to take part in the contest to choose a successor. A contest meant to take four months under SNP rules was squeezed into six weeks. Followers of Sturgeon dominate the upper echelons. Upon Sturgeon's resignation, they altered the rules of the constitution to enable the party's national executive committee to enjoy a free hand to manage the election. Accordingly, the continuity candidate, Humza Yousaf won the hastily-arranged contest (albeit narrowly) and took over as the new First Minister on 29 March 2023.

The way the succession is being organized seems to pave the way for further dissension in nationalist ranks.[65] Sturgeon's influence is bound to remain in various public bodies, civic and cultural organisations, as well as charities campaigning groups that are firmly in the Sturgeonite orbit. But it is hard to see anyone being able to drive forward a radical progressive agenda with as much energy and determination as she was able to summon for the task.

Backing for independence had flatlined during her years at the top. Her response to events like Brexit proved pedestrian, when a more imaginative separatist leader would have sought to gain advantage from the prolonged disarray and strife at Westminster. Aided, however, by a public relations machine, she was able to ensure that much of the political weather in Scotland revolved around whatever was on her mind. In her resignation speech, she asserted that 'I enjoy approval ratings after eight years in government which most leaders would give their right arms for'. But by this point she must have been aware that numerous people were laughing at the ridiculous hole she had dug for herself over the trans issue. Her ascendancy was as much to do with the weakness of the opposition as her impact on the face of Scotland. Arguably, there were none (or very few) of the achievements which nationalist, leaders wishing to take a country on a fresh journey, sought to roll out in the public policy field or in infrastructure. Much was spin and artifice, concentrating on influencing minds rather than improving physical or mental well-being, or transforming the economic face of the land.

'Resign Sturgeon' electronic billboards had been put up at strategic points in Scotland's two largest cities, by the anti-nationalist group The Majority, 48 hours before she announced her departure. On that evening, several hundred delighted pro-Union locals were filmed performing the Conga in Glasgow's George Square. It was imagery emanating from Scotland that the rest of the world had seen little of during sixteen years of nationalist control. But it would be premature to imagine that this movement is now on the way out. The SNP remains a large membership party with a tight grip on key areas of Scottish life, in state and society. Hubris, chronic mismanagement of party and nation, a vendetta outlook, and disdain for the aspirations of perhaps most Scots, when politics is put aside, cut short Sturgeon's time at the top. A leader with such advantageous electoral arithmetic might have expected to carry on for much longer. But her undoubted technical skills in politics and her prowess as a communicator, campaigner and image-maker, proved of no avail. Instead, authoritarian traits, which grew more pronounced the longer she remained in office, capsized her political career, at least in Scotland. She found herself in the invidious position of being out-maneuvered by Rishi Sunak on the gender recognition hill that she chose to die on. It remains to be seen whether her party can put her stubborn adherence to self-rule behind it in order to recover momentum. There remains everything to play for, not least because the opposition in Scotland and the British establishment at Westminster, are bedevilled by severe flaws of their own.

Sturgeon's hasty and ignominious exit is revealing, not only about her failed stewardship, but says much about the shallowness of the claque of well-wishers in metropolitan power-centres across the globe who saluted her as a harbinger of a new progressive order. They wished to reduce world politics to the rolling out of a series of middle-class radical nostrums in which any meaningful control over their own lives was snatched from ordinary striving citizens. Needless to say, they were coldly indifferent to the fiasco that ensued in Scotland when a myopic and driven leader pushed parts of the woke post-modern agenda to breaking point.

Sturgeon had been almost as implacable in imposing her will on her own party as in defying Westminster. Many quit, frustrated at not knowing what her true beliefs are beyond her conviction that what she does is invariably good for Scotland. Her durability was remarkable, not only given the seeds of distrust she has sown in nationalist ranks, but also taking account of her poor record as an administrator even before she took full charge in 2014. She has sidelined the party, whose elected members are mainly compliant careerists, and built up alternative power bases in the media and especially the professional managerial classes. These groups were dazzled by her sense of entitlement and vaulting ambition and also seemed ready to overlook her limited administrative abilities and the shortcomings in integrity, which loomed large, especially after her sudden departure from office. It is quite an accomplishment that she was able to hoodwink party, societal power-holders and indeed much of the British media for so long. Indeed, it makes her perhaps a more intriguing and absorbing object of study than the cause that she claims to represent, which has found itself increasingly becalmed during her years handling devolutionary powers.

Right up to, and even after, her arrest and detention for seven hours as part of the police investigation into the whereabouts of missing party funds, Sturgeon continued to be treated as a celebrity, if not a saint, in different quarters of the mainstream media. On the weekend of 10–11 June 2023, Scottish Television was just one media outlet to publicise the fact that she had just passed her driving theory test with full marks in one section. She had announced the fact on Twitter and 24 hours later, after her release from custody, she said: 'I am grateful that so many continue to show faith in me...I know beyond doubt that I am in fact innocent of any wrongdoing'.[66] Her quasi-imperial presentation of herself as better than anyone else had not deserted her in a difficult hour. In the social media age, she retained the skill of convincing people that she was a friend, a mascot, or a distant but sympathetic force for good in the world, not a ruthless politician whose only cause was herself.

Ironically, the very next day, Silvio Berlusconi, another artful and devious politician, died. Arguably, he was also a master of the black arts of public relations. His passing was treated with a certain sympathetic reverence, even in quarters unimpressed by past examples of his piratical behaviour in public affairs. The fact that an easily manipulable communications industry enabled flawed politicians to appear like minor deities or miracle workers even though their record in government is devoid of any clear achievements, is unsettling—yet another unseemly cloud hanging over Europe's troubled democratic landscape.

---

[1] Andrew Liddle, 'Sturgeon chastised by her former teacher', *Press and Journal,* (Aberdeen), 23 July 2016.
[2] Ben Borland, 'The murky end to the SNP chief's legal career', *Scottish Daily Express,* 5 April 2021.
[3] Mark McLaughlin, 'Nicola Sturgeon ignored SNP bullies, says former MSP', *Times,* 22 March 2021.
[4] See Tom Gallagher, *The Illusion of Freedom, Scotland Under Nationalism,* London: Hurst Publications, 2009.
[5] *Scotland's Future,* Edinburgh: Scottish Government, 2013.
[6] '"Democracy rocks" for Nicola Sturgeon at Glasgow Hydro', *BBC News,* 22 November 2014, https://www.bbc.co.uk/news/uk-scotland-30157986, accessed 15 June 2022.
[7] Chris Green, 'Scotland's top civil servant, Leslie Evans, responsible for Alex Salmond debacle, say MSPs', *Inews,* 23 March 2021, https://inews.co.uk/news/scotland/scotlands-top-civil-servant-leslie-evans-responsible-for-alex-salmond-debacle-say-msps-926479, accessed 17 June 2022.
[8] Rehema Figueiredo, 'More than a third of SNP supporters voted for Brexit in Sturgeon embarrassment', *Scottish Daily Express,* 28 December 2016.
[9] Tom Gallagher 'Sturgeon's Mission is Division', *Think Scotland,* 9 March 2021, https://thinkscotland.org/2021/03/sturgeons-mission-is-division-having-split-the-country-shes-now-working-on-her-party/, accessed 10 March 2022.
[10] Alex Bell, 'Scotland shown to be in rotten state as gang ethos takes over government', *Press and Journal,* 25 March 2021.
[11] Fraser Nelson, 'Sturgeon's establishment stitch-up', *Spectator,* 27 February 2021, https://www.spectator.co.uk/article/sturgeon-s-establishment-stitch-up-should-concern-us-all, accessed 12 March 2021.
[12] Andrew Neil, 'Censorship, bullying, threats of jail... how Nicola Sturgeon's storm troops turned Scotland into a banana republic without the bananas', *Daily Mail,* 25 February 2021.
[13] David Davis, 'Scotland – A deficit of power and accountability', *Spectator Online,* 16 March 2021, https://www.spectator.co.uk/article/david-davis-scotland-a-deficit-of-power-and-accountability, accessed 28 March 2021.
[14] Simon Johnson, 'Nicola Sturgeon faces SNP rebellion over gender 'self-identification'', *Telegraph Online,* 27 February 2002, https://www.telegraph.co.uk/politics/2022/02/27/nicola-sturgeon-faces-snp-rebellion-gender-self-identification/, accessed 10 June 2022.
[15] Mary Wright and George Mair, 'Number of transgender prisoners in Scotland up by a third amid fresh calls for single-sex jails', *Scottish Daily Express,* 23 August 2022.
[16] Hayley Dixon, 'The week Nicola Sturgeon abandoned women', *Daily Telegraph,* 2 March 2022.

[17] Dixon, 'The week'.
[18] 'Nicola Sturgeon: JK Rowling is not a real feminist like me', *Daily Telegraph*, 8 October 2022.
[19] Joanna Williams, 'Why is the SNP So Obsessed with Teenage Sex', *Spiked Online*, 23 February 2022,
https://www.spiked-online.com/2022/02/23/why-is-the-snp-so-obsessed-with-teenage-sex/, accessed 10 June 2022.
[20] Robin McAlpine, 'Now a price will be paid', *Robin McAlpine Org*, 9 June 2022, https://robinmcalpine.org/now-a-price-will-be-paid, accessed 13 June 2022.
[21] Russell Findlay, 'Know your Nicola: A handy guide to the many different versions of "Russian doll' Sturgeon', *Scottish Daily Express*, 15 February 2022.
[22] Paige Beresford, 'Nicola Sturgeon opens up about menopause – as FM feels she has 'responsibility' to talk about it', *Scottish Sun*, 21 January 2022.
[23] George Mair, 'Nicola Sturgeon: I feel less safe in polarised and toxic climate', *Times*, 30 March 2022.
[24] Steerpike, 'More shameless Sturgeon selfie summitry, *Spectator Online*, 11 November 2021,
https://www.spectator.co.uk/article/more-shameless-sturgeon-selfie-summitry, accessed 15 November 2021.
[25] James Heale and Michael Simmons, 'Nicola Sturgeon's secret state', *Spectator*, 9 April 2022.
[26] Reporter, 'Supreme Court blocks Named Person scheme branding elements "unlawful"', *Press and Journal*, 28 July 2016.
[27] Tom Harris, Nicola Sturgeon shamelessly exploited Covid in her war for independence', *Daily Mail*, 17 February 2022.
[28] Reporter, 'Tidal wave' of closures and redundancies expected in hospitality sector', *Scotsman*, 19 May 2020.
[29] Effie Deans, 'The Great Sturgeon', *Lily of St Leonards*, 26 November 2021, https://www.effiedeans.com/2021/11/the-great-sturgeon.html, accessed 27 November 2021.
[30] John Lloyd, 'What the SNP really believes', *UnHerd*, 8 September 2021, https://unherd.com/2021/09/what-the-snp-really-believes/?=refinnar, accessed 8 September 2021.
[31] McAlpine, 'Now a price'. Rory Scothorne, 'Nicola Sturgeon's record reign is a sign of stasis rather than strength', *New Statesman*, 30 May 2022.
[32] Tom Harris, 'Alex Salmond once pioneered the SNP's cynical tricks. Now he's exposing them', *Daily Telegraph*, 25 May 2022, https://www.telegraph.co.uk/news/2022/05/23/alex-salmond-pioneered-sturgeons-cynical-tricks-now-exposing/, accessed 26 May 2022. Editorial, 'Nicola Sturgeon's record: Failing State', *Times*, 16 June 2022.
[33] Brian Monteith, 'Expensive booze pushes Scots towards drugs, *The Critic*, 17 November 2021, https://thecritic.co.uk/dear-booze-makes-scots-druggies/, accessed 18 November 2021.
[34] Brian Monteith, 'The Scottish Government budget that takes Scotland (further) down the road to financial ruin', *Scotsman*, 13 December 2021.
[35] David Walker, 'Indian Council boss warned Sturgeon not to do business with Sanjeev Gupta years before collapse of his steel firm', *Scottish Daily Express*, 2 December 2021.
[36] Susan Dalgety, 'Beware of 'insider Scotland' and Sturgeon's New Model Army', *Scotsman*, 11 June 2022.

[37] Dalgety, 'Beware of'.
[38] Heale and Simmons, 'Nicola Sturgeon's'.
[39] McAlpine, 'Now a price'.
[40] Jill Stephenson, 'The "strong men" and their illusions', *Think Scotland*, 10 June 2022, https://thinkscotland.org/2022/06/the-strong-men-and-their-illusions/, accessed 10 June 2021.
[41] Jill Stephenson, 'Image without substance', *Think Scotland*, 30 November 2021, https://thinkscotland.org/2021/11/image-without-substance-nicola-sturgeon-and-the-snp/, accessed 10 December 2021.
[42] Douglas Dickie, 'Are the Nats brainwashing children? Academic warns Scottish Nationalism "seeping" into education system', *Scottish Daily Express*, 9 January 2022.
[43] David McCann, 'Expert condemns 'pro-independence' study aid with 16 photos of Nicola Sturgeon and other SNP politicians', *Times*, 23 May 2022, https://www.thetimes.co.uk/article/expert-condemns-pro-independence-study-aid-with-16-photos-of-nicola-sturgeon-and-other-snp-politicians-btzzbtlft, accessed 24 May 2022.
[44] Neil Oliver, 'Hogmanay may be hushed but the SNP can't muzzle us all', *Times*, 2 January 2022, https://www.thetimes.co.uk/article/neil-oliver-hogmanay-may-be-hushed-but-the-snp-cant-muzzle-us-all-2css5k8lc,accessed 2 January 2022.
[45] Heale and Simmons, 'Nicola Sturgeon's'.
[46] Jenny Hjul, 'How Scotland became the wokest country in the world', *Daily Telegraph*, 28 January 2023.
[47] Stephen Daisley, 'The fish rots from the head in Sturgeon's Scotland', *Spectator Online*, 31 January 2023, https://www.spectator.co.uk/article/the-fish-rots-from-the-head-in-sturgeons-scotland/.
[48] Michael Glackin, 'You waste it, Nicola Sturgeon, and we'll pick up the tab', *Sunday Times*, 5 June 2022, https://www.thetimes.co.uk/article/you-waste-it-nicola-sturgeon-comment-snp-economy-scotland-2h6fklc08, accessed 5 June 2022.
[49] Simon Johnson, 'Nicola Sturgeon's call for a Ukraine no-fly zone "could trigger World War Three"', *Daily Telegraph*, 10 March 2022, https://www.telegraph.co.uk/politics/2022/03/10/ukraine-no-fly-zone-nato-scotland-nicola-sturgeon-russia-invasion/, accessed 11 March 2022.
[50] Kieran Andrews, 'Independence will not guarantee better future', *Times*, 14 June 2022.
[51] Alex Massie, 'Why Sturgeon has to win over the doubters', Times, 12 June 2022.
[52] Jim Sillars, 'Longest...but?', *Yours for Scotland*, 31 May 2022, https://yoursforscotlandcom.wordpress.com/2022/05/31/longest-but/, accessed 2 June 2022.
[53] *GBNews*, 'Dan Wootton Tonight', 16 February 2023.
[54] Andrew Nicoll, 'I worked alongside Nicola Sturgeon for 20 years – here's what finally pushed her over the edge', *Scottish Sun*, 16 February 2023.
[55] Rob Harris, 'The trans rights row sparking a crisis for Nicola Sturgeon's leadership', *Sydney Morning Herald*, 12 February 2023.
[56] Michael Blackley, 'Fury as under-fire Nicola Sturgeon accuses gender reform critics of "homophobia and racism"', *Daily Mail*, 28 January 2023.
[57] Kirsteen Paterson, 'Lord Ashcroft poll reveals gulf between Scottish Government and voters on independence and gender reforms', *Holyrood Magazine*, 13 February 2023.
[58] @electpoliticsuk, 17 February 2023.

[59] Steerpike, 'Nicola Sturgeon's resignation speech', *Spectator Online*, 15 February 2023, https://www.spectator.co.uk/article/full-text-nicola-sturgeons-resignation-speech/.
[60] 'The Times view on Nicola Sturgeon's resignation: Scot Free', *Times*, 16 February 2023.
[61] Brian Wilson, 'Nicola Sturgeon, First Minister of Failure, chose grievance politics over working hard to improve people's lives', *Scotsma*n, (Edinburgh), 16 February 2023.
[62] Kezia Dugdale, 'I am proud to live in Nicola Sturgeon's Scotland, *The Courier*, (Dundee), 16 February 2023, https://www.thecourier.co.uk/fp/opinion/4148029/kezia-dugdale-nicola-sturgeon-opinion/.
See also @wendy_alexander, @agcolehamilton, @joswinson, @willierennie.
[63] The Editorial Board, 'Trans debacle is the end of the line for Nicola Sturgeon', *Reaction*, 27 January 2023, https://reaction.life/trans-debacle-is-the-end-of-the-line-for-nicola-sturgeon/.
[64] James Hookway and David Luhnow, 'Nicola Sturgeon resigns as Scotland's First Minister', *Wall Street Journal*, 15 February 2023.
[65] Robin McAlpine, 'Stop Murrell's corruption NOW', *RobinMcAlpine.org*, 17 February 2023, https://robinmcalpine.org/stop-murrells-corruption-now/, accessed 17 February 2023.
[66] *Daily Telegraph*, 11 June 2023.

PART 5
CHAPTER 19: THE TRIUMPH OF SELF-ABSORBED LEADERSHIP

Upon the commencement of a new century, a career in politics soon began to lose much of whatever appeal it had previously enjoyed. The 'feel good' atmosphere occasioned by the anti-climactic end to the Cold War, evaporated with the attacks on major targets in the United States, mounted by operatives belonging to Al-Qaeda, on 11 September 2001. The knee-jerk response by ruling politicians in Washington and London, unfamiliar with geopolitics or military affairs and with a sketchy understanding of the roots of religious fundamentalism, led to a series of disastrous entanglements in Iraq and Afghanistan. A hitherto impregnable-seeming Tony Blair had his premiership in Britain shortened by the fall-out from the failed attempt to conjure up stability in Iraq after the removal of Saddam Hussein. When George W. Bush stepped down as US President in 2009, he was seen as one of the most unsuccessful holders of that office. Yet just a few years later, a consortium of European leaders, with David Cameron and Nicholas Sarkozy to the fore, repeated the same mistakes by believing that they could conjure up stability in oil-rich and strategically located Libya by hastening the departure of its leader Muammar Gaddafi.

By the new century's second decade, the Eurozone, which had been created by impetuous Franco-German politicians, was revealed as a half-finished monetary union whose defects had plunged the Mediterranean states of the EU into prolonged turmoil and, in the case of Greece, deep depression. Even leaving aside such calamitous errors, politics and its practitioners were already being viewed with reserve, if not downright scorn. The foundations of the house of European democracy were shifting and masonry was becoming dislodged. The end of nuclear confrontation meant that politicians could no longer appeal for solidarity and restraint from domestic populations in the face of the threat to open societies emanating from the east. More obliquely, the retreat of a previously familiar set of values, once substantially shaped around the Christian religion, meant that appeals from elected elites for stoicism and sacrifice in the face of economic adversity, increasingly fell on deaf ears. Working-class communities, unable to shield themselves from the effects of out-sourcing of jobs or automation, grew disillusioned with social democratic or post-communist parties. The sense of deference towards traditional elites started to melt away.

The alienation of the middle-class from established institutions proved to be a much more drawn-out process. By the early 2020s, it had led to many young people, going through or recently emerged from higher education, viewing national institutions as illegitimate systems of power. Indeed, they were depicted as nothing less than the successors of colonial structures of oppression that continued to block various submerged minorities from enjoying self-realisation. Such a change in bourgeois attitudes on both sides of the Atlantic occurred against the background of a growing convergence between technocracy and identity politics, between the efficient and unsentimental moneyed right and a left shorn of even residual attachment to the interests of the working-class.

As the younger cohorts of middle-class opinion were radicalised, especially in anglophone countries, and lower-income groups by contrast moved rightwards due to their unhappiness with many of the effects of globalisation, it was a bewildering time to engage in the trade of politics. Fresh pressures were heaped on practitioners who found it hard to display endeavour or originality in the face of expectations from the media, corporations, and academia that they should operate within a narrow band of what was politically acceptable. There was a growing scepticism about the ability of political parties to represent wide interests in society. As a result, enrolment in parties sharply decreased. Simultaneously, electoral volatility increased. Voters were likelier to abandon their partisan loyalties and vote for other parties, often new ones specifically catering for the disenchanted. These parties were invariably dubbed dangerously 'populist' in influential quarters, prompting the philosopher John Gray to observe that 'populism' is a liberal pejorative for the unintended consequences of liberalism.[1] Turnout in elections often slumped as voters perceived little real difference in the performance and priorities of ostensibly rival parties when they held office.[2]

It is perhaps no surprise that politicians, unable to draw upon strong reserves of support from an increasingly disgruntled society, instead drew increasingly closer to the state. In most European countries, state-funding was introduced for political parties after the year 2000. Party leaders, in or out of office, were able to fund teams of advisors whose primary role was often to assist them with presentation and messaging. Speeches were written for them and vote-winning strategies devised through relying on focus groups, which were supposed to be a representative section of the electorate. Inevitably, the age of the mass party meeting or the party conference as venues of genuine engagement or debate entered into abeyance. Media advisors became more omniscient in political life—'influencers' often with narrow academic backgrounds which insulated them from knowledge of the wider public. Politicians became increasingly reliant on validation from a media industry. The timing of this development was hardly inspired. It occurred as much of the media was not only failing to reflect popular concerns but was starting also to emulate long-held elitist viewpoints about the essential backwardness of the masses. Instead of 'speaking truth to power', much of the media was endeavouring to impose the views of powerful global lobbies on increasingly restive readers.

In the mid-19th century, Alexis de Tocqueville warned of the possibility that a determined phalanx of ruling interests and their allies would be able to crush the autonomy of citizens by clever manipulation of their emotions and senses. He wrote in *Democracy in America*: 'Such a power does not destroy, but it prevents existence; it does not tyrannize, but it compresses, enervates, extinguishes, and stupefies a people, till each nation is reduced to nothing better than a flock of timid and industrious animals, of which the government is the shepherd.'[3]

Recently, the Scottish philosopher and novelist Ewan Morrison has warned about states, militaries, activist movements and private corporations harnessing the latest technology to influence citizens to accept authoritarian solutions by bombarding them with seductive imagery that emphasises 'cuteness'.[4] As the media have switched from their information role to that of influencer, often being given considerable revenue to perform such a role at the service of the state, it has become bound up with nudging citizens towards behaviour and attitudes which governments are keen to roll out and impose.

The slump in circulation from the paying public has redefined much of the media. As familiar print titles entered into decline, social media platforms sought to succeed them, often more concerned with shaping narratives than providing a regular flow of news. The rise of Twitter, Facebook and other engines of online information and opinion meant that much of the information industry started to grow reliant on niche groups in society not just for profits but for a sense of direction.

As the response to the Covid pandemic showed, mainstream politicians also became increasingly dependent on government and health bureaucracies for guidance and advice. In this crisis, a set of credentialed experts were seen as possessing knowledge far superior to that of elected decision-makers, even though it turned out that many of their decisions turned out to be erroneous ones. It was remarkable that official recommendations leading to lockdowns and mask and vaccine mandates did not result in greater scrutiny or scepticism from government or opposition politicians, despite warnings from others of the profound impact on society and economic stability of these policies.

Across the West, the response to Covid of elected politicians (with the exception of a few countries like Sweden) threw into sharp relief the fact that politicians were separating themselves from society. The exposure some received when managing crises, such as Matthew Hancock, Britain's health minister for most of the pandemic, revealed that they often seemed to be far more concerned with their own egos and reputation than with saving lives, shielding the young from harmful restrictions, or allowing the elderly access to their loved ones, especially in their final moments. The release of 2.3 million words in *WhatsApp* messages from and to Hancock in March 2023, produced outrage that is almost certainly likely to deepen the chasm between the London-centric political classes and the rest of British society. Hancock and others seemed to revel in frightening, or intimidating, the public and there are too many people who feel victimised by a lockdown shaped around political criteria rather than any 'science', for the sense of anger to dissipate.

By now, politicians who often seemed hermetically-sealed from society were growing increasingly reliant not only on an agenda-driven media and state bureaucracies but on international bodies laying down the tramlines for policies, which hitherto had been the almost exclusive prerogative of national governments. The readiness, in turn, of major world bodies to interfere quite deeply in national politics was perhaps well illustrated by the sharp criticism of the British government's mini-budget from the IMF in September 2022, over proposed tax cuts in 2023, involving sums a fraction of those which had been spent on handling the Covid pandemic.[5]

Perhaps understandably, bureaucracies at national and international level rarely show concern about globalising government involved in transferring decision-making to the EU, the IMF or United Nations institutions. With politicians no longer engaging with domestic electorates, the emergence in outline form of world government in the dimension of socio-economic, health or cultural policy considerably increases the freedom of action of law-makers and administrators weary of nation-state confines.

It is very easy for politicians to get lost in the thickets of supra-national governance. Few, at least while in office, have displayed the self-confidence to defy conventional wisdom as laid down by elites in Washington, Brussels, or Davos, and be guided by the primacy of what they see as core national interests. Perhaps one such figure was Shinzo Abe, Prime Minister of Japan from 2007 to 2008 and again from 2012 to 2020. He worked out his own strategy for steering his country through complex times. Writing shortly after his assassination in July 2022, his biographer described him as 'a nationalist' who 'saw his country as engaged in a fierce competition among nations'. Abe himself went on record to say that: 'My mission is none other than to draw a new vision of a nation that can withstand the raging waves for the next 50 to 100 years'.[6]

Abe was heavily involved in seeking to shield Japan, and the rest of East Asia, from threats to regional peace and national sovereignty posed by authoritarian regimes in China and, to a lesser degree, Russia. Europe continues to have its disputed territorial areas, but it is hard to see any of the current generation of leaders possessing the heft to cool tensions such as those that have (at the time of writing) flared up between Turkey and Greece. The main democratic contenders have preferred to be swept along by the cultural *zeitgeist* of the moment. It may explain why an obscure, fervently Green teenage activist, Greta Thunberg of Sweden, was able to influence the direction of European policy on energy matters to a remarkable degree for half-a-decade. It was only the eruption of the war in Ukraine that drove home for millions the inconvenient fact that renewable energy was unable to meet a sudden and long-lasting shortfall in oil and gas supplies.

In reality, Thunberg was very much an invention of the media and environmental pressure groups. She embodied a new secular moralism that offered parallels with waves of puritanism in previous epochs of British and American history.[7] There was an insistent demand for austerity to counter what was seen as excess or licentiousness that had spread greed and irresponsibility across the land. As in the early 17th century and later, it was well-placed minority groups, within what would be seen as middle-class society, which were the engines behind the demand for a fundamental correction in human behaviour.

Thunberg addressed the UN World Climate Action Summit in September 2019. A 16-year-old wouldn't have come so far so early without important political backing. Left-wing parties incorporated the push for a Green economy in their manifestos even though it meant the end of industrialisation, which they had risen on the back of in the previous 150 years. Their centre-right opponents were usually unwilling to resist a fashionable political tide, even though (Germany excepted) Green parties obtained poor election results from voters sceptical about the wider benefits of their anti-materialist ideology.

With one exception, the early 21st century politicians profiled in this section were unwilling to shape the cultural discourse in society around their own beliefs. They went in fear of a media that has grown increasingly sulphurous in its judgment of leaders whom it takes a dislike to.

Leaving aside his own unforced errors, it was media hostility, more than any other factor, that secured the demise of Boris Johnson after three years in power in Britain. He had been very much an irreverent outsider, this time a journalist whose extrovert style won over millions of jaded voters disillusioned with the bland offerings of both Conservative and Labour. He was a populist, anti-establishment Tory whose reputation had been made thanks to his key role in getting a majority of voters to back leaving the EU in 2016. Less than a year into his premiership, it was blown off course by the Covid pandemic. Promises to make the economy more dynamic and competitive, now that Britain no longer had to comply with a raft of EU regulations, were soon forgotten. A blizzard of state spending ensued and his premiership soon became noted for the semi-socialist direction of its policies. Illiberal technocrats, rather than freedom-minded small state enthusiasts, defined policy. Dissension within his coalition of backers mounted, especially when he enthusiastically placed Britain in the vanguard of the net zero revolution. Perhaps only the duration of the Covid pandemic enabled him to get away with such apostasy and stay in office for 32 months. His chaotic style of government revealed a politician increasingly out of his depth. Scandals, intense media hostility, resignations and a full-scale government mutiny, overshadowed his final months in power. Good at capturing power, he was soon dominated by the metropolitan establishment whose agenda he had long decried. Johnson had been a beneficiary of a febrile political culture which prized sound bites and stunts, but when it emerged that, in response to urgent problems, all he had was platitudes and posturing, much of his support base evaporated, and he was soon gone.

France's Emmanuel Macron is far more disciplined and determined than the untidy and irresolute Johnson. However, both rose to power by styling themselves radical outsiders, when in fact their policies when in power were those of elitist liberals. They have urged massive alterations to lifestyles in order to pursue climate goals. These are policies which if ever carried through would likely result in a flow of investment from Europe to China as well as a massive transfer of wealth from lower-income groups to upper-class interests that have acquired a huge financial stake in the Green non-carbon economy.

France has a tradition of popular resistance to elitists schemes which are felt to benefit the privileged alone. Britain so far doesn't. Macron felt the sting of popular disapproval as street unrest overshadowed his first term before the onset of the pandemic. He was re-elected in 2022, but without a parliamentary majority. In a speech delivered in August of that year, he declared that climate change and the war in resource-rich Ukraine meant 'the end of abundance'.[8] Increasingly, he has shown impatience with the limitations on his power imposed by a recalcitrant population. His decision to raise the retirement age by decree in March 2023, sparked a nationwide explosion of anger in which he showed the hauteur which alienates so many French voters from him.

He is unapologetic about wishing to transfer budgetary powers from the nation-state to the centralised EU, leaving voters with little say about where their taxes go. He would seem to be little different in his outlook from the former French foreign minister Hubert Vedrine who said: 'Let us not be afraid to say it...All the major decisions to move towards European integration...were the product of modern forms of enlightened despotism'.[9]

Despite the country being associated with an emblematic revolution, there is a long tradition in France favouring *epistocracy*, rule by betters. Macron was educated in an elite school whose graduates were often seen as possessing the unchallenged right to guide the nation. At times, he has struggled to conceal the view that many of his fellow citizens are too limited in their understanding of political affairs to deserve much control over them. His lofty judgments on the shortcomings of others has often extended to the leaders of smaller European states who are reluctant to follow the French policy lead. Auguste Comte, one of the founders of the doctrine of positivism, remains an important intellectual influence in France and was dismissive of democracy. He argued that just as inferiors shouldn't choose their superiors, the governed cannot select their leaders owing to their natural deficiencies.[10] By overriding the will of parliament and decreeing a rise in the pension age on French citizens in March 2023, Macron seemed happy with the autocratic role that he and liberal EU allies decried when visible in East-Central Europe.

If Macron, unloved at home while taken much more seriously in global economic and political spheres, whose influence and wealth has greatly expanded during and after the Covid years, decides to embrace a variant of such a *dirigiste* philosophy, it will be a watershed point in Europe's political evolution. Numerous figures, not just in the media, but across European governance, argue that a ruler has already gone down this inglorious path.

He is one who leans not towards the cultural left, but towards the political right. This is Viktor Orbán, the winner of four consecutive elections in Hungary since 2010. That he is the object of fierce hostility in international liberal circles is perhaps due to his ability to replicate the hegemony which left-leaning progressives have established over state and society in different parts of the West, *but on a firmly conservative basis*. He refuses to be held to account by the EU, despite its growing tendency to impose heavy fines on Hungary for defying its contested definition of democracy. His supporters argue that he is defying an undemocratic behemoth which allows favoured members in the larger states to flout its rules with impunity. Critics contend that Orbán is a tyrant in the making, whose refusal to disown Vladimir Putin after the launch of his invasion of Ukraine, reveals his true colours. Most of his population has taken his side in wishing to rebuff foreign interference and, if outright EU hostility results in economic hardship, dislodging him is unlikely to be easy.

Hungary is a scene of polarisation between metropolitan groups concentrated in urban spaces and small town and rural dwellers who are mainly conservative in outlook. Rather surprisingly, even higher levels of polarisation have become evident in the Netherlands. Under the durable Mark Rutte, it is citizens from the small towns and provinces, as well as the indigenous working-class, who feel marginalised. Parties, keen to alter lifestyles and economic occupations by ushering in a globally-focused order based on Green social engineering, have made the running during his twelve years of rule. Paradoxically, Rutte belongs to the centre-right. But it is the priorities and world view of the metropolitan left which have shaped key public policies. Bureaucrats and NGOs have been able to impose a 'progressive' design for living on the country while largely disregarding the big swathe of citizens who feel they are being subject to unwelcome top-down experiments.

The Dutch political model, long presumed to be centred on the need to maintain a balanced consensus, is creaking in the face of such an ideological overload. Dissenting forces 'not getting with the programme' feel themselves marginalised. Rutte initially showed flair in seeking to steer the Netherlands in an increasingly post-national direction. However, he increasingly struggles to bridge a gulf of mistrust in Dutch society between supporters and opponents of Green-focused social engineering policies, ones which have emboldened many within government, institutions and corporations. Top-down zealotry is occurring during deepening economic adversity, which is being felt even by middle-class citizens. The state's readiness to close farms (to meet environmental criteria) and enforce a tough lockdown and vaccine policy during the Covid pandemic are sparking an instability which may be hard to overcome. Having been seen as a poised and decisive national manager, Rutte increasingly seems opportunistic and insipid in his reactions to the growing fracture in Dutch society, not least about how far to embrace the Green agenda. There is no guarantee that the densely-populated country can avoid an era of strife similar, or perhaps worse, than ones witnessed occasionally in post-war France, Italy or even Germany, if rulers seek to narrow the political stage to accommodate a select group of interests.

Election results from Italy to Sweden show that the critique from Viktor Orbán and others of the disruptive effects of globalisation, enjoy backing in contrasting parts of Europe. His opposition to progressive elites altering national identity over the heads of citizens, strikes a chord and has turned him into a pillar of conservatism who is far more effective than de Gaulle was in his heyday. He has articulated in a forceful manner the desire of nearly all the former communist states of Eastern Europe, not to fall under the sway of an undeniably more decent form of tutelage exercised from Brussels than what was endured at the hands of the pre-1989 Kremlin. But Hungary stands out owing to the strength of one party, Fidesz, and the unparalleled hold on power of a single man who is unapologetic about his illiberalism.

By contrast, none of the other post-communist states, from the Baltic States to the Black Sea, have witnessed such political durability allied to a concentration of power. Frequent alternations in office have occurred. New parties have risen and fallen. Party leaders have come and gone, although in Poland, figures like the conservative Jaroslav Kaczyński enjoy long-term influence. The democratic contest has been more robust at times than in supposedly consolidated democracies further west. But there have been few signs of deep-seated alienation from the constitutional pluralist regimes which emerged in the 1990s, by contrast with the disaffection now to be found in several of the founder member-states of the EU. This helps to explain why there hasn't been much focus in the book on this part of Europe. If the continent's politics decay before entering full-scale crisis, it is likely that the impetus will come from the states with older systems of democracy, which have been increasingly poorly managed and where electoral backlashes have been fiercer.

Vladimir Putin perhaps gambled in 2022 that, in his confrontation with the West, he would be able to rely on defections from the Euro-Atlantic security alliance among several of the post-communist states which became absorbed in NATO after 2004. But this hasn't happened (not even in the case of Hungary). Instead, irrespective of the complexion of governments, most have been more active than Western heavyweights like France and Germany in their backing for Ukraine. Moreover, they display less fear of the use of nuclear weapons than is the case further west.

---

[1] Dominic Green, 'Europe's "New Right"'.
[2] See Mair, 'Ruling the Void'.
[3] Alexis de Tocqueville, *Democracy in America*, first published 1859, many subsequent editions, Vol. 4, Book 2, Chapter 6.
[4] Ewan Morrison, 'Cute Authoritarianism', *Aero Magazine*, 15 March 2023, https://areomagazine.com/2023/03/15/cute-authoritarianism/, accessed 15 March 2023.
[5] Editorial, 'What went wrong in Britain', *Wall Street Journal*, 30 September 2022.
[6] See Tobias Harris, 'The Postwar Japan That Shinzo Abe Built', *New York Times*, 9 July 2022.
[7] Nigel Jones, 'Wokeism is Latter Day Puritanism', *The Critic*, 9 July 2020, https://thecritic.co.uk/wokeism-is-latter-day-puritanism/, accessed 24 October 2022.
[8] 'Macron warns of sacrifices ahead after the end of abundance', *Barrons*, 25 August 2022, https://www.barrons.com/news/macron-warns-sacrifices-ahead-after-end-of-abundance-01661332507.
[9] Mody, *Euro Tragedy*, p.p. 97-8.
[10] José Adelino Maltez, Tradição e Revolução, Uma Biografia do Portugal Político do Século XIX ao XXI, Vol. II, (1910-2005), Lisbon: Tribuna, 2005, p. 353.

CHAPTER 20: MARK RUTTE

1967-

Mark Rutte is a technocrat, with a background in the human resources industry, who has enjoyed a lengthy span as head of government in The Hague. It makes him one of the few post-war Dutch leaders who is easily recognisable elsewhere in Europe. At home, his emollient style and cool nerves have enabled him to ride out successive governmental crises. For a long time, he displayed the knack of calming Dutch anxieties, which enabled his People's Party for Freedom and Democracy (VVD) to thrive. He suffered no loss of popularity by insisting that creditor countries in the EU should not be expected to prop up financially debtor member-states. At the same time, he backs the drive to shape social and cultural policies of member states around an intrusive template, able to draw upon keen support only among technocratic elites and their urban left-liberal allies.

Rutte's central role in his nation's affairs has coincided with growing political polarisation which has seen the collapse in support for various historic parties and the rapid rise of newcomers. Growing disgruntlement has been traced to the deterioration of the urban environment, demographic pressures on public services, economic insecurity, and collisions over competing rights and ideological agendas. Parties near to power have increasingly forsaken maintenance of balance and consensus in favour of imposing fashionable global prescriptions on Dutch life.

While Rutte has been adroit at managing coalition squalls, he increasingly struggles to soothe public anxieties and disagreements over the direction the Netherlands is going in. Arguably, he mishandled the 2020-22 coronavirus pandemic by displaying an unsure touch and opting for an authoritarian style. The worst social unrest seen anywhere in Northern Europe during the emergency resulted from the declaration of severe lockdowns. Nevertheless, his ability to mobilise voters accustomed to a paternalistic state ensured his re-election in March 2021, though it took nearly a year to form a coalition government.

After a dozen years of power, he now increasingly defers to his main coalition partner the D66, a firm advocate of open borders, by placing climate at the centre of government policy. His party has grown increasingly colourless as Rutte and an inner-circle of allies close down discussion on policy directions. Cosmopolitan liberals prevail while national liberals, wary of runaway social change and keen to limit EU scope for interference in Dutch affairs, are forsaking the VVD in increasing numbers.

The revolt of Dutch farmers over EU directives that threaten to close many farms, poses a threat to the VVD's base. It means that the party could suffer an eclipse, as the Socialists and Christian Democrats have already done. Resistance to state plans to expropriate farms in order to fulfil Net Zero targets has triggered a militant response from a hitherto quiescent element in Dutch society. Rutte increasingly struggles to articulate a coherent vision for Dutch society. His reluctance to rein in coalition allies, who are more interested in carrying out experiments on the Dutch population than in paying close attention to their immediate wishes and longer-term aspirations, suggests he is running out of steam. The political centre has retreated under him, and parties on the radical left and right enjoy greater sway in the Netherlands than at any time in its modern history. The legacy of an outwardly conventional political leader, under whom an increasingly authoritarian state has acquired growing sway, may prove to be an unenviable one. Under him, the rules of politics which made his country a byword of stability have been quietly subverted. It means that the Netherlands increasingly resembles other established European democracies, where there is a gulf of mistrust between the state and a growing number of its citizens, who feel as if they have become outsiders in their own country.

The free market VVD party, which has reflected the libertarian outlook for long visible in urban Dutch society, has been Mark Rutte's political home. Unlike many of its natural supporters, he did not grow up in economically comfortable circumstances. His father had lived in the main colony of the Netherlands, the Dutch East Indies, until being imprisoned in the Second World War by the invading Japanese. His wife did not survive captivity and, upon the reluctant departure of the Dutch, he attempted to continue a business career in what had become the republic of Indonesia. When the Dutch were expelled in 1958, by now re-married, he returned to the Netherlands and worked his way up in a car dealership firm. Mark was the last of six children to be born, in 1967. He grew up in a religious household and he claims to be guided by a strong Protestant faith. After graduating with a liberal arts degree, he joined the Unilever conglomerate and enjoyed a rapid rise in the human resources industry, arguably the fastest growing one in the capitalist West during the last thirty years. Entering the VVD, with its pro-capitalist outlook, was a natural step. He proved adept at the tasks which an ambitious young politician needs to make his mark. His abilities as a networker and organizer, who had entered the lower ranks of government in his mid-thirties, enabled him to become the leader of the VVD in 2006, a year before his fortieth birthday.

The VVD was then in the doldrums after a period of unprecedented success under a leader who had taken it into the top league of Dutch politics. Frits Bolkestein was a strong champion of the EU's internal single market, along with Margaret Thatcher. After retiring from Dutch politics, he was European Commissioner for the Internal Market and Services between 1999 and 2004. This experience, coinciding with a vast expansion in the EU's powers, confirmed his wariness of the ambitions of federalists keen to impose EU taxes and bonds, like the prominent Belgian Liberal figure Guy Verhofstadt. In 2010, along with the former German President Rainer Herzog, he signed a manifesto urging the EU to change course or else risk 'complete collapse'. They complained that 'Brussels legislates regardless of the people's wishes and of long-established traditions and cultures'.[1]

Rutte became Prime Minister in 2010, when the EU was in the grip of the Eurozone crisis. The EU institutions, which now included the European

Central Bank, pursued an inconsistent path in order to shield the most successful national economies from the problems faced by debtor nations, mainly located in Southern Europe. The EU's powers of intervention were increased with the debtor countries, often dismissively termed the PIGS, falling under the tutelage of Brussels and the Franco-German tandem, which more than ever before shaped the policy agenda. In the anxious second decade of the new century, Rutte carved out a distinctive role in often fraught EU deliberations about a seemingly never-ending crisis. He insisted that debtor countries meet stringent conditions in return for receiving aid in the form of loans. When the new challenge posed by the coronavirus pandemic reared up in 2020, his position was unaltered. Initially, he opposed outright a pandemic recovery fund due to its vast size and the fact that, for the first time, it involved the sharing of debt among the bloc's countries. By being prepared to disrupt EU business in return for insisting on serious oversight about the destination of 500 million euros in funding, he boosted his image at home.

Taking such an outwardly intractable stance had contributed to success in three national elections for the VVD, held under his premiership. The Dutch self-image of frugality and a realistic approach to EU finance was being advanced at the heart of government. But in practice, the tougher governance controls which he called for were more apparent than real. Rutte was broadly content to acquiesce in the increasingly German-led conception of the EU as a mercantilist force prepared to interact closely with authoritarian powers, China and Russia, on issues of trade and energy resources, respectively. His pragmatism shaded into dogmatism, however when it came to rule-of-law issues, which increasingly pitted some East-Central European states against Brussels. Thanks to the influence of left-wing NGOs in devising EU templates for social and cultural conventions that were supposed to be reflected in national legislation, there was growing acrimony between Poland and Hungary, in particular, and key EU power centres. Despite his party's centre-right base, Rutte was to the fore in demanding that 'progressive' norms be adopted by this rebel pair on issues such as the appointment of judges and LGBT rights. He supported sanctions against Poland and Hungary for adhering to their conservative agenda, and in 2021 rhetorically asked at one EU summit: 'Can you found an EU without Hungary and Poland?'[2]

Rutte does not seem to have anticipated, or feared, a backlash from VVD activists. He had placed the party at the centre of influence in a highly fragmented political landscape. At the last election, in 2021, 150 parliamentary seats were split between 20 parties and independent MPs. He had also manoeuvred deftly to silence any dissent within the party about his direction. Inevitably, a price was to be paid for taking a side in the culture wars between conservatives and liberals. The highly proportional Dutch electoral system has enabled right-wing conservative parties to establish a permanent presence in national politics. The first one, the Pim Fortuyn List, won 17.6 percent of the vote in the 2002 parliamentary elections, held two days after the murder of its founder, by an environmental militant. It soon broke up, but others have taken its place. In the 2021 election, strongly conservative parties won 28 seats, compared with 26 for the left. VVD supporters, influenced by Bolkestein's *national* liberal vision, have thus been able to find alternative homes if they find Rutte's *global* form of liberalism unpalatable.

The Dutch Labour Party (PvdA) was still strong enough in 2012 for it to be Rutte's main coalition partner. The party was increasingly divorced from its working-class roots and drawn instead to niche issues such as shaping economic policy around environmental priorities. It was Labour which was keenest at this point to place the Netherlands in the vanguard of renewable energy. However, it was to be paid for, not by central government, but by consumers through their power bills.[3]

Labour's past sureness of touch, which placed it in charge of government for many years, now deserted it. Jeroen Disselbloem, the party senior who was head of the Eurozone group of finance ministers at a new stage in the Greek debt crisis, generated much ill-will, albeit mostly abroad, by his refusal to back any relaxation in austerity in order to revive growth in the country: 'You cannot spend all the money on women and drinks and then ask for help', he told fellow left-wingers then in charge in Athens.[4] By 2022, more than one-third of Greece's population was living in poverty and a wage of 800 euros a month after tax, was common.[5]

Rutte shrewdly allowed Labour to own these uncomfortable positions. Unmarried and apparently unmotivated by the acquisition of wealth and possessions, he cultivated a modest, approachable image. Not without success, he convinced large numbers of voters that he was keen to strongly defend the popular self-image of the Netherlands as a *Gidsland,* [good land] sensible, practical, hard-working but with a strong moral compass and keen to play a responsible role beyond its borders. Such a comfortable image was already starting to be frayed during the first phase of his premiership due to the growth of a sense of insecurity. This was particularly noticeable in the Randstad, a roughly crescent-shaped conurbation in the central-western Netherlands, consisting primarily of the four largest Dutch cities; their suburbs, and many towns in between, containing almost half the country's population. The area had long been Labour's political heartland, but catastrophe struck in the 2017 election. The PvdA suffered the biggest election defeat of any party in Dutch history, losing 19 percent of its vote and falling back to single digit support (5.7 percent).[6]

The VVD also lost some seats in this election. But Rutte had impressed many voters when he confronted Turkey's ruler Tayip Erdogan in a spat over a Turkish immigrant turned down for a job as a bus driver for refusing to shake women's hands. In a full-page newspaper ad, Rutte said: 'If you live in a country where you get so annoyed with how we deal with each other, you have a choice: Get out! You don't have to be here!'[7] He had already banned two Turkish ministers from addressing campaign rallies in the Netherlands.

But from 2017 to 2022, it proved increasingly harder for him to act as a flinty champion of what it was to be quintessentially Dutch in a world increasingly beset by growing tensions, some of which spilled over into domestic affairs. As his main coalition partner in his 3rd and 4th governments, Rutte increasingly relied on the D66 party. It was a party that never disguised its emphatically urban and progressive perspectives. On issues like climate policy and managing immigration, it was forthright about replacing identities shaped around loyalty to a fixed territorial community with commitment to building a new progressive global order. It did not flinch from backing schemes which required major adjustments in lifestyle and occupation from Dutch citizens. The farming population was the sector which was required to make the sharpest adjustments to the new Green economic model, committed to slashing carbon emissions and endeavouring to make Europe the poster boy for an environmentally-focused planet. In 2021-22 months of protests ensued due to rural opposition to closing farms in order to fulfil Net Zero targets.

Rutte's skills as a smooth pragmatist able to defuse contentious issues deserted him. He may not even have tried very hard to urge radical coalition partners to see some sense or use his undoubted clout at EU decision-making level to dilute zealous measures bound to cause disruption at home. By now, the solidarity which he seemed most interested in was cementing partnerships with powerful interests at EU, and indeed global, level committed to forms of technocratic governance. He never hid his belief that continued Dutch prosperity must be preserved through a close partnership with global corporations which, increasingly, saw massive profits to be made from championing the Green economy.

With the central state downgrading national sovereignty in different ways, appeals to patriotic solidarity, that Rutte had previously made with some success, fell flat. He preferred to make common cause with similarly-minded leaders such as David Cameron in Britain and Angela Merkel in Germany, who were unafraid to express post-national objectives and insist on their societies making adjustments to comply with global trends laid out by corporations and transnational bureaucracies.

Rutte was stung by Britain's decision to vote to leave the EU in 2016 and he did not hesitate to say that he hated Brexit 'from every angle'.[8] He had some justification. Britain's departure meant that the contribution of the Netherlands to EU funding mechanisms rose substantially. Despite the obstacles in the way of Britain's complete exit from the EU, it gave impetus to political forces keen to assert national sovereignty. In 2019, the Forum for Democracy (FvD), a Eurosceptic party under a frequently outspoken leader Thierry Baudet, caused an upset by sharing the top position in elections for the Senate with the VVD.[9] Despite its intellectual brand of radical conservatism and a split due to the inflammatory utterances of Baudet, it kept its parliamentary presence after the 2021 election. Its offshoot JA21 (short for Just Answer) also established itself thanks to the highly proportional Dutch voting system. Meanwhile, the Party for Freedom (PVV) of anti-Islamic politician Geert Wilders, is the longer-established of the elected forces unambiguously on the right.

The Covid pandemic of 2020-22 provided further evidence that the Netherlands was no longer at ease with itself. The already growing state bureaucracy further expanded in size and power, thanks to the need to take emergency measures to halt the spread of the virus. These included lockdowns and the introduction of coronavirus passports to avail of public services once experimental vaccines with short-term benefits had been manufactured. Rutte was widely viewed as an efficient crisis manager at the start of the pandemic. But this estimation was later dented. After a relaxation of the lockdown in mid-2020, a new spike in infections led to the swift re-imposition of severe restrictions. Unrest resulted and when the first curfew since the 1940s was imposed in January 2021, severe rioting in many urban areas resulted. 'I did not expect it to burn so violently in all the cities', chief of police Willem Woelders confessed.[10]

It was not so much political forces which were behind the unrest, but unaffiliated and alienated younger Dutch citizens who refused to recognise the ruling status quo as a legitimate one. They were alienated from the Binnenhof, the political institutions concentrated in The Hague, as well as the media which, in common with many other Western countries, had been a cheerleader for a policy of restrictions.[11] Many were already facing uncertain employment prospects due to contractions in an already fragile economy, when the sudden eruption of the pandemic made the outlook even bleaker. Middle-class citizens also found their living standards squeezed. With active displays of patriotism having been frowned upon by those in power, the Dutch design for living seemed less attractive than it had been for many decades. It wasn't just the state's response to the pandemic, but also proposed changes in occupation and lifestyle to fit with Green energy targets, which alarmed citizens about the sense of direction being taken. Rutte's smooth manner failed to hide the fact that major changes could be imposed upon citizens without their consent. In a sour atmosphere, few national institutions retained their previously high standing and that included the monarchy, which seemed content to take its lead from the dominant elements in the political class.

Nevertheless, numerous Dutch voters remained keen for a lead from the top in a time of acute danger. Rutte was rewarded politically by nervous citizens at a time when officially 18,000 people died from Covid. In parliamentary elections held in March 2021, the VVD enjoyed a further (albeit slight) increase in support. The endorsement for Rutte was all the more striking since he had been at the centre of a scandal, involving the Dutch tax authorities pursuing thousands of families for child benefit fraud. They had been ordered to repay thousands of euros, without any means of appeal, until it emerged that the charges were groundless. Rutte issued an abject apology but, within months, he plunged into isolation after strong evidence emerged that he had tried to exclude the popular politician Pieter Omtzigt, who had uncovered the scandal, from entering the coalition government.[12] For a while, it seemed that potential partners would refuse to serve under him and it took 271 days before a coalition could be formed at the end of 2021.

A weakened Rutte's standing was further impaired in April 2022, when he faced a storm of criticism for deleting texts which referred to government matters from his Nokia phone, which had room for just 20 messages. This was despite Dutch law stating that correspondence from ministers should be kept to ensure public accountability. He denied that he had ever consciously withheld important matters and promised to use a smartphone in future.[13]

D66, the party which championed the agenda of metropolitan progressives, was content to have a tarnished Rutte in charge of the government. He increasingly deferred to D66 on climate change and open borders and had to struggle to prevent its flagship policy of legalising euthanasia becoming coalition policy. D66 was clear about its vision for the Dutch future. It wished to impose a design for living on the whole of society based on radical precepts that only a minority embraced. However, its adherents were disproportionately to be found in occupations such as academia, the law, the media, as well as the bureaucracy whose power was in the ascendant. Rutte, having hollowed out his party to some degree, had no equivalent power-base. It meant that he was prepared to drift with the prevailing globalist current which had important adherents among politicians, such as Canadian leader Justin Trudeau, who was viewed as a close ally of his on the world stage.

By 2019, the shift in power towards a cosmopolitan elite who believed absolutely that their model was the only one that should be permitted in the Netherlands, was already visible. In that year, Rutte's coalition agreed to reduce carbon emissions by 49 percent by the year 2030. This was a victory for Sigrid Kaag, the D66 leader. The former diplomat, with an extensive background in the work of the United Nations, has been keen to shape policy on contentious issues, such as absorbing refugees and asylum seekers, around liberal transnational models. She has a close ally in the Dutch vice-president of the European Council, Frans Timmermans, arguably the EU decision-maker most in favour of imposing policies, on Net Zero and refugees and asylum seekers, on recalcitrant heads of national governments.14 He is another former diplomat, one who opted for an EU career after his party, the PvdA, entered into decline. He is just one of numerous Euro-Socialists who have been appointed to key positions in this increasingly powerful entity as the left's fortunes have slumped across Western Europe. Known by Dutch opponents as 'the Pope of Climate', he has been most vocal on the need to make his homeland a front-line state in the economic transformation of Europe along broadly Green lines.[15]

With Rutte putting up only token resistance to some of the radical environmental schemes and implicitly accepting others, it has meant that he has forfeited his role as the smooth, unflappable arbiter of Dutch policy. New political forces have emerged to try and slow down or derail the Green globalist juggernaut. For a time, the JA21 party was the one on the right which seemed best able to articulate concerns that those at the heart of the state no longer see themselves as guardians of society but wish instead to bend it to their own revolutionary or utopian agenda. It has an active presence in the European Parliament and has sought to reach out to global business figures like Elon Musk, who are felt to share its objections to the surveillance state.

The Farmer-Citizen Movement (BBB) has come out of the struggle of farmers to hold on to their farms in the face of EU-led policies to slash nitrogen levels in the soil. Its following has spread to the cities among voters who fear that powerful but rootless decision-makers are ready to sweep away farming communities for the sake of abstract goals which enjoy only minority support.[16] On 15 March 2023, it emerged as the big winner in the Dutch provincial elections. This contest decides the composition of the Senate and means that there is a strong possibility that the BBB, along with allies, can delay legislation designed to remove farmers from their land.

Along with the JAS, it has vigorously campaigned against EU plans to oblige member-states to absorb large numbers of immigrants. The political right in general is also nervous that the D66 plans to apologise for the past Dutch role in the slave trade, will lead to the state having to pay large financial reparations to its former colony Surinam. There is also concern (to be found also in the Socialist party which is suspicious of globalism) of the establishment of a digital Euro which will enable the government to determine what citizens can spend their money on.[17]

Growing tensions in Dutch society make Rutte's performance as the imperturbable ringmaster in the sometimes rowdy Dutch political circus, increasingly harder to maintain. Despite surmounting scandals to remain as prime minister, he seems to be just the most adroit member of a trans-party social liberal establishment whose mediocrity is harder to disguise from much of the public. His coalition partners increasingly promote a polarising stance on key issues, which sabotage his effort to present himself as the embodiment of national unity. Dutch citizens are unhappy, with an 'enormous number of inverted tricolors in Dutch villages and cities' sprouting up, according to Wierd Duk, a historian, who is one of the few national commentators prepared to dissect the scale of disenchantment.[18] At the end of 2022, a survey revealed that 50 percent of young people believed that things are 'going in the wrong direction in the Netherlands', up from 38 percent in 2018.[19] Rutte is the symbol of a co-existence whose potency is fast fading, as mutual respect is in decline. Rather pompously, he described the 2023 electoral triumph of the BBB as a 'scream at politics'.[20] His coalition is divided about how to respond to the demand of the farmers, and parliamentary elections could be held long before they are next due in 2025.

The Dutch electoral system enables people to express their grievances more effectively than in nearly any other European country. With the eruption of fierce disagreements over individual and local freedoms and rights, in the face of an interventionist state, Rutte's message is an increasingly insipid one. Looking back on his tenure in office, his achievements seem nebulous. The country has been outwardly stable, but the changes that have been implemented have been driven by a narrow set of domestic players and arguably shaped by wider trans-national interests. Millions of people feel like strangers looking in on a political process where things are done to them without their consent.

The reciprocity between the main actors in Dutch politics, which insulated the Netherlands from storms which rocked European politics in recent centuries, seems to be waning rapidly. A widely held sense of disempowerment is breeding alienation, and the surest legacy of the Rutte years is the likelihood that the Netherlands will be much harder to govern in the future.

---

[1] Gallagher, Europe's Path, p. 102.
[2] Tom Theuns, 'Could we found a new EU without Poland and Hungary', *EU Observer*, 21 September 2020,
https://euobserver.com/opinion/149470.
[3] Gordon Darroch, 'The strange death of the Dutch Labour Party', *Dutch News*, 6 January 2017,
https://www.dutchnews.nl/features/2017/01/blog-gordon-darroch-the-strange-death-of-the-dutch-labour-party-diederik-samsom/.
[4] Mody, *Euro Tragedy*, p. 430.
[5] James Jeffrey, 'Greece's beauty masks untold poverty', *Spectator*, 18 February 2022.
[6] Cas Mudde, 'What happened to the Dutch left', *LSE Blog*, 15 March 2021,
https://blogs.lse.ac.uk/europpblog/2021/03/15/what-happened-to-the-dutch-left/.
[7] Paul Kirby, 'Mark Rutte: Survivor of Dutch politics in fight for political life', *BBC News*, 2 April 2021, https://www.bbc.co.uk/news/world-europe-39289468.
[8] Kirby, 'Mark Rutte'.
[9] Mehreen Khan, 'Dutch Eurosceptic party storms to victory in regional elections', *Financial Times*, 21 March 2019.
[10] Valentina Pop, 'Dutch Rioters Clash With Police for Third Night Over Covid-19 Curfew', *Wall Street Journal*, 26 January 2021.
[11] 'Wierd Duk in Nederland – Paperback', *Wynia's Week*,
https://www.wyniasweek.nl/product/wierd-duk-in-nederland-paperback/, accessed 20 December 2022.
[12] Tom Jan Meeus, 'The man defying Mark Rutte', *Politico EU*, 29 January 2021,
https://www.politico.eu/article/the-man-defying-mark-rutte-the-netherlands-coronavirus-curfew-riots/, accessed 18 December 2022.
[13] Victor Jack, '"Nokiagate": Dutch lawmakers slam Mark Rutte after claims he deleted texts for years', *Politico EU*, 18 May 2022,
https://www.politico.eu/article/nokiagate-lawmakers-mark-rutte-pm-deleted-texts-for-years/, accessed 18 December 2022.

[14] 'European Parliament elections 2019: Who is Frans Timmermans? And what does he stand for?', *Euronews*, 30 April 2019, https://www.euronews.com/2019/04/25/eu-elections-2019-who-is-frans-timmermans-and-what-does-he-stand-for, accessed 18 December 2022.
[15] Elena Sanchez Nicolas, 'Timmermans: high energy prices must speed up transition', *EUobserver*, 15 September 2021, https://euobserver.com/green-economy/152911, accessed 18 December 2022.
[16] Wierd Duk, 'Radicale overheid lokt radicale reacties uit', *De Telegraf*, 30 June 2022, https://www.telegraaf.nl/podcast/1883188905/radicale-overheid-lokt-radicale-reacties-uit, accessed 16 December 2022.
[17] Wierd Duk,'Pas op een overheid die jouw geld controleert!', *De Telegraf*, 22 September 2022, https://www.telegraaf.nl/podcast/644679599/pas-op-een-overheid-die-jouw-geld-controleert, accessed 19 December 2022.
[18] Wierd Duk, ''Niet eerder was burgerlijke onvrede zo zichtbaar', *De Telegraf*, 14 July 2022, https://www.telegraaf.nl/podcast/644679599/pas-op-een-overheid-die-jouw-geld-controleert, accessed 22 December 2022.
[19] @Sonnyspek, 20 December 2022.
[20] Claire Moses, 'Dutch Pro-Farmer Party Sweeps Elections, Upsetting the Status Quo', *New York Times*, 16 March 2023.

CHAPTER 21: VIKTOR ORBÁN

1963-

Viktor Orbán is the best-known figure to have emerged from the politics of East-Central Europe since the fall of communism. Arguably, he is Europe's most successful conservative leader in the last fifty years (Margaret Thatcher included). Ironically, the amount of attention that he receives outweighs the size and importance of his country, Hungary. Under Orbán, the strategically-placed central European country has partly-recovered from a profound communist deformation of society as well as post-communist mismanagement. But it is chiefly thanks to the implacable enemies he has made in parts of the international liberal left, that he has basked in regular publicity. His dedication to building a conservative political order in Hungary continues to provoke outrage. His acquisition and retention of power has been put down to chicanery and authoritarianism. Too often overlooked are his ability to produce good economic results and win electoral victories on such a scale that it strains credulity they have been secured primarily by fraud or malfeasance.

Much of the indignation seems to arise from the fact that he has used parts of the early 21st century progressive blueprint for acquiring sway over the state machine, the media, and academia, to instead establish a conservative hegemony in Hungary. He has broken up a liberal intellectual power base that had seemed entrenched even after the fall of communism and replacing it with a new conservative establishment. Debate rages over whether he has overstepped democratic bounds in his handling of the media, state resources and the private sector. Ruling parties elsewhere in the EU have attempted to assume a proprietorial role over the state and parts of society or have flouted the EU's Maastricht Treaty (see the chapter on Pedro Sánchez). But Spain and France have not attracted such concentrated ire from the European Union or the mainstream media. Orbán is the lightning conductor in a political battle between radical exponents of identity politics who, with strong support in global elites, pursue power through cultural change, and conservatives who rally around Christianity and the nation-state.

With Europe plunged into war after February 2022, he courted fresh controversy by refusing to support an embargo on oil imports from Russia. He refuted the charges of being a tool of Vladimir Putin by asserting that his duty lies in shielding Hungarians from war and that some of his main foes in the EU are insincere about sanctions. Orbán is unabashed about having an ideological agenda. It is one that places him out on a limb, at least within elite circles in Europe. But he is far less isolated in the wider population, and so far he has shown no lack of ambition and skill in pursuing his particular vision for Hungary and the rest of Europe. It is one where he hopes to turn Hungary into 'a regional middle power in Central Europe'. For this to happen, he believes Hungary must not get embroiled in confrontation between antagonistic blocs. Due to its geopolitical location, it risks being a major loser.[1] But such a position is hard to reconcile with Hungary's membership of NATO.

Orbán attracts such ire not just because of his political success, but because of perceived opportunism. It was as a radical firebrand that he first made his mark. On 16 June 1989, in the final stages of communist rule, he delivered an electrifying speech at a ceremony in Budapest's Heroes Square when the remains of prominent victims of communist rule were being laid to rest. The 26-year-old unshaven and casually-dressed activist declared: 'If we trust our own strength, then we will be able to put an end to the communist dictatorship'.[2]

A year earlier, he had helped found the Alliance of Young Democrats, or Fidesz, then a liberal youth movement. His background enabled him to easily stand out from the middle-class youngsters from the capital who were rejecting a communist elite now in its death throes. He spent much of 1990 studying at Oxford University, the beneficiary of a scholarship from the Hungarian-born philanthropist George Soros, who was attempting to nurture an elite governing class in Central Europe. His studies were interrupted later that year when Fidesz won 22 of the 386 seats in Hungary's first truly free elections. Soon after, he reached the conclusion that replacing the communist hegemony with a liberal one was not what he wanted. With the help of activists, mostly from rural areas or small towns, he repositioned Fidesz on the centre-right of politics. His foes rallied around the 'Free Democrat' label and moved leftwards, endorsing the legalisation of cannabis and same sex marriage. They played a pivotal electoral role in 2002, after Orbán's first four-year stint as Prime Minister. The economy had slowly picked up after major factory closures resulting from the state's abandonment of the socialist economic model. But Orbán faced a hostile media still very much dominated by the former ruling left. Thanks to an electoral pact between his former liberal allies and the Socialists, Fidesz went into opposition and would stay there for the next eight years.

Orbán has claimed that the example of liberals making common cause with the former communists had a profound effect on him. He grew increasingly convinced that much of post-Cold War liberalism had shed its belief in pluralism and instead wished to impose a hegemony of opinion.[3] He felt propelled to offer a fresh stance, involving the building of conservative institutions and reinforcing the traditional values of society. In his view, this conservative outlook had made Hungary vigorous and successful, until crashing to defeat in World War I and then becoming a vassal of the Soviet Union in 1945.

On his new political journey, he dropped his previous anti-clericalism and had his children baptised in the family's Calvinist faith. For a critical biographer like Paul Lendvai, his new conservative outlook smacked of opportunism: 'no deep ideological soul-searching [was] involved—just clear-eyed calculations about what it would require to win power'.[4]

Some wrote Orbán's obituary when he lost again in 2006. But, as has often proven to be the case, he was lucky in the unpromising character of his opponents. The Hungarian left went through a succession of unimpressive leaders during eight years in power. The one who damaged its cause the most was Ferenc Gyurcsány, prime minister from 2004 to 2009. He was a former communist youth leader who had done sufficiently well in the 'wild west' economic conditions following the demise of single-party rule, to emerge as 72nd in the list of Hungary's 150 wealthiest persons, by 2006.[5] In the autumn of that year, he provoked deep outrage when the tape of a speech which he had made to a closed party meeting was leaked. For many, his remarks seemed to boldly confirm the charge that the post-communists were unfit to be in charge:

> 'We screwed up. Not just a bit. Big time...It was perfectly clear that what we were saying wasn't true...You cannot mention a single major government measure we can be proud of...I almost died when I had to pretend that we were actually governing. We lied morning, noon and night'.[6]

Five days of often violent protests followed, to which the police responded with harsh measures that resulted in some officers later being placed on trial. In the 2010 election, the ruling left lost two-thirds of its seats and the liberal Free Democrats were completely wiped out (soon to disband). Back in government, and with a two-thirds majority, Orbán commissioned a new constitution that was enacted in 2011. The provision whereby the members of the Constitutional Court were chosen, not by an all-party parliamentary committee but by a vote in parliament, came in for most criticism.[7] But given the primacy enjoyed by Fidesz, whatever the method of selection, it is likely that the result would have been much the same under either system. Fidesz was determined that its governance would not to be impeded by power bases in the hands of liberals within the state and indeed wider society. It sought to emulate left-wing believers in the Italian Marxist António Gramsci's strategy for power by undertaking a march through the institutions of media, education, and civic society promoting its own conservative elite. Inevitably, it faced the scrutiny of the European Court of Justice (ECJ), the most powerful arm of the EU, which is required to promote ever closer union or integration.[8]

The EU's transformative agenda has been based on promoting liberal norms in society, as the Union's powers have expanded in many different directions since the ground-breaking Maastricht Treaty of 1992. Since the early 1990s, social justice, equality and diversity underpin the direction which the EU has taken since it ceased to be mainly concerned with regulating trade. Progressive activists in NGOs have acquired a role in drawing up regulations in areas concerning personal morality, lifestyle and minority concerns, which has made them increasingly important players inside the EU.[9] The ECJ, with its pro-integration outlook, finds in favour of the EU's main decision body, the European Commission in the overwhelming number of cases.

Orbán feels under no obligation to defer to what he regards as a politicised court belonging to an international entity that is often unfriendly towards governments wishing to preserve their sovereignty. In 2022, a hostile ECJ judgment led to the EU triggering Article 7 of the EU Treaty, which means Brussels views Hungary as having a 'systemic deficiency' in the rule of law. He is wily in seeking to resist EU post-nationalism, but ultimately unbending. He had sufficient will-power to take on George Soros, the billionaire philanthropist and currency speculator. The Hungarian-born Soros has used much of his fortune to back pro-minority campaigns on both sides of the Atlantic. Their impact has enabled considerable political power to be placed in the hands of radical activists, particularly in the US. Budapest was the Central European headquarters of his Open Society Foundation but hostility from the government compelled him to retreat from most of his activities there in 2017.[10]

Orbán has swatted away claims that under his 'political-economic clan', Fidesz is exercising a media monopoly in Hungary.[11] Defenders such as Boris Kálnocky point out that the media scene has always been highly politicised in Hungary, and in the first stage of democracy had been dominated by the left. In 2022, he claimed that the media was less one-sided than it had been in 2005, at the height of Socialist rule. Regional papers and public radio can be considered close to the government, but 'the media landscape has remained pluralistic, critical voices remain influential, and the spectrum of published political opinion remains broad'.[12] No media outlet has been closed down for criticism of the government. Nor, he asserts, have journalists been harassed for their views since 2010 (or indeed suffered violent ends, as leading ones have in the Netherlands and Malta).

The war between Orbán and Soros, the respective early 21st century standard-bearers of European conservatism and global progressivism, showed an implacable side to the Hungarian leader. He himself has admitted to having been a horrid child: 'badly misbehaved, cheeky, violent. Not at all likeable'.[13] But, however trenchant his decision-making style, he has formed a durable team of fellow conservatives who he is able to motivate and keep focused on retaining power in the conservative interest. He has so far avoided the walk-outs and recriminations that have beset numerous other European contemporaries wielding power. At home, such cohesion has also been painfully lacking among his challengers on the liberal left and on the far-right where the Jobbik party, after a brief upsurge in 2014, eventually became mired in internal strife.

Orbán's staying power has been reinforced by his ability to cultivate influential allies. Prominent critics have argued that an increasing web of economic contacts with Eurasian autocrats in Moscow, Beijing and Ankara reveal him in his true colours as a despot in the making.[14] But, until the Ukraine war, a whole host of other EU countries sometimes established much closer ties with the likes of Putin and Xi Jinping, with only a fraction of the uproar. The novelist Tibor Fischer asked in 2018: 'Why should it be up to Hungary (whose Soviet-built nuclear reactor provides half its electricity) and Orbán to slap Putin in the face? Orbán does business with Putin, but he's in the queue with everyone else'.[15]

The most crucial economic relationship for Orbán is the one that surprisingly continues to receive very little scrutiny. It was established very early in his governmental career, and his key partners were German power-wielders in politics and business. He was introduced into this world of influence by Count Otto Graf Lambsdorff, the influential liberal politician. He had been a long-standing minister of economic affairs in governments of different political stripes. A strong believer in free market economics, he saw Orbán as a disciple who could carry that torch. Within days of becoming Prime Minister in 1998, Orbán was in Bonn for meetings with executives of German industrial giants like Audi, Bosch and Siemens, that had been arranged by Lambsdorff. He persuaded these moguls that a predictable economic environment awaited them. Hungary's manufacturing base, hollowed out after the collapse of communism, was replenished as a result. German car-makers became 'the number one engine of Hungarian economic growth' and, through this, of the Orbán government's political successes. By 2020, according to the Hungarian

Central Statistical Office, car manufacturing accounted for 4.5 percent of Hungary's GDP and suppliers working for these firms accounted for another 5-8 percent.[16]

Attracted by a favourable investment climate, a close economic relationship grew up between southern Germany, by now the main centre of German manufacturing, and Hungary. Firms such as Axel Springer and Deutsche Telekom made big investments in their turn. They had media holdings, some of which were sold to companies on good terms with Fidesz.[17] These economic ties were not replicated by close political ones, as German politics were swinging left. Orbán established a friendship with Helmut Kohl, but that was when he was out of power and bemoaning how his legacy was being destroyed by his successor as chancellor, Angela Merkel.

Interestingly, when the German-born Pope, Benedict XVI died at the very end of 2022, Orbán was one of the few non-socialist European leaders who paid his respects in Rome before the actual funeral. Until 2021, Fidesz belonged to the European People's Party (EPP), an outwardly centre-right alliance of Members of the European Parliament which lacked a distinctive world view and, at least on ethical and cultural issues, grew indistinguishable from social democracy. The once vigorous Christian Democratic tradition in Europe withered. By 2022, the CDU in Germany was in the process of dropping 'Christian' from its name, a theme which had little appeal for party bosses and image makers.[18]

Orbán had an uneasy relationship with his German counterpart, Angela Merkel, who ruled in coalition with social democrats for most of her sixteen years as chancellor. In 2015, they collided over her abrupt decision to open German borders to large numbers of refugees from the conflict in Syria. She had said: 'For a rich European Union, this is the right thing to do'.[19] He riposted that: 'This is an uncontrolled and unregulated process. We did not get authorisation from [our citizens] for millions to walk into our continent...The German, Hungarian or Austrian way of life is not a basic right of all people on earth. It is only a right for those people who have contributed to it'.[20]

On this occasion, Orbán had read the European room correctly. Merkel suffered a backlash which saw her party steadily lose ground during her remaining years in power. Even the liberal-minded President of the EU Commission, Donald Tusk, soon went on record to say that: 'We cannot pretend any longer that the great tide of migrants is something that we want and that we are conducting a well-thought-out policy...We have lost our ability to control our borders'.[21]

Orbán has repeatedly dissented from the official EU norm on many issues. Defending national governance, Christian family values, solidarity with Hungarian minorities in neighbouring states, and a closed borders policy to untrammelled immigration, are the best-known examples of his defiance. Perhaps ironically, the issue which so far has generated the greatest discord has concerned Hungary's pro-family social policies. Various schemes have been launched to incentivise child-bearing and stem a population decline. Encouraging children to embrace a heterosexual identity has been part of the strategy. In 2021 a law was passed which prohibited the dissemination of ideas promoting homosexuality and gender self-identification in schools. It went further and restricted the promotion of LGBT activity in fields such as advertising, capable of being viewed by children.[22] This highly controversial step was taken as much of the West, especially Anglophone countries, were being convulsed by disputes over whether the age-old view that there are two biological sexes should be replaced by ideas that instead promote gender self-identification. LGBT groups had influential backing in the media and corporate business for children to be allowed to identify as transsexuals. The rainbow flag of LGBT activists sometimes enjoyed as much visibility as the EU flag in countries where radical progressive ideas enjoyed much traction. Accordingly, Hungary's Child Protection Act brought Hungary and the EU on a collision course.

The Christian Democrat politician, Ursula von der Leyen, the President of the European Commission since 2019, had been narrowly elected with the help of Fidesz votes, but she had no hesitation is slamming the new law as a shameful act.[23] It led to the EU withholding €7 billion from its Covid-19 recovery fund. Hungary (along with Poland) became the first EU members to fall foul of a new regulation which enabled Brussels to block EU funds if a member state was found to be in breach of European Court of Justice decisions. On 16 February 2022, in a significant ECJ ruling, the politicised court surprised few by rallying behind the European Commission.

Eight days later, attention was suddenly diverted from this trial-of-strength, over whether national democracy or the tutelary form preferred by officials and NGO advisers in the European Commission, would shape the Europe of the 2020s. Russia marched into Ukraine and, encountering stiff opposition, a devastatingly brutal war on a scale not seen in Europe since 1945, got underway.

Orbán had met Putin in Moscow as recently as 5 February. He had once reportedly related to a top US government official that Hungary has only two really important points of reference, Russia and Germany. Hungary gets its energy from one and jobs from the other.[24] Hungary's decision to hold out against the imposition of a ban on Russian oil imports to the EU generated a storm.[25] He stated that it would scarcely harm the Russian economy but would do great damage to Hungary, whose oil refineries are optimised for Russian oil. He also stood out by refusing to allow Hungary to be used as a transit point for weapons deliveries from other NATO countries.[26] Arms transfers from Hungary to Ukraine would have to pass through Ukraine's Transcarpathia region, which is home to 150,000 Hungarians. Budapest's policy of shielding Hungarians from the war extended to these co-ethnics.

Václav Klaus, the Eurosceptic former president of the Czech Republic, defended Orbán as 'the only credible politician in Europe today. The only one who truly strives to represent his nation and his country. He does not hide this and acts accordingly'.[27] But Poland's Prime Minister, Mateusz Morawiecki, expressed his consternation that Hungary was unwilling to make a forthright condemnation of Russian crimes in Ukraine.[28] Poland's Deputy Prime Minister, Jarosław Kaczyński, a long-standing ally of Orbán, had stated in April that 'we can't continue to cooperate as before'.[29]

By the third month of the war, Hungary was contending that it was not taking a pro-Putin stance. Zsolt Németh, a longstanding ally of Orbán's, wrote in May 2022, that 'the reconstitution of the former Soviet empire is entirely unacceptable to Hungary...It is our position that the Russian troops must be withdrawn from the occupied territories...War crimes must be investigated, perpetrators and accomplices...sentenced, and the costs of reconstruction after the war paid for by the party that caused the damage'.[30] However, such positioning was undermined by reports that Orbán pressurised the EU to remove Russia's kleptocratic church leader Patriarch Kirill from the EU's sanctions list, despite his fierce support for Putin's conduct of the war.[31] More seriously, in May 2022, in return for lifting a veto on the EU's sixth round of sanctions on Russia, Hungary was able to win an exemption enabling it to receive oil supplies from Russia.[32]

On 2 April 2022, a parliamentary election had been held that garnered much international attention. Observers who believed that Hungary had slipped into an authoritarian situation, nevertheless built up hopes that Fidesz could be defeated, thanks to the opposition parties forming a common front, from the Socialists to the once neo-fascist and anti-Semitic Jobbik. Their main candidate, Peter Márki-Zay, contended that voters were presented with a stark choice between Russia and the West.[33] But the opposition was unable to set out an attractive counter-offer to voters. The voters were not divided about the war in Ukraine—46 percent in a Europe-wide poll claiming that it was all or mainly Russia's fault, and 26 percent saying they didn't know.[34] Economic issues and the ability of the incumbent to shield them from the violence that had descended on the region appeared to be primary considerations. On a 70 percent turnout, Fidesz increased its majority, once again winning over two-thirds of seats. But the opposition stayed in control of the capital and several major cities.

Orbán delivered plain speaking in an inauguration speech on 16 May 2022. He warned that 'this decade will be an age of perils, uncertainty and wars'. Russia was slammed for being an aggressor in Ukraine, whose President, Volodymyr Zelensky, was also chided for supporting the opposition in the recent election. He struck an embattled note: 'the Hungarian left and their international allies...all rallied against us. Let us make it clear: Brussels and George Soros were also playing to ensure our downfall'. But he also struck a note of self-confident bravado: 'thirty years ago we thought that Europe was our future; today we think that we are Europe's future. Let us feel the weight of our responsibility'.[35]

He displayed no intention of wishing to leave the EU and indicated, in a later speech to American conservatives, that he would combat 'the ideologically trained faceless people in Brussels and Washington' who were working for a supra-national future by technocrats ready to insulate themselves from public pressure.[36]

Orbán has the brisk efficiency, boundless energy, and forceful personality which would probably enable him to thrive as a dictator, at least for a while. But it is arguably ill-judged to mark him out as an undemocratic ruler. He admits to being illiberal in outlook, but views this as a gesture of self-defence owing to the abandonment by international liberals of much of the democratic terrain, in favour of technocracy and strict regulation of society.[37]

The late Gyorgy Schöpflin, who became a Fidesz MEP after many years teaching politics at London universities, observed in 2020: 'it's a weird monopoly of power where the opposition can win the local elections in Budapest and the 10 largest towns in Hungary (2019), where the courts regularly bring in decisions that are not at all welcome to Orbán's government, [and] where there are regular demonstrations against the government…'[38] The American conservative commentator Rod Dreher conceded that Orbán's regime might have corrupt elements, but he invoked his father's backing for the governorship of 'Huey P. Long [who] ran a similar machine in his home state of Louisiana. He recalled him saying that the choice 'was between crooked government that looked out for the interests of the poor and working class, or crooked government that benefited the rich'.[39]

Critics argue that he has debauched democracy by handing contracts to promote sport to a local friend, with whom he shares a passion for football. But figures like Macron in France and Johnson in Britain have received only a fraction of the criticism for handing out massive sums of public money (set aside to combat Covid-19) to technocratic firms which hover close to power, on a less than transparent basis.[40]

The confrontation with Brussels worsened in the second half of 2022, following a speech in which he defended ethnic homogeneity and stated that 'the motherland must stand together, and Transylvania and the other areas in the Carpathian Basin inhabited by Hungarians, must stand together'. He even asserted that: 'We Hungarians see this war as a war between two Slavic peoples, and as one which we want to stay out of. But the Poles see it as a war in which they are also involved: it is their war, and they are almost fighting it…The Ukrainians will never win a war against Russia with American training and weapons. This is simply because the Russian army has asymmetric superiority'.[41]

A poll taken in November 2022, showed that 57 percent of respondents felt that Orbán needed to be tougher in his stance towards Putin (up from 36 percent in April), given his actions in Ukraine.[42] Yet he showed no sign of abandoning his chosen path and on 9 November stated that he would block a long-term EU aid package to Ukraine as long as the EU continued to freeze substantial post-Covid funding for Hungary. On 15 September 2022, the European Parliament had approved a report saying Hungary had become 'a hybrid regime of electoral autocracy' under Orbán and that it had taken the country out of the community of democracies.[43]

He has also been slow to ratify the accession of Sweden and Finland to NATO, reportedly linking Hungarian approval with a request that the Scandinavian nations work to lift the blockage of EU funds to his country. As for Ukrainian membership of NATO, he reportedly warned in February 2023, that 'we should think ten thousand times about the further expansion of NATO to the east'.[44] He also revived an idea (which he claimed had been first made by him in 2012) that Europe create a security body of its own, without American participation. He is well aware that the requisite degree of unity and resolve hardly exists for such an undertaking to easily get off the ground. It would more likely or not give a huge boost to Russia's neo-imperialist agenda. Silence greeted these manoeuvres by Orbán, who has been cut out of NATO's intelligence loop because of stances seen as inimical to the preservation of European security.

Democracy is in a state of disrepair across much of Europe, and to single out Fidesz under Orbán for particular admonishment is unfair and may well prove to be futile posturing. The EU would likely be rather more forgiving towards autocracy in Budapest if it mirrored its own transnational priorities, rather than championing national sovereignty and social conservatism. He will likely face intensifying pressure from the EU due to the revival of the left in European government and the hostility towards his stance on Ukraine. Angela Merkel was no friend but, as long as she was in power in Berlin, direct confrontation with Budapest was averted. In a visit to Hungary in 2019, she even praised how EU funds were being spent in Hungary. 'If we look at Hungarian economic growth rates, we can see that this money has been well invested by the country, that it benefits the people'.[45] However, if EU funding dries up completely for Hungary due to its apostasy, economic difficulties will accumulate. Reliance on a German car industry, which has an uncertain future in a growing anti-car culture, also hems Orbán in. But he is likely to stand firm rather than retreat. He has an efficient and loyal political movement and can probably rely on substantial social backing, even in the face of economic adversity.

However, his survival is likely to grow less assured unless he can form a rival coalition in the West to match liberal internationalism.[46] This cannot be ruled out. But if Hungary is Carthage to the EU's Rome, it is likely to enjoy as much staying power as this North African kingdom once did, at least while a resourceful and strong-willed Orbán stays in charge.

---

[1] Mariann Ory, 'Hungary's Strategy to Win the Decade', *Hungary Today*, 6 January 2023, https://hungarytoday.hu/here-is-hungarys-strategy-to-win-the-decade/ accessed, 7 January 2023.
[2] Paul Lendvai, *Orbán, Europe's New Strongman*, London: Hurst Publications, 2017, p. 8.
[3] Jaime Nogueira Pinto, 'Viktor Orbán, por ele mesmo', *Expresso* (Lisbon), 5 June 2021, https://expresso.pt/internacional/2021-06-05-Viktor-Orban-por-ele-mesmo--em-passeio-pelo-Porto-e-a-conversa-com-Jaime-Nogueira-Pinto--4b319aa2, accessed 6 June 2021.
[4] Lendvai, *Orbán*, p. 51.
[5] The Economist Intelligence Unit, 10 May 2006.
[6] 'Hungarian dances; Charlemagne', *Economist*, 23 September 2006.
[7] See Paul Lendvai, 'The Transformer: Orbán's Evolution and Hungary's Demise', *Foreign Affairs*, Vol. 98, No. 5, September-October 2019, p. 50.
[8] Aris Roussinos, 'Has the Ukraine war saved Orbán?', *UnHerd*, 2 April 2022, https://unherd.com/2022/04/has-the-ukraine-war-saved-orban/, accessed 2 April 2022.
[9] William Nattrass, 'How deep does the EU's corruption scandal go', *UnHerd*, 12 December 2022, https://unherd.com/thepost/how-deep-does-the-eus-corruption-scandal-go/, accessed 4 January 2023.
[10] Jack Grove, 'Ignatieff: Central European University "forced out" of Hungary', *Times Higher Education*, 3 December 2018,

https://www.timeshighereducation.com/news/ignatieff-central-european-university-forced-out-hungary, accessed 26 May 2022.
[11] Lendvai, 'The Transformer', p. 51.
[12] Boris Kálnocky, 'Media Freedom in Hungary', *Hungarian Review,* Vol. 12, No. 4, 9 March 2022.
[13] Lendvai, 'The Transformer', p. 51.
[14] See Timothy Garton Ash, 'Viktor Orbán's victory adds to the darkness engulfing Hungary', *Guardian,* 4 April 2022.
[15] Tibor Fischer, 'The problem with Hungary', *Spectator,* 14 October 2017.
[16] Information for this paragraph was obtained from Panyi Szabolcs. 'How Orbán played Germany, Europe's Great Power', *Direkt36,* 18 September 2020, https://www.direkt36.hu/en/a-magyar-nemet-kapcsolatok-rejtett-tortenete/, accessed 20 June 2022.
[17] Szabolcs, 'How Orbán'.
[18] Jan-Werner Mueller, 'Has Christian Democracy reached a dead end in Europe?', *Guardian,* 10 June 2010.
[19] 'Orbanism Ascendant', American Interest, 23 October 2015, http://www.the-american-interest.com/2015/10/23/orbanism-ascendant, accessed 19 June 2022.
[20] Ryan Heath, 'We are in trouble', *Politico,* 22 October 2015.
[21] 'Orbanism Ascendent'.
[22] William Nattrass, 'What's driving Hungary's culture war', *Spiked onlin*e, 25 June 2021, https://www.spiked-online.com/2021/06/25/whats-driving-hungarys-culture-war/, accessed 11 April 2022.
[23] Jennifer Rankin, 'ECJ dismisses Hungary and Poland's complaints over rule-of-law measure', *Guardian,* 16 February 2022, https://www.theguardian.com/law/2022/feb/16/ecj-dismisses-hungary-poland-complaints-eu-rule-of-law-measure, accessed 6 June 2022. Frank Furedi, 'The EU's neo-colonial assault on Hungary', *Spiked online,* 17 February 2022, accessed 28 October 2022.
[24] Szabolcs, 'How Orbán'.
[25] Attila Demko, 'Hungary is not doing Putin's bidding', *Spiked onlin*e, 6 May 2022, https://www.spiked-online.com/2022/05/06/no-hungary-is-not-doing-putins-bidding/, accessed 7 May 2022.
[26] Roussinos, 'Has the Ukraine war'.
[27] 'Václav Klaus: Viktor Orbán is the only credible politician in Europe', Hir Magazin, 10 April 2022, https://hirmagazin.eu/en/vaclav-klaus-orban-viktor-az-egyeduli-hiteles-politikus-europaban-video, accessed 27 October 2022.
[28] Eszter Zalan, 'Visegrád will survive but as a fractured alliance', EUobserver, 9 May 2022, https://euobserver.com/ukraine/154898, accessed 2 June 2022
[29] Laurence Norman, 'Hungary's Orban Threatens EU Unity on Russia', *Wall Street Journal,* 10 May 2022.
[30] Zsolt Németh, 'On Ukraine and Poland, Soberly', *Hungarian Conservative,* 13 May 2022, https://www.hungarianconservative.com/articles/current/on-ukraine-and-poland-soberly/, accessed 16 May 2022.
[31] 'EU Drops Russian Patriarch From Sanctions Package To Gain Hungarian Acceptance', RFE-RL, 2 June 2022, https://www.rferl.org/a/patriarch-kirill-sanctions-eu-ukraine-hungary/31880523.html, accessed 3 June 2022.

---

[32] William Nattrass, 'Viktor Orban defeats the EU – again', *UnHerd*, 31 May 2022, https://unherd.com/thepost/viktor-orban-defeats-the-eu-again/, accessed 1 June 2022.
[33] Wojciech Przybylski, 'The End of the Budapest-Warsaw Alliance', *EUobserver*, 2 April 2022, https://www.politico.eu/article/hungary-poland-axis-diplomacy-ukraine-russia-war-vikto0r-orban-fidesz-pis-visegrad-group/, accessed 3 April 2022.
[34] *YouGov* poll quoted by @HusaJaakko, 8 May 2022.
[35] 'Speech given by Prime Minister Viktor Orbán after swearing his prime ministerial oath', *About Hungary*, 17 May 2022, https://abouthungary.hu/news-in-brief/speech-given-by-prime-minister-viktor-orban-after-swearing-his-prime-ministerial-oath, accessed 24 May 2022.
[36] 'Cele 12 porunci ale lui Viktor Orban, în lupta pentru "salvarea civilizației occidentale": Ungaria are o rețetă împotriva dominației progresiste', G4Media, (Bucharest), 20 May 2022, https://www.g4media.ro/cele-12-porunci-ale-lui-viktor-orban-in-lupta-pentru-salvarea-civilizatiei-occidentale-ungaria-are-o-reteta-impotriva-dominatiei-progresiste.html.
[37] His political philosophy has been set out in Ryzard Legutko's, *The Demon in Democracy: Totalitarian Temptations in Free Societies*, New York and London: Encounter Books, 2018.
[38] Gyorgy Schőpflin, 'A flawed analysis on the rise of transnational authoritarianism', *The Critic*, 19 August 2020, https://thecritic.co.uk/a-flawed-analysis-on-the-rise-of-transnational-authoritarianism/, accessed 9 April 2022.
[39] Rod Dreher, 'Defender of the Normies', *American Conservative*, 29 June 2022, https://www.theamericanconservative.com/dreher/viktor-orban-new-yorker-american-orbanism/, accessed 6 July 2022.
[40] Jonathan Miller, '"McKinseygate" won't bring down Macron', *Spectator Online*, 31 March 2022, https://www.spectator.co.uk/article/macron-is-plodding-towards-re-election, accessed 31 March 2022.
[41] Cabinet Office of the Prime Minister, Tusnádfürdő/Băile Tuşnad speech by Prime Minister Viktor Orbán at the 31st Bálványos Summer Free University and Student Camp, 23 July 2022.
https://miniszterelnok.hu/speech-by-prime-minister-viktor-orban-at-the-31st-balvanyos-summer-free-university-and-student-camp/, accessed 6 August 2022.
[42] Redactie, 'Sondaj de opinie: majoritate cetăţenilor ungari susţin că Viktor Orbán ar trebuie să adopte o posiţie mai fermă împotriva Rusie', *G4Media*, 15 November 2022, https://www.g4media.ro/sondaj-de-opinie-majoritatea-cetatenilor-ungari-sustin-ca-viktor-orban-ar-trebui-sa-adopte-o-pozitie-mai-ferma-impotriva-rusiei.html, accessed 15 November 2022.
[43] 'Hungary's Ruling Party Reacts Angrily To European Parliament Ruling Country Not A "Full Democracy"', *Radio Free Europe*, 16 September 2022, https://www.rferl.org/a/hungary-fidesz-angry-ep-ruling-not-full-democracy/32036575.html, accessed 18 September 2022.
[44] Ukraine Today, 22 February 2023, https://ukrainetoday.org/2023/02/27/we-have-to-think-ten-thousand-times-orban-spoke-about-ukraines-membership-in-nato/, accessed 4 March 2023.
[45] Szabolcs, 'How Orban'.
[46] Sumantra Maitra, 'Hungary and the new reactionary vanguardism', *National Interest*, September 2022.

CHAPTER 22: EMMANUEL MACRON & BORIS JOHNSON

1977- and 1964-

Emmanuel Macron and Boris Johnson have presented themselves as radical outsiders. But they quickly ended up presiding and reacting rather than innovating or reforming. In their defence, the onrush of events foreclosed their chances of making a deep mark on national affairs. But even without the Covid pandemic and the war in Ukraine, Johnson seemed pre-disposed to having a decorative role. Unlike Macron, he showed more interest in pleasing individuals and groups who matter to him emotionally and materially, than in the exercise of power.

They are both elitist liberals who instinctively display progressive cosmopolitan instincts, as when they condemned the decision of the US Supreme Court in 2022, to rule that abortion laws would be decided by the electoral process in each of the fifty US states and not by an un-elected court.[1] To no small degree, their political careers took off because of the valuable connections that they made in liberal social circles. After being at Eton, Johnson progressed to Oxford, where he stood out as a member of a privileged set sometimes known for self-indulgent behaviour.

Macron's lightning rise occurred as a political vacuum opened up in France, plunging two long-dominant-parties, the Gaullists and the Socialists, into a protracted crisis. An ability to appear and sound innovative while mobilising forces committed to preserving the dominance of entrenched elite groups drawn from Paris and a few other cities, worked in his favour. Macron's eloquence and approachability enabled him to transmit a vague populist message. Johnson would also rise to the top of the Conservatives without spending much time on party matters or as a minister. He was a chameleon figure who appeared a refreshingly unconventional antidote to a London elite of which much of the rest of the country was tiring. He sought to channel a restless spirit to his advantage, while Macron set out to reassert the primacy of the centre by appearing as a vague saviour figure. These were far from easy roles to perform. It is no surprise that both were extremely competitive and prepared to be reckless and unorthodox at times.

Macron grew up in the nicest quarter of the northern city of Amiens, the son of two doctors. The family environment was stable, whereas Johnson's was turbulent. At the age of ten, he witnessed the break-up of the marriage between his sensitive, artistic mother and a father ambitious for professional success. A biographer has argued that he inherited from his father 'disloyalty, ambition and breathtaking narcissism. And also, Stanley's lack of self-criticism, indiscipline and insensitivity to others'.[2] It was, however, Macron who showed remarkable impetuousness aged only 16 when he started an affair with his married drama teacher, then a mother-of-three called Brigitte Auzière. Despite their 24-year age gap, they went on to make a successful marriage.[3]

Johnson acquired a semblance of domestic stability when he married Marina Wheeler, a successful lawyer. She has been recalled as someone who is very intelligent, who cared, and instilled some order in Johnson's life.[4] But his affairs and illegitimate children brought the marriage to an end in 2019.[5] The disappearance of her 'steadying influence' was seen as a loss by someone who knew them. He 'traded that in for a demanding girlfriend and strong disapproval from his children'.[6]

The early trauma faced by Macron mainly centred around his failure to gain admission to the École Nationale d'Administration, the French school of public administration. It was the best known of a series of elite training schools that for the last 150 years have been dedicated to state service. They have instilled the view that, despite periodic turmoil France, in the words of de Gaulle, is dedicated to fulfilling 'an eminent and exceptional destiny'.[7] Their graduates obtain posts in civil service agencies and nationalised companies. Thanks to a desire to wield power and influence, the self-willed Macron had fewer problems than most in rising to become a government insider. Once he became familiar with public service practices in the centralised French state, he built a political network and obtained rapid advancement.

After graduating in 2004, he became an inspector in the finance ministry, followed by a stint with the Rothschild & Cie Banque, where he led several lucrative mergers and acquisitions.[8] A member of the Socialist party from the age of 24, he attached himself to Jacques Attali, an assiduous political operator who had been close to François Mitterrand. In 2010, he joined the staff of François Hollande, the same year that he declined an invite to be the deputy chief of staff of the centre-right prime minister François Fillon. He was kept on by Hollande as an adviser upon him being elected President of France in 2012. He advocated measures to strengthen competition and cut back on social entitlements. But they fell on deaf ears. Simultaneously, he was pursuing opportunities in private business and higher education. His breakthrough came in August 2014, when he was appointed economy minister, being dedicated to introducing business-friendly measures. He withdrew from the Socialists in 2015 when it was becoming ever clearer that the Hollande presidency was a failure. His frenetic networking was crowned a year later when he formed a new party *En Marche* with a liberal and pro-EU manifesto.

Macron's insider status garnered him very supportive media coverage and, when he quit the government and announced his candidacy, the left dubbed him the media candidate. His chances were transformed when the Gaullist front-runner Fillon was beset by scandal. Macron became the candidate whom a large swathe of opinion rallied around in order to thwart the challenge from Marine Le Pen on the far-right. His support extended from left-wingers like Daniel Cohn-Bendit to the Grand Mufti of Paris, and it united centre-left and parts of the centre-right. He was elected President on 7 May 2017, with 66 percent of the vote. There was, however, a record abstention rate of 25 percent and 8 percent of the ballots were blank or spoiled.

Johnson's rise to the top was the slower of the two. He won the British premiership in July 2019, at the age of 56. For the previous three years, there had been unusual levels of turbulence in British politics over the extent to which Britain should move beyond the EU's orbit. The referendum held on 23 June 2016 had given victory to the 'Leave' side. But the 'Remainers' were dominant in influential sectors of state and society. A majority in parliament was determined to delay, dilute or overturn the withdrawal process.

Johnson had only decided late in the day to identify with the Leave camp. It is widely assumed that his campaigning skills, enabling him to win over sceptical or apathetic voters, played a crucial role in securing a victory of just over one million votes. His informal brand of showmanship had already been enough to win him the post of Mayor of London in 2008, one of the most left-wing parts of Britain. This had seemed a feat beyond someone who had been an MP for one of the most affluent constituencies in the country and who had already edited the right-wing *Spectator* magazine. Johnson's administrative record was patchy and he delegated many key tasks to able lieutenants. But he generated 'a feel good' atmosphere which enabled him to be re-elected in 2012, the year London hosted the Olympics.

In December 2019, Johnson's anti-establishment credentials would ensure that he obtained the biggest majority the Conservatives had had in thirty-two years. Unlike other Tory party leaders from John Major to David Cameron who had relied upon 'technocrats, Eurocrats or paternalistic do-gooders', he was seen as a leader who reflected the outlook not only of 'Middle England' but of the formerly Labour 'Red Wall' seats, mainly in the English North, which had secured him an 80-seat majority.[9]

Johnson promised a decisive break from what had gone before. Britain formerly left the EU on 27 January 2020. His main advisor Dominic Cummings was given the job of shaking up an under-performing civil service. But two months later, the Covid pandemic struck. By the end of the year, Cummings had staged an acrimonious departure. Those now advising Johnson were big state planners and metropolitan liberals, not least his partner, and later wife, Carrie Symonds, whose priorities of Net Zero and launching expensive economic projects of uncertain worth were far removed from his previous concerns. An editorial in the political magazine formerly edited by Johnson described her as 'a person with no mandate to make policy and personnel decisions [who is] constantly being permitted to make them'.[10]

His policies of raising taxes and boosting state spending increasingly resembled those of a Labour government. One disenchanted supporter dismissed him in mid-2022 as 'a freedom-loving conservative' who governed as an illiberal technocrat and who 'moved his party closer to socialism than any Prime Minister' since the 1970s.[11]

The failure of his advisers to abide by the social-distancing measures imposed on the public, which marked the two pandemic years, was instrumental in damaging his popularity and enabling a hostile media to contribute to bringing his premiership to a premature conclusion in 2022. A full-scale mutiny gripped his party due to many allies joining long-standing foes in urging him to stand down. Rebels argued that Johnson was an egotist whose only true agenda concerned him winning political power, and enjoying the fruits of office, and that Brexit had been merely the means to accomplish this personal end. An occasionally tumultuous personal life often overshadowed an erratic leadership style. Neither could be said of Macron. However, both struggled to live up to what many in their respective populations regarded as proper conduct in their leaders.

Both damaged their standing by side-stepping or flouting conventions designed to prevent elected leaders overstepping their authority. With Johnson, the controversies placed in sharp relief his preference for an informal style of rule and the sway exercised by an allegedly disruptive spouse. He faced criticism in the media, and from a growing number of his own MPs, for allegedly trying to secure a major advisory position in government for her;[12] for the runaway costs of decorating No.10 Downing Street; for trying to erect a tree-house for his son, costing £150,000 at Chequers (his official weekend seat);[13] and not least, for giving priority to the evacuation of cats and dogs in the British evacuation of Afghanistan in 2021.[14]

Macron was under fire for more systematic exploitation of his powers of patronage. He received fierce criticism for side-stepping French ministries and institutions and commissioning major global consultancy firms to formulate policy on everything from the environment to health, often at a steep cost.[15] In 2018, his presidency was rocked by the revelation that he had created what some called a private militia to supersede the security organs of the presidency (the so-called Benalla affair).[16] His liking for unorthodox parallel arrangements designed to consolidate his hold on power was seen as a throw-back to other high-handed eras of personal rule.

It may have helped intensify the serious unrest that gripped large areas of provincial France during the middle of his first term. Street protests, some of which were harshly dealt with by paramilitary police, erupted against ill-thought-out price liberalisations and cuts to social entitlements.[17] They were an imposition by the mobile and satisfied 'Anywhere' elites on the rooted and precarious 'Somewheres' living in overlooked France.[18] Macron retreated before this militant anti-elite outburst staged by the *Gilets Jaunes* (Yellow Vests). Tax increases on low income pensions and end-of-5year bonuses were withdrawn. He conceded that many grievances were legitimate. But the eruption of the crisis was a sign of how far decision-makers had separated themselves from the lives of a big segment of the population.

Pressures on living standards were slower to make themselves felt under Johnson. But from early on, he tended to marginalise the cabinet and rely on personal advisers. Few of them proved to be hard-headed counsellors able to steer an easily distracted prime minster in prudent directions.

In the third year of his premiership, the educationalist and writer Toby Young (who had been on friendly terms with Johnson for decades), was frank about his un-prime-ministerial mindset: 'he's the most chaotic, disorganised man I've ever known. His nickname in No.10 is "trolley" because he zig-zags around like a wonky shopping cart'.[19]

According to his biographer Tom Bower, despite being respected as a classicist, he displayed an ignorance of British history and the importance of dominating the Whitehall civil service machine: 'key departments...were staffed by incompetent, illiterate, woke antagonists' who were ready to thwart proposals that offended their outlook.[20] It was only Johnson's penchant for higher spending that they readily implemented. It was not hard for despairing economic analysts to show that much of this financial outlay was wasted due to poor planning, or else purloined by hostile devolved administrations or outright fraudsters, which happened during the Covid pandemic.[21] The Tories were jeopardising their reputation as competent economic managers, which they eventually lost to the hitherto struggling Labour Party in 2022.

Lasting almost two years (from March 2020 to early 2022), the Covid pandemic suspended normal political activity as Britain was contemplating life outside the regulatory embrace of the EU. This public health emergency threw the underlying political natures of both Johnson and Macron into sharp relief. Johnson's initial instinct had been to roll out contingency plans already prepared to deal with such an emergency. The unwell would be treated, the vulnerable shielded, while British society and the national economy were allowed to function as far as possible.

Sweden practised such a strategy, avoiding draconian restrictions, and keeping schools open along with much of the economy. Reliant on information from a state bureaucracy and a medical establishment prone to extreme caution, Johnson quickly discarded his libertarian instincts. He proved receptive to the warnings of statisticians, scientists and an influential wing of health opinion, which asserted that the pandemic posed a mortal peril that could only be averted by confining society and freezing the economy. Thus, restrictions on everyday living soon saw the relationship between the individual and the state tilt massively in favour of the latter. A massive administrative state sprung up, which engorged itself on ambitious and expensive schemes to contain Covid. Spending £12 billion on a vaccine which mitigated the worst effects of the virus was a gamble that paid off. On the other hand, the £37 billion spent on 'the track-and-trace' mass monitoring scheme had no discernible benefit.[22] Opinion remained divided on the merits of the furlough scheme, in which millions of business owners and their employees were compensated for economic inactivity (the scheme having cost an estimated £70 billion by November 2021).[23]

Johnson was a big spender by instinct and he was deferential to the world view of experts, ready to fling much of the wealth of the state into this battle. In dozens of televised media briefings, in which he was flanked by top medics and functionaries, he came across more as a legate selling their crisis agenda and less as a leader. Whatever reputation he once had as an effective communicator gradually faded as he repeated the formulaic homily, 'Stay safe, protect the NHS and save lives'. He showed no evidence of thinking long-term about of the impact of closing down an advanced urban capitalist society for months on end, nor did he encourage debate about other policy options among his ministers. The emergency left him free from the supervision of his party, but a stark reckoning could not be avoided. In 2020, Britain saw the biggest fall of economic activity since the Great Frost of 1709. Record spending and borrowing saw public sector debt rise from 80 percent of GDP to around 100 percent. A spike in job losses occurred, especially in the service sector, but there were also job shortages and a reluctance of many in the public sector to return to their desks. Treatment of serious medical conditions was shelved to enable the NHS to function as a 'Covid Service'. The closure of educational institutions impacted not only on the education of a generation of young people, but also on their psychological well-being.

Johnson (who was very ill with Covid in the spring of 2020) slotted into a public relations role during the crisis, whereas Macron cultivated an image of decisiveness. He used the full panoply of the centralised French state and acted far more on his own volition than Johnson did. He defied expert advice by easing restrictions in the summer of 2020. But he was ready to impose draconian measures even when it was apparent that the pandemic was on the wane. On 24 January 2022 (with the Omicron variant resulting in far fewer deaths), he introduced a vaccine passport that effectively shut out from much of society anyone who was not triple jabbed. On 4 January of that year, referring to the unvaccinated, he had said: 'I really want to hassle them. And so, we will continue to do it, until the end'.[24] Arguably, he helped detoxify Marine Le Pen, his main challenger in the 2022 presidential election, by revealing to many, through his liking for emergency measures, that he posed a bigger danger to freedom than she did.[25]

Wider afield, he caused controversy when, at the start of 2021, he claimed that the British-developed Astra Zeneca vaccine appeared to be ineffective for the over-65 age group (the ones seen as most at risk from the virus)[26] He later backtracked but, according to Sir John Bell, Regius Professor of

Medicine at the University of Oxford, 'the European politicians who cast doubt on Astra Zeneca probably killed hundreds of thousands of people'.[27]

More positively, Macron did secure Germany's backing for an €800 billion Covid recovery fund. But it is quite possible that a funding stream being channeled through a sclerotic EU bureaucracy in Brussels will end up recycling old projects that soak up much money for little useful purpose, rather than stimulating an economic revival in different parts of Europe.[28]

Relations were frosty between Macron and Johnson until the outbreak of the war in Ukraine. The French leader was more opposed in public to Brexit than any of his EU colleagues. It was seen as an unhelpful diversion from the drive to deepen the powers of a French-designed European community. But they were both globally-minded centrists happy to pursue ambitious schemes via international institutions. If it meant inconveniencing their party backers, then so be it. This was hardly a problem for Macron. He saw an early exodus of radical deputies unhappy at his rightward economic turn. En Marche had been his creation in 2016 and he had renamed it twice, its latest incarnation, *Renaissance*, being 'a change in packaging obscuring the lack of new content'.[29]

Books appeared not long after Macron's presidential tenure began, in which he was depicted as the only person on the European stage with the vision and determination to press ahead with further integration of the EU, a quarter of a century after the path-breaking Maastricht Treaty.[30] He himself wrote *Revolution* in 2017, where he scarcely bothers to disguise his ambition to rank as a historical figure, or a 'Jupiter', as he once dubbed himself.[31] But whatever plans he had to be 'the spiritual leader of Europe', as one admiring journalist described him in 2022, they were constantly frustrated.[32] Resistance at home put paid to plans to tighten the economic purse strings in a country where public spending remained steady at 57 percent, one of the highest levels in the West. One long-term France watcher observed that Macron had hoped that 'a Thatcherite shake-up, sugared by cultural leftism', would restore France as a serious partner in the eyes of Germany, Europe's reluctant paymaster.[33] Even before becoming President, he had spoken up for the mutualisation of debt, which meant 'the switch of French obligations on to the German credit card'.[34]

But France's disorderly domestic politics made the creation of an EU Treasury with tax-raising powers seem a complete overreach. Macron's first term was spent fighting fires ranging from the Gilets Jaunes agitation to Covid rather than planning the architecture of a more unified Europe. At least as a consolation prize, France would have the Presidency of the European Council in the midst of his re-election bid in the first half of 2022.

A packed calendar of events was planned, not least to project the role of the EU as a first-rank foreign policy actor, with potential martial clout that could enable it to surpass NATO. But the Russian invasion of Ukraine in February 2022 rudely shattered such ambitions. The US-led alliance, which Macron had described as 'brain dead' in 2019, regained its relevance overnight as it rushed aid to prevent Ukraine being pulverised by Putin's forces, and mobilised to deter attacks on NATO states near the front line of this conflict. The new war in Europe also coincided with the collapse of French-led military operation in Mali against Islamist terrorism, the kind of in-house EU operation which Macron had predicted was the way ahead for a Europe flexing its military muscles.[35]

An embattled Macron struggled to keep his composure even in dealings with fellow EU leaders. On 8 April 2022, he lashed out at the Prime Minister of Poland, Mateusz Morawiecki, remarking that 'he is an anti-Semite of the far-right who has banned the LGBT movement...and, on several occasions, has received Marine Le Pen'.[36] He was more respectful towards Viktor Orbán of Hungary, but during campaigning he argued that France would become like Hungary if she came to power, where 'rights are meticulously and progressively reduced'.[37]

Johnson increasingly resembled Macron as 2022 got underway. His popularity with the public was fast waning, especially as a hostile electronic media capitalised on the contrasting ways in which the lockdown was flouted at the heart of government while often rigorously imposed on ordinary citizens. As scandals mounted in the ranks of his party, leading to by-election losses for the Conservatives, he was described as 'a pre-Christian figure' who 'leads a sybaritic patrician class enjoying the pleasures of the flesh while denying them to the plebeian masses'.[38] However exaggerated such a claim may seem, he showed no interest in establishing strong connections with his electoral base, and his lack of enthusiasm for energetic reform meant he had no reserves of affection to drawn on when his difficulties mounted.[39]

He and Macron were drawn to globalist institutions. But it was increasingly unclear what Johnson stood for in domestic politics. He used opaque populist language, but increasingly appeared to govern from the left. The ex-libertarian seemed more and more comfortable with corporate socialism. He dragged his feet on issues that were dear to many who had voted for him in 2019. There was no sign of any concerted effort to take advantage of being outside the EU's regulatory regime by liberalising the economy in order to increase inward investment. An effective plan to thwart the gangs of people smugglers who were bringing large numbers of illegal immigrants across the English Channel was slow to emerge. Supporters told him that it would require Britain leaving, or replacing, the European Court of Human Rights, but he shrunk from doing it. Renewable technology continued to be preferred to using Britain's own ample carbon assets, even as energy bills surged and the possibility of power cuts increased. On 6 June 2022, 41 percent of Conservative MPs withheld their backing in a vote of confidence, including a clear majority of backbenchers. Despite a string of previous party leaders urging him to step down, Johnson clung on. Exercising power for its own sake seemed to be his main political aim, as a coherent agenda for government showed no sign of emerging beyond the midway point of his administration.

He had played a notable role in mobilising the West to save Ukraine. But he inherited this pro-Ukrainian stance from predecessors and it is one that a successor was likely to maintain. The exercise of power increasingly seemed to be a holding operation for him as he struggled, in the midst of darkening economic prospects, to prevent his party ditching him.

Two by-election defeats in safe seats showed that he was no longer an electoral asset. The idea that he was a politician on the side of ordinary folk evaporated as he brushed away difficulties at home and became a convert to international causes preferred by his liberal left opponents. His MPs were unable to explain or defend his high tax, high spending agenda to the public. His quixotic embrace of radical environmentalism meant increasing costs were placed on businesses and ordinary households, which faced mounting financial burdens, in order for Britain to be the poster boy of Net Zero. Campaigning on the right but governing from the left in a time of crisis was bound to alienate him from much of his base but win him no friends on the left, where he continued to be loathed and disparaged. Consumers, meat eaters, drivers and many with a suburban lifestyle grew confused and then angry by his incontinence as a ruler in a time of crisis.[40] Finally, on 7 July 2022, he resigned after dozens of ministers mutinied and walked out on him. He had struggled to hang on with more tenacity than he had shown in ruling the country. But his authority melted away and, following the appointment of a successor Liz Truss on 5 September and the death of Queen Elizabeth II just three days later, he was starting to become a forgotten and largely unmourned figure.

It is perhaps wrong to see his three years in office as a quixotic interlude in British politics. Instead, it may have some significance due to inaugurating a new era in public affairs where politicians in office cede authority to managers, technocrats and big business.[41] Johnson cut loose from his own party, which unceremoniously dumped him. The turbulence persisted under his successor Liz Truss, who it soon turned out, lacked the political poise and intellectual heft to re-introduce free market policies after a long period in which financial policy had focused on balanced budgets and fiscal discipline.[42] Cornered by the trans-Atlantic financial establishment, she quit on 20 October 2022, after just 47 days in office. Within two days, Johnson was rushing back from a holiday in the Caribbean to indicate that despite misgivings among his MPs and his unpopularity in the country, he was ready to fill the vacancy. A frantic 48 hours followed in which he tried to obtain the requisite backing of 100 of his party's MPs which would enable his candidacy to be placed before Tory Party members in the country. To the puzzlement of many, his standing among many of the faithful remained high. This was despite the fact that he had consistently failed to deliver policies to match the centre-right positions that he had campaigned on. But the conditions for a Johnson comeback were fast receding. There had just been a markets crisis, with turbulence continuing, and Johnson showed no more understanding of economics than he had displayed in the past. As many as sixty Tory MPs seemed ready to deny him backing if he became Prime Minister again. There was also the threat that he would face a recall petition and a by-election due to his enemies in the House of Commons being determined to find that he had lied to that body.

On 23 October, he surprised many of his followers by announcing that he was quitting the race. Two days later, his foe Rishi Sunak became Prime Minister but, in his withdrawal statement, Johnson included the line that 'now is not the time' for a comeback, a clear indication that he hoped another opportunity might arise in the future. It might well do but it will be thanks to the enemies of Johnson in the left-leaning Westminster establishment if they resolve to make a martyr of him by attempting to drive him out of public life. That is the only way he could engineer a comeback, appealing to the underlying sympathy towards Johnson in sections of the public who regard him as a likeable rogue.

No senior politician with Johnson's record of failure in British politics has ever returned to high office. Jonathan Sumption, a former judge and respected commentator on Britain's crisis of governance, has explained why he was so ineffective during the Covid crisis:

> 'The role of the prime minister is critical. He is the only person in a position to decide between the rival claims of public health, education, social policy, economic survival and financial solvency. For that he needs a clear idea of what he is trying to achieve and a strategy for achieving it. He needs strength of personality and the public stature to persuade the public rather than just appease them. He must have command of the detail, and the respect of his subordinates. Boris Johnson had none of these things.'43

The political landscape in France was also fractious and polarised but Macron could rely on the resources of the French state, which was obvious during his spring 2002 re-election effort. But his campaign was a subdued one. Voters were offered subsidies on gas and electricity, and the long-held commitment to increasing the retirement age from 62 to 65 was only timidly referred to. He was petulant in his second-round debate with Le Pen, whom he defeated by 58.6 to 41.5 percent of the votes on 24 April. According to the political calendar, the elections for the French national assembly were due in June. He did not campaign actively. Nor did he grasp that millions of French voters endorsed him because he was the least bad option.[44] His dramatic trip to Kyiv on 16 June, seems to have had no more impact on self-absorbed voters than his decision, in April, to pose for photos with the trademark special forces garb and unshaven face that had turned Ukraine's President Zelensky into a rare leader, able to use his eloquence and fortitude to motivate a nation in adversity. In the event, his re-branded Renaissance suffered a heavy reverse on 19 June, falling well short of an overall majority. At 53 percent, the election marked a record abstention in the history of the 5th Republic. Le Pen's rebranded National Rally got 89 seats (up from 14). There was a record result for the coalition of the populist left put together by Jean-Luc Mélanchon. Both Le Pen and Mélanchon's formations now eclipsed Macron's liberal centrist party in the national assembly, which meant he had to fight for every new policy. In a terse television address, he betrayed no willingness to contemplate a new start beyond saying: 'I am determined to take charge of the desire for change that the country has clearly expressed because it is my role as the guarantor of our institutions'.[45]

The Gaullists and the mainstream Socialists, hitherto the pillars of the political order, had been crushed. A year before the elections, Philippe de Villiers, a seasoned operator who had broken with the Gaullists, had been blunt about the young President: 'Emmanuel Macron is not up to his job, he does not inhabit the body of the king; like Giscard he does not know that History is tragic'. He depicted him not as a hoarder of power but as a frenetic salesman for powerful state interests, global corporations, the Brussels bureaucracy, and various Green and hi-tech lobbies.[46]

Perhaps Macron will grow distracted with a French presidency in which a parliament, in opposition hands, prevents him from being the master of all he surveys. In London, Johnson could still rely on a parliamentary majority. But it was small comfort as the wolves circled and his control over the machinery of state became increasingly questionable. He and Macron spent three days in close proximity during the G7 summit held in the Bavarian Alps from 26 to 28 June. Their expressions and body language betrayed a sense of relief about escaping, at least temporarily, from accumulating woes at home. There was room for common ground on Ukraine, which dominated the agenda. Johnson eschewed triumphalism about having been vindicated in backing Ukraine, and Macron seemed to have given up trying to reason with Putin. Photos showed the pair arm in arm, and there was talk of a 'bromance' between them.[47] The rivalry between these two highly competitive figures may well have started to abate because the political tides were receding for both of them. Less and less did there appear to be a coherent purpose to their administrations. The chorus of voices proclaiming that France and Britain were in existential distress steadily grew. Perhaps as compensation, he busied himself with portentous speeches. In 2017, he was delivering ones in which he talked about launching 'democratic conventions' aimed at 'refounding Europe' or constructing a 'European sovereignty'.[48] By September 2022, with troubling socio-economic indicators showing that its profile was increasingly southern European, he was telling a gathering of French ambassadors that France needs to be a 'strong nation which...knows what the price of freedom is'.[49]

Unfortunately for Macron, most French citizens possess little affinity with his vision of greatness, which has seemed too bound up with personal aggrandisement allied to the pursuit of global technocracy, in which France (though not him) can only enjoy a negligible role. This was shown in the spring of 2023 by his decision to raise the pension age from 62 to 64. In most countries there would have been disgruntlement but not the outpouring of rage against a step felt to be necessary because of a fast-ageing population. Macron, the most ambitious president in the 75-year history of the 5th Republic, found himself the object of intense hatred, far more than the measure itself. Its imposition by presidential decree, due to the absence of sufficient votes in parliament, was seen as proof of his illegitimacy. While being interviewed on television at the height of fierce riots that fanned beyond Paris, he surreptitiously removed a luxury watch from his wrist, presumably due to the unfavourable impression it might give.[50] Such artful guile has too often proven self-defeating. He acts like an undeniably clever but disdainful overseer towards a population who sense his lack of sympathy allied to a readiness to interfere in their lives. He may be acutely aware of the 'malaise of a country haunted by its economic decline, its cultural fragmentation, its ageing population' but is powerless to offer remedies or improvements because of a brittle and adversarial relationship with much of the French people.[51]

Easter week 2023, which led to a pause in the crisis at home, was chosen by Macron to pay a high-profile visit to China. He spoke indulgently about his host Xi Jinping and was even filmed at a staged event, fraternising with a pro-regime crowd. He insisted that Europe should not be 'a vassal' of the United States while displaying neutrality about China's increasingly bellicose actions in East Asia, especially towards Taiwan.[52] He called for Europe to build up its strategic autonomy even though this would require a huge increase in defence expenditure for which support is to be found only in certain states which acutely feel the danger from the east. He seemed oblivious of the fact that the Russo-Ukraine war, more than ever, showed how reliant Europe was on the security shield provided by the United States. His fatuous comment that the reception he had been given in China showed that France is 'not just a country like any other', once again offered a display of narcissism, but at a perilous stage in international relations. Chairman Xi, no doubt satisfied by the fissures in the Western security alliance which his guest had opened up, smugly remarked to him: 'If you stay longer, you are welcome to live here'.[53] Perhaps he could see that Macron was an ambitious freelancer, absorbed by manoeuvres and procedures, that enabled him to sit at the top table rather than being prepared to defend values essential for the survival of free societies. To the dismay of a growing numbers of allies of France, he was more interested in garnering prestige even if it meant colluding with authoritarians looking for any chance to defeat and overwhelm the West.

With every passing day, it looks increasingly unlikely that 'Johnsonism' or 'Macronism' will enter the lexicon of politics as terms denoting a political project or an outlook. The pair were past masters at delivering platitudes that often bore little resemblance to how they exercised power. They did not worry about a lack of political consistency or about being occasionally seen to lack probity. Perhaps true fulfilment only awaits two classic exponents of shapeshifting in politics outside this field of activity. Macron will step down in 2027, with a bulging contacts book and the distinct possibility of walking into any number of international positions as a globally-minded left-liberal. Johnson may have to content himself with being an author, media celebrity and after-dinner speaker, relieved to extract a lucrative income from multiple reiterations of his eventful career in politics.

Johnson announced his resignation from parliament on 9 June, 2023, denouncing what he termed a bureaucratic coup designed to drive him from public life—one he strongly hinted that Rishi Sunak was quietly colluding in.[52] He had just received notification that the Privileges Committee of the House of Commons was going to impose a heavy penalty for violating the Covid lockdown rules. It would mean his suspension from parliament and a by-election, which the Tories were unlikely to win. His melodramatic gesture was a sign of boundless self-absorption. But it was noted that Keir Starmer, in perhaps a more serious breach of the lockdown rules, had been deemed to be blameless by a Labour ally sitting in judgment. Moreover, the impartiality of Sue Gray, the civil servant who had headed the Whitehall investigation into what was known as 'Cakegate' was soon questioned when it transpired that she had been negotiating to become Starmer's Chief of Staff, while likely still in this inquisitorial role. Johnson leaves parliament undefeated, his allies claiming that he was the victim of an anti-democratic coup, and his more numerous detractors insisting that his downfall was largely his own work.

Both men assumed high office at a fraught period in European and world affairs. Both were unable to fulfill the hopes invested in them. It is surely not unfair to argue that their failures were as much due to personal shortcomings as to the sheer weight of the challenges that were soon placed on their shoulders. They are thus emblematic figures in an era where an absence of vision, discipline and purpose have intensified the maladies of democratic politics in Europe and the wider West.

---

[1] Kurt Zindulka, 'Who Asked? Boris, Macron, European Leaders Rush to Condemn Roe v Wade Ruling on Abortion', *Breitbart News,* 25 June 2022, https://www.breitbart.com/europe/2022/06/25/boris-macron-european-leaders-rush-to-condemn-roe-v-wade-ruling/, accessed 30 June 2022.
[2] Tom Bower, 'Can Boris save himself?', *Spectator,* 16 January 2022, https://www.spectator.co.uk/article/can-boris-save-himself/, accessed 9 August 2022.
[3] Peter Allen, 'How Macron's hometown betrayed him', *UnHerd,* 21 April 2022, https://unherd.com/2022/04/how-macrons-hometown-betrayed-him/, accessed 16 May 2022.
[4] Lord Ashcroft, 'Carrie uncovered', *Daily Mail,* 6 February 2022.

[5] Tom Newton Dunn, 'All of Boris Johnson's women – a rundown of the affairs, flings and love-children left in the former Foreign Secretary's wake', *The Sun*, (London), 8 September 2018.
[6] Ashcroft, 'Carrie uncovered'.
[7] Robert Tombs, How Macron manipulates Europe', *UnHerd*, 24 January 2022, https://unherd.com/2022/01/how-macron-manipulates-europe/, accessed 6 August 2022.
[8] Mody, *Euro Tragedy*, p.p. 402-3.
[9] Allister Heath, 'Tory Britain faces extinction at the hands of a radical hard-Left alliance', *Daily Telegraph*, 25 May 2022.
[10] Editorial, 'Carrie Symonds and the first girlfriend problem', *Spectator*, 1 May 2021.
[11] Madeline Grant, 'The politics of nothingness has engulfed Britain', *Daily Telegraph*, 29 June 2022.
[12] Mason Boycott-Owen, 'Boris Johnson fails to deny that Carrie was considered for Foreign Office and royal jobs', *Daily Telegraph*, 22 June 2022.
[13] Adam May, 'Boris Johnson 'planned to build £150,000 treehouse for son Wilf' at Chequers', *Daily Mirror*, 25 June 2022.
[14] Melanie McDonough, 'Should we really be airlifting pets out of Kabul?', *Spectator*, 26 August 2021.
[15] Yves Mamou, 'French Presidential Election: Macron v. Le Pen... Again', *Gatestone Institute*, 11 April 2022, https://www.gatestoneinstitute.org/18420/france-presidential-election, accessed 14 April 2022.
[16] John Lichfield, 'Could Macron prove more dangerous than Trump?' *UnHerd*, 2 August 2018, https://unherd.com/2018/08/macron-prove-dangerous-trump/, accessed 6 August 2022.
[17] See Frédéric Royall (2020), 'The Gilets Jaunes protests: mobilisation without third-party support,' *Modern & Contemporary France*, Vol. 28, No. 1, 2020.
[18] See François Valenti, 'The poison in France's veins', *UnHerd*, 19 April 2022, https://unherd.com/2022/04/the-poison-in-frances-veins/, accessed 23 April 2022.
[19] Toby Young, 'Plan B isn't a conspiracy to hide the Downing St party', *Daily Mail*, 9 December 2021.
[20] Bower, 'Can Boris'.
[21] Allister Heath, 'Basket-case Britain is the definitive proof lockdown was an epic mistake', *Daily Telegraph*, 23 June 2022. Ian Murray MP, 'Covid lockdown: Why is SNP government holding back billions of pounds that could help businesses now?' *Edinburgh Evening News*, 25 February 2021.
[22] Martin Bagot, 'Test and trace's 'eye-watering' £37billion shambles laid bare in damning report', *Daily Mirror*, 27 October 2021.
[23] 'How did COVID affect government revenues, spending, borrowing and debt?' https://ifs.org.uk/taxlab/key-questions/how-did-covid-affect-government-revenues-spending-borrowing-and-debt, accessed 27 October 2022.
[24] https://www.cnbc.com/2022/01/05/macron-french-president-wants-to-annoy-the-unvaccinated-.html, accessed 19 January 2022.
[25] Gavin Mortimer, 'The days of Macron's Covid tyranny are officially over', *Spectator Online*, 24 June 2022, https://www.spectator.co.uk/article/the-days-of-macron-s-covid-tyranny-are-officially-over, accessed 9 August 2022.
[26] 29 January 2021, https://www.france24.com/en/live-news/20210129-macron-astrazeneca-vaccine-quasi-ineffective-for-over-65s, accessed 10 August 2022.

[27] Newton Emerson, 'Brussels remains intoxicated by EU nationalism Brexit helped create', *Irish Times*, 23 June 2022, https://www.irishtimes.com/opinion/2022/06/23/newton-emerson-eus-misguided-action-on-astrazeneca-was-driven-by-brexit/.
[28] Ambrose Evans Pritchard, 'Emmanuel Macron's "grand bargain" with Germany', *Daily Telegraph*, 1 July 2022.
[29] Charles Devellennes, 'Emmanuel Macron's authoritarian liberalism', *Spiked Online*, 15 May 2022, https://www.spiked-online.com/2022/05/15/emmanuel-macrons-authoritarian-liberalism/, accessed 15 May 2022.
[30] See for instance William Drozdiak, The Last President of Europe: Emmanuel Macron's Race to Revive France and Save the World, New York: Public Affairs, 2020.
[31] Emmanuel Macron, *Revolution: the bestselling memoir by France's recently elected president*, London: Scribe UK, 2017. It was published in numerous other European languages as well as Chinese and Vietnamese.
[32] Luke McGee, 8 April 2022, https://edition.cnn.com/2022/04/08/europe/macron-putin-french-election-analysis-intl-cmd/index.html, accessed 9 April 2022.
[33] Evans Pritchard, 'Emmanuel Macron's'.
[34] Charles Grant, 'Macron's' plans for the Euro', *Centre for European Reform*, 23 February 2018.
[35] Paul Taylor, 'Why Macron is failing on strategic autonomy', *PoliticoEU*, 26 May 2022, https://www.politico.eu/article/macron-fail-strategic-autonomy-france-eu-presidency-2022/, accessed 28 May 2022.
[36] 'Emmanuel Macron face á nos lecteurs', *Le Parisien*, 7 April 2022, https://www.leparisien.fr/elections/presidentielle/emmanuel-macron-face-a-nos-lecteurs-jai-envie-de-donner-envie-07-04-2022-HADZ4DZNABDANLHKZ2GPULFA5I.php, accessed 8 April 2022.
[37] Tom Evans, 'Emmanuel Macron told he's a "rubbish president' and 'Machiavellian manipulator" by furious voter', *GBNews*, 13 April 2022, https://www.gbnews.uk/news/emmanuel-macron-told-hes-a-rubbish-president-and-machiavellian-manipulator-by-furious-voter/270918, accessed 13 April 2022.
[38] Andrew Cadman, 'Nero and the Johnson empire', *TCW*, 28 June 2021, https://www.conservativewoman.co.uk/nero-and-the-johnson-empire/, accessed 29 June 2022.
[39] See Matthew Goodwin, 'A tale of two realignments', *Matt Goodwin Substack*, 28 October 2022.
[40] Allister Heath, 'His premiership is ending in disaster, but I don't regret backing Boris in 2019', *Daily Telegraph*, 7 July 2022.
[41] Frank Furedi, 'How ideology works in the 21st century', *Frank Furedi Substack*, 13 October 2022, https://frankfuredi.substack.com/p/how-ideology-works-in-the-21st-century, accessed 14 October 2022.
[42] Thomas Fazi,'Why the Left shouldn't be celebrating', *UnHerd*, 24 October 2022, https://unherd.com/2022/10/why-the-left-shouldnt-be-celebrating/, accessed 25 October 2022.
[43] Jonathan Sumption, 'Matt Hancock was never a policy maker – he was a fanatic, *Daily Telegraph*, 11 March 2023.
[44] Anne-Elisabeth Moutet, 'Emmanuel Macron's humiliation will get worse', *Daily Telegraph*, 21 June 2021.

---

[45] Jonathan Miller, 'Macron's state of denial', *Spectator Online*, 22 June 2022, https://www.spectator.co.uk/article/macron-s-credibility-is-in-danger-following-france-s-election, accessed 22 June 2022.
[46] Philippe de Villiers, 'Macron n'est pas à la hauteur de sa fonction', *Memorabilia*, 8 April 2021, https://artofuss.blog/2021/04/08/philippe-de-villiers-macron-nest-pas-a-la-hauteur-de-sa-fonction/, accessed 30 July 2022.
[47] John Keiger, 'Boris and Macron's 'bromance' is rooted in despair', *Spectator online*, 29 June 2022, https://www.spectator.co.uk/article/boris-and-macron-s-bromance-is-rooted-in-despair, accessed 30 June 2022.
[48] Mody, *Euro Tragedy*, p.p. 405, 427.
[49] Aris Roussinos, 'Can Europe survive the age of strongmen?' *UnHerd*, 21 September 2022, https://unherd.com/2022/09/can-europe-survive-the-age-of-strongmen/, accessed 22 September 2022.
[50] Henry Samuel, 'Moment Emmanuel Macron removes luxury watch during pensions interview', *Daily Telegraph*, 24 March 2023.
[51] Angélique Négroni, 'Hántes par le déclassement, ces français qui pleurent la fin d'un monde', *Le Figaro*, 22 January 2023, https://www.lefigaro.fr/actualite-france/hantes-par-le-declassement-ces-francais-qui-pleurent-la-fin-d-un-monde-2023012025, accessed March 2023.
[52] Editorial, 'Macron blunders on Taiwan – and Ukraine', *Wall Street Journal*, 8 Ap 2023.
[53] Roger Cohen, 'If you stay longer, you are welcome to live here', *New York Times*, 8 Apr 2023.
[52] Boris Johnson, 'Why I resigned', *Spectator*, 9 June 2023.

CHAPTER 23: ZELENSKY AND SCHOLZ

Leadership and the Ukraine War

In terms of the quality of leadership exhibited by Europe, there is a possibility that the year 2022 may constitute a fork in the road. As war raged in Ukraine, the transactional leaders in charge of the two main EU players, France and Germany, were reluctant to shun Vladimir Putin, despite the murderous attacks on civilians that increasingly were at the centre of his flailing war effort. Both Emmanuel Macron and Olaf Scholz were reluctant to cast out Putin from the club of civilized nations. They dwelled on the danger of nuclear war. But it wasn't hard to see that they had other grounds for their amenable outlook. Not only were they concerned with the damaging economic fall-out from the war. But they feared that their dominant role inside the EU was being placed in jeopardy.

By successfully affirming Ukraine's commitment to democracy and sovereignty in the most arduous circumstances, its leader Volodymyr Zelensky emerged as a new figure of authority in Europe. His bravery and charisma rallied his own nation and won him respect among fellow leaders in northern and Eastern Europe as well as Italy, who were unambiguous in the support that they offered. It remains to be seen if Zelensky is a dazzling, if transitory, meteor, or else someone who can play a role in arresting the drift in leadership which has plagued Europe for a long period.

Until the eve of the Russian invasion, launched on 24 February 2022, the key players in the EU were disinclined to challenge what was seen as the inexorable course of history in a traditionally Moscow-dominated part of the world. Initially, Ukraine was given days, or at best weeks, to hold out. There seemed little hope of human agency derailing the Russian juggernaut.

In this sombre atmosphere, it was hard to spot popular leaders who were in close touch with their populations. During the coronavirus pandemic, French, German and Dutch leaders had not flinched from advancing state power at the expense of individual liberties even as the health danger was fast receding. It was not unknown for threatening language to be used towards citizens who rejected vaccine passports.

Putin would have been relieved by the unflinching pacifist stance and undiminished mercantile instincts of sections of the Euro elite. Germany continued to contribute little to NATO, being content to allow others in the Alliance to defend Germany in the event of a military crisis. Russian gas flowing across the Baltic Sea and oil being unloaded at German refineries, was viewed as vital to power German industry and homes, irrespective of the steadily increasing drumbeat of war. Olaf Scholz's coalition had blocked sales of weapons to the under-equipped Ukrainians in December 2021. On the war's eve, when he travelled to Moscow for talks with Putin, he told EU ambassadors that it might be appropriate for Ukraine to be more accommodating to Russia.[1]

Macron, at this stage, was even more compliant to Russian perspectives. Having floated the idea of a security pact between the EU and Russia in 2019, he now returned to the presumed desirability of EU states decoupling from the USA in defence matters. Speaking to the European Parliament on 19 January 2022, he called on EU states to embark upon a competing dialogue with Russia, thus superseding the Washington-led negotiations with the Kremlin, in order to avert conflict in Ukraine.[2]

On 7 February, Macron had five hours of fruitless talks with Putin in Moscow where they sat at opposite ends of an unusually long table. He persisted in striving 'to demonstrate deep concern for Russia's needs and interests'. Putin was unbending, warning that if Ukraine ever joined NATO, European countries would 'automatically' be at war with Russia.[3]

Putin might have been forgiven for assuming that Franco-German overtures after 24 February were proof of limited Western resolve. But it is likely that he was also discomfited at the revulsion in free societies towards the type of war he was waging. His methods made it harder for expedient Western leaders to forge a deal with him at Ukraine's expense.

The creation of a vast refugee exodus in the face of massacres and rapes in the areas seized by his forces, the bombing of residential areas and attacks on hospitals, the deliberate destruction of vital infrastructure, the blockade of food supplies at Ukraine's ports, the abduction of over two million Ukrainians who were taken deep into Russia, and the carrying out of deliberate mass murder after the bombing of a jail containing dozens of Ukrainian prisoners, were some of the consequences of his war.

The tweet sent on 4 April 2022, by Wolfgang Ischinger, the doyen of German diplomats, who served as chairman of the Munich Security Conference from 2008 to 2022, indicated that a watershed moment had occurred:

> 'Truly horrible. But quite revealing: so it was not and is not about NATO? It is instead about eliminating the existence of Ukraine? Those in the West who blame the mess on the US because of NATO enlargement should please take note. This is pure fascism. Nothing else'.[4]

After the atrocities against civilians carried out by Russian forces in Bucha, Irpin, Mariupol, Izium and other places, the old cliches in Berlin about how Russia was entitled to protect its 'security interests' were set aside. Merkel refused to disavow past policies but Wolfgang Schäuble, her long-time CDU finance minister declared: 'I was wrong, we were all wrong'.[5]

On 24 February, Chancellor Scholz stood up in the Bundestag to announce 'a watershed in the history of our continent'. He added that the issue is whether brute power is allowed to prevail 'or whether we have it in us to keep warmongers like Putin in check. That requires strength of our own'.[6] The *New York Time*s described it as Germany's biggest foreign policy shift since World War II. It was what Scholz himself proclaimed as a

Zeitenwende, epochal shift.[7] It had quickly followed Berlin's decision to freeze the recently completed Nord 2 gas pipeline.

Almost as big a turnaround was the admission by President Steinmeier, five weeks into the war, that he had badly misread Putin:

> 'We clung on to bridges that Russia no longer believed in, despite warnings from our partners. My impression was that Vladimir Putin wouldn't risk the complete economic, political and moral ruin of his country in his imperial madness. On that point I, like others, was wrong'.[8] He had been an ally of Gerhard Schröder's for decades but showed no sign of publicly disassociating himself with the unrepentant architect of Germany's Russia-dependent energy strategy who, in 1998, had reassuringly informed him that 'You fit in with us'.[9]

Once the dust had settled, it turned out that there was a conspicuous lack of enthusiasm at the top of German politics to match words with action. There was no desire to launch an enquiry into deep policy failures or act on re-armament promises.[10] The reception for the online address of Volodymyr Zelensky in the German Bundestag on 17 March was instructive. It was described as 'a courteous yet devastating oration of less than ten minutes' in which he 'exposed the fictions on which German policy has been based since the Cold War: that it was safe to become dependent on Russian energy; that repeating the mantra "never again" meant that war and genocide could not return to Europe'. Yet the applause was short lived and perfunctory, and nobody was inclined to ask him any questions.[11] Indeed, the video link with their guest was cut while there was still clapping, and the order of business continued.[12]

The German commentator Stefan Meist was soon expressing doubts about the 'policy revolution'. He reflected on 18 June that: 'To change a political culture which is lacking any strategic thinking is not possible with one decision, it is a process which takes place at the moment with external pressure. Only a fundamental, irreversible policy change will bring a cultural change, with Germany leading Europe in this fundamental crisis'.[13]

Three months into the war, the evidence was mounting that the change in the official German outlook might be based on theatrical role-playing to ward off scorn from an audience shocked by Germany's negligent attitude towards Russia.

In late May 2022, German leverage within the EU remained strong enough for the European Commission to issue guidelines on sanctions, effectively allowing European states to pay for Russian gas in roubles as Putin had demanded. Germany promised that an embargo was coming, but not before the end of 2022. In the wake of this decision, a German commentator observed that 'it has become obvious in recent months that many European states care more about ending the war than about who wins'.[14] He went on to claim that France and Germany were determined not to let go of the reins. They 'have jealously guarded their position as the ultimate decision makers in Europe'. But open impatience about how a Franco-German agenda dominated EU affairs was articulated by other sizeable member-states, notably Italy and Poland.[15]

Sweden and Finland quickly took steps to be received into NATO, with backing at home transcending normal party divisions. They could all too easily imagine themselves as countries in danger of assault by Russia because of their proximity. But in Germany especially, it was difficult to let go of the habit of viewing Ukraine as an ill-defined territory or a problem impeding the normalisation of ties between countries with different social systems and even moral codes but which had a powerful incentive to trade with one another. The prominent Ukraine historical expert Timothy Snyder countered what he saw as continued myopia in Berlin:

> 'As a former colonial power in Ukraine, and as the economic partner of the current colonial power in Ukraine, Germans were doubly obliged to listen to Ukrainians, ideally before the war, and at the very latest in the days and weeks after the war broke out. This simply did not take place'.[16]

Much of the blame for German numbness to the march of events was directed at Jürgen Habermas, Germany's best-known intellectual who had long argued that his nation needed to be in the vanguard of removing nationalism from the European consciousness. He wrote a long article in mid-2022, clearly meant to dampen down active solidarity for Ukraine, by arguing that Ukraine's hopes of victory were hopeless and there was no point in providing armed support. In his piece only one East European had 'a name and a voice...Vladimir Putin'. Snyder observed that 'it is the first rule of post-colonial discourse that the colonized are to be allowed to speak. Yet Habermas gives no Ukrainian a name, let alone a voice'.[17]

When a package of sanctions designed to inflict severe damage on the Russian economy was announced by the EU in April 2022, no plan for powering Europe, that didn't involve buying from Putin, was placed on the table. Thanks to pressure from the junior government partner, the Greens, Germany remained stubbornly on course to phase out the country's nuclear power industry. By 2020, Germany had reduced the nuclear proportion of its energy supply from 30 percent to 11 percent. Then, on the last day of 2021, even as the possibility of a conflict in Ukraine grew ever likelier, half of its remaining six nuclear reactors were shut down.[18]

The emphasis on Green economics, not just in Germany, helps to explain why the percentage of Russian gas consumed in the EU rose from 30 percent in 2016 to nearly 47 percent by early 2021.[19] Powerful business lobbies, committed to maintaining trade connections with Moscow and Beijing in all seasons, were unwilling to retreat as war returned to Europe. On 9 April 2022, Herbert Diess, the chief executive of Volkswagen called for a negotiated settlement between Russia and Ukraine so that sanctions could be lifted to avoid damaging the German economy.[20]

Arguments raged about Germany's reluctance to supply Ukraine with the means to defend itself. What was seen as Scholz's obstructionism and double-speak, produced mounting fury not only among Ukraine's allies but also at home. The German weekly *Der Spiegel* believed that initially his reluctance to send arms to Ukraine stemmed from the belief that its cause was hopeless.[21] After Ukraine surprised most of the world by repelling most attacks, his obduracy persisted. Writing on 21 April 2022, Wolfgang Münchau believed that this was due to both he and his Social Democratic Party (SPD) remaining 'heavily invested in the bilateral relationship with Russia, which is arguably the most important strategic relationship in post-war Europe'.[22]

Scholz displayed extraordinary chutzpah as the storm over his stance intensified. In early June 2022, he was claiming that 'no other country gives as much military aid to Ukraine as Germany does'.[23] Earlier, the conservative opposition leader Friedrich Merz lambasted him as a miserable friend to Ukraine and speculated that he might even be pursuing a 'hidden agenda'.[24] Bringing about a shorter war and quicker negotiations by slow-walking military help, has been widely seen as a key plank of this agenda.[25]

According to Ulrich Speck, another German foreign-policy analyst, 'taken as a whole, the West [in mid-2022] is providing Ukraine [with] "just enough" weaponry to survive, not enough to regain territory. The idea seems to be that Russia should not win, but also not lose'.[26]

It was surprising how swiftly the *Zeitenwende* which was supposed to define a morally-grounded approach to a war-making Russia, dropped from Scholz's vocabulary. He successfully lobbied his fellow German head of the European Commission to relax the sanctions regime to enable Russian goods to cross Lithuania and enter Kaliningrad by that route. For at least one seasoned commentator, it was a clear sign that Merkel-style 'deviousness in indecision remains the prevailing norm of German politics'.[27] Another, the British historian Timothy Garton Ash, helped popularise the term *scholzing* which came to be described as communicating good *intentions* only to use/*find*/invent any reasons imaginable to *delay these* or prevent them from happening.[28]

Increasingly, the main bedrock of the German Chancellor's support, lay with the left-wing of the SPD from which emanated much 'navel gazing, moralizing hand-wringing and impotent hyperventilating over the Russo-Ukraine war'. It cleaved to a 'nostalgia-driven foreign policy discourse that eschews any kind of actual analysis of Russian behaviour or ideology'.[29]

Rather brazenly, he chose to ignore the low standing in which Germany was held by other EU members and in July 2022, demanded a change in the decision-making process of the EU which would strengthen the grip of the most powerful states. His call for the abolition of national vetoes on foreign policy decisions is seen in some quarters as a bid to prevent other states frustrating neo-mercantilist foreign policies involving first Russia and later China.[30] Poland's Prime Minister Morawiecki went as far as calling it a bid to ensure 'the tyranny of the strongest' prevails in the EU.[31]

Germany was also a key driver of the European Commission proposal, in the same month, that member states reduce their demand for natural gas by 15 percent over the coming winter months. EU Commission chief Von der Leyen called for the entity to be given special powers to enforce cuts if Russia halted gas supplies.[32] The measure clearly benefited Germany while countries like Spain, whose gas was supplied from North Africa, would need to make sacrifices. However, European solidarity had frayed ever since Merkel had insisted that a 'prudent' Germany would not share the pain disproportionately borne by the Mediterranean EU states during the post-2009 Eurozone crisis. Spain's energy minister borrowed from the Merkel playbook and crisply declared that energy rationing was unnecessary because Spain had not lived beyond its means from an energy point of view.[33]

The longer it stayed in office, Scholz's government revealed an inclination to be didactic towards less powerful EU states and towards the home population on the environment and health issues. The autocratic tinge may have been a legacy of his own much earlier immersion in far-left politics. As deputy leader of the Young Socialists, for much of the 1980s, he had visited East Germany a total of nine times between September 1983 and June 1988.[34] Due to his then markedly anti-NATO stance, he was received by the second most important functionary in East Germany, Egon Krenz, on two of the visits.[35]

Immediately prior to the invasion, the disposition of leading EU decision-makers suggested an inclination to accept the fate of Ukraine being decided according to 'the might is right principle'. But this reaction was quickly replaced by astonishment at the extent of the national popular mobilization to try and repel the invaders. Combined with the acute shortcomings quickly exposed in the numerically vastly superior Russian side, the depth of the resistance foiled the planned conquest.

Perhaps almost as remarkable was the fact that Ukraine produced a leader for the critical hour. Volodymyr Zelensky seemed a highly unlikely warrior President when he was elected in April 2019, with 72 percent of the vote. He was an actor of Jewish origin from a Russian-speaking part of south-east Ukraine. Until he acquired enduring fame in 2015, by playing a schoolteacher who declaimed on a video about the everyday corruption affecting many Ukrainians, he had, prior to launching a political career, been best-known for his roles in comedy.[36] When Russian forces tried to seize Kyiv, he spurned an American offer to spirit him and his family out of Ukraine, answering, 'I need weapons, not a ride'. He then rallied the population and the army during the first terrible hours of war.[37]

Four months earlier, less than ten percent of Ukrainians had felt he was doing a good job.[38] His refusal to flee, in face of forces who had been given orders to kill him and members of his government, transformed his image. No other European leaders had faced such an ordeal. In the months that followed, he delivered nightly video addresses on social media to stiffen resolve. His actor-trained voice led to his eloquence being compared with the wartime addresses of Winston Churchill. He forsook his trademark dark suit and tie and dressed in various shades of army green. His unshaven face and determined expression became internationally-known symbols of the resistance. He usually only left his fortified government offices to visit troops on the front line or wounded soldiers in hospital. He was turning his prowess in communications into a weapon of war, making himself in the process a surprisingly effective wartime leader who might in time become known as a great one.

Putin's failure to take the measure of Zelensky and imagine that the Ukrainian leader would soon turn into a figure of global renown, while eventually he would be indicted by the International Criminal Court at The Hague for the abduction of countless numbers of Ukrainians, was perhaps the greatest miscalculation of his political career. The journalist Owen Matthews has written:

> 'What Putin did not understand when he chose to launch his invasion in February was that behind the comic Mr. Nice Guy exterior, Zelensky was actually a trained lawyer who had ruthlessly built his Kvartal 95

entertainment company into Ukraine's biggest TV production house and earned himself tens of millions in the process'.[39]

In the first months of the war, he made it clear that he would never accept a dictated peace imposed over the heads of his people. According to polls, his public determination to fight for the recovery of all occupied lands was a sentiment shared by the overwhelming majority.

His global visibility was not only due to his particular skill set. The revolution in media communications enabled his rallying calls to reach far and wide through mobile phones, laptops, and more traditional media, providing a crucial advantage in propaganda terms for the initially poorly-armed Ukrainians. In what has been described by David Patrikarakos as 'digital statesmanship', he used 'humour, pathos and bathos to make Ukraine's case, and in so doing, he created a new form of wartime leadership'.[40]

Western leaders, keen to shield themselves from Putin's aggression or avert their gaze from the full horrors of his assault on civilians, were stupefied by the emergence of Zelensky as a potent symbol of defiance against armed might. During a global recession in democratic leadership, he proved to be an *affirmer* of personal liberty and national self-determination while increasingly, many in the political classes in the West preferred to *ration* or surreptitiously *curtail* individual freedoms.

For several decades at least, important countries had been governed by colourless technocrats who kept a distance from the people and often seemed to regard elections as ordeals meant to be got over as quickly as possible. They had a managerial world view and increasingly viewed citizens with the visage of an impatient overseer. The electorate were not their democratic masters, but instead subjects who were required to follow instructions being drawn up in seats of corporate power about how to live their lives in a new post-carbon world committed to net zero green energy. With increasing boldness, global campaigns were launched to de-industrialise national economies and even phase out animal farming in the name of eco-purity.

Zelensky has kept a prudent silence about such intra-Western struggles. His discourse suggests that he regards the Ukrainian people as the country's greatest asset. If true, it means that he's unlikely in the future to evangelise in favour of a carbon-free future in a country which needs to restore its industry and agriculture in order to be viable.

He has been unafraid to cross verbal swords with venerable figures, like Henry Kissinger as well as the procrastinating German leadership, if he felt that their public stance harmed Ukraine.[41] In a remarkably short time, he acquired far stronger recognition on the world stage than any other contemporary European political figure. He beamed messages explaining Ukraine's struggle to mass audiences at cultural events across continents. Global celebrities from Bono to Piers Morgan and politicians from Rishi Sunak to Justin Trudeau lionised him. He was seen as the 'New Thing' and they and many others strove to ensure that some of his stardust rubbed off on them. But conspiracy theories also proliferated about Zelensky. Left and right, as well as those who saw Putin as some crusader for Western traditionalism, branded the Ukrainian as: an unscrupulous money-making adventurer; a warmonger seeking to bring about nuclear war; and a pawn for neo-conservatives and the Western arms industry. In summary, in these quarters, he had no agency but was an accessory of various dark forces.

Such views emanated from a left which saw Putin as a successor of Soviet power and capable of delivering a knock-out blow to the West. They also gripped others on the political right opposed to US involvement in foreign conflicts, or who saw Zelensky as discredited because of his close association with ruling US Democrats. But on his visit to the United States on 21 December 2022, when he held talks with the President and addressed Congress, he very much showed that he was his own man. He gracefully received the plaudits of the political establishment and skillfully made the case for continued US and NATO help to repulse Russian aggression, but he carefully refrained from implicating himself in divisive internal US conflicts by any word or gesture.

In his previous encounters with European leaders, this independence of spirit had already been on display. He had shown how it was possible for someone who had once played clowns for a living to evolve into a tough leader. On 17 June 2022, as host to France's Emmanuel Macron, he recoiled as his visitor attempted to pull him into a PR-friendly embrace. Displaying Chaplinesque wiles, he 'looked as though he'd rather be fighting in the trenches...when the smarmy French leader...wrapped a crisply-laundered sleeve around his torso. Zelensky simply scowled at the floor, evidently displeased with the posturing'.[42]

In previous weeks, the Ukrainian had openly rebuked Macron for wishing to force Ukraine to the negotiating table'.[43] In May 2022, with France then holding the EU Presidency, Macron poured cold water over Ukraine's hopes of early EU membership after the EU had extended a formal invitation. He made it plain that there would be no EU membership for Ukraine for decades, and that Kyiv would have to be content to belong to a meaningless annex.[44] Common ground between the Franco-German duopoly would be steadily eroded in 2022. But they remained opposed to any 'system transformation' brought about by Russia's war on Ukraine. They feared that as more and more of the post-1994 EU member states surpassed the Mediterranean states in economic vigour, the EU's centre of gravity would shift eastwards. A Ukraine exporting key products and knocking at the EU's door for membership would simply confirm the steady erosion of Franco-German hegemony. Thus, there may have been an unspoken but very real meeting of minds between Russia and the key EU players about the need to relegate Ukraine to secondary status.

Ukraine fears that Macron might be capable of imposing a negotiated peace that devalues the huge battlefield sacrifice, with an estimated 100,000 military having been killed in 2022. Some solace is obtained by his current political weakness. He lost his parliamentary majority in mid-2022, and his vision of a European defense community independent of the United States, largely evaporated. His fortunes may yet revive but in the first stages of the Ukraine war his political reputation seems to have followed the downward trajectory of another once young and ambitious leader, Tony Blair, who was a dominating presence in the EU until his fateful miscalculation over Iraq in 2003.

Tensions with Germany showed no signs of abating, however. 'Peace politicians' were public figures committed to a Russophile *Ostpolitik* in all seasons and they were visible in nearly all the mainstream parties, but especially the SPD. For years, Sigmar Gabriel, a former party leader and foreign minister, had been assiduous in promoting the view that Germany's special ties with Russia must never be jeopardised, whatever misconduct could be laid at Putin's door. He was the most egregious of a number of SPD leaders who combined left-wing rhetoric with acquiring a bulging portfolio of financial interests. He secured a place on the board of Deutsche Bank, through the good offices of Qatar, a major shareholder in the troubled German institution.[45]

SPD ideologues and wheeler-dealers in the corporate business world gave the party a seedy image. They were among the chief actors who ensured that Scholz's supposed historic shift in foreign and security policy remained still-born. On 22 October 2022, it was revealed that the planned increases in defense spending were being substantially cut back. On 2 December, Scholz talked of returning 'to a peace order that worked...if there is a willingness in Russia to go back to this peace order'.[46] He had only recently returned from a visit to China, where he did not disguise his wish to enjoy economic cooperation on preferential terms with a China that increasingly was behaving like a rogue power rather than a country with an interest in maintaining a predictable global environment. (In March 2023, he was the only Western leader to send congratulations to Xi Jinping upon embarking upon a third term as China's leader, widely seen as acquiring the job for life).

Scholz was very much the antithesis of Zelensky. Politics had occupied his entire professional existence and he was married to someone with a similar profile who was a minister in a regional government in what had formerly been East Germany. His formative years had been spent on the far-left, whereas Zelensky was fortunate to come of age when the hold of Marxist indoctrination was weakening in Ukraine. Scholz had risen in a party that increasingly relished lecturing the citizenry on lifestyle, consumption patterns, private behaviour, and moral outlook. Gone were the days when the SPD hoped to be judged by its skill in protecting the public well-being. Increasingly, it stood for a moral agenda based on cultural and environmental issues, upon which it did not expect to be questioned.

It was by issuing reassuring appeals to the hard left voters of the ex-communist party, now known as Die Linke, that he enabled the previously declining SPD to become the largest party in the 2021 elections.[47] Such a political force, nostalgic to some degree for features of communist life, now existed nowhere else in the former Soviet bloc.

The political environment in which Scholz had long operated meant that he may not have found it unduly arduous to trade with the Kremlin during times of uneasy peace or seek to mollify its occupant once he had embarked on outright war. The Chancellor was disinclined to sanction or demote compromised figures, despite the opprobrium that they faced for their pre-war roles. By contrast, Zelensky moved firmly against the oligarch Igor Kolomoisky, who was his business ally prior to his election as President.[48] Three top-level resignations occurred at the start of 2023, leading the economist and government adviser Tymofiy Mylovanov to claim that corruption is episodic while the fight against it is systemic.[49]

It remains to be seen how long Zelensky's political ascendancy will last in the face of the shifting sands of war. Troubling choices inevitably lie ahead for him. Does he defy many at home by opting for a compromise peace that leaves territory originally Ukrainian in the hands of invaders? Or does he risk losing active Western backing by holding out for the complete expulsion of Russian forces from Ukrainian lands? He knows there are lukewarm well-wishers in the chancelleries of Europe who, as Scholz's rhetoric indicates, have no qualms about treating brutal leaders as respectable partners. They have as good as said that they do not wish a Ukraine, which Zelensky told the US Congress was 'alive and kicking', to be a strong force in continental affairs. Thus, the principle of anti-selection, the preference for the drab and the mediocre to occupy leadership, remains entrenched even in the face of an elemental conflict sending shock waves across Europe. Zelensky's flair in directing a global influence campaign to keep his nation alive, invites suspicion in influential quarters when admiration might be a more appropriate reaction from the main European democracies.

Time may well show that Zelensky's global reach is probably far greater than his domestic strength. The war may have revealed a spirit of unity at home but, inevitably, enormous tensions will have built up during the course of it. Post-conflict Ukrainian politics is likely to be messy and disputatious, and Zelensky may prove a successful war leader who finds reconciling different demands and interests in a ravaged landscape hard to accomplish. It may well be that no single individual can perform such a task, which will ensure that he remains head and shoulders above everyone else, in the estimation of most Ukrainians.

President Biden's visit to Kyiv on 20 February 2023 was a sign that Ukraine was getting closer to being integrated into Euro-Atlantic security structures. But even if Ukraine obtained the entry keys to sit at the main table in European counsels, what would it find? Three decades after communism unraveled in Europe, epic institutional groupthink is easy to detect. A self-absorbed political class, full of schemes to dragoon citizens to accept costly and unpalatable experiments, seems to have re-occupied many of the seats of power.

Britain, ironically the main West European champion of Ukraine, has left largely unused the freedoms acquired from leaving the EU's rules and structures. Instead of building a distinctive British economy based on free trade and renewed emphasis on science and technology, it seems intent to replicate the state-led corporatist model of the European entity which it left in 2020. The drab profiles and uninspiring approach to their duties of elite figures in national capitals, as well as Brussels, has eroded the legitimacy of this managerial brand of politics, involving the concentration of power and the imposition of suffocating norms on the general population. Their assumptions about how to plan for challenges and handle crises have too often been found painfully wanting. Efforts to preserve important aspects of post-Cold War order and prosperity have been incoherent and low-grade in the face of mounting challenges to a rules-based international order.

Whatever its exact outcome, the war in Ukraine is likely to have multiple impacts on Europe. Civil, and especially military, leaders in Ukraine have shown the valour and determination that has been in painfully short supply in Western Europe for a long time. It will be no surprise if the largely Franco-German dominated Europe, shaped by figures who are profiled in this book, is reconfigured. What may hasten a political realignment is the realisation that however much Ukraine suffered in 2022, Europe as a whole had a lucky escape. Given the dangerous state of the world and the advantages that tyrants and fanatics enjoy outside a shrinking number of democracies, Europe may not easily obtain a second chance if leadership remains so deficient in the face of looming threats. The unheroic herd behaviour that characterised the stance of many of the key European decision-makers in the countdown to war could have enabled Putin to accomplish his goals if he had been better prepared militarily. On 11 October 2022, looking back at how Europe had lost its way, the EU's foreign affairs chief Josep Borrell acknowledged that failed policies towards Russia had left Europe vulnerable, but he refused to dwell on individuals or countries.[50]

In August 2022, one of the turn-of-the-century European statesmen Wolfgang Schäuble, a veteran of German governments for decades, bared his soul. He said that Lech Kaczynski, President of Poland, was right in 2008 to say that Putin will first attack 'Georgia, then Ukraine, then the Baltic States and then Poland...we knew everything, and we refused to see it'.[51]

He was as good as admitting that, in governing circles, there was a great aversion to independent thinking that was based on acquiring information from multiple sources.[52] The reliance on group think was indeed strong and it is unlikely to be easily broken. This was shown on 18 January 2023 when Olaf Scholz defied a clamor from European NATO allies to allow Ukraine the use of German-made Leopard tanks. One of the world's best tanks, more than 2,000 of them were then in service in Europe, meaning Ukraine would have a large pool to draw on.[53] Germany's permission was needed before other countries could send them. Scholz was reported as saying that he would only lift his objections if the US agreed to send its own tanks. Poland said it would defy Germany and send them anyway, while Zelensky declared: it is 'not the right strategy to say we will deliver the weapons if someone else outside Europe does… Ukraine is fighting for Europe. We need all the strength we can.[54] Six days later, Scholz bowed to pressure from NATO and indeed from coalition members. He announced that Germany would send a company of Leopard tanks to Ukraine and grant licenses allowing allies to do likewise with the ones in their possession. This step was belatedly taken only after Germany's credibility, as a reliable international actor, had taken a fierce battering.

The GDP of the ten East European candidate countries for EU membership in 2002 was a mere 5 percent of the EU total but, by 2023, it stood at 15 percent.[55] Perhaps if the centre of gravity in the Euro-Atlantic sphere extends outwards from Paris and Berlin, networks of power that colonised positions in the EU will be challenged. In the Baltic area, women politicians have emerged as outspoken advocates of resolute steps to protect against Russian aggression. Finland's prime minister Sanna Marin has been unequivocal about the need for Russia to relinquish its conquests. Her counterpart in Estonia, Kaja Kallas, whose mother was deported far into Russia when she was six months old, shares her view and has publicly upbraided French and German leaders for their readiness to appease Russia in the past.[56] They insist that Russia must not be humiliated, in order to avoid disequilibrium and a power vacuum in Eastern Europe. But they are incapable of showing how 'a small, poor state in a big, large country with an exaggerated sense of its own power and influence' can provide stable continental ballast.[57]

However, such figures from the Baltic region continue to be relegated by the world's media in favour of the Swedish environmental radical Greta Thunberg. In October 2022, despite being tireless in demanding that the public drastically reduce its consumption of animal foods and energy, she insisted that: 'I don't want to go into politics because it's too toxic'.[58]

This is probably a sensible position for Thunberg to take as closing down industrial production or restricting the output of farms is unlikely to be a vote-winner, however well-regarded the advocates of such steps find themselves in influential wings of the media. Her Malthusian view that humans have over-reached and grown too dominant and possibly numerous, is one with powerful intellectual backing in Europe. If state electorates were confined to university towns and cities, the manifesto offering an ecological hair shirt for humanity would quite possibly obtain a sweeping endorsement. But there is a war raging in Europe and philosophers who think that Europe should tend its own organic garden, irrespective of the horrors that may spill over the perimeter fence, face unexpected opposition.

Estonia's Kaja Kallas sees herself as someone who is part of the community of national voters who elected her, rather than as someone who is apart from them and entitled to interfere profoundly in their lives. Her part of the world saw too many experiments in which citizens were treated as disposable fools or inconvenient obstacles to a questionable progress. It is possible that the upheavals in Ukraine will tilt the balance away from remote elites, whose record as clear-eyed decision-makers has been increasingly found wanting. In the pre-Ukraine-war decades, mercantilism and mediocrity in West European power centres, at times almost seemed to match the malevolence and megalomania that gradually became entrenched in Russian power centres after the year 2000. Neither part of Europe can realistically expect to recover easily, or hope to thrive, unless both West and East manage to transcend these failings.

---

[1] Melanie Amann, 'The Calamitous Errors of Germany's Russia Policy', *Der Spiegel*, 25 February 2022.
[2] Mehreen Khan et al, 'Macron floats EU security pact with Russia in split from US calls for unity', *Financial Times*, 19 January 2022.
[3] David M. Herszenhorn and Giorgio Leali, 'Defiant Putin mauls Macron in Moscow', *EUobserver*, 8 February 2022, https://www.politico.eu/article/vladimir-putin-russia-welcomes-emmanuel-macron-france-into-his-lair-kremlin-ukraine/, accessed 9 February 2022.
[4] Twitter, @Ischinger, 4 April 2022.
[5] Matthew Karnitschnig, 'Putin's useful German idiots', *PoliticoEU*, 28 March 2022. https://www.politico.eu/article/putin-merkel-germany-scholz-foreign-policy-ukraine-war-invasion-nord-stream-2/, accessed 28 March 2022.
[6] Bruno Macaes, 'Europe's Illusion of Peace Has Been Irrevocably Shattered', *Time magazine*, 2 March 2022, https://time.com/6153168/ukraine-invasion-europe-war/, accessed 3 March 2022.
[7] Katrin Beholden and Steve Erlanger, 'Ukrainian war pushes Germans to change', *New York Times*, 12 April 2022.
[8] Oliver Moody, 'Germany's Toxic Legacy', *Times*, 6 April 2022.
[9] Florian Kain, 'Das is Schröder's Macht-Netzwerk', *Die Bild*, 14 March 2023, https://www.bild.de/politik/inland/politik-inland/brisantes-buch-so-trieb-schroeders-macht-netzwerk-uns-in-die-russland-abhaengigk-83196354.bild.html, accessed 22 March 2023.
[10] See Charlemagne, 'Germans have been living in a dream', *Economist*, 21 July 2022.
[11] Daniel Johnson, 'This war is a shameful episode in German history', *Daily Telegraph*, 19 March 2022.
[12] Katharina Roll, 'Germany and Ukraine—solidarity without action is not enough', *Deutsche Welle*, 18 March 2022.
[13] Twitter, Stefan Meister, @meistefan1 18 June 2022.
[14] Ralph Gertz Sledgehammer, 'Why Europe hedges its support for Ukraine', *Wall Street Journa*l, 22 May 2022.

---

[15] Wilhelmina Pressmen, 'Poland and Italy "fed up" with EU bureaucracy, PM Morawiecki says', *Politico EU*, 22 December 2022, https://www.politico.eu/article/poland-and-italy-fed-up-with-eu-bureaucracy-polish-pm-says/, accessed 22 December 2022.
[16] Timothy Snyder, 'Germans have been involved in the war, chiefly on the wrong side', *Frankfurter Allgemeine Zeitung*, 27 June 2022, https://www.faz.net/aktuell/politik/ausland/ukraine-germans-have-been-involved-in-the-war-an-answer-to-juergen-habermas-18131718.html, accessed 30 June 2022.
[17] Snyder, 'Germans have been involved'.
[18] Michael Shellenberger, 'The West's Green Delusions Empowered Putin', *Common Sense*, 1 March 2022, https://www.thefp.com/p/the-wests-green-delusions-empowered, accessed 3 March 2022.
[19] Shellenberger, 'The West's Green'.
[20] Giulia Bottaro, 'Ukraine should negotiate with Putin to protect German economy, VW boss says', *Daily Telegraph*, 9 May 2022.
[21] Melanie Amann, 'Why has Germany been so slow to deliver weapons', *Der Spiegel,* 3 June 2022, https://www.spiegel.de/international/germany/olaf-scholz-and-ukraine-why-has-germany-been-so-slow-to-deliver-weapons-a-7cc8397b-2448-49e6-afa5-00311c8fedce, accessed 5 June 2022.
[22] Wolfgang Münchau, 'Olaf Scholz is becoming Putin's most valuable ally', *Spectator,* 21 April 2022.
[23] Twitter, *Dw Politics*, @dw_politics, 7 June 2022.
[24] Amann, 'Why has Germany'.
[25] Michael Nienaber, 'Germany's Scholz accused of slow-walking Ukraine arms supplies', *Bloomberg*, 14 April 2022, https://www.bloomberg.com/news/articles/2022-04-14/germany-s-scholz-accused-of-slow-walking-ukraine-weapon-supplies, accessed 14 April 2022.
[26] Steve Erlanger, 'Gaps in Arms Supplies to Ukraine Point to Countries' Divergent Strategies', *New York Times*, 15 July 2022.
[27] Holman W. Jenkins Jr, 'Germany's Energy Crisis and Surrender', *Wall Street Journal*, 20 July 2022.
[28] Twitter, @fromTGA, 19 January 2023.
[29] Georg Löfflmann, Department of Political and International studies, University of Warwick, Twitter, @gloefflmann, 2 September 2022.
See also Georg Löfflmann, 'Germany's military muddle over Ukraine', *Spectator Online*, 24 April 2022, https://www.spectator.co.uk/article/germany-s-military-muddle-over-ukraine/, accessed 2 May 2022.
[30] Wolfgang Münchau, 'Herr Scholz goes to Europe', *Euro Intelligence*, 30 August 2022.
[31] Preussen, 'Poland and Italy'.
[32] 'Russian gas again flowing into Europe via Nord Stream 1 pipeline', *Deutsche Welle*, 21 July 2022, https://www.dw.com/en/russian-gas-again-flowing-into-europe-via-nord-stream-1-pipeline/a-62545705, accessed 27 July 2022.
[33] Ignacio Fariza, 'No podemos asumir um sacrificio sobre el que no nos han pedido opinion', *El Pais*, 21 July 2022.
[34] Katja Hoyer, 'Germany grapples with the limits of pacifism', *Financial Times*, 4 February 2023.

[35] Dr Hubertus Knabe, 'Is Germany's leader so soft on Russia because he's an ex-Marxist who savaged NATO and bowed to Moscow?' *Daily Mail*, 17 May 2022.
[36] James Hookway, 'Who Is Volodymyr Zelensky' *Wall Street Journal*, 24 March 2022.
[37] Brendan O'Neill, 'The leadership and bravery of Volodymyr Zelensky', *Spectator*, 27 February 2022.
[38] 'The Righteous Glorification of Volodymyr Zelenskyy', *CEPA*, 28 July 2022, https://cepa.org/the-righteous-glorification-of-volodymyr-zelesnkyy/, accessed 1 August 2022.
[39] Owen Matthews, 'What Zelensky has taken from his former TV career', *Spectator*, 29 October 2022.
[40] David Patrikarakos, 'Ukraine and the myth of peace', *UnHerd*, https://unherd.com/2023/02/ukraine-and-the-myth-of-peace/, accessed 24 February 2023.
[41] Ron Kampeas, 'Zelensky to Kissinger: The world didn't adapt to the Nazis, we're not adapting to Putin', *Jewish Journa*l, 26 May 2022. https://jewishjournal.org/2022/05/26/zelensky-to-kissinger-the-world-didnt-adapt-to-the-nazis-were-not-adapting-to-putin/, accessed 29 May 2022.
[42] David Averre, 'Macron leans in for an awkward hug', *Daily Mail*, 17 June 2022.
[43] Dominic Lawson, 'Boris Johnson is right and Emmanuel Macron is wrong. Saving Vladimir Putin's face is a mug's game', *Daily Mail*, 6 June 2022.
[44] Ann-Elisabeth Moutet, 'I defended Emmanuel Macron's approach to Russia - now it's unforgivable', *Daily Telegrap*h, 14 May 2022, https://www.telegraph.co.uk/news/2022/05/14/defended-emmanuel-macrons-approach-russia-now-unforgivable/.
[45] Reinhard Bingener, 'Russland und die SPD: Die Moskau-Connection', *Frankfurter Allgemeine Zeitung*, 13 March 2023, https://www.msn.com/de-de/nachrichten/politik/russland-und-die-spd-die-moskau-connection/ar-AA18zjYy.
[46] *Times* (London), 2 December 2022.
[47] James Hawes, 'The real reason Germany is always afraid', *Foreign Policy*, 19 April 2022, https://foreignpolicy.com/2022/04/19/the-real-reason-germany-is-always-afraid/, accessed 20 April 2022.
[48] Black, 'The demonisation'.
[49] Twitter, @TymofiyMylovanov, 24 January 2023. See also Tom Balmforth and Olena Harmash, 'Ukraine purges officials and governors in biggest shake-up of war', *Reuters*, 23 January 2023.
[50] 'EU Ambassadors Annual Conference 2022: Opening speech by High Representative Josep Borrell', *European Union External Action*, 10 October 2010, https://www.eeas.europa.eu/eeas/eu-ambassadors-annual-conference-2022-opening-speech-high-representative-josep-borrell_en, accessed 12 October 2010 .
[51] Stephan-Andreas Casdorff et al, 'Wolfgang Schäuble zum Ukraine-Krieg: Wir haben alles gewusst – und wollten es nicht sehen', *Tagesspiege*l, 18 September 2022, https://www.tagesspiegel.de/politik/wolfgang-schauble-kritisiert-krisenhilfe-der-staat-darf-nicht-die-illusion-erwecken-dass-das-grenzenlos-sei-8645221.html, accessed 20 December 2022.
[52] Martin Kulldorff provided this insight, Twitter, @MartinKulldorff.
[53] Guy Chazan and Laura Pitel, 'Free the Leopards!', *Financial Time*s, 23 January 2023.
[54] *Times of Israel*, 19 January 2023.
[55] Twitter, Daniel Foubert, @d_foubert, 5 March 2023.

---

[56] James Crisp, 'Europe's new 'Iron Lady' Kaja Kallas says the West mustn't negotiate with Putin', *Daily Telegraph*, 9 October 2022.
[57] Julian Lindley-French, 'Kontesting Kissinger', *The Lindley-French Analysi*s, 27 December 2022, https://lindleyfrench.blogspot.com/2022/12/kontesting-kissinger.html, accessed 29 December 2022.
[58] Twitter @GretaThunberg.

CONCLUSION

The five sections making up the book examine the careers of a cross-section of politicians and seek to show what their acquisition, retention, and (in most cases) retreat from power might reveal about the shifting contours of democracy over a seventy-year period.

The Cold War era politicians assessed in the first section were well aware that they could not rule or influence national conditions without acknowledging the desire for populations to enjoy some degree of leverage over decisions made in their name. Even Tito, an anti-democrat, was prepared to offer a Yugoslav road to socialism which offered more opportunity for citizens to control their own lives than anything seen in the heartlands of communism. The threat posed by Soviet communism to those parts of Europe that remained outside its orbit meant that competitive democracy could not be eroded or diluted, at least not overtly. Belgium, Finland, Italy, and Yugoslavia had just emerged from foreign occupation, the threat of such an occupation, a lengthy dictatorship, and civil war and Spaak, Kekkonen, Andreotti and Tito were aware that there were limits to how they exercised their control. Each of them was prepared to lower the temperature and make accommodation across the political spectrum. They operated in an era where left-right rivalry ceased to be as toxic as it had previously been, despite the continuation of the Cold War. They were politicians who were ready to be seen and to inform themselves about the conditions of the country. Their visibility and approachability were meant to cement their authority and underscore the claim that their actions were based on a defence of the national interest. Of course, self-interest also coloured their actions which were not always transparent or designed to ensure long-term stability. They were flawed individuals but arguably the international situation and the turbulent times their countries had lived through meant that they faced restraints, impeding abuses of power.

Such limitations were less evident in the careers of the four politicians from France and Germany who exercised sway towards the close of the Cold War and into the new century. France and Germany (even in its divided state between 1949 and 1990), never ceased to be pivotal countries influencing developments in *uncaptive* Europe from 1945 onwards. Attempts to heal internal traumas and cleavages were affected by partition and by France's painful retreat from empire. It was no small achievement that both countries managed to replace corrosive mutual rivalry with growing cooperation. The European institutions which both states heavily invested in, proved to be the means by which this historic breakthrough was consolidated. But the seemingly successful efforts at reconciliation failed to release energies capable of having a transformative effect on the political condition of Europe.

Leaderships in both countries used their weight in what, by 1993, had become the European Union, to pursue their own national interests rather than devote their energies towards creating a new post-national European order. Rhetoric notwithstanding, neither was able to find the political leaders ready to try to construct a different paradigm for the future. Much of the French elite clearly wished the EU to be the power that France alone could no longer be and sought to use the entity as a platform for unbridled French interests. Divided Germany sought to avoid such a proprietorial stance but after reunification it became one that increasingly defined Berlin's stance towards the common institutions. The management of the post-1999 single currency increasingly seemed to revolve around the needs of German industry as indeed did the common foreign and security policy. For several decades, those shaping the EU's geopolitical orientation ignored the danger from Russia, without whose oil and gas Germany would not have acquired such economic ascendancy over the rest of Europe.

Stagnation and drift soon overtook France after a period of recovery that occurred under de Gaulle's newly-established Fifth Republic. Presidents for over twenty years, Giscard and Mitterrand presided over a fractious political scene, with their tenures in office much influenced by personal considerations. The political class as a whole was resolved to satisfy its own appetites rather than show resolution and flair in tackling mounting social and economic problems. As a result, the gulf between the political world and much of French society started to look like a chasm before the century's close. The parties were all-too-obviously concerned with occupying power rather than doing anything of lasting value with it. The left in France and Germany diluted their effectiveness by declining to offer a class appeal based on the *social solidarity* of the people. Their right-wing rivals increasingly retreated from appealing to the citizenry on *national* grounds. Both instead 'converged in a common European project' which enabled coalitions to become the norm in both countries but at the price of destabilising the main parties.[1]

The two long-established political forces on the French left and right effectively vanished from the forefront of politics twenty years after Mitterrand's death in 1996. In Germany, the familiar red (SPD) and black (CDU) rivals slumped in appeal, though in less dramatic fashion. Gerhard Schröder and Angela Merkel, occupants of the chancellery between 1998 and 2020, increasingly detached themselves from their own parties. They resolved to stake Germany's economic fortunes and Europe's wider security on an energy compact with Russia, giving its tyrannical ruler sway over much of Europe, which no Soviet general-secretary had ever enjoyed. Parties grew remote from the lives of citizens as narrow lobbies, cliques and influential economic corporations filled the void left by the retreat of popular participation.

The encouraging journey embarked upon by both countries after 1950, proved to be an overdue burial of mutual enmity rather than the prelude for the transformation of European politics. The impact of Franco-German elites on their own national politics as well as on the emerging continental political order was of doubtful merit. The calibre of politicians reaching high office failed to stand out from that of predecessor generations in eras of representative rule. The decline in the quality of elective leadership impaired the quality of democracy at home and contributed to a growing political malaise across Europe.

Much of southern Europe suffered from the failure of the EU to be an effective agent of development and improved political standards. It meant that there was no external counter-balance to ensure that the retreat from dictatorship in the 1970s was not followed by a return to destabilising political practices. Countries where industrialisation had been patchy or non-existent and whose growth was undermined by class, regional or caste divisions, had fallen behind northern Europe between 1850 and 1914. The failure to define a national agenda for progress around which core groups could unite, led to instability and chronic bouts of unrest and dictatorship (in the case of Spain via a disastrous civil-war). In the late 20th century, it is possible to contend that there was a failure to make a fresh start and much of southern Europe slipped back into sterile partisanship and low-grade governmental decision-making.

Entropy revived even though the conditions for a break with the past seemed to be promising ones. The desire to bury authoritarian rule had been widely felt. The visionary possibilities presented by the European integration process seemed to herald the real possibility of a fresh start in Europe's south. Instead, the EU failed to be a guardian of progress. Its instruments of integration, such as transfer funds, were too unwieldy and easily diverted to be modernising agents. Instead, they scratched the surface of the political economy of Mediterranean Europe and failed to dislodge parasitic interests. The strategies employed by these interests in order to misuse or squander EU funding were often sophisticated ones. Thus, EU structural and cohesion funds (along with subsequent funding programmes) failed to stimulate the emergence of modern economies. The goal of narrowing the economic gap between Europe's north and south remained out-of-reach. Politics all too easily became orientated towards diverting this bounty from Brussels to favourite interests and flashy infrastructure projects of dubious long-term value. The reformist momentum of post-dictatorial politics sagged. Parties, disinclined to stick with a modernisation agenda, instead revived ideological disputes or else piled into new controversies around human identity imported from America. (This has been particularly evident in Spain). Politics became heavily personalised as an ethos of public service became hard to detect in an era of mounting economic adversity.

CONCLUSION

It was a bad omen for Greece that a confrontational figure like Andreas Papandreou was its leader during much of the 1980s, someone who treated the state as his plaything and relished disrupting EU business. Silvio Berlusconi, belonging to the right, provoked outrage with melodramatic stunts and attempts to enhance his economic power by using the state in a discretionary manner. In neither country did a reputation for probity and a temperate style of rule survive their periods in office. Djukanović of Montenegro and Sanchez of Spain were, on balance, less vulgar but a personalistic approach to power characterised their rule. Before the onset of the long post-2008 crisis in the Eurozone, such picturesque figures might have been seen as anachronisms, but it looks increasingly likely that mountebanks and manipulators will enjoy staying-power elsewhere in Europe as the struggle for power grows increasingly uninhibited.

Second only to the invasion of Ukraine, the mishandling of the Eurozone debt crisis arguably proved to be the worst calamity faced by Europe since the integration process got underway. It wasn't just in the Mediterranean zone that economic retrenchment and decline destabilised politics, but it was here that shortcomings in EU governance and crisis management, combining with local problems, were most acutely felt. Iberia, Italy and Greece were doing better before they became part of a financial supervisory process that was geared towards the interests of stronger northern members. Especially after the massive expenditure of state funds on the Covid crisis, the precarious financial state of a growing list of countries is now beginning to resemble that of the European South. The acute financial turbulence in Britain during the autumn of 2022 suggests that it could possibly be added to the list. Accordingly, Southern Europe might already be a showcase for the polarising, low-grade style of politics that could become the norms elsewhere, denting optimistic scenarios about Europe being able to put a politically disastrous twentieth-century safely behind it. Western and southern European growth rates have been among the lowest in the world. The decline cannot continue without a reduction in social programmes, which remain among the most extensive anywhere in the developed world. Strong welfare states have been a key legitimising factor for increasingly unloved European democracies, and if they are cut back, all bets may be off about the long-term survival of democracy.

Politics has grown more unpredictable and turbulent in various parts of Europe thanks, in part, to the retreat of the major twentieth-century ideologies, from the communist left to the traditional right and including liberalism and social democracy. In an era of growing polarisation, it is forgotten that advocates of these ideologies often competed with relative decorum. These contrasting doctrines once provided important parties with coherence and motivation, but no longer do so. New social movements with radical agendas, involving sharp adjustments to human identification, lifestyles and consumption patterns, are increasingly on the rise. Their approach is usually not characterised by restraint. They have started to fill the political vacuum, and their core appeal is to educated youth in urban areas. Electorally, they have yet to break through in most places and there is growing evidence that they do not see the need for elections in order to legitimise their power. Instead, it is minority nationalist movements, usually with an agenda of territorial autonomy or separation, which have emerged as the main 'anti-system' forces capable of winning elections in Britain and Spain. These 'independence' movements are replete with paradoxes. They wish to secede from old nation-states, but only to dissolve their fate in European or global arrangements which would allow them less autonomy than currently enjoyed under systems of sweeping devolution. They are really anti-nation-state movements masquerading as anti-centralist ones.

The central authority is assailed for its remoteness and unresponsiveness to local needs. Yet, once in charge of devolved institutions, they lose no time in usually centralising power and colonising institutions hitherto removed from political control, ranging from civic bodies, charities, and even the business sector. As the Scottish and Catalan examples shows, heavily personal leaderships are the norm, meaning that ruling parties lack any kind of serious interior life. Much energy is invested by leaders in promoting themselves as figures in the vanguard of cultural change for a new global era. This performative display of 'radical awareness' is often superficial and contrived but, thanks to social media, separatists can often win new converts with such a giddy approach.[2]

Challenges to the authority and legitimacy of nation-states are emerging on almost all sides. They are coming from global bureaucracies, powerful corporations, radical social campaigners, as well as assertive regions or non-state nations. So, despite the lack of success in turning the places that they govern into showcases for independence, minority nationalist movements enjoy staying power. Their dogmatism and intransigence reflect the tenor of much of the discussion about the contemporary world in academia and the media. Their gleeful expressions of ingratitude towards, often benevolently-inclined, nation-states mirror increasingly fashionable cultural attitudes that the young are exposed to. It would not be surprising if left-leaning parties, losing working-class appeal, similarly focus on personal identity and lifestyle in order to stay afloat politically. This has happened in Spain, in Italy it was attempted by the left without much success before the 2022 election, and the British Labour Party's pro-Green policies and identification with the radical trans movement, suggest it may have better prospects of reaching out to disaffected middle-class youth in the future.[3]

It would be understandable if worsening economic conditions and the diminishing ability of parties in government to improve them (whatever steps they take), reduced the appeal of holding office for political contenders. Machiavelli advised in Chapter IX of his 1513 work, *The Prince, that*: 'He who becomes a Prince through the favour of the people should always keep on good terms with them; which it is easy for him to do, since all they ask is not to be oppressed'.[4] But it now seems increasingly harder, upon reaching office, for democratic figures to establish such a compact with society. A time of economic crisis imposes strain and hardship on society, which, across Europe, are proving beyond the capacity of politicians in office to deal with. The lack of preparedness and indifferent calibre of politicians often adds to the problem. Too many quickly reveal how self-absorbed they are, or else become unduly focused on niche concerns. Such stances detach them from society where issues to do with lifestyle or the welfare of the planet continue to preoccupy small, albeit well-connected and often determined, portions of voters. Thoughtful manifestos tackling major societal problems are increasingly rare. Too many politicians eager for office prefer a 'depoliticised regime of technocratic governance [that] emphasises processes and rules and relegates ideals to the margins'.[5]

Increasingly, politicians lack real life experience due to the way they have been recruited. Disproportionate numbers now spring from the hot house atmosphere of academia, journalism, public relations, and full-time political activism. The numbers possessing useful skills or with experience in managing workforces, making things, rearing animals or growing crops, or serving in the military—perhaps never that high in some places—have slumped. It means that too many politicians depend on the state for status and income, rather than having a broader implantation in society. Such a stunted background deprives them of the hinterland needed to display authority and nerve in the sudden crises which are erupting with increasing frequency. It means ruling politicians are likelier to be buffeted by events, inclined to appease the views of the loudest voices in venomous disputes over personal identity, and shrink from the task of appealing to solidarity across a fractured social and economic landscape. In not a few cases, it is hard to avoid the conclusion that ambitious politicians, keen to benefit from their careers and give little back, simply do not like human beings very much. They have few attachments to Abrahamic religions that urge altruism or modesty in behaviour. Their connections with groups seeking improvements in society are tenuous at best. For such single-minded managerial types, it is not hard to endorse global moves designed to create a universal health regime supervised by the United Nations, or a globally-agreed taxation system which means elections cease to determine the fiscal policies of nation-states. Hubristic politicians obsessed with their own personal star, and who sometimes view humanity itself as a burden or an obstacle to progress, are increasingly noticeable especially in Anglosphere countries such as Scotland, New Zealand and Canada.

In such a blighted atmosphere, individuals with talents as administrators, business leaders, orators, or campaigners for reform, often find excuses to avoid a political career. The strain, uncertainty, exposure to often hostile saturation media coverage, and absorption in superficiality a great deal of the time, repel many. It is harder to see how, once in office, politicians can accomplish serious undertakings that make a positive difference to the country, due to external constraints and the decline in effectiveness of bureaucracies that they are supposed to rely on. The dissatisfaction of voters with their performance is more easily brought to bear than before, owing to the arrival of the 24 hours news cycle, and the explosion in media platforms that specialise in controlling narratives and in denouncing various shortcomings of the political order. An occupation possessing arguably fewer psychological compensations than in the past plunges the holder into dealing with problems that grow steadily far more complex as a turbulent new century advances. The intractable Eurozone crisis and the damage caused to a string of national economies, the political warfare in Britain initiated after the decision to quit the EU, the costly and divisive approach to the Covid pandemic, and the war in Ukraine, are only the most prominent issues that have bedevilled the practice of politics. Each of these may prove to be ultimately passing afflictions. But it will be possibly much harder to prevent the democratic order being swamped by the sheer incompatibility between the agenda of elites and what ordinary citizens prefer.

The preference for remote and costly technocratic solutions for problems, real or imagined, particularly in the environmental sphere, ones that leave little room for considering the wishes of citizens who fail to see any advantage in it for them, threatens to derail democratic politics.[6] It is striking that technocratic environmentalism, involving urban-inspired plans for transforming the countryside, has so little space for individual human beings. Instead, it often sees them as an obstacle in the way of big-tech solutions for whatever is seen as ailing the planet.[7] The danger exists that the politically-engaged owners of capital in the bio-tech and digital economy will conclude that a mulish and uncomprehending electorate is an obstacle to the realisation of their ambitious plans for global development. Many of them focus on the transition to a green economy. It is supposed to be the salvation of the planet. By contrast, industry and economic growth are its nemesis, even though they have raised countless millions from poverty.

The planetary cause, and not human welfare and progress, now enjoys the backing of administrative elites, much of the media, as well as activist groups. Weak governments often comply with the prescriptions of this mobilised phalanx. They have shown scant inclination to limit the explosion in wealth and influence of a new set of moneyed forces who have prospered by marketing green solutions. By contrast, the profits of smaller business firms have contracted along with the incomes of non-elite groups and the amount of wealth that they possess. The danger is that parts of Europe, along with North America, will see violent collisions between winners and losers in the polarised economic conditions that are opening up. Conflict between bureaucratic elites keen to project their power through various schemes of social engineering, from combating climate change to instituting world, or at least European, government, risk promoting a backlash that extends beyond the ballot box and may spill over into the streets.

The survival of a spirit of consensus is indispensable to prevent a descent into a spiral of conflict over the division of wealth and the rules for governing societies. But such a temperate outlook may be disappearing in older democracies, due not least to the absence of any contact points between dominant elites and the mass of society. Twenty-first century information platforms and higher education, in which uniformity of thought can be prized over debate and exploration of ideas, have cocooned many in their own opinion bubbles. Opinion surveys show that the commitment of educated younger generations to plural democracy has fallen sharply within a relatively short space of time.[8] In one poll, 61 percent of young people in Britain expressed a preference for dictatorship over democracy.[9] Such a perspective makes the search for common ground, and even civility in politics, all the harder. Unless attitudes change, it means leaders of the future will spring from this disillusioned cohort. In the absence of any strong democratic memory, it is quite possible that disastrous and demeaning pacts will be entered into with despotic states. Poland's Prime Minister Mateusz Morawiecki warned in October 2022, that Europe might already be going down this path when he observed that some European Union leaders are not averse to ending the war that Russia launched, with Ukraine's defeat.[10]

In this era of uncertainty, the most assured occupants of the political stage often seem to be adventurers who are prepared to devise fresh rules in order to ensure they can count or prevail amidst the confusion and mayhem. With persistent tremors convulsing economic systems, social structures and the political environment, it is increasingly left to strong-willed figures with unorthodox approaches to politics, to try and make their mark. Macron, Orbán, Johnson and Rutte have had contrasting agendas and beliefs. But they adopted quite similar stances to the exercise of politics. They style themselves as pragmatists or innovators who have special insights into what is needed to restore good times and successfully adapt their countries to complex challenges. Self-belief, strong reserves of energy and manipulative skills, as well as indifference to the customary political rules, enable them to appear as men of destiny able to fashion an appeal across the customary political boundaries. Their efforts at projecting, or more likely manufacturing, charisma are meant to turn emotional attachment, and not policy direction, into the main basis for loyalty.

Some detachment might enable such figures to see that, however talented they are for this disruptive age, they are the mere beneficiaries of altered political conditions which permit new forces to come to the surface. The last thirty years have seen the slow dissolution of economic and social structures and agreement about codes of public behaviour, which provided a degree of political stability in the West for much of that time. The twenty-first century mavericks profiled in the final section are beneficiaries of an age of dissonance that could soon lead to sizeable upheavals. Perhaps only Orbán has a secure enough territorial base to withstand the political storms that are gathering force in Europe, and even that is far from certain. If economic and social disruption intensify, will democracy itself (and not just parties, ideologies and party systems), become a casualty of the time of troubles? Certainly, in the supposed heartlands of democracy, it is increasingly harder to find those prerequisites that were once recommended by think-tanks in order to ensure that post-dictatorial states in East-Central Europe and elsewhere could stand a chance of consolidating the politics of free choice.

509 years after the appearance of Machiavelli's *The Prince*, Munira Mirza, the former head of Boris Johnson's Policy Unit when he was Prime Minister, was sufficiently alarmed by the deficit in leadership that she glimpsed at first hand, that she decided to offer a training manual to provide advice on how to run an increasingly hard-to-govern Britain.[11] Two of his ministers, Kemi Badenoch and Michael Gove, roundly praised her initiative.

National democracies are ceding power and authority to other interests, both globally and internally. Few contenders for office seem able to halt the trend by appealing to the common good and a sense of community transcending partisan divides. Among the young, belief that electoral democracy within national state boundaries offers little of value, is growing. So, to worry about even the short-term durability of democracy may not be as outlandish as it once seemed. In Ukraine, at the time of writing, there is a desire for pluralist self-rule that provides a contrast to the decay of democratic politics in other parts of Europe. But in time, the critical danger for Ukraine might come to be seen as not the presence of a determined adversary on its doorstep, but the absence of anything resembling a vigorous democratic neighbourhood in which it can hope to take its place. Europe's voice is no longer heard much in the rest of the world. The views of many, that Europe's history is a litany of oppression and exploitation visited on much of the rest of the world, received a highly visible endorsement from the lawyer Gianni Infantino, the head of the world football association FIFA, at the start of the 2022 football world cup in Qatar.[12] In the UN General Assembly, it is dictatorships and patrimonial states which have by far the louder voice. Shibboleths pour forth from the Vatican, where a papacy in its twilight phase is busy endorsing radical elite nostrums for overhauling the planet, rather than daring to offer a spiritual reference point at a time when millions of disorientated and hard pressed citizens seek such guidance.

This book has been written thirty-three years after the collapse of the Berlin Wall and the retreat of dictatorial rule from Eastern Europe (Russia obviously excluded). The Soviet backed system collapsed because of its lack of political legitimacy, its despotic methods of control, and its failure to construct an efficient economic system which delivered growth and prosperity. The democratic system of government in Europe has been in increasing disrepair (not everywhere admittedly, but certainly in countries that in the past were crucial for its success). Increasingly, ideological priorities, particularly in the environmental sphere, take precedence over the need to govern in the interests of citizens whose taxes and votes underpin national democracies. In the absence of the technology required to make it work, much of the West is now investing vast sums in renewable energy as an alternative to hydrocarbons. Decision-makers are almost in as much of a headlong rush as Stalin was in when he converted the Soviet Union from agriculture to heavy industry. Even within the democratic context, they show as much disdain for the concerns of numerous citizens well able to grasp that the latest march to utopia (this time ecologically-focused) is a tool of the ruling power structure which will leave many stripped of freedoms and impoverished. The resultant disruption could easily result in today's political forces and the institutions guaranteeing a degree of political competition, unravelling. Any vacuum will not necessarily be filled by benevolent alternatives that will pay any more attention to citizens wishes than the pre-1989 single-party rulers did. The leaders whose careers are explored in this book were often self-absorbed, philistine or short-term in outlook and complacent about the democratic responsibilities placed on their shoulders. Europe cannot afford a repeat performance if liberty and order are to be sustained. It is a small area of the world with diminishing ability to repulse individuals and forces who have scant respect for democratic ways. They include predatory nations, home-grown radical forces, and individuals with enormous wealth keen to leave their mark on history not by philanthropy but by schemes of social engineering which leave little room for humans. Unless the recession in democratic leadership is replaced by replenishment and renewal, the ability of free societies to hold out against these assorted enemies is likely to be steadily diminished.

---

[1] See Manent, 'Populist Demagogy'.
[2] See Frank Furedi, 'The Ruling Elites- How They Justify Their Role. The ideology of cultural power', *Frank Furedi Substack*, 21 October 2022, https://frankfuredi.substack.com/p/the-ideology-of-the-ruling-elites, accessed 21 October 2022
[3] Joan Smith, 'What Starmer told Pink News is a sign of things to come', *UnHerd*, 20 October 2022, https://unherd.com/thepost/what-keir-starmer-told-pink-news-is-a-sign-of-things-to-come/, accessed 21 October 2022.
[4] Niccolo Machiavelli, *The Prince*, (translated by W.K. Marriott), London: Aegypan, 2007, Chapter IX.
[5] Frank Furedi, 'Who's afraid of ideology?' *Spectator Online*, 30 October 2022, https://www.spectator.co.uk/article/whos-afraid-of-ideology-2/, accessed 6 November 2022.

---

[6] Joel Kotkin, 'Welcome to the end of democracy', *Spectator*, 8 January 2022, https://www.spectator.co.uk/article/welcome-to-the-end-of-democracy, accessed 24 October 2022.
[7] Paul Kingsnorth, 'The Truth about Eco-fascism', *UnHerd*, 12 November 2022, https://unherd.com/2022/11/the-truth-about-eco-fascism/, accessed 13 November 2022.
[8] Daniella Wenger and Roberto Foa, 'Young voters are disconnecting from democracy – but who can blame them?' *Guardian*, 23 October 2020.
[9] Matthew Syed, 'The West's loss of faith in liberalism risks opening the door to great evils', *Sunday Times*, 30 October 2022, https://www.thetimes.co.uk/article/8bc3a6bc-56d5-11ed-8e9a-37443e2955cd, accessed 30 October 2022.
[10] 'Polish Prime Minister Morawiecki: the leaders of some EU countries allow the defeat of Ukraine', *Teller Report*, 28 October 2022, https://www.tellerreport.com/news/2022-10-28-polish-prime-minister-morawiecki--the-leaders-of-some-eu-countries-allow-the-defeat-of-ukraine.HJBHMwtNo.html, accessed 28 October 2022.
[11] Munira Mirza, 'How to train our leaders to run the country', *Times*, 10 November 2022.
[12] Matt Lawton, 'Fifa president Gianni Infantino denounces West's hypocrisy against Qatar', *Sunday Times*, 20 November 2022.

INDEX

ABOUT THE AUTHOR

Tom Gallagher is a Scot who pursued an academic career as a historian in England for over three decades and is currently Emeritus Professor of Politics at the University of Bradford. He lives in the Lake District and travels widely in Europe and further afield.

Among his books are:

Glasgow The Uneasy Peace: Religious Tension in Modern Scotland
Manchester University Press, 1987.

The Balkans Since The Cold War: From Tyranny to Tragedy
Routledge, 2003.

Romania and the European Union: How the Weak Conquered the Strong
Manchester University Press, 2010.

Scotland Now: A Warning to the World
Scotview Press, 2015.

Salazar: The Dictator Who Refused to Die
Hurst Publications, 2020

Printed in Great Britain
by Amazon